The POWER *of* PRINTS

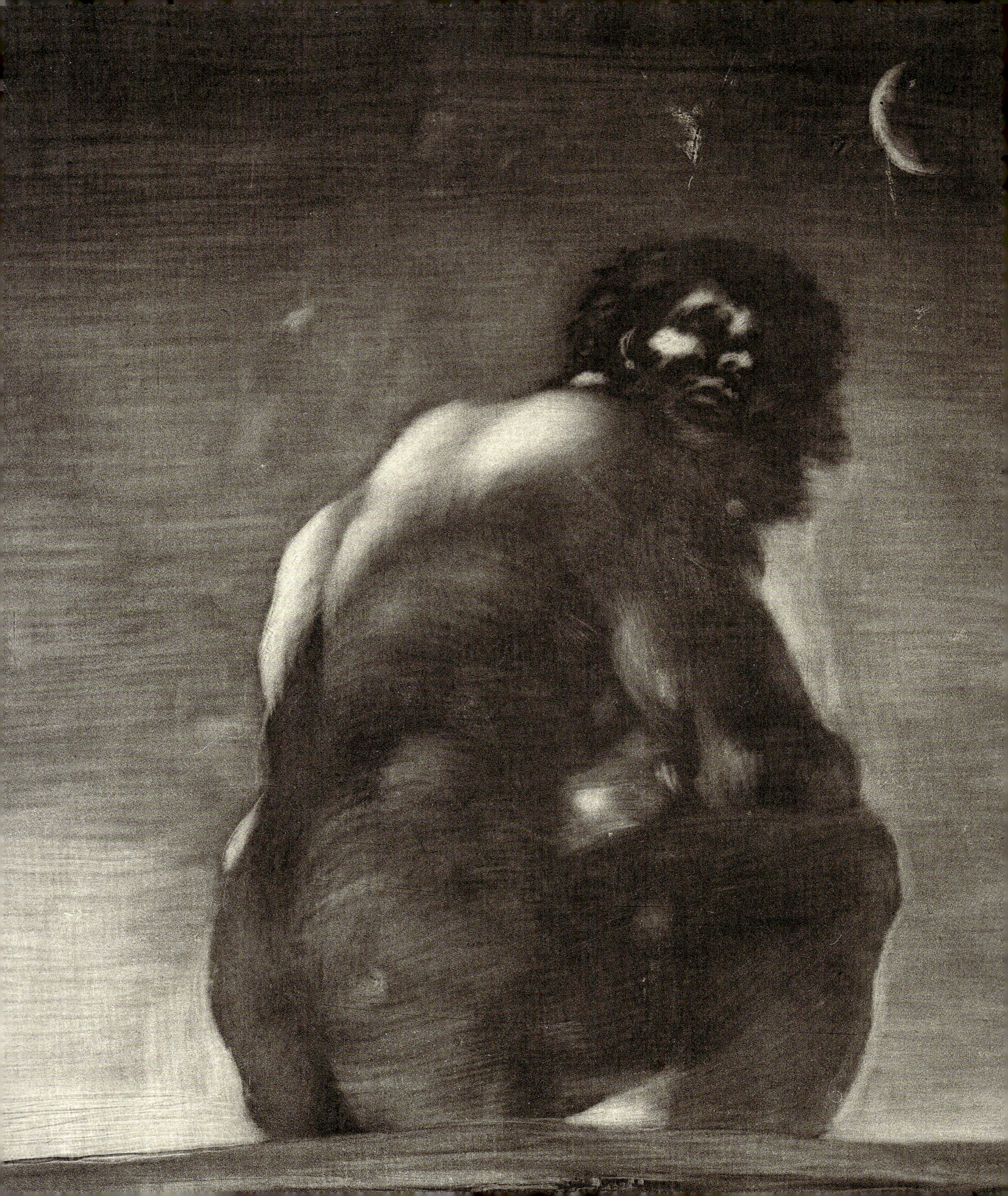

The POWER of PRINTS

The Legacy of WILLIAM M. IVINS and A. HYATT MAYOR

FREYDA SPIRA

with PETER PARSHALL

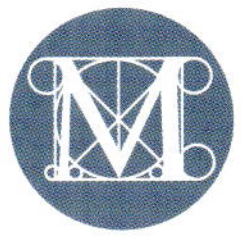

THE METROPOLITAN MUSEUM OF ART, NEW YORK

DISTRIBUTED BY YALE UNIVERSITY PRESS

NEW HAVEN AND LONDON

This catalogue is published in conjunction with "The Power of Prints: The Legacy of William M. Ivins and A. Hyatt Mayor," on view at The Metropolitan Museum of Art, New York, from January 26 through May 22, 2016.

The exhibition is made possible by The Schiff Foundation.

The catalogue is made possible by the Drue E. Heinz Fund.

Published by The Metropolitan Museum of Art, New York
Mark Polizzotti, Publisher and Editor in Chief
Gwen Roginsky, Associate Publisher and General Manager of Publications
Peter Antony, Chief Production Manager
Michael Sittenfeld, Senior Managing Editor
Robert Weisberg, Senior Project Manager

Edited by Nancy E. Cohen
Designed by Christopher Kuntze
Production by Christopher Zichello
Bibliography and notes edited by Leslie Geddes

Photographs of works in the Metropolitan Museum's collection are by The Photograph Studio, The Metropolitan Museum of Art, unless otherwise noted.

Additional photo credits: © 2016 Delaware Art Museum / Artists Rights Society (ARS), New York: cat. 43; © Estate of Martin Lewis: cat. 47; © 2016 Estate of John Marin / Artists Rights Society (ARS), New York: fig. 21; © 2016 Estate of Reginald Marsh / Art Students League, New York / Artists Rights Society (ARS), New York: cat. 48; © The Museum of Modern Art / Licensed by SCALA / Art Resource, New York: fig. 20

Typeset in MVB Verdigris and Bernhard Modern
Printed on 150 gsm Phoenixmotion Xantur
Printed and bound by Verona Libri, Verona, Italy

Cover illustrations: front, Rembrandt van Rijn, *The Three Trees* (detail), 1643, cat. 15; back, Night View of World's Fair Grounds (detail), from the Chicago World's Fair series, 1933 (Burdick 435, PC225-1.26), see pages 164–65
Frontispiece: Francisco de Goya y Lucientes, *Seated Giant* (detail), by 1818, cat. 26

Additional illustrations: page vi: Mary Cassatt, *The Letter* (detail), 1890–91, cat. 36; page x: Hendrick Goltzius, *The Great Hercules* (detail), 1589, cat. 74; page 2: woodcut (detail) from *De Aritmetica*, 1491, cat. 81; page 12: Lucas van Leyden, *Panel of Ornament with Two Sirens* (detail), 1528, cat. 65; page 28: Benjamin Pollock, Characters and Scenes from *Jack the Giant Killer* for a Toy Theater, scene 8 (detail), 1870–90 (52.541.1[16]), see pages 164–65; pages 42–43: James McNeill Whistler, *Black Lion Wharf* (detail), 1859, cat. 29; page 44: Rembrandt van Rijn, *Christ Crucified between the Two Thieves: The Three Crosses* (detail), 1653, cat. 17; page 82: Albrecht Dürer, *Saint Eustace* (detail), ca. 1501, cat. 55; page 110: woodcut (detail of eclipses) from *Sphaera Mundi*, 1485, cat. 79; page 136: William Henry Bradley, *The Echo, Chicago's Humorous and Artistic Fortnightly* (detail), 1895, cat. 115; pages 166–67: Sir Francis Seymour Haden, *The Mouth of a Brook* (detail), 1859, cat. 28

The Metropolitan Museum of Art endeavors to respect copyright in a manner consistent with its nonprofit educational mission. If you believe any material has been included in this publication improperly, please contact the Editorial Department.

The Metropolitan Museum of Art
1000 Fifth Avenue
New York, New York 10028
metmuseum.org

Distributed by
Yale University Press, New Haven and London
yalebooks.com/art
yalebooks.co.uk

Cataloging-in-Publication Data is available from the Library of Congress.
ISBN 978-1-58839-585-6

CONTENTS

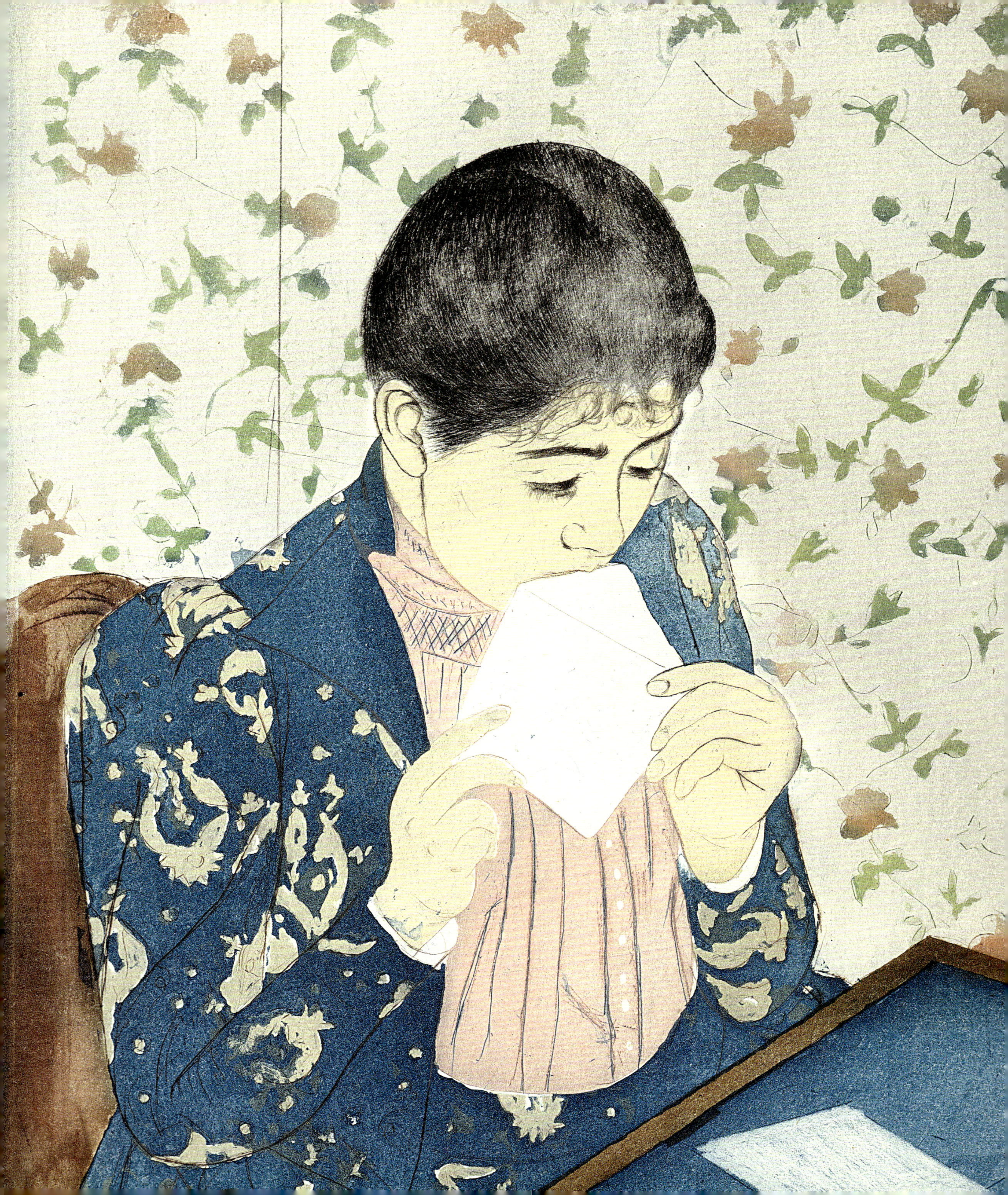

DIRECTOR'S FOREWORD

The Power of Prints commemorates the centennial of the Department of Prints at The Metropolitan Museum of Art by celebrating the legacy of its founding curator, William Mills Ivins Jr., and his protégé, Alpheus Hyatt Mayor. Together, during their combined fifty-year tenure, Ivins and Mayor amassed a collection of many hundreds of thousands of prints. The result is both encyclopedic in its scope and scholarly in its areas of focus.

By drawing on the Met's vast holdings, this exhibition and its accompanying catalogue reveal how the Museum's print collection was artfully constructed according to Ivins's and Mayor's shared vision. It displays the most beautiful, rare, and exceptional prints alongside the equally important popular and ephemeral works they collected during the first fifty years of the department's history. Because works on paper cannot endure long exposure to light, many of these works have not recently been shown. Certainly no exhibition before has told the full story of this great American collection through prints by Andrea Mantegna, Albrecht Dürer, Marcantonio Raimondi, Jacques Callot, Rembrandt van Rijn, Francisco de Goya y Lucientes, Honoré Daumier, James McNeill Whistler, Henri de Toulouse-Lautrec, Mary Cassatt, Edward Penfield, and Edward Hopper, to name just a few of the artists whose works are on display.

Organized by Freyda Spira, Associate Curator in the Department of Drawings and Prints, *The Power of Prints* explores how the evolution of curatorial priorities—notably, from purely aesthetic concerns to those of content and context—affected the assembling of the department's remarkable collection of etchings and engravings. As did Ivins and Mayor, the exhibition also considers printed matter as the entrée to the information age: prints as functional objects that spread ideas to an ever-expanding audience and reflected a changing society. In the age of digital photography and the Internet, the power of prints, or the ability to disseminate images in identical form to a mass market, has special relevance to how we see, understand, and engage with works of art.

The Metropolitan Museum's mission to share its permanent collection with the broadest possible public is realized only through the support of our sponsors. We would like to recognize the generosity of The Schiff Foundation for its support of this exhibition and its enduring commitment to the Museum's work. We are also deeply grateful to Mrs. Henry J. Heinz II for her important contribution toward the publication of this catalogue.

Thomas P. Campbell
Director
The Metropolitan Museum of Art

ACKNOWLEDGMENTS

This endeavor has been made immensely richer by the contributions of Peter Parshall, whose essay offers considerable insight into the life and career of William M. Ivins. I also benefited enormously from our discussions and from Peter's perceptions and observations, which helped shape this catalogue and the selection of works in the exhibition it accompanies.

One of the great advantages of working at The Metropolitan Museum of Art is the professional support and encouragement of my colleagues. I am deeply grateful to George R. Goldner, former Drue Heinz Chairman of the Department of Drawings and Prints, for his enthusiasm for this project from the very beginning and his advice throughout the process. With the recent appointment of Nadine M. Orenstein to the position of Drue Heinz Curator in Charge of the Department of Drawings and Prints, the project has thrived. I feel lucky to be working with someone so passionate about both the collection's history and its future. I am thankful for the unending generosity and ideas of past and present members of the Department of Drawings and Prints: Stijn Alsteens, Rebekah Burgess, John Byck, David del Gaizo, Erin Florence, Colta Ives, Catherine Jenkins, Julia Lillie, Ricky Luna, Mark McDonald, Constance McPhee, Mary L. Myers, Samantha Rippner, Femke Speelberg, Perrin Stein, Elizabeth Zanis, and Mary Zuber. I am fortunate too for the help of my talented colleagues in Paper Conservation: Marjorie Shelley, Sherman Fairchild Conservator in Charge, Rachel Mustalish, and Rebecca Capua. I relied heavily on the Museum's archives to get a glimpse into the personal and professional histories of Ivins and Mayor and was assisted by the incredibly accommodating and affable Melissa Bowling. I gratefully acknowledge Kenneth Soehner, Arthur K. Watson Chief Librarian, and the staff of the Thomas J. Watson Library, who are always professional and extremely helpful.

Research into the lives and careers of Ivins and Mayor led me to Bernard Berenson's home, I Tatti, outside of Florence. The villa and its contents are now part of Harvard University, and working in the archives there was deeply pleasurable because of the assistance and enthusiasm of Jonathan Nelson, Assistant Director for Academic Programs and Publications, and the archivist Ilaria Della Monica. I also thank the staffs of the Archives of American Art, Smithsonian Institution; the Grolier Club, New York; Syracuse University Libraries; Harvard Art Museums Archives and Special Collections; Columbia University Rare Book and Manuscript Library; and the New York Public Library Archives and Manuscripts.

My research led to many connections with print people and those interested in the intellectual history of the field. I received enthusiastic help from Elisabeth Hodermarsky, the Sutphin Family Senior Associate Curator of Prints and Drawings at the Yale University Art Gallery, who shared her previous work on Ivins and Theodore "Tubby" Sizer. I greatly benefited from discussions about Ivins and Mayor with Maryan Ainsworth, Jonathan Bober, Suzanne Boorsch, Shira Brisman, Marjorie B. Cohn, Susan Dackerman, Colin Eisler, Jennifer Hallam, Morrison H. Heckscher, John Ittmann, Patrick Murphy, Nathaniel Prottas, Andrew Robison, Elizabeth Rudy, Victoria Sancho Lobis, Susan Schulman, Larry Silver, Susan Alyson Stein, and Naoko Takahatake.

The thoughtful installation in the galleries is the work of members of the Design and Exhibitions Departments: Linda Sylling, Patricia Gilkison, Zoe Florence, and Ria Roberts.

The publication took shape under the guidance of the Editorial Department, led by Mark Polizzotti, Gwen Roginsky, Peter Antony, and Michael Sittenfeld. Christopher Kuntze's book design and Christopher Zichello's careful attention to the images and production allowed us to make interesting juxtapositions and show works in detail where possible. I was especially thankful for my editor, Nancy E. Cohen, who was always happy and willing to discuss and debate issues and move the publication forward.

An exhibition ultimately draws on every corner of the Museum, beginning with the support of Thomas P. Campbell, Director; Jennifer Russell, Associate Director for Exhibitions (and a former student of Mayor's); and Carrie Rebora Barratt, Deputy Director for Collections and Administration. Barbara J. Bridgers, Mark Morosse, William Scott Geffert, Hyla Skopitz, and Erica Allen are responsible for the beautiful photography of the works in the Museum's collection. I thank Martha Deese in the Exhibitions Department, Jennifer Mock in Education, and Mary Flanagan in Communications. I have been lucky to have the assistance of two capable interns, Theresa Ketterer and Thomas Brown.

Special recognition goes to our generous donors. I am grateful to The Schiff Foundation for its support of the exhibition and to Mrs. Henry J. Heinz II for her support of this catalogue.

Last, I would like to acknowledge that this book would not have been possible without the love and continuous support of Ben Slavin, and the laughter of our children, Hannah and Toby.

Freyda Spira

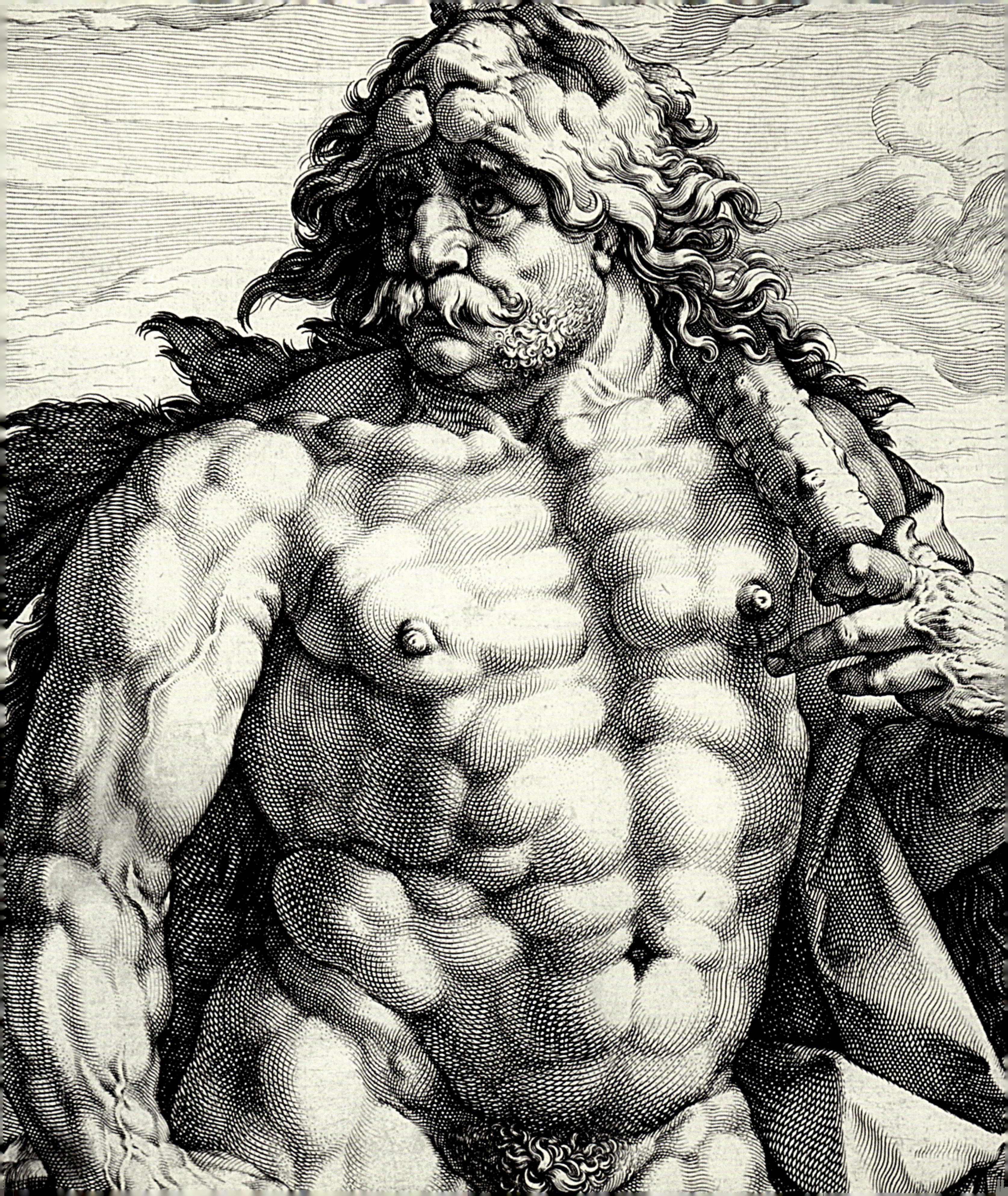

The POWER of PRINTS

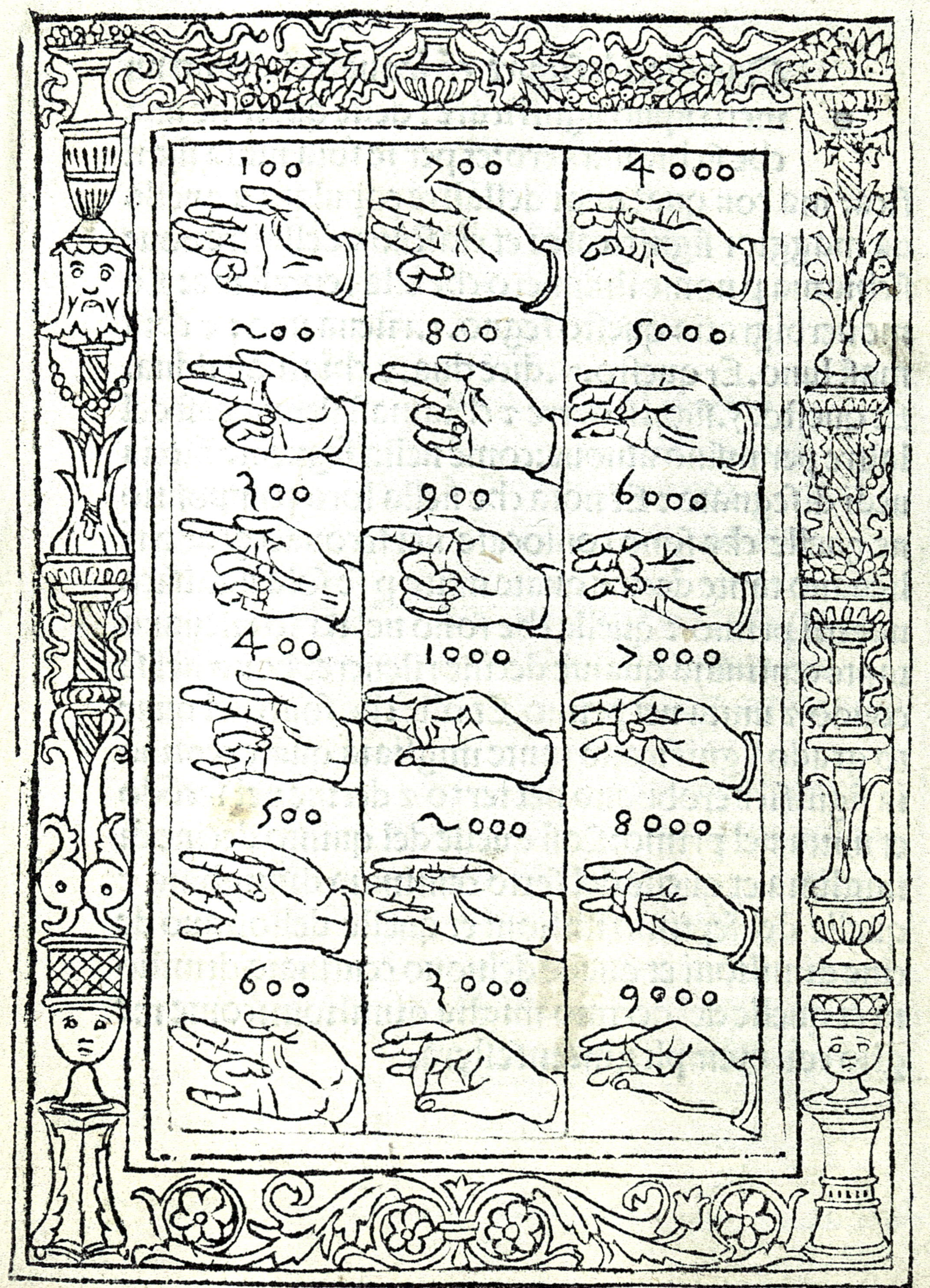

100
200
4000
200
800
5000
300
900
6000
400
1000
7000
500
2000
8000
600
3000
9000

Introduction: Printed Matter

FREYDA SPIRA

Prints "throw open to their student with the most complete abandon the whole gamut of human life and endeavor, from the most ephemeral of courtesies to the loftiest pictorial presentations of man's spiritual aspirations,"[1] declared William Mills Ivins, founding curator of The Metropolitan Museum of Art's Department of Prints, soon after assuming that position. If Ivins's lifelong passion for prints was manifest from the outset of what was to be an illustrious career as a curator, critic, social scientist, and picture historian, the great accomplishment of Ivins and his successor Alpheus Hyatt Mayor was as yet unforeseen: they not only built one of the world's most important and unprecedentedly diverse collections of prints but in so doing revolutionized the field.

For years before hiring Ivins, the Museum had only haphazardly acquired prints, but in 1916, following the acquisition of more than thirty-five hundred prints from the paper manufacturer Harris Brisbane Dick, its trustees brought him in to create a collection that rivaled its other departments. Preceded in the United States only by the print collections at the Museum of Fine Arts, Boston, and the Fogg Museum at Harvard University,[2] the Museum's department was envisioned as a collection of prints of "artistic" quality. The trustees published their now-anachronistic desiderata in early 1917: the collection was to encompass etchings by both old masters, including Rembrandt van Rijn, and nineteenth-century artists, such as James McNeill Whistler, Anders Zorn, and the now relatively unknown Sir David Young Cameron, who had experimented with the medium's artistic and expressive possibilities (fig. 1). It was to exclude the kinds of objects that were being actively collected by libraries, athenaeums, and archives: maps and city views, portraits, costume books, anatomical prints, botanicals, and anything else that appeared to be of historical rather than aesthetic interest.[3] But Ivins and, later, Mayor flouted both those

instructions and then-standard practice as they amassed many hundreds of thousands of prints and photographs from Europe and the Americas for the Museum, seeking richness of content as well as of form. As Ivins asserted at the beginning of his tenure: "The print collection of a museum cannot be formed solely upon Yes and No answers to the question: Is it a work of art? Rather must it be, like the library of a professor of literature, composed of a corpus of prints in themselves distinctly works of art, filled out and illustrated by many prints which have only a technical historical importance."[4] To that end, the collection they assembled includes the most beautiful, rare, and exceptional examples, lauded for their aesthetic appeal, as well as popular prints, such as posters and trade cards, that were printed in large numbers, widely circulated, and never intended to last. Collecting ephemera and popular prints was unprecedented in American museums, but, as Ivins recognized to some extent and Mayor ardently believed, these more common, more ephemeral prints are storehouses of information about their time and place that belonged in the Museum. The two curators' prescient understanding of the value of printed works across a wide spectrum, and the intellectual framework from which their collecting practice arose, transformed the field of prints by broadening its scope beyond the aesthetic, formal, and technical aspects and asking new questions about the function of works of art, their historical and cultural context, and their active role as both containers and purveyors of knowledge.

Yet when the Museum set out to develop its own collection, it aimed to emulate the traditional aesthetic-based prints programs in Boston, even seeking the advice of the Fogg's newly installed assistant director, Paul J. Sachs, whose connoisseur-style courses and mentoring fostered an entire generation of museum professionals. He strongly recommended Ivins, a fellow Harvard graduate, as an "ideal curator," although Ivins's professional background was not

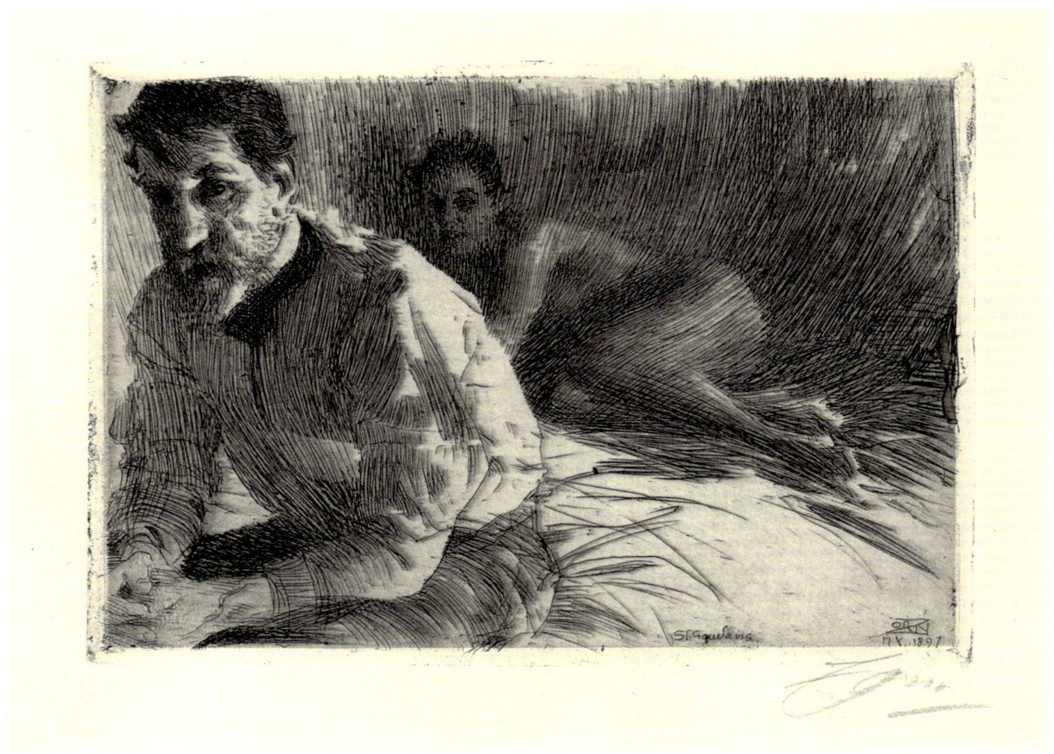

Fig. 1. Anders Zorn (Swedish, 1860–1920). *Augustus Saint Gaudens II (Saint Gaudens and His Model)*, 1897. Etching and possibly drypoint, 10 × 12¾ in. (25.2 × 32.4 cm). Harris Brisbane Dick Fund, 1917 (17.3.726)

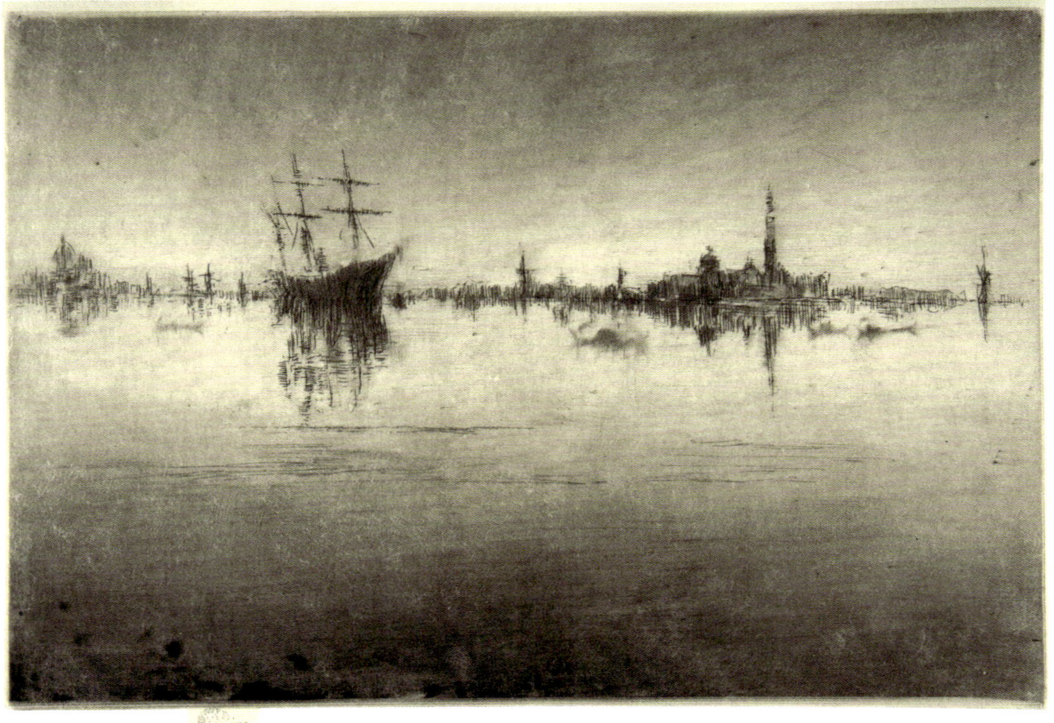

Fig. 2. James McNeill Whistler (American, 1834–1903). *Nocturne*, from First Venice Set, 1879–80. Etching and drypoint, sixth state of nine, 8 × 11⅝ in. (20.3 × 29.6 cm). Harris Brisbane Dick Fund, 1917 (17.3.86)

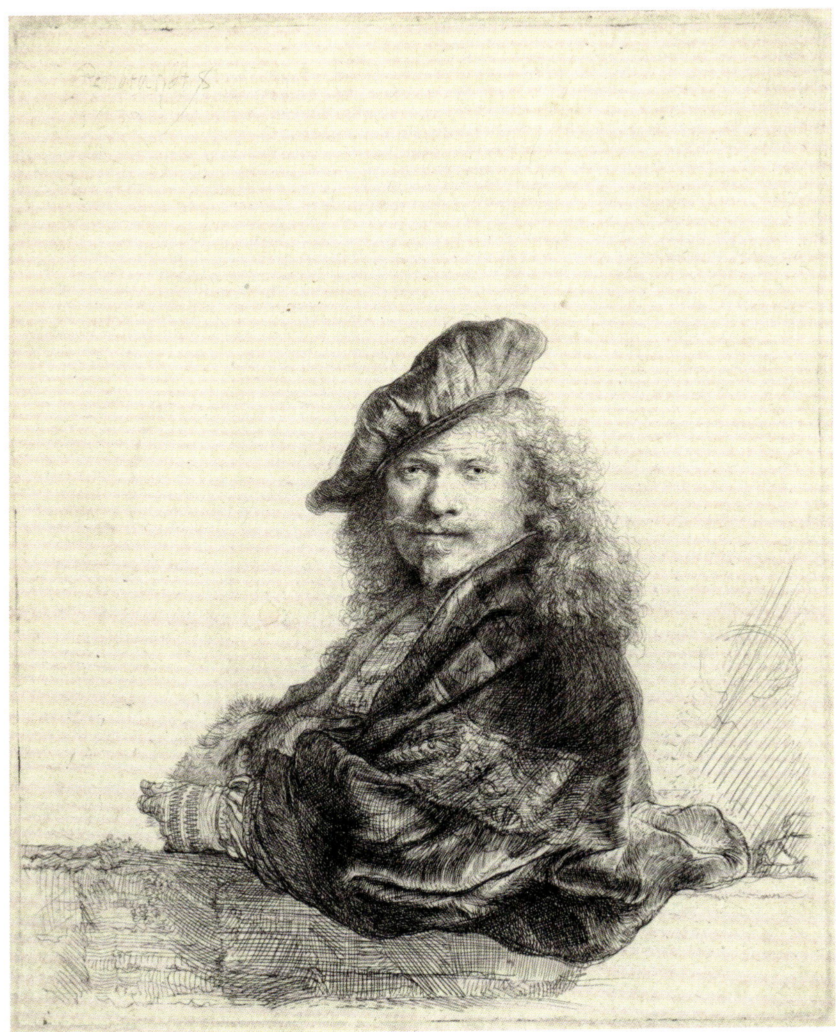

Fig. 3. Rembrandt van Rijn (Dutch, 1606–1669). *Self-Portrait Leaning on a Stone Sill*, 1639. Etching, drypoint, and burin, second state of two, 8⅜ × 6⅝ in. (21.1 × 16.8 cm). H. O. Havemeyer Collection, Bequest of Mrs. H. O. Havemeyer, 1929 (29.107.25)

in the arts.[5] As Sachs wrote in a letter to the Museum's director, Edward Robinson, Ivins's "knowledge of the black and white, considering the little time he has been able to give it, is extraordinary, and with his memory and more opportunity to see things, he would, I am sure, develop into an excellent, interesting and inspiring curator, who would attract the public and understand it."[6] Ivins readily abandoned a successful career as a lawyer, which had given him the wherewithal to buy prints and illustrated books but provided little intellectual or spiritual inspiration.

Ivins arrived at the Museum determined to expand the collection beyond the trustees' stated goals: "To make a museum collection on strictly aesthetic grounds would perforce end in amassing a body of material which would reflect rather the immediate personal predilections of the group of men who formed it than anything else."[7] Nevertheless,

the taste of the day—in the form of Harris Brisbane Dick's fashionable yet predictable collection of French, British, and American nineteenth-century etchings—unquestionably shaped the Museum's early collection. Typical of Dick's holdings were prints with sensuous appeal and high artistry, such as Whistler's supple *Nocturne*, from the First Venice Set, a series of twelve etchings that trace through tone and texture the effects of light as it plays along the city's buildings and waterways (fig. 2). Ivins and Mayor sought to build on Dick's gift by accumulating works by other artists and from other periods that were in vogue with American collectors; for example, they amassed a near-complete collection of the celebrated etchings of Rembrandt, many skillfully acquired through gifts (fig. 3). They also negotiated with living artists, such as Edward Hopper and Martin Lewis, to acquire their new etchings about modern life (fig. 4). Their acquisition of

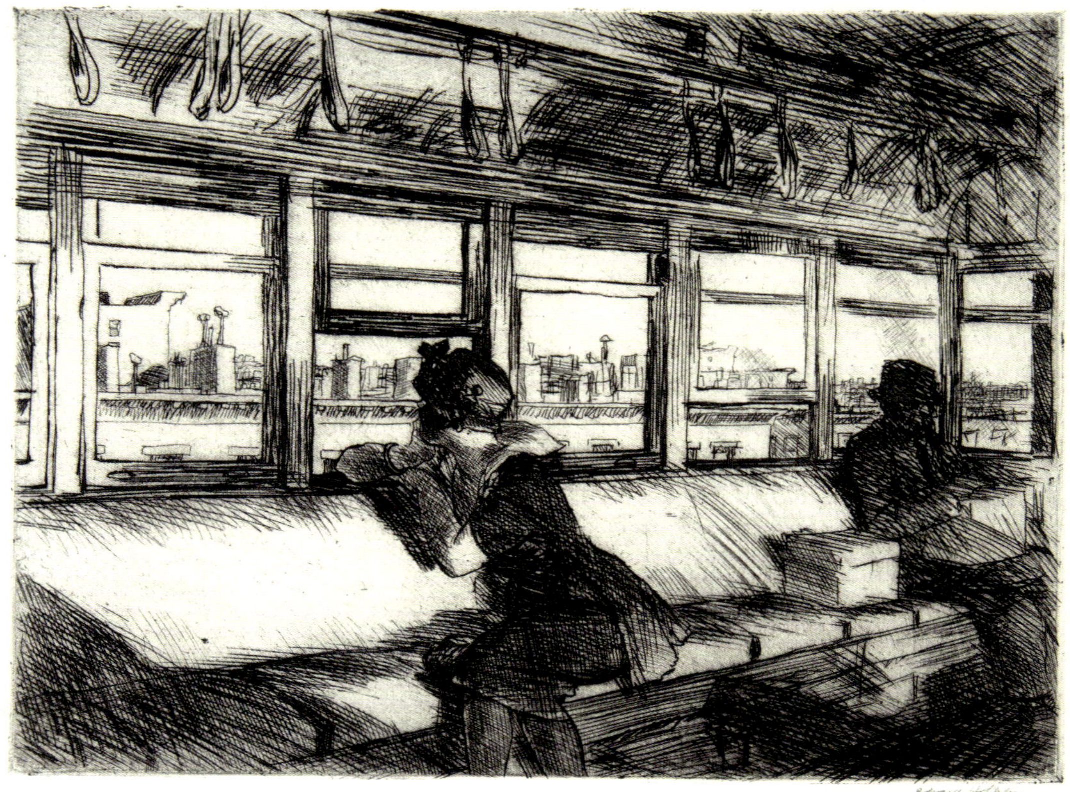

Fig. 4. Edward Hopper (American 1882–1967). *House Tops*, 1921. Etching, 9⅛ × 11⅛ in. (23.2 × 28.3 cm). Harris Brisbane Dick Fund, 1925 (25.31.10)

contemporary art was a radical shift for the Met and demonstrated Ivins's and Mayor's confidence as collectors and their authority as tastemakers.

They further challenged convention by acquiring and ultimately making markets for then-underappreciated artists such as Goya. At the time, the American public derided the Spanish artist's work across media as too personal and definitely not beautiful. Only prints from Goya's imaginative and bizarre series Los Caprichos (fig. 5), which critiques the folly of contemporary Spanish society, had found an audience; Romantic artists and European collectors had sought them out in the nineteenth century. Ivins had been exposed to Goya's prints during his student days in Paris and deeply affected by their ability to express "this world here and now, this world of dirt and weariness and strength."[8] For Ivins, Goya was a fine technician, but his power came from skillfully communicating emotions, ideas, and a sense of his own time and place. Ivins believed Goya's visual expression of humankind's cruelty would always be relevant to a broad public. In Ivins's first five years as curator, the Museum acquired

fifty-seven Goya prints in addition to an entire set of eighty Caprichos. By 1936 the Goya collection of prints was almost complete; with nearly three hundred prints, the Met's is one of the world's most comprehensive Goya collections. While Mayor did not significantly increase the Goya holdings, his superb interpretive studies and exhibitions demonstrate his zeal for the artist and for Spanish culture more generally, as was also reflected by his role as president (1955–80) of the Hispanic Society of America after the death of its founder, Mayor's uncle Archer Huntington.

In championing Goya, Ivins not only spurred a reappraisal of the master's work; he may have helped set in motion the overthrow of taste, a criterion that was central to art collecting during the early twentieth century and is anathema today. Taste's subjective nature preoccupied Ivins, whose article "A Note on Aesthetic Theory" (1925) argues that objective beauty does not exist—that "perception and valuation of qualities are an essentially personal thing"—and that aesthetic assessments of artistic merit tell us nothing about art but only about the person who expounded upon it. Quoting

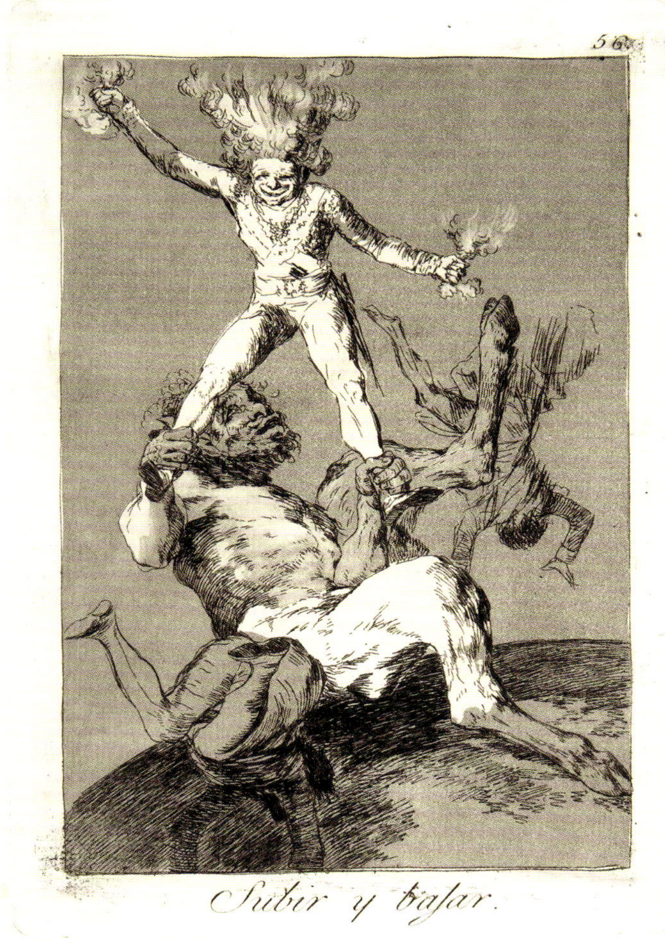

Fig. 5. Francisco de Goya y Lucientes (Spanish, 1746–1828). *To Rise and to Fall* (*Subir y bajar*), plate 56 from Los Caprichos, 1799. Etching and burnished aquatint, 11⅝ × 8⅜ in. (29.5 × 21.1 cm). Gift of M. Knoedler & Co., 1918 (18.64[56])

the father of American psychology, William James, the article concluded: "The typical aesthetic judgment was 'lemon juice goes well with oysters.' All anyone can do is to go try for himself."[9] Personal reactions to art and aesthetic appreciation of technical mastery were not enough for Ivins; a consummate humanist, he responded to work that took him on an intellectual journey, connecting him with its maker, its subject matter, its function within a larger historical context. Ivins was drawn to Italian Renaissance masters such as Andrea Mantegna, one of the first painters to experiment with engraving, who created a handful of narrative prints that inventively portray humankind's pleasures and discontents. Ivins called Mantegna's print *The Risen Christ between Saint Andrew and Saint Longinus* (see cat. 51) "the single most desirable item" to have entered the Museum's collection.[10]

Collectors had always sought after Mantegna's engraving, for reasons ranging from its technique to its rarity, but its appeal to Ivins stemmed from its pivotal role in the intellectual history of Renaissance Italy: one of the earliest engravings, it used ancient sculptural models and demonstrated an understanding of human proportions, the unfolding of perspective space, and artistic self-promotion—this talented painter made prints to advertise his expertise! In his appreciation of Mantegna's engraving, Ivins exemplifies a broader shift away from a focus solely on traditional connoisseurial concerns about attribution and quality of impression and toward the exploration of objects' meaning and context.

Mayor shared Ivins's appetite for prints that told stories and disseminated information. Like Ivins, Mayor was not a trained art historian but happily a print amateur; before joining the Museum in 1932 he had studied modern languages, literature, and poetry and worked as an arts critic, teacher, and an occasional actor. Both men were avid bibliophiles with wide-ranging interests whose voracity for knowledge and passion for social history defined their approach to art. The two assiduously collected and exhibited the masters of Renaissance engraving—Mantegna, Marcantonio Raimondi, Albrecht Dürer, and Lucas van Leyden—but Mayor realized that so-called reproductive engravings were equally important to understanding the Renaissance, among other periods. The practice of making reproductive engravings stemmed from Marcantonio's brilliant engravings after Raphael's paintings and drawings; widely circulated, they broadcast Raphael's style and masterpieces to the world. Yet in the nineteenth and early twentieth centuries, reproductive engravings were derided as derivative, mere copies far from the master's hand. Such engravings went unnoticed in the market until Mayor recognized their significance in documenting the history of a popular market for prints, as evidenced, for example, by the myriad works by the likes of Cherubino Alberti, Niccolò della Casa, Domenico del Barbiere, and Giulio Bonasone after Michelangelo's famed fresco of *The Last Judgment* (Sistine Chapel). He saw too that they could be valuable records of unknown or unique works, such as Hendrick Goltzius's erotically charged *Mars and Venus*, after a lost drawing by Bartholomeus Spranger (fig. 6). Making two large purchases of reproductive engravings from the venerable European collections of the Princes of Liechtenstein and the Albertina in Vienna, Mayor brought into the Museum thousands of works by now-celebrated printmakers, including Cornelis Cort, Aegidius Sadeler, Nicolas

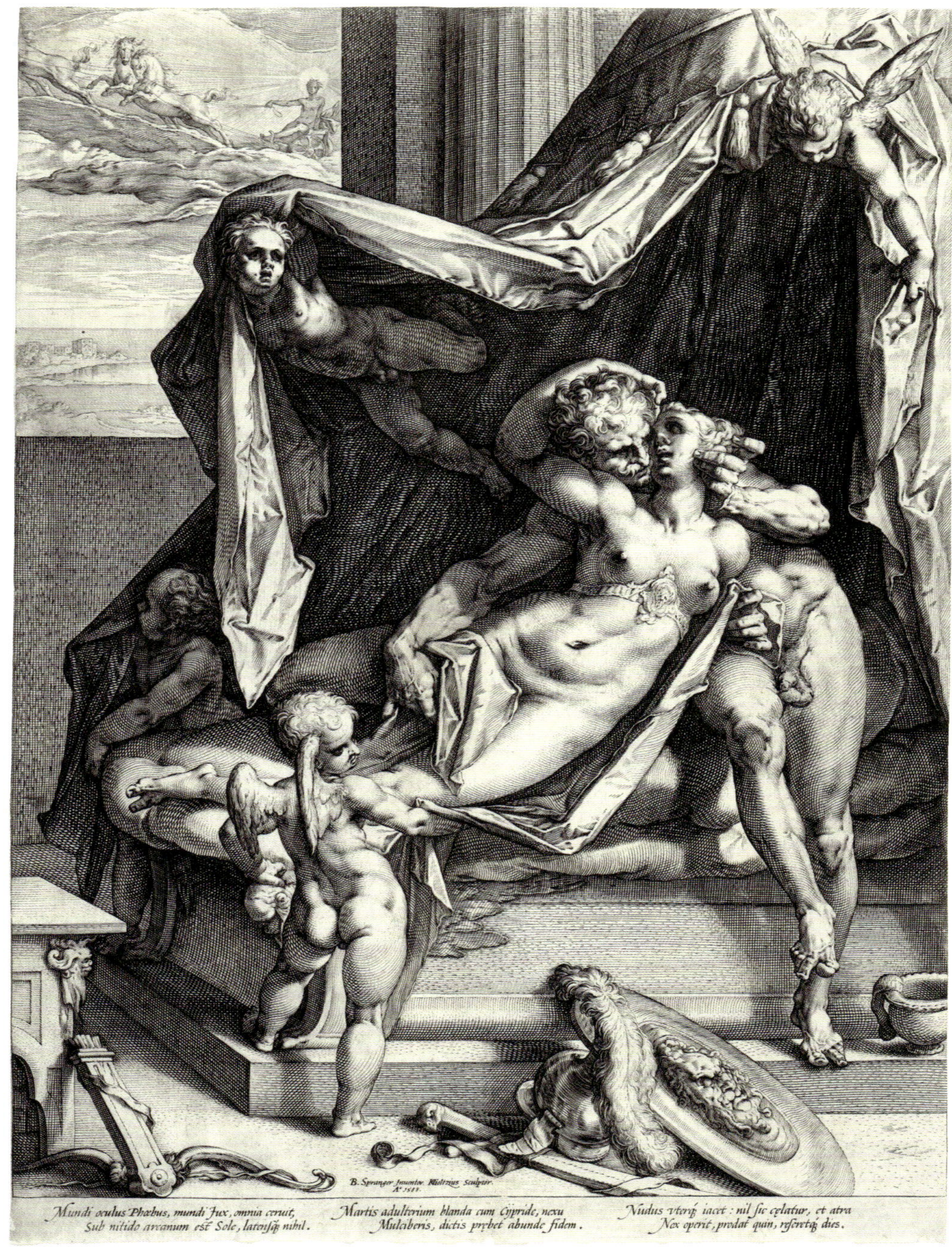

Fig. 6. Hendrick Goltzius (Netherlandish, 1558–1617) after Bartholomeus Spranger (Netherlandish, 1546–1611). *Mars and Venus*, 1588. Engraving, first state of four, 17⅛ × 12⅞ in. (43.5 × 32.7 cm). The Elisha Whittelsey Collection, The Elisha Whittelsey Fund, 1949 (49.97.681)

Beatrizet, Agostino Veneziano, Giorgio Ghisi, and Antonio Tempesta.

Ivins and Mayor thus pioneered a new appreciation in America for prints beyond the merely beautiful. They supplanted the conventional approach to prints as interesting foremost for their technical mastery with an understanding of prints as representatives of their time and place, objects that ask and answer questions to provide a broader historical, political, religious, or intellectual understanding of a given culture. They saw prints not only as an individual's creative acts but also as documents of whole communities that were endowed with vast social importance.[11] Ivins explained, "In the making of anything, from a pot to a picture, its maker informs it not only with his personal skill and sensibility but with the whole attitude towards life of his period and group and country."[12]

Ivins and Mayor were also influential in raising awareness of prints' value not only for the information they contained but also for their ability to communicate it widely. They contended that, because prints on paper are inherently multiple, relatively inexpensive, and extremely portable, they played a central role in disseminating information and ideas to an ever-growing audience. In the age before the Internet and digital photography, prints truly were the most democratic art form. Ivins was fascinated by one of the earliest manifestations of this phenomenon, the appearance of woodcuts in early illustrated books dating from the mid-fifteenth to the sixteenth century. In his groundbreaking examination of printmaking, *Prints and Visual Communication* (1953), he explored how the books' woodcut illustrations revolutionized the spread of knowledge about topics as varied as architecture, astronomy, perspective, machines, currency, costume, and anatomy during the Renaissance and beyond.[13]

Books historically had been collected as exquisite objects, but Ivins and Mayor approached them as repositories of information. They amassed a collection of books that tell the history of scientific, technical, and other advances. For example, two volumes in the Museum, produced just half a century apart, demonstrate the evolution of botany into a science. The images in the first illustrated book devoted to plants and flowers, the Pseudo-Apuleius of 1481, bear no resemblance to actual plants; the woodcuts were based on degraded medieval manuscript copies of pictures that may date to the first century B.C. (see cat. 76). Then, in 1530, Otto Brunfels's *Herbarum vivae eicones* (*Living Pictures of Plants*) helped catapult botany forward with Hans Weiditz's pioneering illustrations made by firsthand study (see cat. 86).

While Ivins focused on woodcuts' impact on how people presented and received information in the period of discovery known as the Renaissance, Mayor was invested in the relatively modern technology of lithography. In the nineteenth century, lithography was widely used for popular imagery such as posters, advertisements, newspapers, magazines, and trade cards that had both the visual power and the distribution to affect a truly mass market. For example, Edward Penfield's distinctive monthly posters advertising *Harper's Magazine*, which featured his bold and witty illustrations of emerging fashions, modes of transportation, and leisure activities,

defined the American middle class of the 1890s (fig. 7). These commercially printed posters appealed to Mayor, whose foundational text, *Prints & People: A Social History of Printed Pictures* (1971), examined how new techniques were devised, for what purpose, and with what new markets in mind. By exploring the shifts in perspective that result from print-making innovations—such as the ability to print a work in large quantities to show on the streets and in shops across the country—Mayor made print history part and parcel of human history.

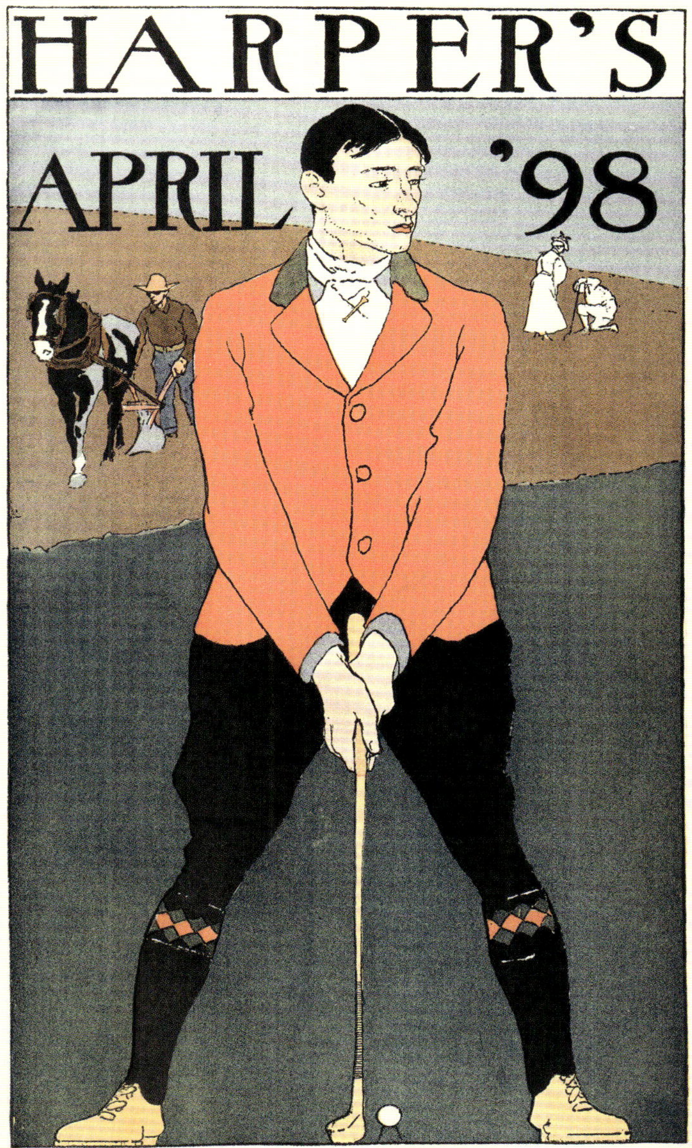

Fig. 7. Edward Penfield (American, 1866–1925). *Harper's, April*, 1898. Lithograph, 16⅛ × 9⅝ in. (40.9 × 24.5 cm). Museum Accession, transferred from the Library (57.627.9[29])

Both as scholars and as curators presenting exhibitions to the public, Ivins and Mayor sought to expose readers and viewers to new experiences and styles, complicated subject matter, and long-forgotten or just-emerging stories, themes, and cultures. In addition to their books, they produced important writing on a much smaller scale, transforming the curatorial approach to exhibition labels. Such labels traditionally included basic information about a work's title, maker, medium, and place and date of creation, sometimes with formal, descriptive texts. Because, as Ivins observed, the museum "is the only place where one is supposed to learn standing up,"[14] he began early in his tenure to write explanatory labels in a conversational style, "essays compact enough to fit onto the mats of prints on exhibition, and sparkling enough to arrest a gallery stroller in his restless drifting."[15] Ivins's label for Edgar Degas's *Mlle Bécat at the Café des Ambassadeurs, Paris* (fig. 8), which shows the famous performer at work in an outdoor café-concert, lays out the influences on Degas's subject and use of light: they are as disparate as Honoré Daumier and Kitagawa Utamaro. The text concludes, "it is doubtful whether any other man has ever so combined bitter wit and great learning with acid realism and artistry."[16]

Mayor built upon Ivins's approach to labels and descriptions of works in his own distinctive style. For example, in his entry on Degas in *Prints & People*, Mayor too summarized the artist's wide-ranging influences: "[He] learned from quattrocento Tuscans to color lucidly and draw clearly, from Japanese woodcuts to spot pictures in patterns never imagined by Giotto or Raphael, from Ingres to control distortions of line, and from Daumier to spy from ambush for the gesture that sparks drama into somebody crossing the street, listening to music, or ironing a shirt."[17]

Whether or not one agrees with their assessments, Ivins's and Mayor's labels are challenging, clever, and expansive yet nonacademic. They were the first conversational labels meant to engage a broad audience of museumgoers, a practice that was widely adopted by American museums in the late 1970s. Through their delightfully colloquial labels Ivins and Mayor conveyed the importance of prints to a generation of collectors, students, and would-be print amateurs.

These transformative labels, as well as the hundreds of books, articles, reviews, calendars, and other publications they wrote, are only part of Ivins's and Mayor's legacy. Their most extraordinary contribution remains the vast, even dizzyingly diverse print collection they assembled over fifty years. The Museum's astounding collection now numbers more than 1.5 million prints that represent the full scope of printmaking in Europe and the Americas from about 1400 to the present day; it ranges from the earliest known European woodcuts of the fifteenth century to Rembrandt's and Goya's experimental etchings, Pablo Picasso's linocuts, Mexican broadsides, and Kara Walker's offset lithographs. Brilliantly mixing the exceptional with the everyday, the Museum's collection is the most comprehensive in the United States and rivals the eminent and much older collections at the British Museum, London, the Bibliothèque Nationale de France, Paris, and the Albertina, Vienna, from which Ivins and Mayor learned much. Ivins and Mayor built the collection with the foresight to satisfy any conceivable interest, answer innumerable questions, highlight the masterpieces of each printmaking medium as it evolved through history, foster debate, and submit to multidisciplinary inquiries—and with the hope that everyone would be as astonished by the power of prints as they remained throughout their long careers.

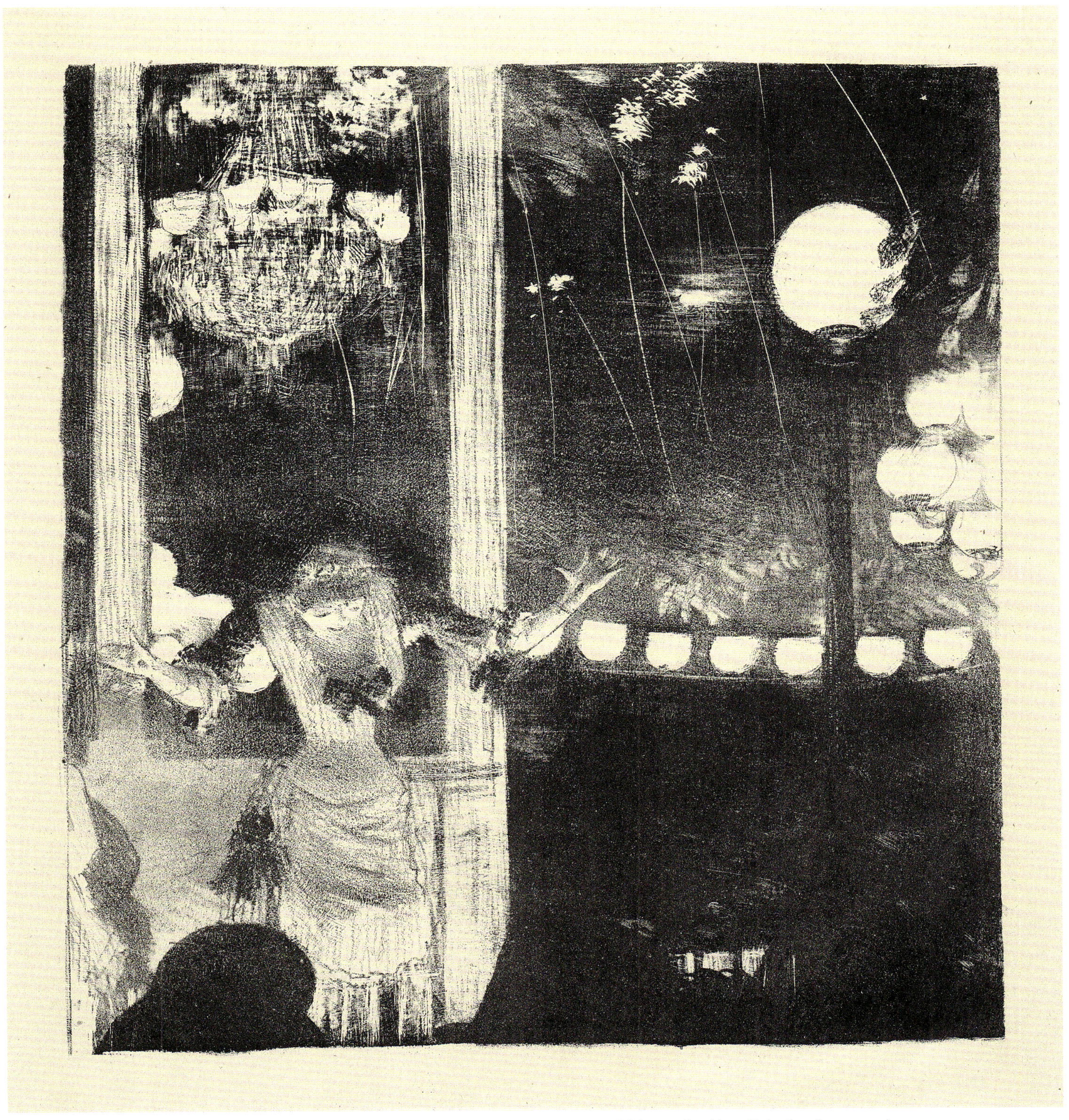

Fig. 8. Edgar Degas (French, 1834–1917). *Mlle Bécat at the Café des Ambassadeurs, Paris,* 1877–78. Lithograph, 8⅛ × 7⅝ in. (20.6 × 19.4 cm). Rogers Fund, 1919 (19.29.3)

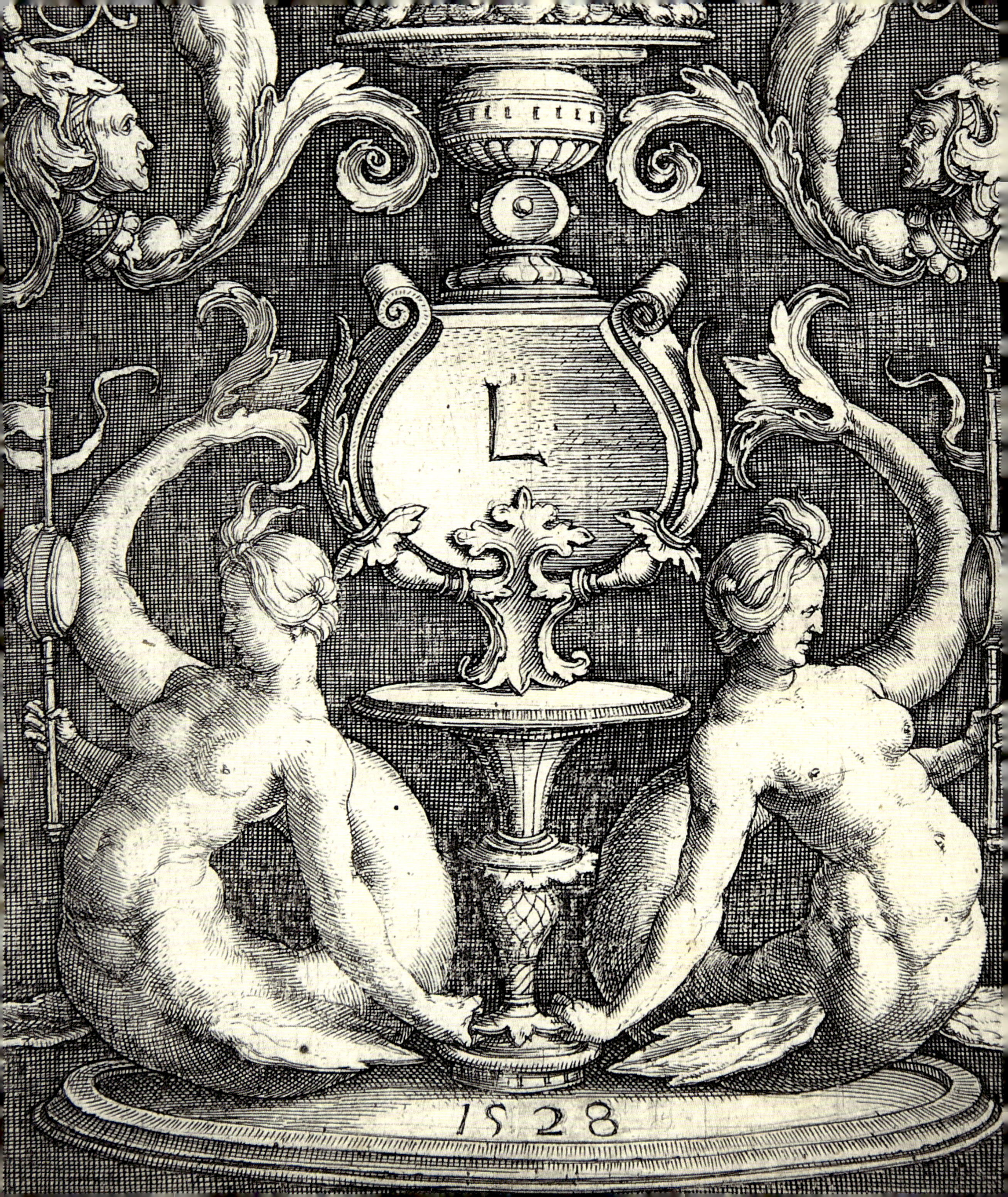
L
1528

The Education of a Curator: William Mills Ivins Jr. at the Met

PETER PARSHALL

What can be shown cannot be said.

—Ludwig Wittgenstein

WILLIAM M. IVINS (1881–1961) was thirty-five years old in 1916, when he abandoned his career in the law to become curator of the newly formed Department of Prints at The Metropolitan Museum of Art. At that time the Museum had a mere sampling of European and American prints, meager holdings that could hardly be deemed a collection. By 1946, when Ivins retired, the department had acquired what was arguably the most significant collection of prints and rare books in the country. With the additional acquisitions made under his successor, A. Hyatt Mayor, the breadth and depth of the collection, numbering hundreds of thousands of objects, earned it a position among the finest print rooms in the world. This is all the more remarkable for the fact that other institutions renowned for their print collections—the British Museum in London, the Albertina in Vienna, and the Bibliothèque Nationale de France in Paris, for example—had been amassing prints for at least two or three centuries.

Who was William Ivins, and how did undertaking such a daunting challenge gradually come to shape his principles and practices as a curator?[1] Ivins came from a well-established New York City family. His father, William M. Ivins Sr. (1851–1915), was a lawyer, businessman, and politician who traveled extensively in Europe and Latin America. A political reformer, he held several civic offices and in 1907 ran unsuccessfully for mayor. Ivins's mother, Emma Yard Ivins (1857–1940), an amateur photographer and an associate of Susan B. Anthony, was herself involved in social and political causes, notably the women's suffrage movement. Their son was educated in private schools, first in Connecticut, then at St. Paul's School in Concord, New Hampshire. Although by Ivins's account he was a good student, he remembers receiving no prizes upon graduation save a copy of *Don Quixote*, in retrospect a surprisingly apt choice that he later confessed had left him somewhat bewildered. Ivins enrolled at Harvard University in 1897, concentrating on economics and political philosophy. After graduating in 1901, he went to Europe at his father's behest to begin studies for a doctorate in economics at the University of Munich, with a possible academic career in mind. During that year he came to the decision that this was not the right path for him. Returning to New York, Ivins took a job under Walter H. Page at *The World's Work*, a periodical concerned mainly with international economic and political issues. After two years as a journalist he decided to attend law school at Columbia University, and in 1907 embarked on a legal career.[2]

Old master prints and early printed books had been a meaningful diversion ever since his undergraduate years at Harvard, where he took courses in art history and, alongside his friend Paul J. Sachs (who would become assistant director of the Fogg Museum), began collecting prints. Since 1903 Ivins had been an active member of the Grolier Club, a society devoted to books and the graphic arts, and he occasionally wrote essays for *The Print Collector's Quarterly* as well as exhibition notes for galleries, all before being asked to join the Museum. He also seems to have developed an early interest in photography as an art form. Sometime in his early twenties, the leading Pictorialist photographer Gertrude Käsebier made a portrait of him (fig. 9), a study that quietly alludes to Ivins's affection for the art of Rembrandt (fig. 10).

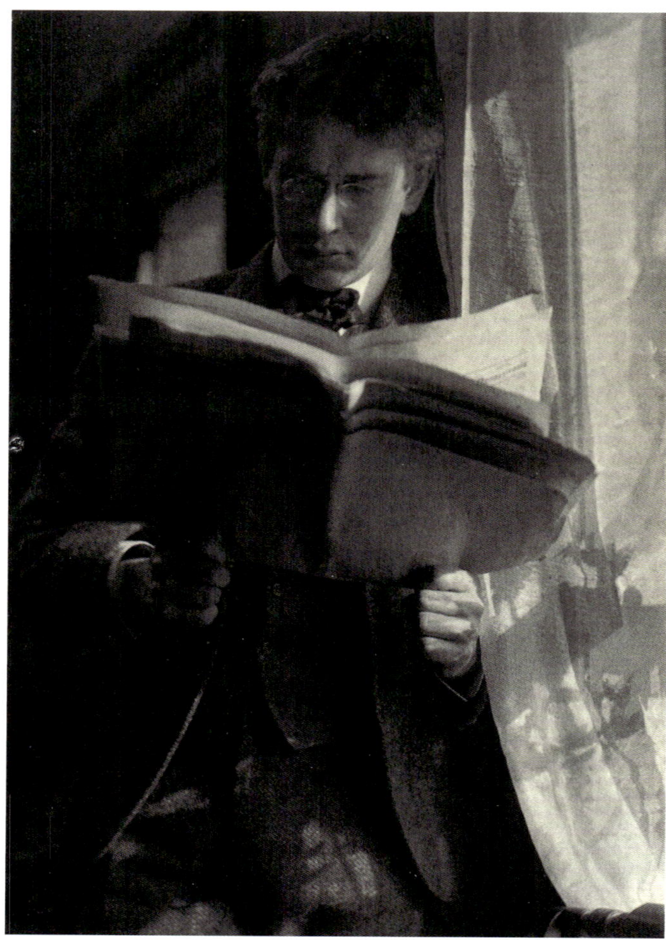

Fig. 9. Gertrude Käsebier (American, 1852–1934). William M. Ivins Jr., ca. 1910. Platinum print, 7⅝ × 5⅜ in. (19.3 × 13.5 cm). Gift of Barbara Ivins, 1984 (1984.1024.1)

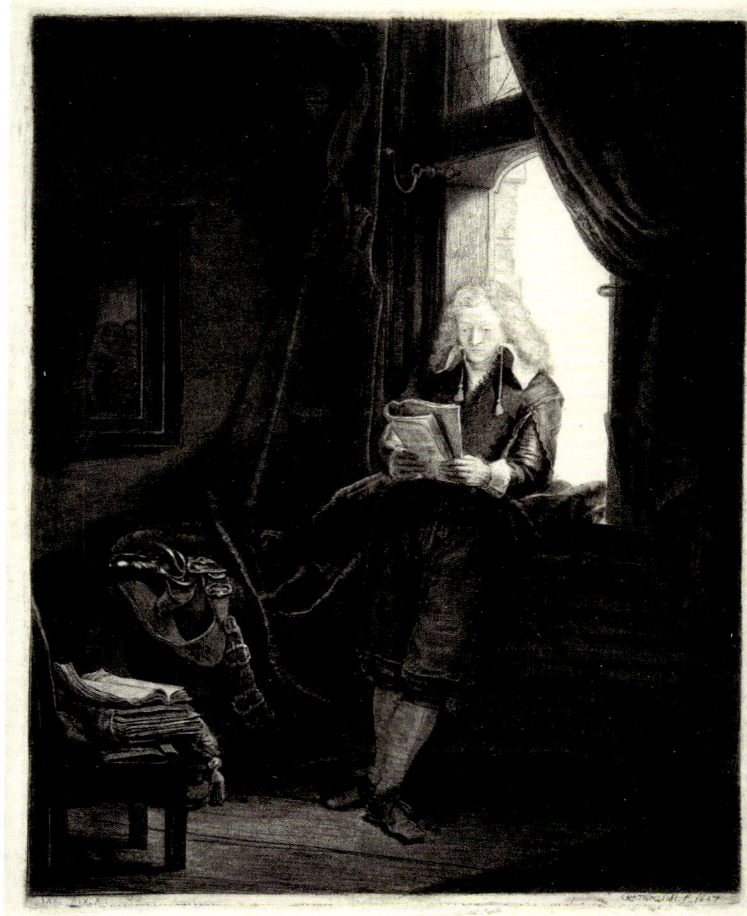

Fig. 10. Rembrandt van Rijn (Dutch, 1606–1669). *Jan Six*, 1647. Etching, drypoint, and burin, fourth state of four, 10¾ × 8⅜ in. (27.2 × 21.1 cm). Gift of Felix M. Warburg and his family, 1941 (41.1.10)

Ivins thus stands within a long tradition of museum curators who began learning their subject as private collectors and independent scholars. Unlike the study of ancient sculpture or Renaissance painting, there were no structured opportunities to be academically trained in ways applicable to the many dimensions of print history. Indeed, the academic study of art history was in its infancy in America, and research on prints was largely restricted to cataloguing and technical description. In this regard Ivins's qualifications to be a print curator would have been typical of the time. Yet he himself was by no means typical, and in recognizing this distinction the Metropolitan Museum made a brilliant appointment.

Later in life Ivins recalled a long moment of revelation that does much to explain his deepest sensibilities when it came to the experience of works of art. Whether we take the recollection at face value or not, it is so consistent with the opinions he expressed in many nuanced variations over the

years that it proves itself genuine in spirit. During the summer of 1901, on his way to Munich, Ivins spent some time in Paris, where he bought Francisco de Goya's suite of etchings titled The Disasters of War (fig. 11). As he tells it, over that year he kept returning to these prints, finding them so inexhaustible, so compelling an expression of human pathos, that he renounced the contemplative life of an academic to follow some other more engaged, although as yet undefined, path. In the thrall of Romantic transport and with characteristic hyperbole, Ivins insisted that the images had taught him more than all the university lectures on economics he attended that year. "The lad began to live, it having for the first time been brought home to him that his eyes were there to see with."[3] This declared bias against the academic would color Ivins's entire career.

The Goya story captures one dominant component of Ivins's thinking as a student of prints. He concluded at an early stage that this medium gave vast and subtle access to the history of human experience, especially human suffering. He believed these modest sheets could reveal far more about individual sentiment, about political and social movements, and about communication and persuasion than a gallery full of masterpieces by Titian and Boucher. For this reason he judged prints by artists like Pieter Bruegel the Elder, Rembrandt, and Honoré Daumier, along with Goya, as representing what art might accomplish for the betterment of civilization. Those masters remained for him in a category of their own; he sensed that they understood tragedy because they were acute observers and lived active lives close to the ground.[4] Ivins held that great works of art had to have content, by which he meant a subject, a narrative, and palpable emotion. He did not place much value in landscape or still life, for example, and had a hard time giving credence to abstraction.[5]

In all of this there is a discernible association with Ivins's liberal upbringing, his education in the social sciences, and probably a youthful inclination toward socialism shared by many among the well educated of his time.[6] He maintained a serious interest in public affairs, politics, and social issues throughout his life. Moreover, he was a self-consciously intellectual man with a clear sense of the importance of engaged citizenship among the privileged elite, an obligation that applied equally to the building and ministration of a museum collection. Ivins saw that prints and printmaking were exceptional in this respect and had to be granted a history of their own. Such a collection as the Met required would need to be managed differently from the others in the institution.

When Ivins took his seat at the foot of the curatorial high table, these larger convictions must have strengthened his resolve. An exceptional articulateness, a willingness to express opinions with a minimum of restraint, and incisive

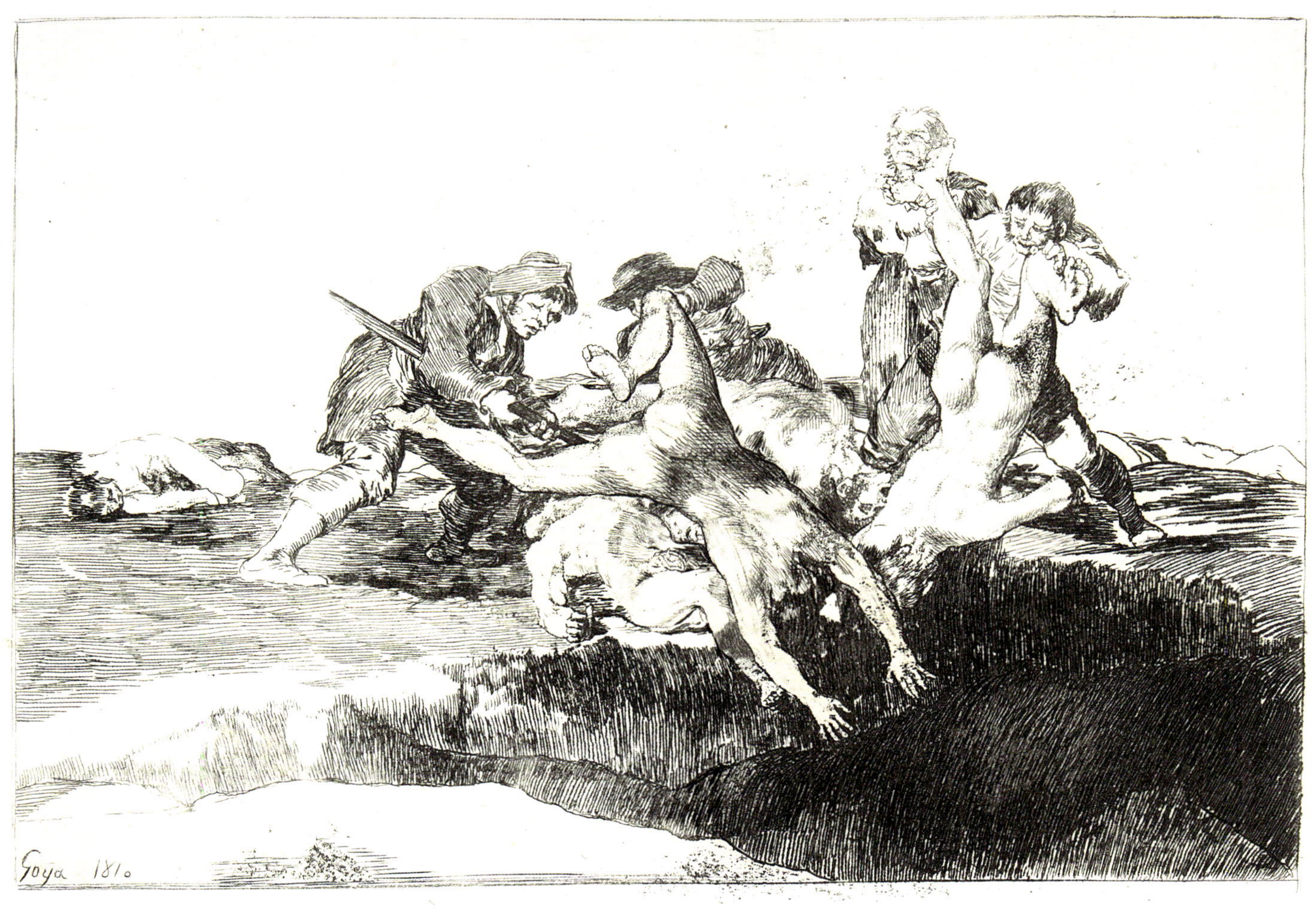

Fig. 11. Francisco de Goya y Lucientes (Spanish, 1746–1828). *Charity* (*Caridad*), plate 27 from The Disasters of War (Los Desastres de la Guerra), 1810. Etching, drypoint, and burin, 6½ × 9⅛ in. (16.3 × 23.2 cm). Harris Brisbane Dick Fund, 1932 (32.62.1)

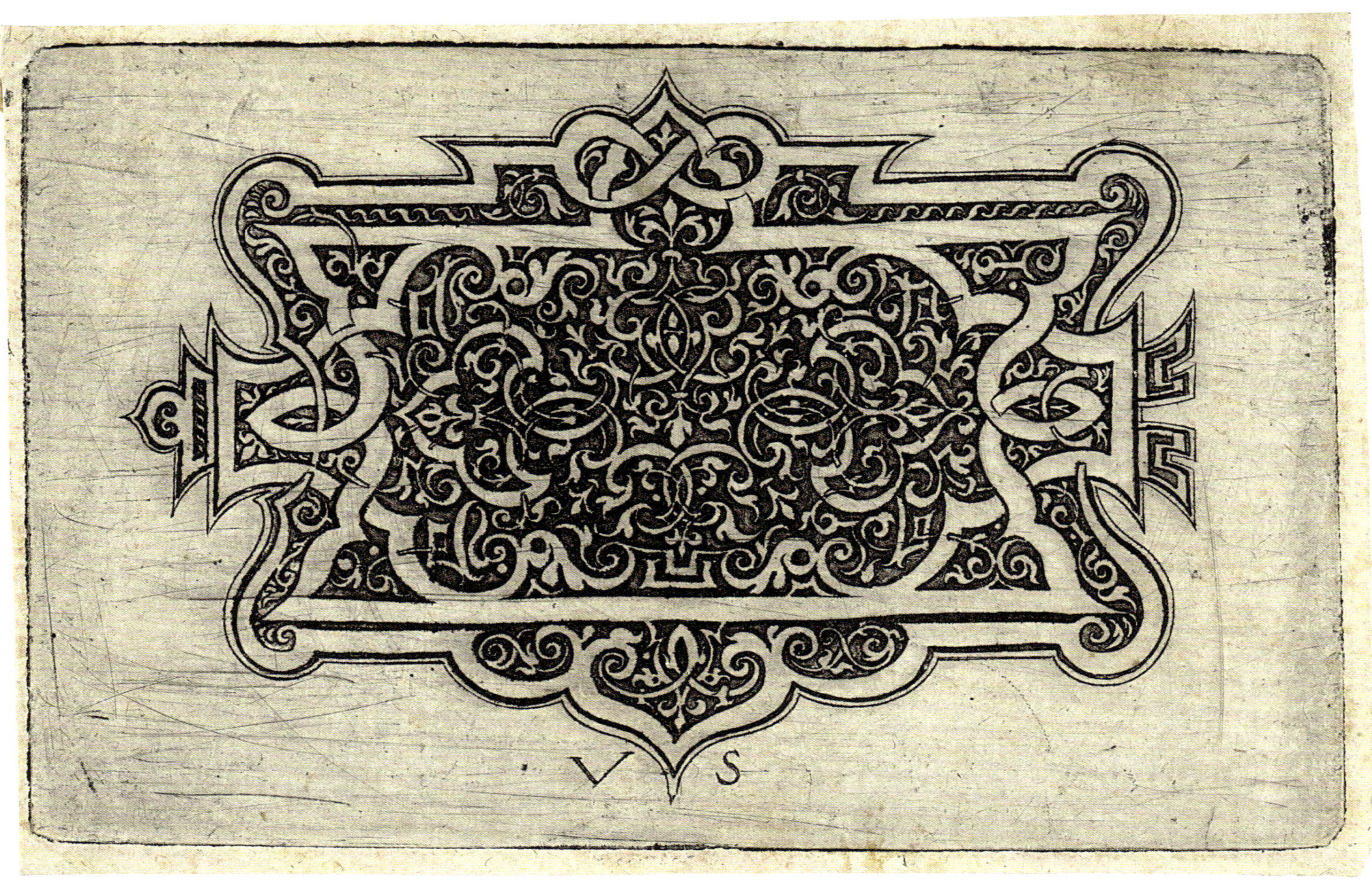

Fig. 12. Virgil Solis (German, 1514?–1562). Arabesque design on dark ground, 1534–62. Etching and engraving, 2⅞ × 4⅜ in. (7.2 × 11.1 cm). Harris Brisbane Dick Fund, 1933 (33.70.39)

views about the conduct of art history and its priorities quickly made him feared as much as respected among his fellow curators. For Ivins, authority lay not in seniority but in arguing one's case effectively and being right about it. He was an unapologetic gadfly let loose upon the field, and one cannot but sympathize with his colleagues as they confronted yet another memorandum finding fault with some seemingly uncontroversial aspect of museum practice.[7] His disputatious self was inseparable from his commitment to the intellectual life. For Ivins a university education was not a credential but the beginning of a lifetime of inquiry, and one's chief responsibility to an institution was to improve it. Accordingly, he regarded a museum's most important contributing asset to be its library, which should be for general reading by a cultivated staff and not just a resource for art historical minutiae.[8] Notwithstanding his contrariness Ivins remained highly regarded for his honesty and acumen as an administrator and a curator, and he eventually was appointed assistant director (in 1933), acting director (1938–40), counsel (1940–46), and, upon his retirement, honorary fellow for life.

Ivins believed close communion with an object, whether a book or a work of art, was the best means of understanding it. At the extreme he held that adopting a secondhand interpretation of a work of art was a concession to received authority and thereby a refusal to engage in independent thinking. On this principle he declared himself averse to composing extended analyses of artworks and to reading much of what we would term secondary literature. Hence, although Ivins wrote about Albrecht Dürer's technique for cutting woodblocks and his understanding of mathematical perspective, both topics being forms of technical investigation, he never attempted a monograph. Doing so would have meant addressing the fullness of the artist's achievement and entering into psychological speculations and private motives that are ultimately inaccessible to the historian. Such matters Ivins was reluctant to consider. No doubt largely for this

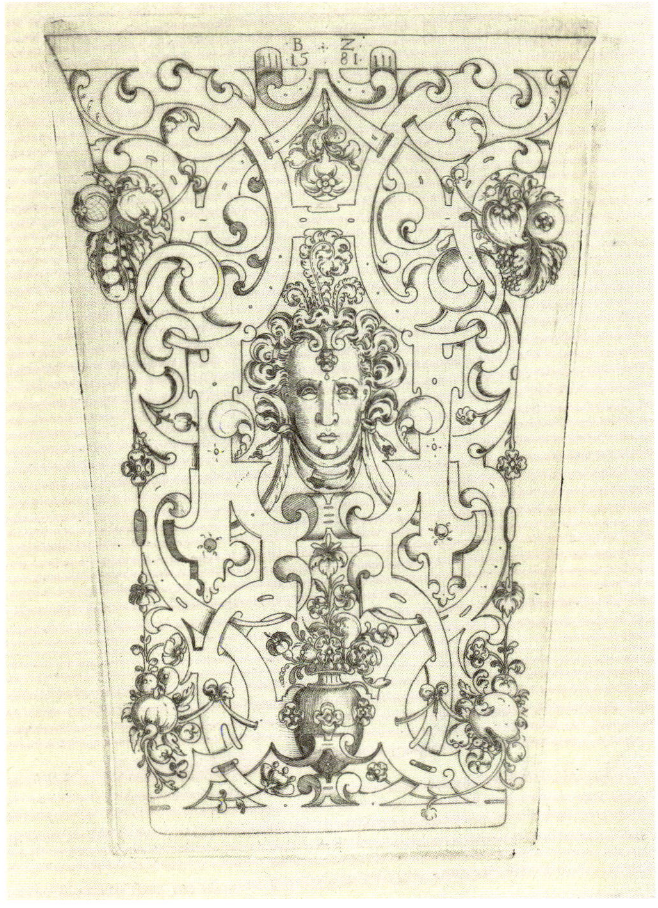

Fig. 13. Bernhard Zan (German, active 1580–81). Design for a beaker, 1581. Engraving, 11⅝ × 7¼ in. (29.4 × 18.4 cm). Rogers Fund, 1934 (34.27.3)

reason those masters whose works he found most deeply moving were not the ones he chose to write about in more than an occasional essay.

Apropos, among Ivins's early interests was the history of ornament prints, a subject he wrote about on several occasions in the 1920s and 1930s. He saw ornament design as an index of cultural priorities, a way of taking the measure of a particular aesthetic language through its formal enciphering. A pattern designed by the sixteenth-century engraver Virgil Solis for, as Ivins supposes, the stolid middle class of the German trading cities provides "a vocabulary of design but no syntax. . . . [F]or all its charm [it is] just a bit inchoate, in its unordered richness resembling the German prose of the time" (fig. 12). In contrast, a set of silversmith's patterns made a few decades later by Bernhard Zan evokes an "attitude toward life . . . humanly pleasant rather than intellectually logical"[9] (fig. 13). Such generalizations, which Ivins characterized as "comparative psychology," are in retrospect more

stereotypical than revealing, but they indicate his wish to embed prints within subconscious operations of the societies that generated them. It was a way of investing abstraction with content.

Illustrated perspective books, geometries, herbals, and anatomies were also among Ivins's protracted interests because they shed light on the efficacy of the print as a means of standardizing information. He became convinced of the importance of printing as the key to disseminating technical and scientific knowledge, and especially of the value of printed illustration to advances in technology. Typical of his time, Ivins saw technological progress as the foundation of the modern world, and his scholarly interests in the history of printmaking were largely driven by this conviction. His long-term research projects, most of them occupying Ivins to the end of his life, involved extended correspondence with scholars in related fields and, above all, the close study of primary sources, as much as possible in their original language. As would become evident in his investigations into the history of geometry, Ivins's cross-disciplinary studies were also attempts to understand larger gravitations in the history of European thought. The topics extended below and beyond individual expression or the personal gratification of an emotional encounter with an artwork.

Ivins's most congenial means of communication was with pen and paper, hence reading his letters is the most effective way to become acquainted with how his mind worked and where his deeper sentiments lay. His letters are invariably perceptive and affable, often showing an understanding of character that can be dazzling in its clarity. But he also had a biting wit and was uncompromising in his personal and professional judgments. The same qualities, although tempered, are evident in Ivins's essays, his preferred medium for the formal expression of his thoughts. For this the *Metropolitan Museum of Art Bulletin*, issued monthly to all Museum members, provided the ideal venue. Over the course of his career at the Museum Ivins published more than 180 short pieces. Graceful and clever, these essays presuppose that all his readers have minds as agile as his own.

Ivins's topics range from departmental activities to new acquisitions and exhibition ideas, from detailed considerations of individual works of art in context to personal reflections on the responsibilities of a curator. Never fearful of giving offense, he pronounced on such subjects as current taste in interior decoration, the symptoms of false erudition, academic small-mindedness, and the failings of contemporary art. These were rarely in themselves his declared topics. In the process of writing about an exhibition or an object he would broach some larger or tangential question that happened to be occupying his attention. His essays are of a frankly pedagogical nature, tightly focused, and intended to make an original point; each is a keenly honed example of what an essay ought to be—a personal, often autobiographical meditation on a subject of general importance and free to take its own course. Ivins had no hesitation in giving his private opinion in a public setting and showed little patience for writers who hid behind what he considered the standard rules of academic address. Mere reportage was not his thing. He had already begun to transform expectations for readers of the *Bulletin*, and by providing them with as much to disagree with as not, he acquired an avid following. As he was often playing out his own thoughts, the highly opinionated disposition of his writings is essential to their message.

When an idea expanded beyond the confines of the *Bulletin* or began to look less suitable for a house publication, he took it elsewhere. In 1918 Ivins drafted a scathing review of a new book on aesthetics and museum education by Benjamin Ives Gilman, the secretary of the Museum of Fine Arts, Boston, and submitted it to *The Nation*, which saw it as overheated and unsuitable. It was eventually published as an independent article after the second edition of Gilman's book appeared in 1923.[10] Still highly combative, the review includes Ivins's first digressions on important questions regarding idealist aesthetics: the problematic status of the masterpiece, the cultural origins of beauty, and the historically contingent nature of artistic judgment. He had no patience for transcendent notions of aesthetic value and, accordingly, despised the elitism of Matthew Arnold's sanctified vision of high culture, an ideology Gilman embraced.[11] Ivins was fearless in denouncing such thinking even if it issued from a well-regarded member of a sister institution. Consistent with his preference for the direct experience of objects unburdened by borrowed opinion, Ivins's aesthetics were grounded in social and historical context rather than in the authority of an inherited intellectual canon. According to him, a work of art will reveal its human secrets to the inquiring mind and across generations merely by resonating with our common humanity.

An antiauthoritarian principle is at work here. Ivins was not prepared to yield any ground to universal aesthetic values as a justification for including a work of art in a museum. There is likewise an implication that the artists who really matter are those deeply enough engaged in their own world to convey something of its reality to the present. The notion of a decontextualized masterpiece was anathema to him. Rather, his position was that a museum should provide the experience of the work without telling us what we are supposed to think about it: "What can be shown cannot be said." Ivins often cited this proposition from Wittgenstein's *Tractatus*; it was in effect his credo and went to the heart of what he valued in a work of art.[12] The museum's foremost educational mission, as he saw it, was to honor that principle: do not attempt to express in words what the work alone can say for itself. Ivins believed in a kind of immanence in the experience of art that fueled his suspicion of rhetoric, and especially academic prolixity. As he put it, "[W]e can describe the work of art only as being itself,—which is a complete and empty circularity."[13]

At first Ivins was vehemently opposed to educational programming in the Museum, even though he occasionally praised those efforts in print. Later the director asked him to take an interest in it, and characteristically he did so.

> The educational side especially fills me with preoccupation—and at times both exultation and disgust. Everyone has a different theory, everyone a different faith—and most of the faiths are in mechanical tricks and instrumentalities, the big final aim taken for granted and almost never mentioned or discussed. . . . But somehow I have a feeling that the art museum in this country is the last citadel of personality in the fight against regimented Philistinism—the only thing that still stands for the dream and hope of doing one's own thing in one's own way—the only institution that stands for a certain curious balance of thought, emotion, sensuality, without which human life becomes merely an ant hill affair without values or meanings save to the man in the moon.[14]

For Ivins the solution to museum education became a matter of training the right people to encourage visitors to discover art for themselves. Ivins had an aversion to institutionalized education (for example, the idea that there were "techniques" for teaching)—in short, anything that seemed predigested or prescriptive. He once employed a charming metaphor to make this point in an essay about the individual discovery of art in a museum.

> Making the acquaintance of a work of art is . . . more like making the acquaintance of a shy child. . . . The rules of this technique consist chiefly of advice about things not to do. Thus, if we would know a work of art, whether or not we ultimately like it, we must not, in the beginning, take an unfriendly or intolerant attitude towards it. Like a timid child a work of art rarely talks to the person who flusters and blusters at it.[15]

Such feints of anti-intellectualism permeate Ivins's writings, and as far as one takes them seriously they provoke the question of how such a concertedly intellectual creature understood this rhetorical posture. Ivins's letters—especially those responding to queries or criticisms—often begin with some form of apologia claiming his ignorance of a subject and how he is doing his best to make the most of it. Although partly a mock version of the Socratic method, behind the protestations of ignorance lay a genuine discomfort with what he deemed sterile academicism and ungrounded theorization—an unease he shared with many other scholars confronted by the daunting edifice of *Kunstwissenschaft*, the version of German art history then entering American universities.[16]

Ivins's trajectory as an art historian is difficult to plot, not least because he was disinclined to refer to the writings of others and indeed took a certain, perhaps perverse, pleasure in citing the *Encyclopedia Britannica* as an authoritative source. In retrospect, Ivins's disenchantment with academic art history centered mainly on the iconological research emerging from the University of Berlin and the Warburg Institute in Hamburg, which is to say academic studies by those scholars being aggressively recruited by American institutions in the 1930s and 1940s. When Erwin Panofsky first traveled from Hamburg to New York to lecture in 1932, presumably auditioning for a professorship at the Institute of Fine Arts, it was Ivins's pleasure to introduce him. He so deeply impressed Panofsky that an intimate exchange of mutual appreciation followed.[17] The two seem to have remained friends but, despite many common interests, never developed a close scholarly connection. Panofsky read and admired Ivins's work on Dürer, but Ivins barely acknowledged Panofsky's sweeping essay on perspective as symbolic form, a treatise directly relevant to the argument of Ivins's *Art and Geometry*.[18] Nor did he do more than refer to Panofsky's magisterial writings on Dürer.[19] As Ivins was inclined to diminish Dürer's standing, deeming him an artist who thought too much and felt too little, the likelihood is that he did not admire the laudatory tone of Panofsky's monograph, although he must have recognized its monumental contribution to scholarship.

Ivins's emphasis on the material aspects of craft reflects his aversion to an art history heavily invested in the history of ideas. His sympathies were more closely aligned with the socially and psychologically oriented work being done at the University of Vienna, best known from the writings of Alois Riegl, Franz Wickhoff, Julius von Schlosser, Wilhelm Worringer, and later Ernst Gombrich.[20] Having evolved in an intellectual community influenced by phenomenology and psychology, the Vienna School was primarily concerned with the social construction and reception of works of art, deemphasizing individual genius and the potentialities of the masterpiece, topics that had always made Ivins uncomfortable. Both Riegl and Wickhoff sought to recuperate the art of late antiquity, maintaining that it was not the degeneration of a lost high art but had a distinct integrity of its own. Ivins may have recognized a parallel here with the evaluation of prints, which were likewise widely regarded as a secondary and reflective rather than a primary and generative force in Western art.

Ivins's principal legacy as a practicing art historian and curator is twofold: the wealth of the Metropolitan Museum's collection of prints and books above all, and a slate of important publications on prints and printmaking. Ivins's major research projects concern the history of perspective, the illustration of early scientific books, and the transmission of knowledge by graphic means: *On the Rationalization of Sight* (1938); "À Propos of the *Fabrica* of Vesalius" (1943); "What about the *Fabrica* of Vesalius?" (1952); *Art and Geometry* (1946); and *Prints and Visual Communication* (1953).

Each of these studies opens a debate and slowly gathers into a highly original thesis. Ivins could not conceal his passion for a subject that captivated him, and this vigorous aspect of his research lends his writings an undeniable flair of excitement. In retrospect, however, Ivins seems often to be convincing himself as much as his audience. A proclivity for tilting against windmills, that quixotic factor his prep school teachers had observed so long ago, only increased with time.

Ivins was repeatedly drawn to the history of science and mathematics, where it seemed possible to measure an accomplishment against a framework of identifiable historical progress. Thus his intellectual models were not Bernard Berenson and Erwin Panofsky but Bertrand Russell and Alfred North Whitehead. The attraction of science explains why Ivins's projects were so heavily invested in materials and techniques: in the technical aspects of woodblock cutting, the accuracy of botanical and anatomical data, the history of geometry, and the systematized languages of visual encoding. Ivins took pride in investigating a problem from the ground up, which usually meant learning a subject's basic mechanics before any consideration of abstract ideas. For instance, when he decided to undertake a study of the history of perspective he began by giving himself a refresher course in geometry and reading Euclid. Similarly, he spent time learning the craft of woodcutting and becoming minimally competent in the basic skills of printmaking, although never to his own satisfaction. And in his retirement he became caught up in photography, including developing and printing his own negatives. Photography for him was the medium that solved the fundamental problem of representation, an opinion that now appears much oversimplified but at the time seemed to clinch the story Ivins sought to tell about the history of mechanical reproduction. His knowledge of practicalities informed his writings, among the most brilliant of which was his study of the cutting of Dürer's early woodblocks.[21] The acute observation and rigorous thinking he brought to bear on the analysis of these tattered blocks remain a benchmark of technical connoisseurship in printmaking. Ivins's conclusion—that only Dürer could have cut these blocks—still pervades the debate over the artist's involvement in the execution of his woodcuts.

Ivins's empirical measure of proof determined the direction of his research. Therefore, in his examination of early perspective books he found fault with Dürer's procedure for establishing the distance-point construction, a lapse that helps explain the dramatically compressed and decentralized perspective of the engraving *Saint Jerome in His Study*. For Ivins this could only be a matter of getting the calculation wrong.[22] He did not substantively entertain the possibility that Dürer may have consciously or subconsciously violated a law of geometry for effect, or that his adaptation of the one-point perspective system might have resulted from a desire to create an atmosphere or a particular relationship to the scene—subjective choices, after all. Although artistic motives were fundamental to Ivins's thinking, he preferred to tackle historical questions that in principle could be proven or disproven on material evidence.[23]

Accordingly, Ivins's most sustained research projects did not concern the art that he most loved, but rather the art that lent itself best to dispassionate inquiry. When he turned to a study of Andreas Vesalius's illustrated anatomies, specifically the seven-volume *De humani corporis fabrica* of 1543, he focused on the practical relationship between the text and the accompanying illustrations (fig. 14). Characteristically, Ivins concentrated not on the physician Vesalius's written remarks but on the skill of the unknown draftsman (or draftsmen) responsible for making the drawings and overseeing the cutting of the blocks. That was something about which Ivins knew a great deal, and it led him to a heretical conclusion: an artist capable of making illustrations of such quality and accuracy must, through intense observation, have come to understand human anatomy as well as or better than a physician who had merely studied it from a distance. Thus Ivins reasoned that Jan van Calcar, considered the most likely illustrator of the *Fabrica*, must have been in charge of the entire publication. This reduced the medical doctor Vesalius, who conducted the dissections, to the marginal role of providing routine commentaries on the illustrations. Although Ivins's proposal has gained little favor among historians of science, his point is that the knowledge and skill required to successfully accomplish such a project extended well beyond medical training.[24] In addition to the draftsmanship, the illustrations required an understanding of the limits of woodcut for registering detail. If you do not know what the medium is capable of, you cannot translate the relevant information into images that are useful. In essence, someone who spent hundreds of hours drawing all parts of the body would have understood human anatomy better than anyone.

While Ivins proclaimed himself a mere investigator of material facts, he ended up adopting some surprisingly unorthodox views that tended to solidify into unassailable convictions as he faced criticism from scholars in the relevant fields. Most notorious of these iconoclastic hobbyhorses is his low regard for the ancient Greeks. Ivins came to believe that an overestimation of Greek culture had retarded scientific progress by privileging ancient authority and abstract ideas over technical and scientific innovation. The burden of the argument rests on what Ivins saw as the limitations of Euclidian geometry, a system based on congruence and what he considered a "tactile-muscular" conception of space.[25] By contrast the visually based, or virtual, geometry of Renaissance perspective, a system later advanced by Girard Desargues (1591–1661), signaled a monumental shift in what Ivins called "space intuitions."[26] Ivins may have found support for such a conclusion in Alois Riegl's conception of the evolution from ancient to modern art forms as a shift from tactile (haptic) to visual (optic) thinking.[27] This is an obvious precedent for Ivins's view of the evolution from Greek to Renaissance art, although for Ivins this evolution meant breaking out of a reactionary mode of seeing into a progressive one. The inhibition of geometry was thus another result of the undue respect accorded to the Greeks, a bias that Ivins

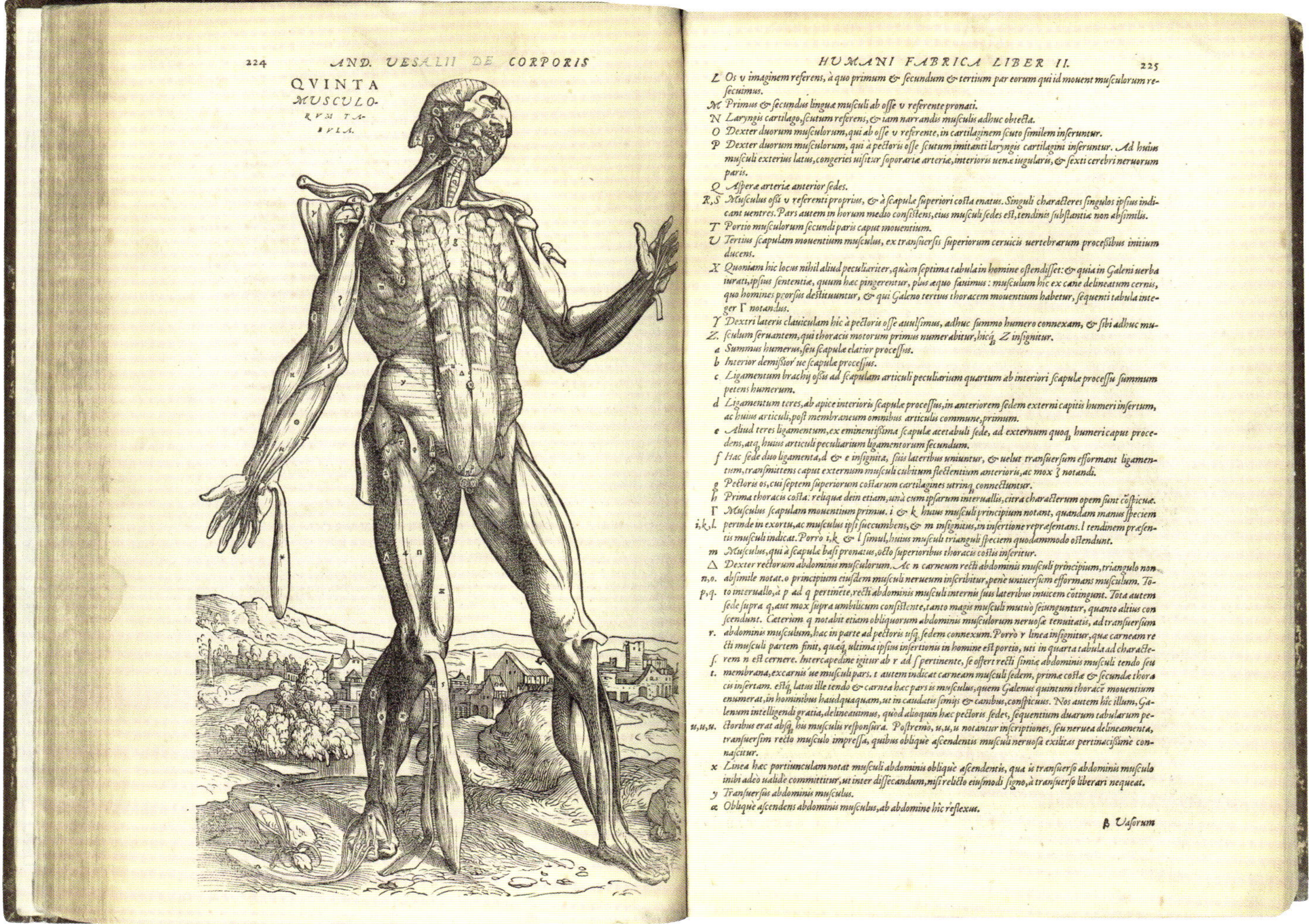

Fig. 14. The fifth muscle man, from *De humani corporis fabrica* by Andreas Vesalius (Flemish, 1514–1564). Published in Basel, 1555. Book overall: 15⅝ × 10½ × 3¼ in. (39.5 × 26.7 × 8.3 cm). Gift of Dr. Alfred E. Cohn, in honor of William M. Ivins Jr., 1953 (53.682)

saw persisting in his own time in the reverence for Greek art and, more consequentially, in the totalitarian drift of political idealism.

Typical of Ivins, he advanced his arguments by slaughtering sacred cows, a move guaranteed to provoke both applause and hostility.[28] He insisted that classical archaeologists had construed entire artistic chronologies from unprovenanced and undatable fragments and that the outline of Greek philosophy taught in the schools was largely a fabrication based on hopelessly splintered bits of evidence. In brief, Ivins held that we know next to nothing about the Greeks and should not pretend otherwise. Like many a combative rhetorician he adopted extreme positions, but centuries of classical studies were not easily swept aside. Ironically, Ivins's proclivity for reductive argument was something he shared with Socrates, and it exposed him to challenges that a more cautious writer might have avoided.[29]

The intensity of Ivins's anti-Hellenic stance must also be understood in light of his abiding attention to political philosophy. His criticism of the ancient Greeks, particularly of Plato's vision of an ideal society in *The Republic*, can be related to a broader change of opinion among social scientists of his generation. Like Ivins, many of his friends grew up in liberal households, often with socialist leanings, and eventually had to confront the catastrophic consequences of totalitarianism on both the left and the right during the 1930s and

1940s. What in some intellectual circles was perceived as a misappropriation of the Platonic strain of classical political theory led to a reevaluation of the ancient precedents. In Ivins's world this case was most forcefully prosecuted by Karl Popper in his now-canonical work of political philosophy, *The Open Society and Its Enemies* (1945). Popper's book is a frontal assault on the authoritarian implications of *The Republic* and what Popper identifies as its most lethal offspring, the theories of historical determinism developed by Georg Wilhelm Friedrich Hegel and Karl Marx.[30] Popper's argument resonated powerfully in the immediate postwar climate of opinion, and his case against Plato reinforced Ivins's own conviction that all bad things descended from the Greeks.[31]

Against that backdrop Ivins's seemingly aberrant arguments can be understood as a good deal more than the writings of an amateur mathematician and sometime student of logic who had misgivings about the limits of archaeological evidence. Rather, he approached fundamental philosophical questions as matters of great consequence to daily life and the future of civilization: the essential humanity embodied in works of art; the contingent nature of beauty; the importance of educating the museum public; the tyranny of received opinion; and the soundness of our historical knowledge. On such topics Ivins expressed himself with passion and often disconcerting bluntness. A committed skeptic, his life was a crusade of persistent questioning that required him to disrupt complacency wherever he found it.

Ivins's last twenty years bore many personal and professional disappointments, but they were also in substantial ways the most productive of his scholarly career. In 1940, after two years as the Museum's acting director, he was denied the directorship, an unsurprising decision given his prickliness. Nonetheless, he had committed himself to the Museum and must have felt that rejection deeply. Returning to his position as a curator, he continued to argue his own opinions, especially in regard to the presentation of the collections and the various educational programs being promoted. Ivins later judged his career as a "museum man" to have been a failure, but it is difficult to accept this dejected declaration straightforwardly. There can be no question that, in addition to having built an astonishing collection, he transformed and redirected the curatorial affairs of the Museum. He set a standard of curatorial responsibility and reflection that would not be ignored. In his last years of employment he began to invest more time in his research, which led, in 1946, to the publication of his second short book on geometry and,

in the same year, an honorary degree from Yale University. Ivins's studies of Vesalius (1943 and 1952), as well as the prestigious Lowell Lectures delivered at the Boston Public Library (1950) and their subsequent publication as *Prints and Visual Communication*, all fell within the decade spanning his last few years in the department and the beginning of his retirement in Woodbury, Connecticut.

In the midst of this rush of productivity Ivins confronted what must have been his harshest personal trial—the death of his wife, Florence, in 1948, after thirty-eight years of marriage. Although comforted by visits to and from his daughter Barbara, to whom he was deeply devoted, Ivins chose to sequester himself in Woodbury, a preference that diminished regular human contact. It has been generally agreed that, in this period of greater isolation, a taint of bitterness afflicted many of his personal and professional relationships. The tenor of his correspondence from that time, however, suggests this is at best a half-truth. In many ways privacy had always suited him, and he wrote most comfortably from his retreats in the country. Although his letters postretirement exhibit his usual impatience with people and with what he considered to be the misdirection of academic and curatorial life, he also maintained a loyal, affectionate, and often electric correspondence with friends and colleagues. And he continued to acquire new epistolary acquaintances, most of them gained through mutual scholarly interests.

Perhaps tellingly, Ivins often found his most stimulating colleagues in other disciplines: the ophthalmologist Adelbert Ames Jr.; the eccentric poet, literary cryptographer, and collector Walter Arensberg; the philosopher and student of ancient thought George Boas; the medical researcher Alfred E. Cohn; the legal scholar and Supreme Court justice Felix Frankfurter; the classical philosopher, historian, and rabbi Henry A. Rosenthal; and, to a lesser degree, the historian of science George Sarton. Given the surviving letters—which appear to be relatively representative of Ivins's long-standing relationships—others whom one might have expected him to befriend are little in evidence. The decades of faithful correspondence with Bernard Berenson reflect a relationship that was close, but in the end not respectful on Ivins's part, as he came to see the aging Berenson's shallow and self-serving side.[32] Ivins's fascination with the history of technology should have drawn him into the circle of Lewis Mumford, an increasingly important figure in New York intellectual circles. Ivins did in fact appear with Mumford in 1928 in a forum on taste in architecture,[33] and much later made disparaging remarks about his writings, but there is nothing to suggest a deeper connection. In later years he might also have more fully engaged the art historian Meyer Schapiro.[34] The list could go on, although in the end negative evidence has at best an unstable bearing on how Ivins may have construed his own circle. Conscious of his chronic misbehavior, he was at the same time a prolific, honest, often intimate correspondent. In many ways this more private means of communication perfectly suited his need for conversation. Moreover, it accommodated his exceptional skill as a writer, allowed for his piercing wit to play freely, and likely provided him and his epistolary companions plenty of laughs. These talents were also effective in public and institutional debate, but there they proved costly.

The last and by far most influential of Ivins's contributions to the larger history of printmaking is *Prints and Visual Communication*, an analysis of the techniques of pictorial representation through the printed medium. Although this project finally appeared in 1953, its essential themes can be traced back in Ivins's writings as early as the 1920s.[35] The basic thesis is that significant advances in science and technology from the Renaissance onward, and our knowledge of many other areas as well, depend heavily on the fact that certain ideas can be expressed only in pictures; they are those things that can be shown but not said. Equally important, to be effective such pictures must be replicable in order to be disseminated in identical form—in Ivins's bulky phrase, as "exactly repeatable pictorial statements." In pursuit of this phenomenon Ivins traces the history of representation in prints from the fifteenth through the nineteenth century, from the earliest woodcuts to engraving, lithography, and finally photography, which he regarded as the culminating solution to the problem of adequate reproduction. In interpreting the history of the replicated image, Ivins identifies the various schemes of what he termed "pictorial syntax" that printmakers developed to convey different kinds of visual information in black and white: technical diagrams, the contours of the human body, surface textures, representations of other works of art, and so on (figs. 15, 16). The manipulation and refinement of these syntaxes made possible the transmission of certain kinds of

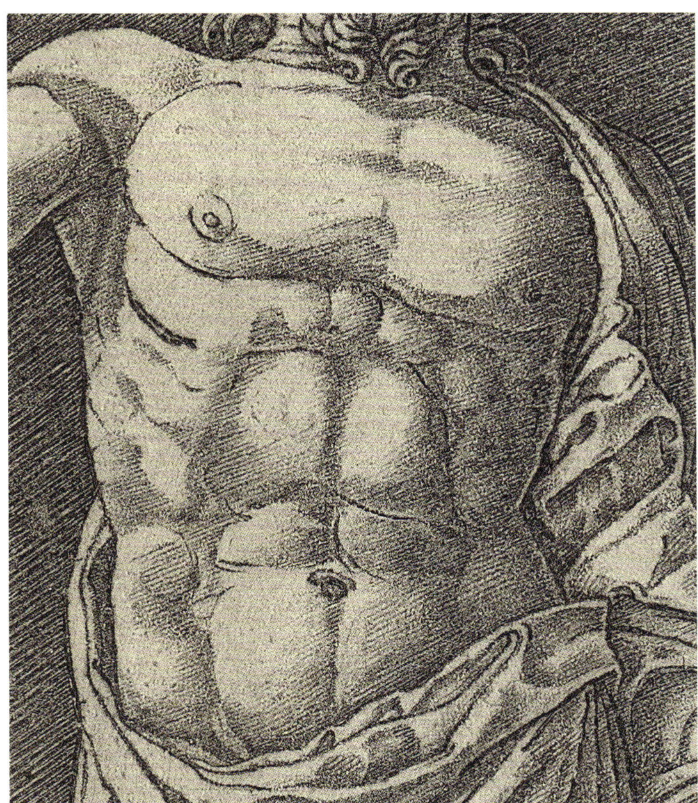

Fig. 15. Andrea Mantegna (Italian, 1430/31–1506). *The Risen Christ between Saint Andrew and Saint Longinus* (detail), ca. 1472. Engraving, overall 12⅜ × 11⅜ in. (31.5 × 28.9 cm). Rogers Fund, 1921 (21.28)

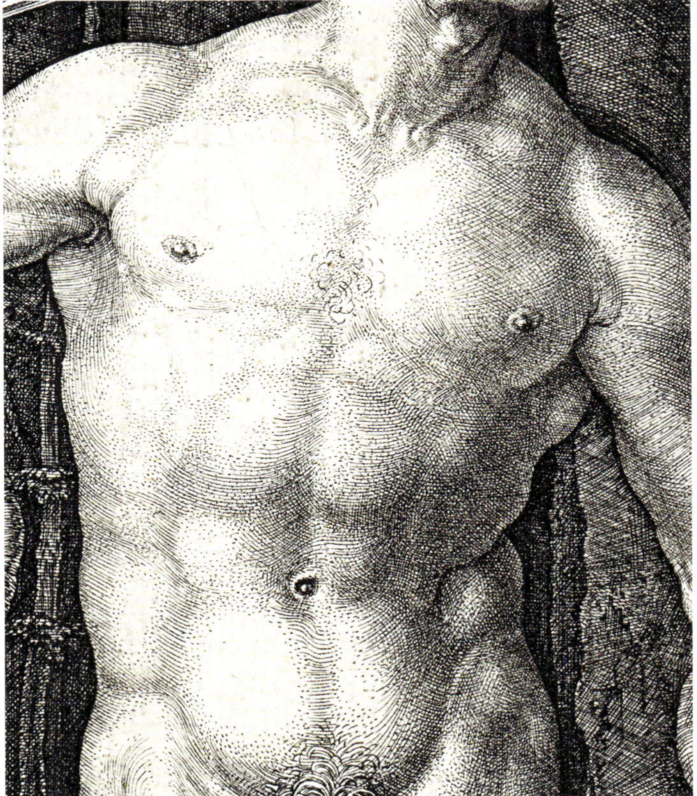

Fig. 16. Albrecht Dürer (German, 1471–1528). *Adam and Eve* (detail), 1504. Engraving, overall 9⅞ × 7⅞ in. (25.1 × 20 cm). Fletcher Fund, 1919 (19.73.1)

information and not others and so came to determine what could and could not be communicated: the medium is the message, *avant la lettre*. Ivins makes a rigorous case for the printed image as a determining force in the history of communication in general, thereby granting a major role in the propagation of knowledge to a relatively rudimentary slate of reproductive techniques.[36]

Prints and Visual Communication appeared almost contemporaneously with André Malraux's *Voices of Silence* (1951; English translation 1953), which proposes that the institution of museums completely restructured our understanding of art. Malraux speculates that the ability to see objects from widely divergent cultures in a uniform setting such as a museum transforms them into works of art regardless of their original purpose. He further argues that photographic reproduction made works of art universally accessible for the first time, an advance he credits with bringing about a second revolution on the same order as the institution of public museums in the eighteenth century.[37] Malraux sees this newfound accessibility through reproduction not as decontextualizing the object but rather as liberating it, allowing the artwork to be assimilated into the totality of human experience. Malraux's claims for photography are in many ways the cultural counterpart to Ivins's claims for transmitting visual information, both arguments suggesting a salutary effect of democratic leveling through mass reproduction.

In several respects *Prints and Visual Communication* was a precocious, even radically topical book when it entered the slipstream of contemporary social scientific thinking. It anticipated by nearly a decade Marshall McLuhan's *The Gutenberg Galaxy* (1962), an analysis of the transforming effects of the mass media in modern society.[38] Also a decade later, Thomas Kuhn argued that the overall direction of scientific research is governed more by received assumptions than free, objective inquiry and that the history of science is marked by long periods of channeled investigation punctuated by hugely consequential breakthroughs that initiate what Kuhn termed "paradigm shifts." This idea has much in common with Ivins's argument that the authority of Euclid's mathematics constituted a "blocked road" that for centuries obscured the way to projective geometry and thereby impeded a spatial mentality capable of making the modern world possible.[39]

How does Ivins's career as a scholar, and to some degree as a public intellectual, bear on his achievements in building the Department of Prints at The Metropolitan Museum of Art?

There are many dimensions to this question and no single answer. As a private collector Ivins's interests were multiple yet inevitably determined by individual preference and means. As a curator his scope was vastly greater. He rarely ever seems to have discussed his acquisition tactics apart from recognizing that some things needed to be hunted down and others would come to the Museum through gifts. Ivins took the hunting very seriously, however, and particularly in his early years made several buying trips to Europe. His career spanned two World Wars, the Wall Street crash, and the Great Depression; even so, opportunities were considerable, but it took energy to realize them.

In any event, what Ivins acquired is more interesting than how he acquired it. Early on he adopted the view that a print collection bore many different responsibilities in a museum with global ambitions. He was of course aware of the encyclopedic character of many early European collections of prints, and he believed that a department of prints should position itself somewhere between the museum proper and its library. That is, a print collection needed to be a resource as well as an assembly of works of art. Moreover, he recognized that illustrated books had a history that could not be separated from the history of prints, so these too were an essential part of his brief. And with remarkable foresight he recognized that a collection of photography was critical to a serious representation of the graphic arts.[40]

This integrated approach to the history of a medium and its value for understanding the past compelled Ivins to think more broadly than perhaps any of his peers at the Museum were inclined to do, given their better established responsibilities. Meanwhile, Ivins's training in the social sciences equipped him to look beyond aesthetic criteria in imagining the future value of such a wide-ranging collection. Thus he endeavored to construct a pictorial history not just of art but of society itself. Indeed, he sought to represent a history of political and social thinking, of scientific research and technical experiment, of narrative literature, of commerce and topography, and, not least, the scattered evidence of printed ephemera. The outstanding strength of the Museum's print collection is its breadth, a result of Ivins's having conceived it from the start as more than a connoisseur's portfolio. Ivins's scholarly interests in themselves proceed logically from the rationale for such an inclusive collection, and as he built it his interests became even more determined by its scope. Ivins's understanding of the collection came to be fully endorsed by his colleague and successor Hyatt Mayor, who carried it into

still wider domains. But Ivins's strengths as a curator were by
no means restricted to accumulating historical documenta-
tion and recognizing the socially redeeming content of works
of art. He was indisputably a superior judge of quality and of
the technical refinements and physical condition of prints.[41]
However much he read and wrote, Ivins must have spent even
more time just looking intently.

Like Candide, in his last years Ivins spent much time
cultivating his own garden, about which he wrote with great
affection.[42] He had a special interest in peonies and, as one
would expect of him, seems to have developed considerable
expertise in the subject (fig. 17). Ivins was anyhow not a little
melancholic—certainly so when he began to suffer chronic
physical difficulties—and despite his persistent dismissal of
how things were going in the art world, not to say the world
at large, he may have grown genuinely doubtful about the
strength and originality of his own opinions. One senses
from his letters that he was gaining greater distance on life
as he entered his seventies. It was likely during a visit to his
daughter in New York City that he wrote the following lines
to a friend: "Here I do little or nothing—but in walking
the streets take pleasure and comfort in watching the very
young—so funny, so charming, in gait and gesture—and
their little mugs so full of expression. Find myself standing over them and looking down at them like some ancient
stork. Somehow they give me a pleasant feeling of benevo-
lence—'specially as they are completely unaware of my pres-
ence and care nothing about me or my feelings."[43] These are
the words of a man who did not lack self-knowledge, a man
who carried within him much of the humanity he esteemed in
the art he held most dear. Ivins's reputation for irascibility has
not served him well with posterity, yet a sustained acquaintance with his private correspondence (much of it written
with quill pens he cut himself) reveals a sentimentality that
must have remained invisible to many of those who knew him
less well. A declared skeptic in all matters of importance, over
time he also acquired the disposition of a stoic. And although
he never seems to have lost his critical edge, those qualities
that many found endearing remained very much alive as well.

Ivins's most lasting contribution to the methods of art
history and curatorial practice are a direct result of his
breadth of interest and his conviction about the singular
importance of printed matter to Western culture. We can
trace the idea that printmaking had a special role in the history of art to at least the seventeenth century, but it was
principally Ivins who integrated that notion into a subtle and

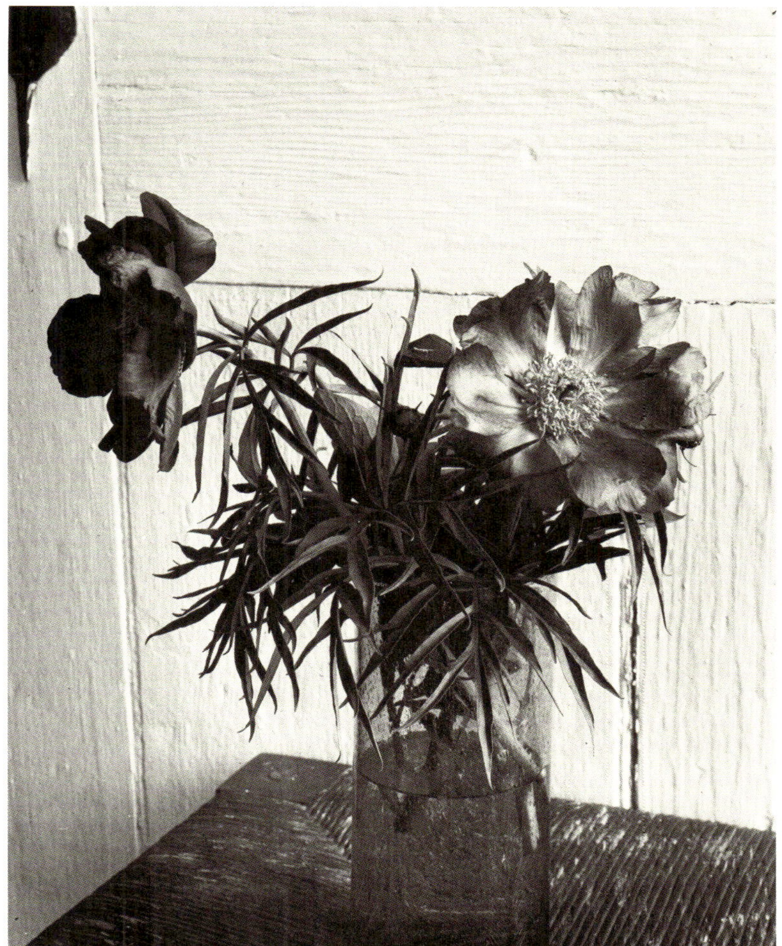

Fig. 17. William M. Ivins Jr. (American, 1881–1961). Peonies, ca. 1950s. Photograph.
Archives of American Art, Smithsonian Institution

original account of the medium itself. Most important, he
approached the phenomenon of prints in more than formal
respects. For him the impact of the print was both intellectual
and pragmatic. Prints changed the way people saw things and
changed the way in which information was exchanged. What
is now a flourishing area of study in the relationship between
art and descriptive science owes a considerable debt to his
writings. Ivins likewise anticipated much of what was later
explored under the aegis of social and intellectual history,
semiotics and information theory, and the history of taste.
What he offered was not so much a contained method in itself
as a way of asking direct questions about how and why things
were made and to what use they might have been put. It was
an empirical approach, beginning with the object and working outward to larger speculations. Most important, he never
lost sight of the connection between object and idea.

1881: William Mills Ivins Jr. is born to William Mills Ivins, a lawyer active in political reform, and Emma Yard Ivins, an amateur photographer, in Flatbush, New York.

1890–93: Ivins attends King's School, Stamford, Connecticut.

1893–97: Ivins attends St. Paul's School, Concord, New Hampshire.

1896: Ivins travels to South America with his father and a group of engineers.

1897–1901: Ivins attends Harvard University, graduating in 1901 with a degree in economics. He takes courses in art history and architecture and has his initial encounters with prints at Harvard's Fogg Museum and the Museum of Fine Arts, Boston.

1901–2: Ivins travels to Europe and enrolls at the University of Munich. His nominal purpose is to study economics, but he remains focused on prints. While visiting Paris Ivins buys, for sixty francs, an edition of Goya's Disasters of War (now in the collection of the University of San Diego), a purchase that shifts his understanding of the impact of prints and ignites his passion for collecting them.

1902–4: Ivins settles in New York and is employed by *The World's Work*, a monthly magazine. His articles include "Russia and the Nations" (July 1903) and "South America and Our Responsibility" (February 1904).

1903: Ivins joins the Grolier Club. He will remain an active member until his death.

1903–16: Ivins makes regular one- to three-month trips to Europe, largely to study prints in Paris, London, Oxford, and Amsterdam. In London he makes the acquaintance of Campbell Dodgson and Arthur Hind, both future Keepers of Prints and Drawings at the British Museum. He plans a monograph on the early development of color printing, etching, and engraving but abandons the project when he learns that both Dodgson and Hind are at work on similar books. In New York and abroad he makes an effort to

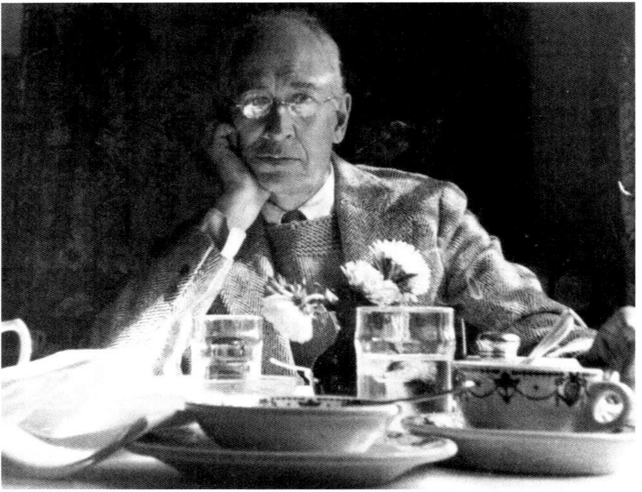

Fig. 18. Photographer unknown (possibly Barbara Ivins). William M. Ivins Jr., Woodbury, Conn., after 1946. Photograph. Archives of American Art, Smithsonian Institution

meet contemporary printmakers such as Rudolph Ruzicka. He also attempts to learn printmaking techniques.

1904–7: Ivins attends Columbia University Law School in New York. He often can be found in Columbia's Avery Architectural and Fine Arts Library looking through art periodicals.

1907–16: Ivins works as a lawyer, first with Ivins, Wolff, and Hoguet for the New York Public Service Commission (1907–8). He then works for Strong and Cadwallader (1908–9) and Cravath, Henderson and de Gersdorff (1909–16). He works on corporate mortgages and is involved with the introduction of American securities to the Paris Bourse.

1908: In November Ivins arranges his first exhibition of prints, "Engravings and Etchings by Albrecht Dürer," at Frederick Keppel & Co., the New York print dealer.

1910: Ivins marries Florence Wyman, a watercolor portraitist and book illustrator in New York who had studied Japanese color printing in Paris.

1911: In April Ivins's first article on prints, "A Note on Goya," appears in the second issue of *The Print-Collector's Quarterly*, a new periodical published by Frederick Keppel & Co.

1913: The Ivinses' daughter, Barbara, is born.

1915: In November Ivins assists his friend the curator Paul J. Sachs with an exhibition and catalogue for the Fogg Museum, *A Loan Exhibition of Early Italian Engravings*.

1916: In December Ivins is appointed the first curator of Prints at The Metropolitan Museum of Art.

1919: Ivins joins the Century Association and is a member until 1961. In November the Met's Department of Prints acquires Junius

Spencer Morgan's almost comprehensive collection of Albrecht Dürer's engravings and woodcuts. The collection also includes two of Dürer's woodblocks.

1921: Watercolors, drawings, and woodcuts by Ivins's wife, Florence Wyman Ivins, are shown in the Education Department (July 15–November 19), the Metropolitan Museum's first solo exhibition of works by a female artist.

1927: Ivins and his wife write and illustrate a small booklet for their friends for New Year's Day, *A Parable of Art Critics and of Collectors by Hans Christian* [sic] *Andersen*, an adaptation of Andersen's tale of pride and intellectual vanity "The Emperor's New Clothes."

1929: The Havemeyer Bequest comes to the Museum. Best known for its nineteenth-century French paintings and decorative arts, it also includes a substantial collection of prints by Degas and Rembrandt, among others.

1930: The Museum publishes Ivins's *Notes on Prints*, a compilation of label texts from the 1929 exhibition "Prints—Selected Masterpieces."

1932–35: Ivins serves as president of the Grolier Club.

1933–38: Ivins serves as assistant director of The Metropolitan Museum of Art.

1936: Ivins gives a series of lectures on illustrated books of the Renaissance at the Pierpont Morgan Library.

1938: Ivins is named honorary curator of prints and drawings at the Pierpont Morgan Library. His *On the Rationalization of Sight: With an Examination of Three Renaissance Texts on Perspective* is published as an appendix to a facsimile of the French text of Viator's *De artificiali perspectiva* (1505).

1938–40: Ivins serves as acting director of The Metropolitan Museum of Art.

1941: The family of Felix Warburg, who had made many smaller gifts to the Department of Prints prior to his death in 1937, donates a substantial portion of Warburg's collection, including prints by Rembrandt, Dürer, and Marcantonio Raimondi.

1943: Ivins's book *How Prints Look* is published.

1946: In June Ivins retires from the Museum. He and his wife move to Woodbury, Connecticut. Ivins's book *Art and Geometry: A Study in Space Intuitions* is published. Ivins is named honorary fellow for life of The Metropolitan Museum of Art, and Yale University awards him an honorary doctorate of fine arts.

1947: Ivins, a lifelong photographer, begins to play with the effects of light and to explore the textures of objects, often flowers from his beloved garden, with his camera.

1950: In January Ivins delivers eight lectures on the history of printed images at the Lowell Institute, Boston.

1953: Ivins's book based on the Lowell Lectures, *Prints and Visual Communication*, is published.

1961: On June 14, Ivins dies in White Plains, New York, aged eighty.

1962: Ivins's daughter, Barbara, sells nearly eight hundred items from Ivins's collection of prints and books to the Department of Prints (accessioned as 62.650.1–.790). In addition to this sale, Ivins had made many small gifts to the museum over the course of his career.

1963: The remainder of Ivins's collection of prints and illustrated books is sold at auction by Parke-Bernet Galleries, New York. The main sales include Modern Graphic Art and Drawings, Estate of the Late William M. Ivins, Jr. (Jan. 11); Rare Books and Manuscripts, Early Illustrated Books & Incunabula, American & English Literature, Slavery and the Civil War, Belonging to the Estate of the Late William M. Ivins, Woodbury, Connecticut (Jan. 15–16); Important Old Master Engravings, Etchings, Woodcuts, Drawings from the Estate of the Late William M. Ivins, Jr., Woodbury, Connecticut (March 14); and Rare Manuscripts, Maps, and Books from the Library of the Czars and from the Aldine Press, Western Americana, from Various Owners, Including Mrs. Carl H. Stone, Estates of the Late William M. Ivins, Jr., The Rev. Dr. Anson Phelps Stokes (March 19).

London, Published by B. Pollock, 73, Hoxton Street, Hoxton

A. Hyatt Mayor's Life in Art and Letters

FREYDA SPIRA

An excursion into the past is sometimes the road to the future.

—Hyatt Mayor

IN AN ADDRESS AT Princeton University in 1977, Alpheus Hyatt Mayor (1901–1980) advocated the following method for confronting and truly seeing a work of art: "Plant yourself in front of the original and start looking. . . . After about half an hour, a fog will lift, like breath leaving a windowpane, and you will enter. You will never forget the thrill."[1] For Mayor, a curator of prints who spent his long career immersed in art of all media, periods, and cultures, that thrill never diminished. His lectures, catalogues, articles, and other writings—notably his now-canonical *Prints & People: A Social History of Printed Pictures* (1971)—explore how works of art are an expression of humanity, "magic windows on history and human life"[2] that conjure and communicate vivid narratives about the people who created, engaged with, and were represented in them. In *Prints & People* Mayor departs from the traditional focus on artistic merit and quality of impressions to present the social history of prints, beginning with a series of fundamental questions: Why were prints made? How? Who bought them? How did they travel? What new techniques were devised? What new subject matter appeared? How did print publishers attract new audiences? Which printmakers discovered new ways of seeing? What resulted from innovation?[3] With this deceptively simple approach, Mayor explores the complex history of prints, from the Chinese invention of paper making to a 1960 lithograph by Jasper Johns, via short, masterfully written essays as disparate in scope and focus as "Playing Cards and Others," "Life in France," "Aesop," and "Dutch Etchers before Rembrandt." The texts are woven through with images of 752 remarkable objects, selected mainly from The Metropolitan Museum of Art's expansive print collection. The outgrowth of Mayor's immersion in the collection and his experience working in "the stimulating disquiet of William M. Ivins' questioning,"[4] *Prints & People* was simultaneously a primer for the general reader and a touchstone for scholars, as it remains to this day.

The Backdrop

Mayor was born into a house of cultured intellectuals. His father and grandfather were eminent marine biologists, his mother and her sister, Anna Hyatt, sculptors. His beloved aunt Anna would marry Archer Huntington, heir to a railroad fortune and a major supporter of the arts, in 1923.[5] Mayor spent his early summers wandering between the coves and around the coastal village of Annisquam, near Gloucester, Massachusetts. During the winters his family traveled extensively, trailing his father and his work for the Carnegie Institute. As a young boy Mayor spent time in the Dry Tortugas off the Florida Keys, in Penzance on the English Channel, and in Germany, France, and Italy.

After exhibiting at the Paris Salon in 1910,[6] his aunt Anna invited Mayor's family to spend the summer with her in Auvers-sur-Oise, France. Anna took over the studio of the Barbizon artist Charles-François Daubigny and worked in the shadow of its former residents Vincent van Gogh, Paul Cézanne, and Camille Pissarro. Happily ensconced in such a beautiful landscape, Mayor spent his days hovering near his aunt in her studio or learning French from the landlady, Madame de Plantier, among the cornflowers in the fields above the town. When the First World War broke out in 1914, Mayor's family ceased their European jaunts and settled in Princeton, New Jersey. Mayor remained in Princeton and went to the university there, receiving a classical liberal arts education.

Throughout college and his later travels, Mayor sent a steady stream of richly detailed letters to his grandmother Audella Hyatt and his aunt Anna that capture his boundless enthusiasms, including his early interest in art. A letter from 1919, the year Mayor turned eighteen, exudes youthful exuberance following a trip to New York and the Pierpont Morgan Library: "The last few days have been so full of happenings that I hardly know where to begin. I have seen the Morgan's things in the Museum. I should need all Madame de [Sévigné's] 27 adjectives to describe them. I try to get past his Byzantine enamels to see something else, but I always get stuck there, like a fly in honey." He continued, "I know now what it feels like to be drunk. I am drunk. I have just returned from the Morgan library."[7]

After graduating from Princeton with honors in modern languages in 1922, Mayor briefly taught art history at Vassar College; in 1923 he pursued literature as a Rhodes Scholar at Oxford University and soon after attended the American School of Classical Studies in Athens. The insatiable curiosity evident from his course of studies would characterize Mayor's career. During his time abroad Mayor established acquaintances with literary aesthetes including Harold Acton, Ezra Pound, and W. H. Auden and spent several school breaks with the eminent art historian Bernard Berenson at his home I Tatti, just outside Florence. In a diary entry from 1925 Mayor recounted how Berenson, in pursuit of his newest acolyte, wanted "someone who will try to assimilate, not his information, but his criterion, someone who will be first a humanist and tackle the thing in its big aspects. This, [Mrs. Berenson] says, they half hope I may have. So do I, gosh darn it. That is just what I want from him to nourish myself from that rich effluvium of knowledge-become-wisdom he exudes."[8]

Although Mayor relished the history and beauty of Europe, he returned to New York in 1928 intent on being "part of the sweaty, active show, which is kind of a comfort after life abroad had forced me to be a spectator only."[9] Soon after his arrival, Mayor sought out his Oxford classmate Francis Fergusson, who would become a prominent theater critic and author of the celebrated *The Idea of Theater* (1949). Mayor joined him as a lecturer and an occasional performer at the American Laboratory Theatre (the Lab), a drama school and theatrical company in New York. Mayor had always been fascinated by the theater, as is apparent in his joyful account, nearly half a century later, of a visit to his aunt Anna in New York during high school.

> She got tickets in the top balcony for all the current plays. . . . [T]hat was her Christmas present and it was the best Christmas present that I've ever had in my whole life. Oh! She was wonderful. So I'd spend my days at the Metropolitan Museum, or Cooper Union, or places like that; and in the evening we would go and see all the plays there were. And in those days that meant the Moscow Art Theater, the Provincetown Players with Eugene O'Neill's original productions, and things that have become absolutely historic.[10]

The Lab, founded by Richard Boleslavsky and Maria Ouspenskaya, was based on their experiences in the Moscow Art Theater, its First Studio, and the teachings of Konstantin Stanislavsky. For Boleslavsky, art was as indispensable as food—man's attempt "to embellish his life, his eternal striving toward beauty [that is] the seed of the divine in human nature"[11]—and an essential aspect of the actor's education. Embracing Boleslavsky's principles, Mayor developed an arts curriculum specifically for actors, intending not only to develop their intellectual and cultural comprehension but also to nourish their souls according to Stanislavsky's meditative and sensory methods. Finding that combining words and images made each more potent, Mayor presented photographs along with evocative readings, an approach that resonated deeply with the actors. He described his course, Style and Background, this way.

> I would borrow photographs from the Metropolitan Museum, from their lending collection, that showed—well, it showed how you wore a toga or a farthingale or whatever it may be. Then I would read extracts from some play or other illustrating them with these photographs. . . . In other words, a bit of the visual with the literary. It was just a fascinating thing to do. It taught me an immense amount.[12]

Mayor's work at the Lab, though brief, exposed him to Stanislavsky's immersive method of actor training; it also brought him into contact with his lifelong friend, Lincoln Kirstein, then a senior at Harvard University. Kirstein would later become a prolific writer, collector, and cofounder of the New York City Ballet, among other accomplishments, but at this young age Kirstein ran, from his dorm room, the independent left-leaning literary magazine *Hound & Horn*. Mayor began writing for the magazine in 1929, including its short-lived Art Chronicle. His first article focused on the

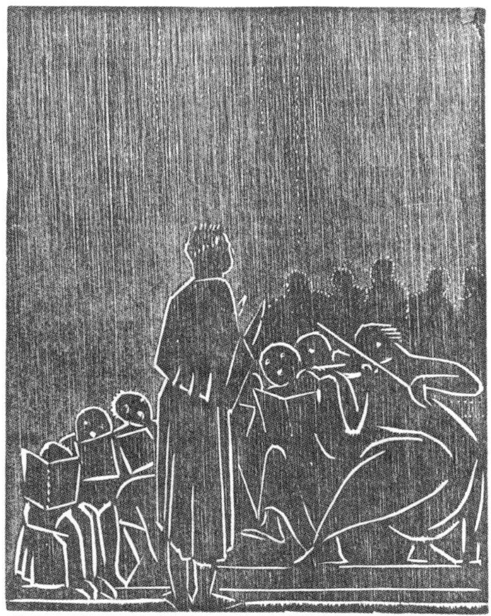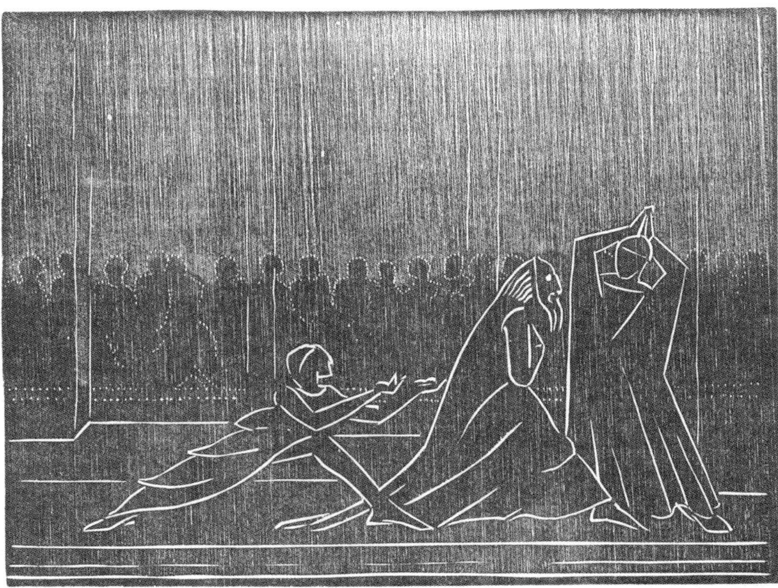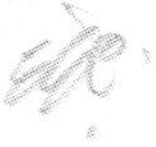

Fig. 19. (Edward) Gordon Craig (British, 1872–1966). *For Hamlet*, ca. 1912. Wood engraving, 9⅛ × 14 in. (23 × 35.5 cm). Gift of Lincoln Kirstein, 1953 (53.648.10)

English modernist director and theorist (Edward) Gordon Craig.[13] Craig approached theater as a new medium of art, revolutionizing set designs and unifying the production through sound, lighting, and costume (fig. 19). Likewise, Mayor—whose early interest in theater only intensified as he grew older—was especially fascinated by how its various aspects combined to bring art to life.

In a 1930 column, "Museums Modern and Metropolitan," Mayor insisted that museums should surprise and stimulate in their arrangements and show a range of objects, each "alive for its time."[14] This idea of artworks as living beings able to communicate ideas about the people and places of their production would echo throughout Mayor's writings. In the article, he argued that the Museum of Modern Art should "show us our own time and leave us to judge," whereas the Metropolitan Museum, an encyclopedic collection, should "select only what is still of interest"—art that remained relevant and in a sense modern. Highly critical of the Met for its loss of an important Titian at auction, its inert display of paintings, and its dearth of shows like the 1928 "Spanish Paintings," which caused people to "[come] out with other eyes than those we had brought in, reconsidering Goya in the light of el Greco,

and settling a whole new hierarchy in our heads,"[15] Mayor ended his article with "Quis custodiet [ipsos] custodes?" (Who shall watch the watchers themselves?).[16] Nevertheless, he joined the Met just two years later, beginning his own career as one of the guardians of printed matter.

According to Mayor's own account, he had stumbled into the Met's Department of Prints in 1932 in the "draggy depths of the Depression," in need of work but without relevant qualifications.[17] Mayor reasoned that Ivins took a chance on hiring him because he was a voracious reader in many disciplines and several languages and could in fact teach himself. He later endorsed this approach of learning about art by reading widely: "Read all the great poems, plays, and novels that you can, for Dante will lead you into the dramatic economy of Giotto, Racine will help you find the balanced organization of Poussin, Flaubert will show you how the Impressionists looked at life. Read general history, the history of science, of economics, of ideas, for these, like the history of art are all peek holes into the central mystery of man."[18] In keeping with Mayor's prodigious appetite for knowledge, he chose upon joining the Met to first catalogue more than three thousand engravings from Denis Diderot's eleven-volume *Encyclopédie*

(1751–72), which describes the essential principles of the arts and sciences.

Another of Mayor's early projects was a small show on the history of theater prints.[19] A lifelong interest in theater led him to explore the subject in depth over the course of his career through a number of writing projects and many exhibitions. They included a book on the Bibiena family of eighteenth-century scenic designers, which may have been inspired by Kirstein's use of their designs for the backdrop of George Balanchine's *Concerto Barocco*;[20] the exhibition "Carpentry and Candlelight in the Theater," which celebrated the origins of stage design in Italian Renaissance treatises on architecture;[21] and a show honoring the New York debut of the fabled Comédie-Française in 1955.[22]

Mayor's first large-scale exhibition and catalogue—*Life in America*—coincided with the 1939 World's Fair in New York. As acting director of the Museum, Ivins had had the idea to show American life through genre pictures; beyond that, Mayor and his cocurator Hermann Warner Williams Jr. were free to travel, meet with donors and museums, and ultimately choose the nearly three hundred objects, almost exclusively paintings, for the exhibition. It was to be one of Mayor's favorite projects, and it was exceptionally well attended by a diverse public—and not just by art lovers—as the *New York Times* reported.[23] Breaking entirely new ground, Mayor and Williams chose "stuff that everybody had forgotten for a century."[24] From Civil War scenes such as *General Doubleday Crossing the Potomac*, by David G. Blythe, to Richard Caton Woodville's depiction of two men talking politics in an oyster house, to *New England Country School*, an interior by Winslow Homer, the selection was a visual account of America over three hundred years.[25] Eschewing aesthetic concerns, Mayor and Williams refocused interest from the merely beautiful to objects that also tell the stories of everyday life in all its variety. As Williams noted, "Although the exhibition incidentally traces the development of painting in this country, the pictures have been chosen because of their subject matter."[26] Mayor later pointed out that the exhibition had shifted taste for certain types of American art and thereby changed how it was collected: "All this collecting that's done nowadays, the Hudson River School and things like that, is the direct outcome of that exhibition."[27] It also was the impetus for new lines of scholarly inquiry, resulting in such works as the curator Marshall B. Davidson's *Life in America* (1951), which examined the pictorial history of the country since the arrival of Columbus's ships in the fifteenth century.

Mayor took over the Department of Prints after Ivins retired in 1946. In the midst of the Second World War, and after the stock market crash and the Great Depression, the United States was a vastly different place than it had been at the department's inception thirty years before. Mayor's focus on art that conveyed information about people and his embrace of the vast range of artistic productions beyond the conventional canon epitomized the humanism and anti-authoritarianism that had emerged in the wake of the war. In literature, the clarity of classical traditions was splintering into a "predilection for ruthlessly subjectivistic perspectives," wrote the renowned philologist and critic Erich Auerbach, an exile from his native Germany.[28] Similar ruptures were taking place in art history; in the United States, a new generation of scholars began exploring undervalued and neglected styles, periods, and media—for example, rejecting classical Roman ideals and proportions in favor of Late Antique art, notable for its decadence and deficient originality.

The art historian James Ackerman lambasted the field for having become too professionalized and cloistered in its elite institutions and for teaching the same theories and practices to the already initiated.[29] Given the larger changes taking place in society, he called on the art historian to cease being "a disinterested interpreter of the past, and [become] an active participant in the effort to reform society by challenging its values and ameliorating its ills."[30]

Edward J. Steichen's revolutionary "The Family of Man" exhibition at the Museum of Modern Art in 1955 exemplifies Ackerman's directive. Steichen (director of MoMA's photography department from 1947 to 1962) creatively displayed more than five hundred amateur and documentary photographs from sixty-eight countries, accompanied by text by the poet Carl Sandburg (fig. 20). Arranged in groupings around themes such as love, birth, work, joy, and death, the exhibition illustrated through everyday images the universality of the human experience among diverse peoples at a time when nuclear annihilation was a constant threat. It was one of the most influential photography exhibitions of all time.

Although none of Mayor's exhibitions achieved the legendary stature of "The Family of Man," his collecting practices, which encompassed popular, reproductive, and ephemeral prints, and his scholarship, notably *Prints & People* and *Popular Prints of the Americas* (1973), echoed its humanist ideals. His books juxtaposed large, readable images with evocative but brief texts, to reach the broadest possible audience and to inspire a new understanding of prints as critical

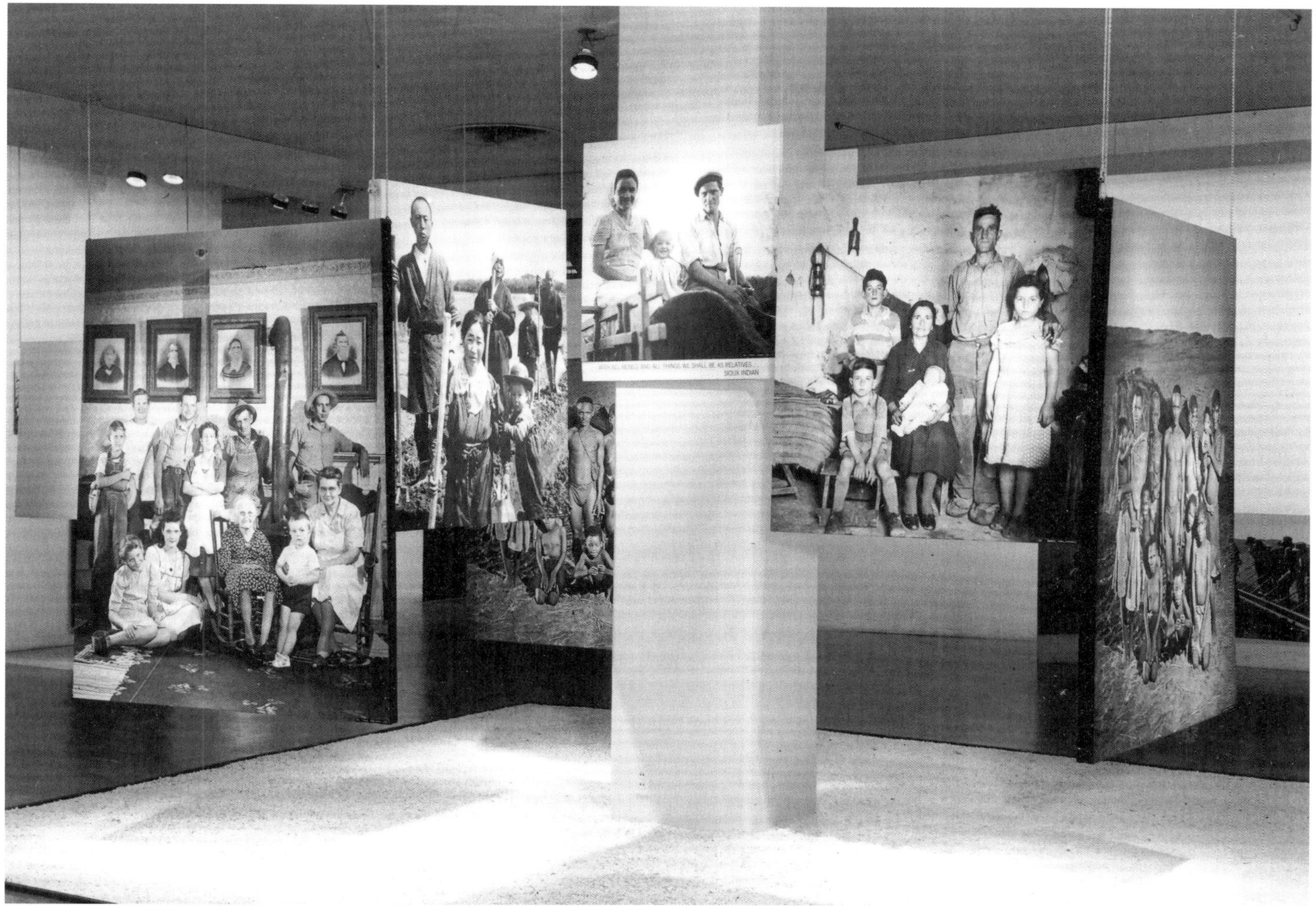

Fig. 20. Installation view of "The Family of Man" exhibition, Jan. 24–May 8, 1955. Photographic Archive, the Museum of Modern Art Archives, New York

to the stories of both art and, more widely, humankind. Mayor himself embodied the very principles he espoused. The Met's director, Francis Henry Taylor, called him "the most intelligent and well-rounded humanist we have in the building"[31] when making the case in 1943 to the president, William Church Osborn, for designating Mayor curator at large, free to pursue interdisciplinary interests across the Museum. Mayor's wide-ranging intellect was impossible to confine and thus was well suited to the study of prints. As he observed: "I'm happy to say that I was never specialized. One can't be in prints. Because they leak out into everything, into city planning, into the law, into dynastic history, into all the technologies."[32]

Mayor strongly believed that the Met's print collection should mirror New York City's breadth and complexity, and so he set out to create a collection of "a variety so endlessly weaving, waving, flowing and evolving that it is nothing less than history itself made visible through things created by all our possible ancestors."[33] In an attempt to reflect the city through prints, he collected, for example, contemporary works by now-celebrated artists such as John Sloan, Edward Hopper, Martin Lewis, and John Marin, as well as trade catalogues about ironworks, brassware, lighting, and fashion, posters printed by New York magazines and book publishers, views and maps of the city and its environs, subway advertisements, collectors' bookplates, and any other kind of printed matter that related to the city's constantly shifting lifeblood (figs. 21, 22, 23). Mayor's methodology was to collect the full spectrum of prints that could answer an "incalculable diversity of questions."[34]

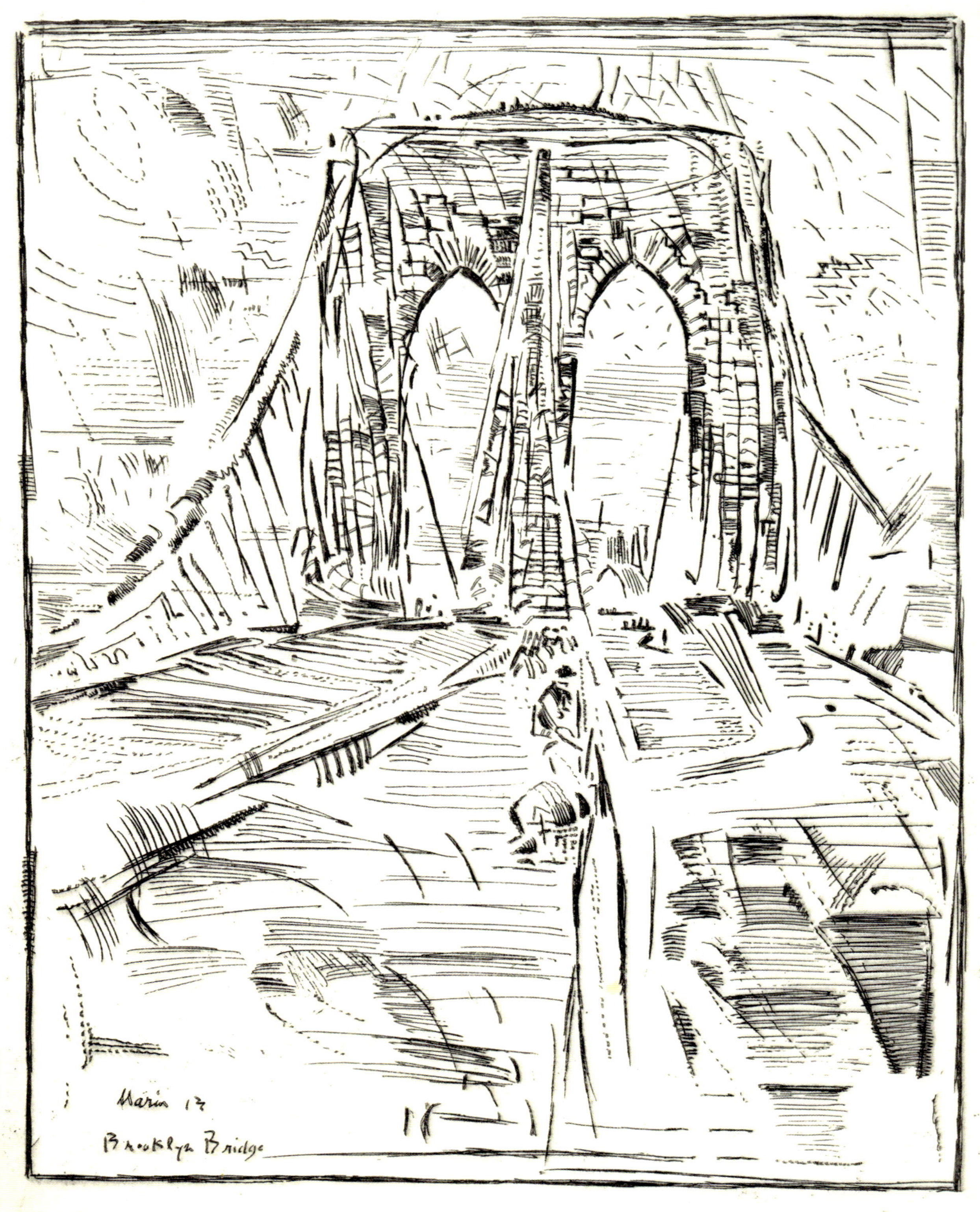

Fig. 21. John Marin (American, 1871–1951). *Brooklyn Bridge (Mosaic)*, 1913. Etching, 12⅞ × 10⅞ in. (32.5 × 27.7 cm). Alfred Stieglitz Collection, 1949 (49.55.132)

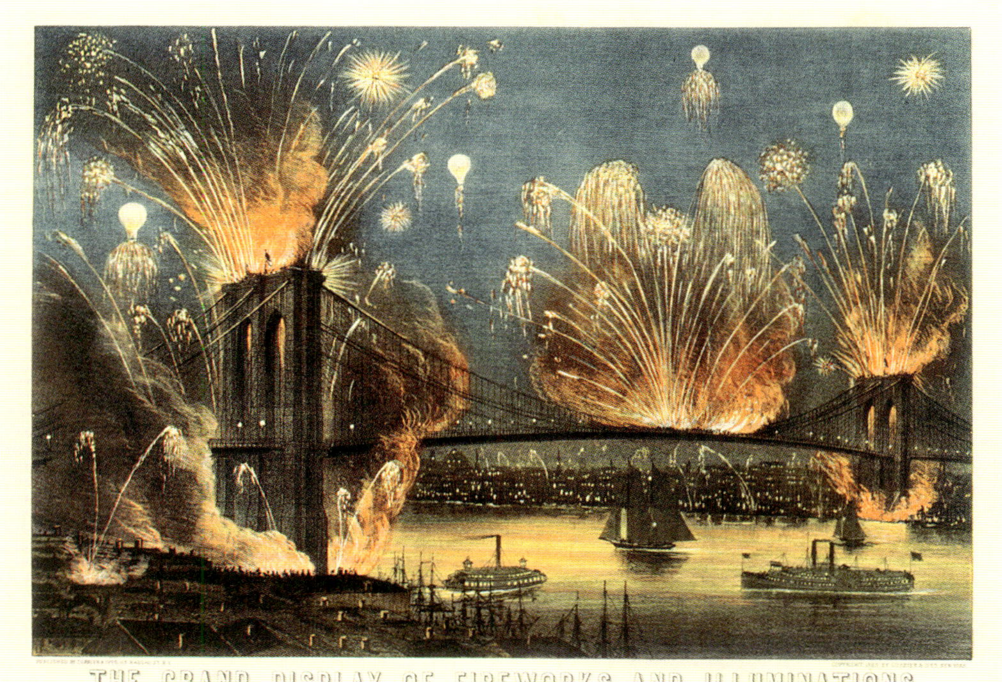

Fig. 22. Currier & Ives (American, active 1837–1907). *The Grand Display of Fireworks and Illuminations at the Opening of the Great Suspension Bridge between New York and Brooklyn on the Evening of May 24, 1883*, 1883. Lithograph, 17⅞ × 23⅝ in. (45.4 × 59.8 cm). The Edward W. C. Arnold Collection of New York Prints, Maps, and Pictures, Bequest of Edward W. C. Arnold, 1954 (54.90.779)

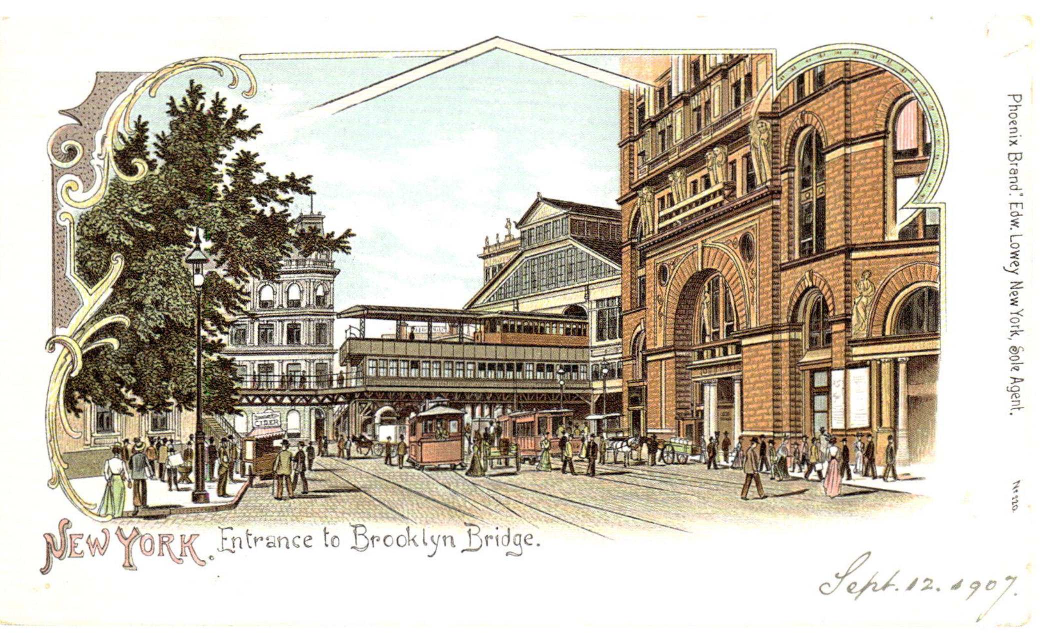

Fig. 23. New York, Entrance to the Brooklyn Bridge. Published by Phoenix Brand Post Card Co., Germany, ca. 1907. Lithograph, 3½ × 5¼ in. (8.9 × 13.1 cm). The Jefferson R. Burdick Collection, Gift of Jefferson R. Burdick (Burdick 405, PC70.57)

With an expansive view about what the collection should include, Mayor ultimately became known as the master of the omnium-gatherum.[35] Building on Ivins's legacy and also pushing the boundaries of what had traditionally been collected as printed matter, Mayor amassed treatises and prints on architecture, furniture, ornament, anatomy, and perspective, as well as fête books, theater designs, trade cards, children's books, silhouettes, posters, valentines, bookplates and book covers, sheet music, postcards, and matchboxes.[36] He acquired some of the most renowned American collections of popular prints, including Adele S. Colgate's comprehensive collection of Currier & Ives, Edward W. C. Arnold's collection of New York prints, maps, and pictures, Bessie Potter Vonnoh's American and French posters from the 1890s, and Bella C. Landauer's and Jefferson R. Burdick's collections of trade cards and postcards.[37] To Mayor, this kind of imagery had value because it contained a wealth of social and historical information, defined the parameters of a culture, and could serve as source material for endless future research in fields as varied as sociology, anthropology, engineering, urban planning, medicine, material culture, and gender studies. For example, within Burdick's massive gift of more than three hundred thousand objects is a large group of tobacco advertising inserts that show the evolution of American women in sports from the late nineteenth to the mid-twentieth century; their depictions developed from merely attractive performers in a sort of burlesque to competitive athletes in a variety of sports, including swimming, baseball, cycling, and tennis (figs. 24, 25).

Mayor recognized the urgency of collecting ephemera while it was relatively new and still abundant, as popular prints tend to be lost to the future through use. Though the skeptical director, Francis Henry Taylor, often teased Mayor, calling the department the "trash basket" of the Museum,[38] Taylor did not make him stop. In fact, Mayor's collecting accelerated, resulting in perhaps the most complete assemblage of popular American prints of the nineteenth and twentieth centuries and the greatest collection of printed ephemera in any museum.

He also built an enormous collection of so-called reproductive prints, which had been pilloried since the nineteenth century as lacking originality and were still overlooked by most collectors and curators.[39] Mayor was attracted not by their aesthetic value but rather by their subject matter,

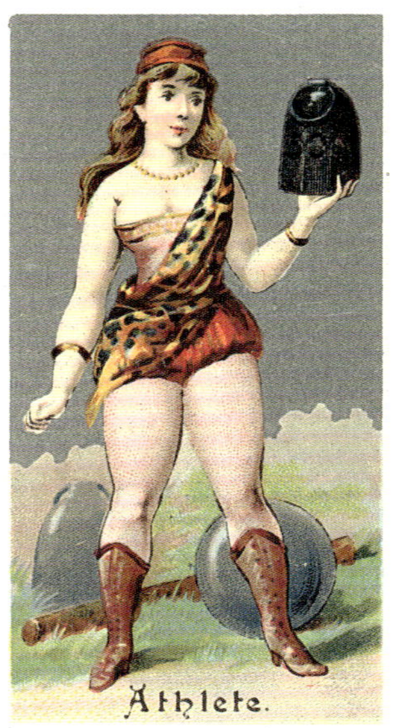

Fig. 24. Athlete from the Occupations for Women series for Old Judge and Dog's Head Cigarettes. Published by Goodwin & Co., New York, 1887. Lithograph, 2¾ × 1½ in. (6.9 × 3.8 cm). The Jefferson R. Burdick Collection, Gift of Jefferson R. Burdick (63.350.214.166.37)

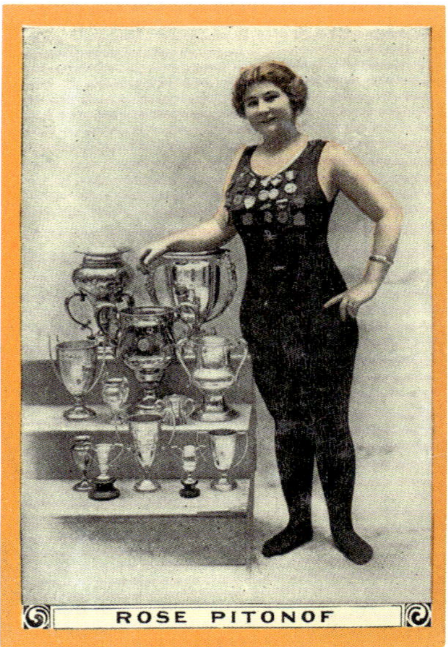

Fig. 25. Rose Pitonof, No. 8, from the Champion Women Swimmers series, issued by Pan Handle Scrap Co., 1913. Lithograph, 3¾ × 2½ in. (9.3 × 6.3 cm). The Jefferson R. Burdick Collection, Gift of Jefferson R. Burdick (63.350.247.221.8)

context, or technical feats, realizing that many such prints were "indispensable for tracing lost works of art and for a thorough study of a [certain] century in all its aspects, artistic, political, literary, etc."[40] In 1949, Mayor—taking advantage of Europe's straitened postwar economy—purchased almost seven hundred prints directly from the Albertina in Vienna.[41] Seizing a rare opportunity to procure parts of the famed princely collection, Mayor focused on works from the golden age of reproductive printmaking, choosing engravings by Marcantonio Raimondi and his followers after paintings and drawings by Raphael, Giulio Romano, Michelangelo, and other Renaissance artists (fig. 26). In works such as these he found answers to myriad questions about the history of art, social history, material culture, technique, and ever-changing notions of taste. As Mayor remarked:

> Marcantonio established the copying of other men's designs as a specialty that was eventually to absorb most of the effort that went into printmaking until the 1870's, when the task was taken over by the photographic processes. The prints he and his school began to make in the early 1500's carried the Italian High Renaissance to its sudden triumph throughout Europe and taught Western art a manner of drawing and of

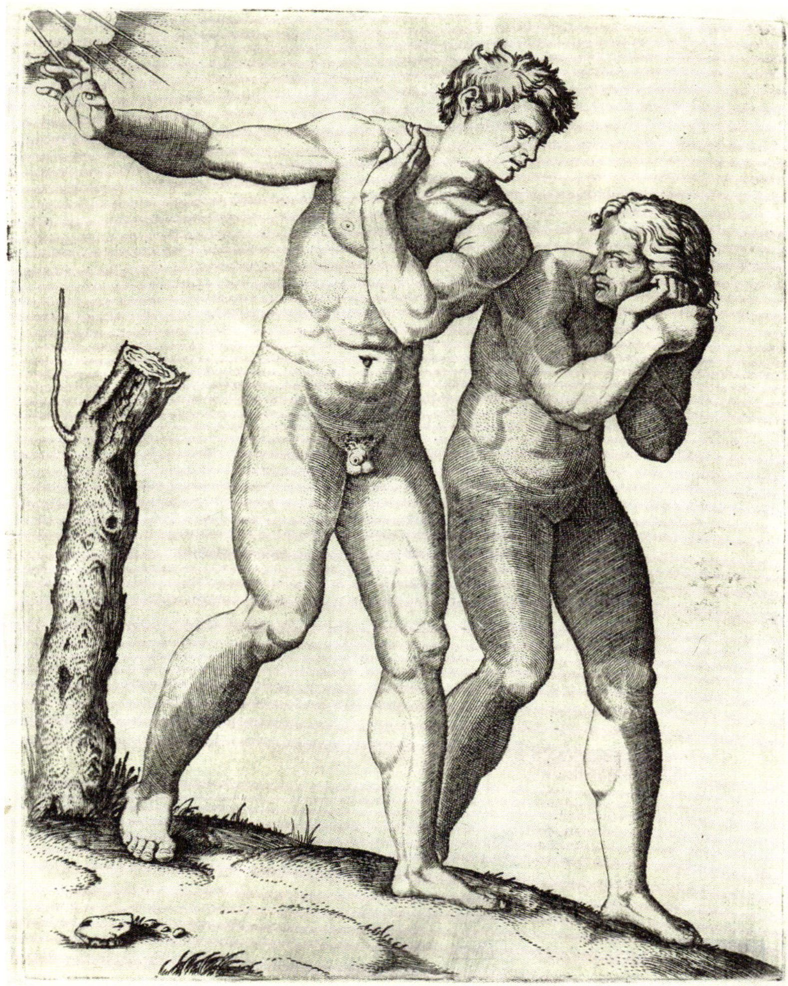

Fig. 26. Marcantonio Raimondi (Italian, ca. 1480–before 1534). After Michelangelo Buonarroti (Italian, 1475–1564). Adam and Eve being expelled from Paradise, ca. 1515–25. Engraving, 7½ × 5⅝ in. (19 × 14.1 cm). The Elisha Whittelsey Collection, The Elisha Whittelsey Fund, 1949 (49.97.1)

figure composition that remained standard until Picasso and his fellows started a revision of values about 1905. The engravings and woodcuts by Marcantonio and his contemporaries changed European art more widely and more thoroughly than any other group of prints ever produced. . . . Their prints now furnish attributions for unidentified paintings and explain many strange subjects, poems, customs, and habits of thought.[42]

Mayor significantly added to the reproductive engravings he acquired from the Albertina with a series of purchases made between 1949 and 1962 through P. & D. Colnaghi & Co. in London. Through these landmark purchases of what Mayor irreverently referred to as "all the unsaleable things,"[43] the Met acquired more than sixteen thousand engravings,

etchings, woodcuts, and mezzotints from Franz Joseph II, prince of Liechtenstein.[44] Though Liechtenstein's collection contained masterpieces of printmaking by artists such as Dürer, Rembrandt, and Mantegna, it also contained an enormous number of reproductive engravings, bringing to the Museum works by the likes of Hendrick Goltzius, Aegidius Sadeler, Jean Mignon, Ugo da Carpi, Agostino Veneziano, Giorgio Ghisi, and Antonio Tempesta, among hundreds of other now-celebrated Renaissance printmakers. Mayor's acquisition of the Liechtenstein and Albertina reproductive prints transformed the Museum's collection, filling in a significant gap and enabling it to tell the full history of printmaking to a largely American audience that remained unexposed to the broader scope of Europe's centuries-old

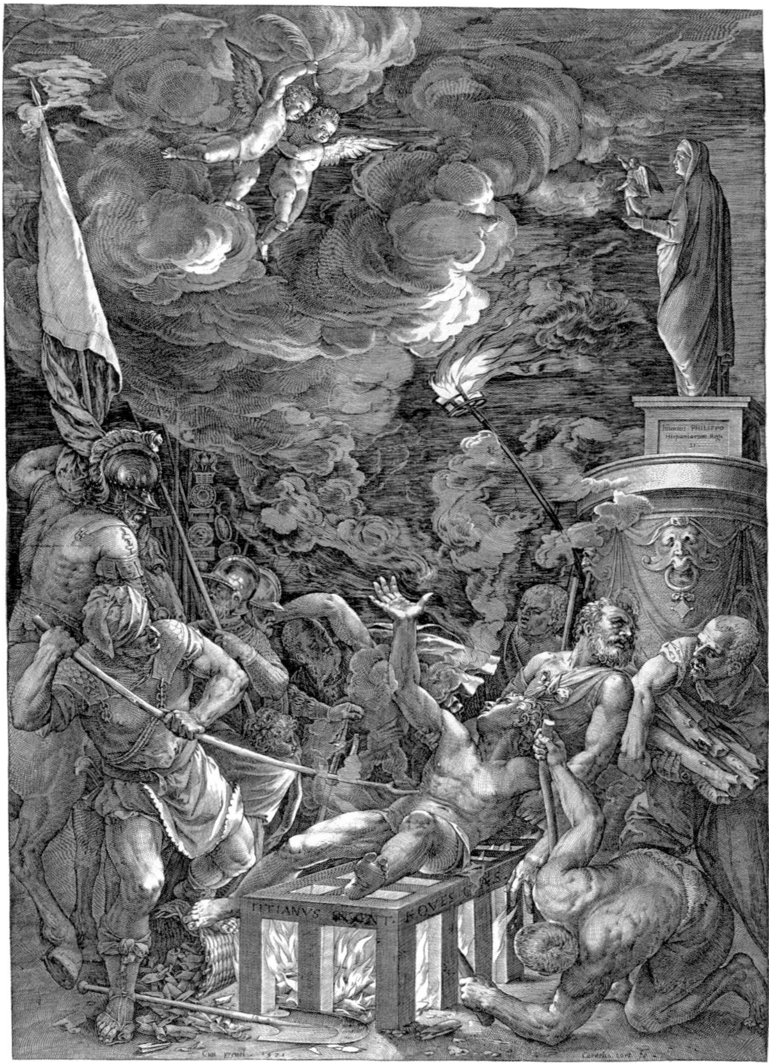

Fig. 27. Cornelis Cort (Netherlandish, ca. 1533–1578). After Titian (Tiziano Vecellio) (Italian, ca. 1485/90?–1576). *Martyrdom of Saint Lawrence*, 1571. Engraving, 19⅞ × 13¾ in. (50.3 × 34.9 cm). The Elisha Whittelsey Collection, The Elisha Whittelsey Fund, 1949 (49.97.537)

collections. In 1950 he staged two exhibitions in conjunction with each other—"1949 Print Accessions" and "Art Treasures from the Vienna Collections"—to showcase the exceptional nature of the Liechtenstein and Albertina purchases. The exhibitions defined the parameters of Renaissance printmaking, including magnificent works such as Cornelis Cort's *Martyrdom of Saint Lawrence*, which combines elements from two paintings by Titian (fig. 27).

Mayor's salvific exploration of reproductive prints was mirrored in academia by a group of art historians, including Walter Friedlaender, Sydney Joseph Freedberg, Frederick Hartt, and Craig Hugh Smyth; many of those scholars had experienced the war firsthand. Seeking art that was relevant to a world in crisis, they looked beyond the noble equilibrium of the Renaissance their predecessors had so deeply studied, reclaiming derided styles like Mannerism, which embraced ambiguity and anxiety and was characteristic of the Italian, French, and Netherlandish reproductive engravings that Mayor coveted.[45] Although their work complemented Mayor's reassessment of this disparaged category as historically significant, the first scholarly examination of reproductive prints came only in 1976 with Gerhard Langemeyer and Reinhart Schleier's exhibition and catalogue *Bilder nach Bildern*.[46]

Beyond his travels in pursuit of prints, Mayor played his role as curator essentially behind the scenes, cloistered in the museum organizing exhibitions, cataloguing, and writing. He found a more public outlet for his enduring enthusiasms in teaching, for which he'd developed a passion at Vassar and the Lab. In 1950 he pursued an adjunct position at New York University's Institute of Fine Arts, which was then as now affiliated with the Museum. He taught courses on connoisseurship, the history of collecting, and museum administration. He directed the first year of the Museum Training program that continues to bring students from the IFA into the Museum to work with objects, hear from curators, and see how a museum operates. Beyond his faculty role, Mayor gave innumerable lectures to the public. Mayor always undertook teaching as a theatrical performance, guided by the mechanics of acting. He was acutely aware of needing to find the right moment for a pause, to be sure his column of air was robust enough to launch vowels to the back of the lecture hall, and to engage those whose attention might be wandering by pointing out something on the screen or launching his voice from the other side of the stage.[47] He was hailed as a captivating teacher who spoke with intelligence, generosity, and humor.[48] "When I listen to your wonderfully graphic and warmly human discourse I am in despair," wrote Frederick B. Adams Jr., the director of the Pierpont Morgan Library and president of the Grolier Club, following one of Mayor's lectures. "Who else is ever as good, who can possibly follow you as a speaker without letting the audience collapse into a plane of mundanities. . . . And to think that you did this for love, when it involved so much labor."[49]

A natural educator, Mayor had had no formal training in teaching. Having taken only two art history courses at Princeton, Mayor spent his early days teaching the subject at Vassar in ignorance and terror.[50] He was reticent about the position even a few years later, when he discussed it with an encouraging Berenson, as he explained in a letter to his grandmother.

> He started by asking me what I had done and when I admitted that I had taught at Vassar, and taught art, he instead of making some jibe about ignorance, said: "Good, good. That is the time to teach, when you are learning. European professors are good teachers because they only lecture on what they are studying at the time, taking the public into their confidence. . . . Ignorance gives you zest."[51]

Mayor took Berenson's comment to heart. He came to delight in ignorance, avidly seeking out knowledge from guidebooks and trade catalogues, documentary materials and contemporary literature. He also relished the experience of learning by teaching, savoring questions that "[knocked] you off your perch" and forced investigation of new media, artists, or contexts.[52] Although most of Mayor's lectures were fleeting performances, unrecorded and leaving no trace except on those in attendance, his publications palpably express the pleasure he took in all provinces of art and knowledge. From mass-produced calendars juxtaposing well-chosen quotations from Shakespeare and the *Bhagavad Gita* with works from the Met's collection, to articles such as "Change and Permanence in Men's Clothes," "How to Bake an Exhibition," and "Prints in Elizabethan Poetry," to books on Giovanni Battista Piranesi, Goya, and Rembrandt, Mayor's writings vividly communicate the scope of his interests and vision.

The polymathic Mayor wrote ceaselessly until the day he died, when he was working on a text about a fifteenth-century Japanese sculpture of a Zen Buddhist monk; it is pictured across from the letter *H* in a charming address book published by the Museum.[53] Perhaps recalling his days at the Lab, whose curriculum incorporated yoga and meditation, Mayor described how the meditating mind surrenders to stillness, allowing the "fidgety ego to stop sparking projects, idle talks, and trivia that distract the approach to basic questions."[54]

Asking basic questions was Mayor's own approach to "the vivid world of images,"[55] one that could lead in unexpected directions, as he demonstrated in *Prints & People*. The same year he published that enduring history of printmaking, he modestly reflected on his career in a letter to a museum colleague. His words reveal that Mayor, a towering intellect who transformed the Met's collection into one of the world's greatest repositories of the vast range of printed matter, was a true populist, sensitive to his diverse audience.

> I loved curating prints because I enjoyed the chase for things, the chance to complete series, to stock up for future exhibitions, to anticipate developments of taste, to discover new aspects of prints. . . . The taste of New York counted for more than my own. Half the things I bought for the museum, I would not hang on my own walls, but they belong in a public collection for as many reasons as there are people coming to [look at them].[56]

1901: Alpheus Hyatt Mayor is born June 28 in the Norwood-Hyatt House in Annisquam, near Gloucester, Massachusetts. He is the oldest of four children of Alfred Goldsborough Mayor, a marine biologist, and Harriet Hyatt Mayor, a sculptor. The Norwood-Hyatt House, which dates to the seventeenth century, was the original site of the Marine Biological Laboratory, which was founded by Mayor's grandfather, the paleontologist and zoologist Alpheus Hyatt. It remained in the Hyatt family until 1987 and was listed on the National Register of Historic Places in 2000.

1907: In June Harriet Mayor and her children travel to Europe, where they remain for the next year to be with Alfred Mayor, who is working in Penzance, England, and at the renowned Stazione Zoologica in Naples.

1910: Mayor's family spends the summer with his aunt Anna Hyatt, who had rented the former studio of Barbizon School painter Charles-François Daubigny at Auvers-sur-Oise, France.

1911: Harriet Mayor is diagnosed with tuberculosis and enters a sanatorium in Sharon, Massachusetts.

1912: Nearly recovered, Harriet travels to Europe with her children in July to complete her tuberculosis treatment, settling in Freiburg, Germany.

1914: Harriet and her children move to Normandy, France, but return to Freiburg after six weeks. In July, however, when war begins to seem likely, they leave Freiburg for Paris. They return to the United States in September, settling in Princeton, New Jersey.

1915: Mayor spends the summer with his father at the Dry Tortugas Marine Biology Laboratory. He assists his father by mounting butterflies and collecting specimens from coral reefs.

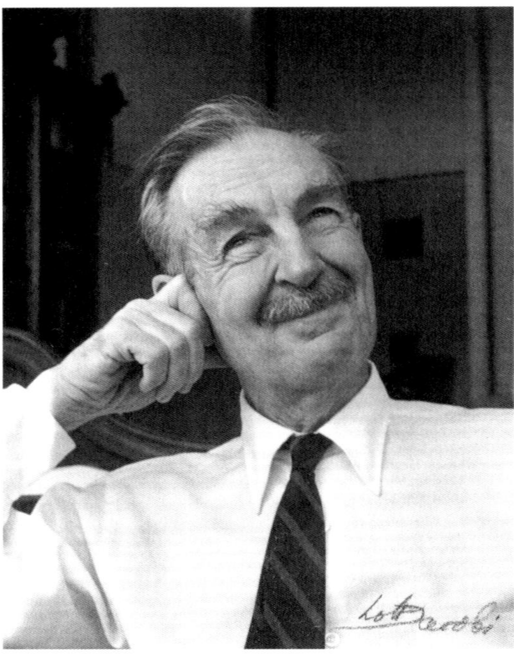

Fig. 28. Lotte Jacobi (American, born Germany, 1896–1990). *Hyatt Mayor*, ca. 1960. Platinum print. David Hunter McAlpin Fund, 1983 (1983.1016)

1918–22: Mayor attends Princeton University, graduating with high honors in modern languages, having taken only two classes in art history.

1922–23: Mayor teaches art history at Vassar College.

1923: On March 10 Mayor's aunt Anna marries Archer M. Huntington, founder of the Hispanic Society of America (1904) and heir to the railroad fortune of Collis Potter Huntington.

1923–28: Mayor is awarded a Rhodes Scholarship and enrolls at the college of Christ Church, Oxford, in the fall of 1923. On his first Christmas break he travels to Florence and while there visits Bernard Berenson at his villa, I Tatti. He makes additional Christmas visits to Florence in 1924 and 1925. After completing his doctoral thesis, on the influence of *Don Quixote* in English literature, Mayor enrolls for a semester at the American School of Classical Studies in Athens. Before returning to the United States in 1928 Mayor travels to Egypt, Istanbul, and Provence.

1928–32: Mayor settles in New York City and begins teaching an art-related course, Style and Background, at the American Laboratory Theatre. He also works as an editor for and contributes articles to Lincoln Kirstein's quarterly, *Hound & Horn*.

1932: Mayor and Virginia Sluder are married in June. In October, after an extended and unsuccessful search for full-time employment, Mayor is hired by William Ivins to work in the Department of Prints of The Metropolitan Museum of Art, despite his lack of experience with works on paper.

1933: Mayor arranges his first exhibition, a small show on the history of the theater.

1934: The Mayors' son, Alfred, is born.

1936: The Mayors' daughter, Martha, is born.

1939: With Hermann Warner Williams Jr. (future director of the Corcoran Gallery, Washington, D.C.) Mayor organizes "Life in America," an exhibition of American genre paintings, which coincides with the 1939 World's Fair in Flushing, Queens.

1941: Mayor joins the Grolier Club. He will remain a member until his death.

1941–46: Mayor serves as acting librarian of the Museum.

1946: Mayor is promoted to curator of Prints on William Ivins's retirement.

1947–49: Mayor initiates discussions with and undertakes a series of purchases of reproductive prints from the Albertina, Vienna.

1949: Mayor makes the first of four major acquisitions from the collection of the Princes of Liechtenstein.

1950: Mayor teaches his first course, Prints in The Metropolitan Museum of Art, at the Institute of Fine Arts.

1955: Upon the death in December of his uncle Archer M. Huntington, Mayor becomes president and acting director of the Hispanic Society.

1958: For the fall semester, Mayor teaches a seminar, Sixteenth-Century Italian Prints, at the Institute of Fine Arts.

1962: Mayor completes the final Liechtenstein acquisition. Altogether, the series of purchases added more than 16,000 prints to the collection.

1963–79: Mayor is a member of the Century Club.

1964: Mayor becomes a fellow for life of The Metropolitan Museum of Art.

1965: After a long search, Mayor appoints Theodore Sterling Beardsley Jr. as director of the Hispanic Society. Mayor retains the position of president until his death.

1965–70: Mayor serves as a trustee of the American Federation of the Arts.

1966: Mayor retires from the Met on June 30.

1967–76: Mayor teaches Museum Training and Connoisseurship I: An Introduction at the Institute of Fine Arts every spring semester except 1972.

1971: Mayor's book *Prints & People: A Social History of Printed Pictures* is published.

1973: Mayor's book *Popular Prints of the Americas* is published.

1975: Mayor returns to the subject of his 1939 "Life in America" exhibition with a Museum calendar, *Life in America*, which features popular prints and ephemera.

1977: Mayor's book *American Art at the Century* (coauthored with Mark Davis) is published.

1980: On February 28 Mayor dies in New York City, aged seventy-eight.

1981: Mayor's widow, Virginia, gives more than sixty photographs, including seven by Walker Evans, to the Department of Prints (1981.1158.1–.61). Mayor gave numerous other prints, books, and photographs to the Museum over the course of his career.

1984: Mayor's book *Artists and Anatomists* is posthumously published with the help of his former colleagues Colta Ives and Mary L. Myers.

1998: On April 2 an auction of Mayor's collection of prints, drawings, and books is held at Waverly Auctions, Bethesda, Md.: A. Hyatt Mayor Collection of Old Master Prints & Drawings & 19th & 20th Century Works on Paper & Canvas & Miscellaneous Books.

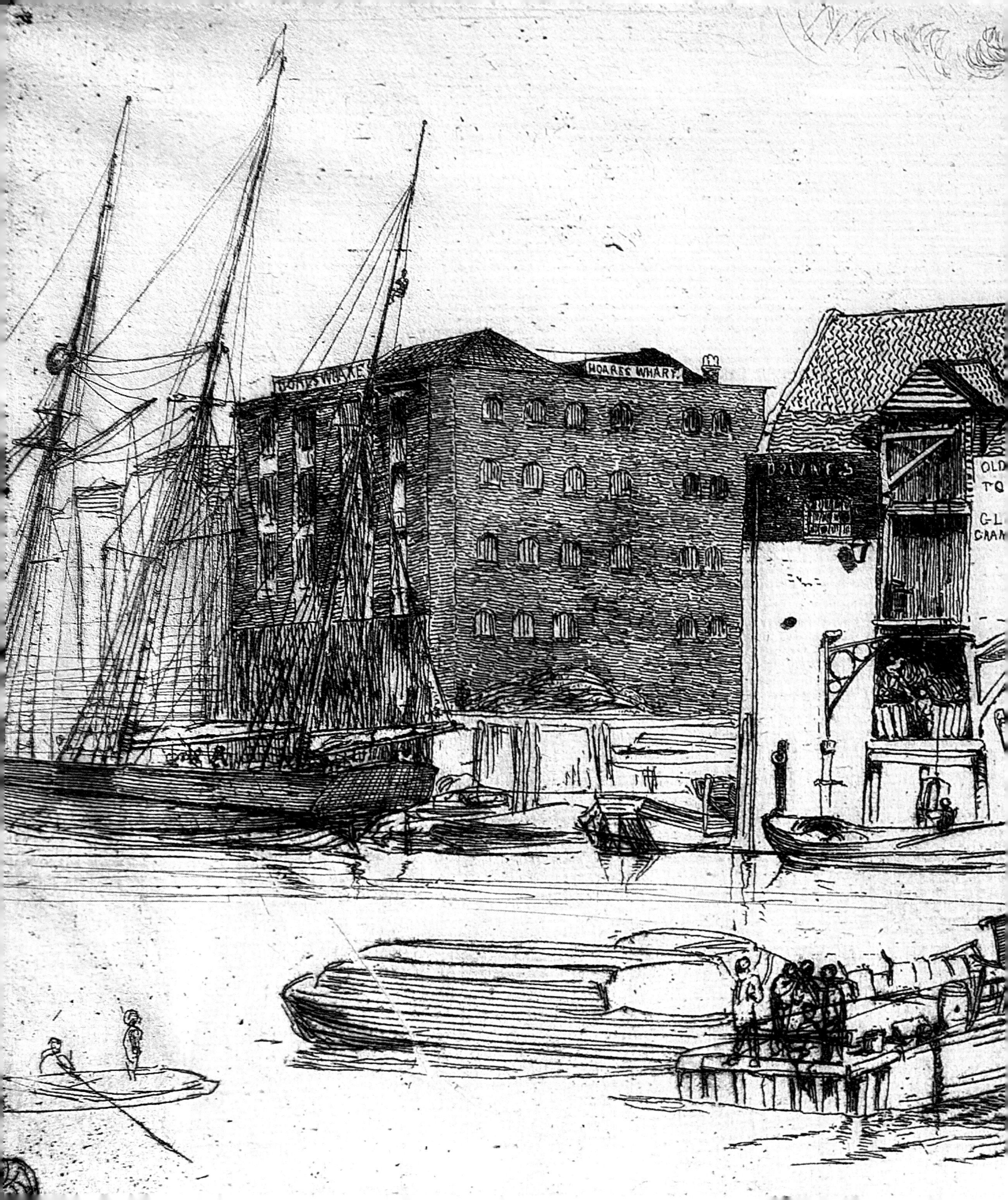
LYON'S WHARF
HOARE'S WHARF.
DOWNE'S
OLD
TO
G-L
GRAN

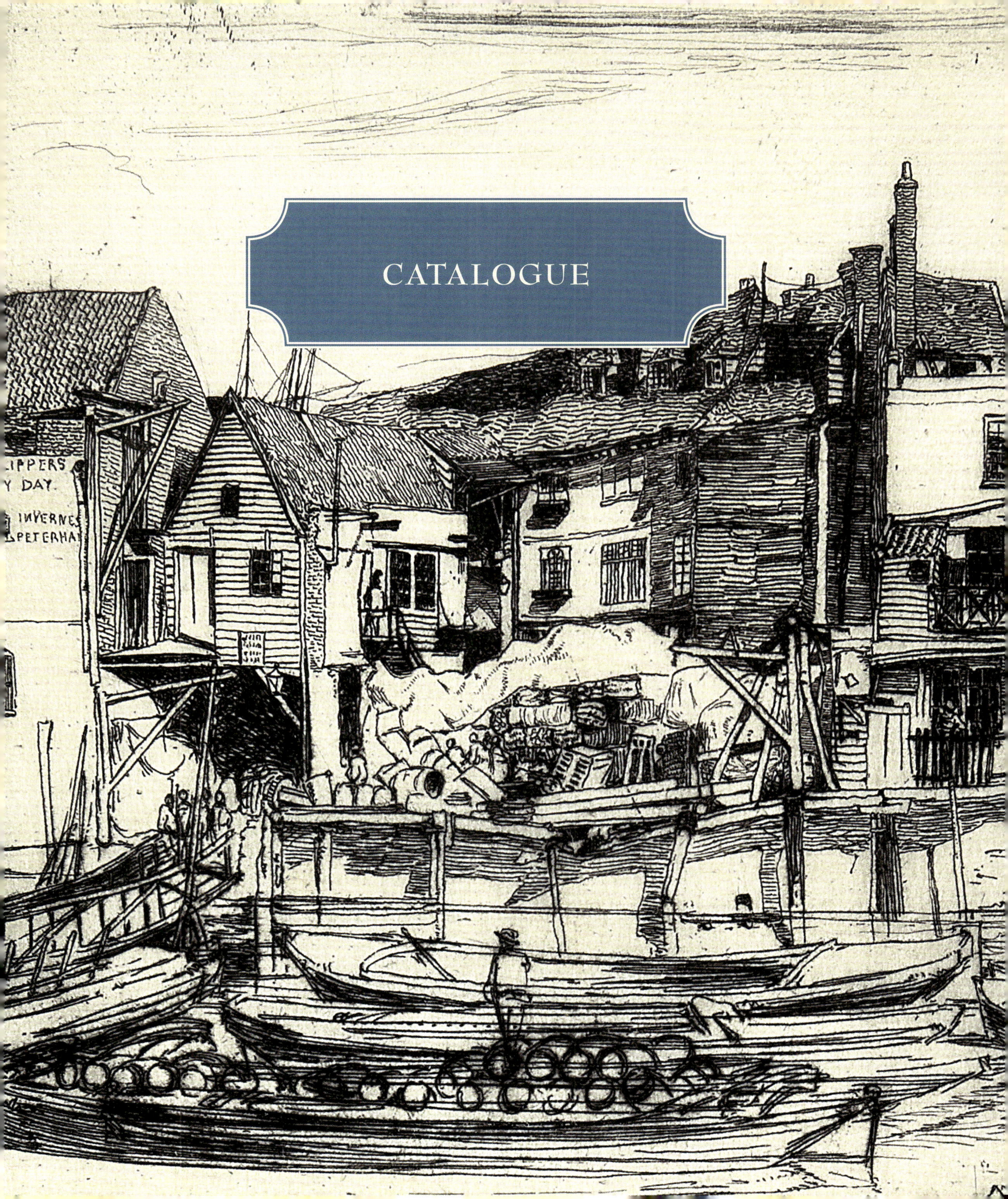

CATALOGUE

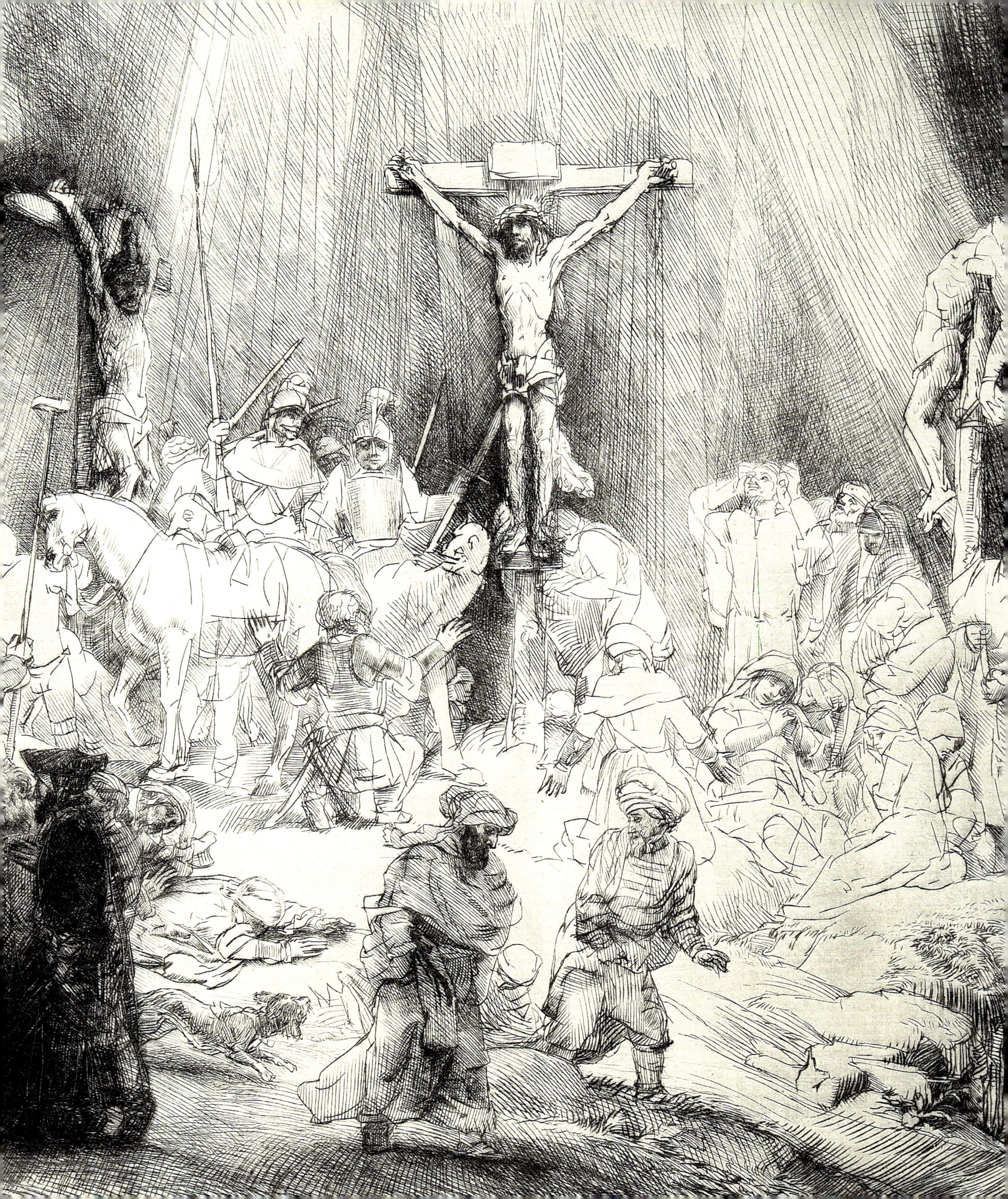

Etchings

THE HARRIS BRISBANE DICK bequest that had been the impetus for founding the Department of Prints in 1916 included etchings by "fourteen fashionable contemporary artists"[1] whose works had been furiously collected by Americans in the last two decades of the nineteenth century. Among them were the principal heroes of the French and British etching revival: James McNeill Whistler, Sir Francis Seymour Haden, Sir David Young Cameron, Anders Zorn, Sir Muirhead Bone, James McBey, Alphonse Legros, August Lepère, Hester Frood, Joseph Pennell, Charles Meryon, and Francis Dodd.[2] They were exploiting a technique that originally had been used to draw designs onto armor and then, in Germany in the early sixteenth century, had been applied to printmaking. Drawing with an etching needle on a metal (usually copper) plate coated with a wax or varnish, artists reveled in the speed and ease of creation and in their ability to mimic the drawn line. Etching developed further in the seventeenth century, notably in the hands of Rembrandt, who experimented with changing compositions and the combination of techniques to create dramatic images. At roughly the same time, technical innovations by artists like Jacques Callot led to greater precision in creating lines, which helped lead to the professionalization of the medium. Both strands of etching persisted into the nineteenth century, when printmakers of the so-called etching revival became primarily interested in the medium's potential to be manipulated to create visual effects.

In Europe the etching revival had gathered momentum in the 1850s with the Barbizon School artists and their circle, but in the United States a passion for these highly aesthetic works developed only in the 1880s. An early proponent of etching, the New York dealer Samuel Avery, began purchasing works by Whistler and other contemporary etchers in Paris. Avery was highly influential in exposing the American market to etchings, and his extensive collection served as the foundation of the New York Public Library's print collection.[3] The records of another New York dealer, Frederick Keppel & Co., demonstrate the burgeoning interest in the medium:

modern etchings had comprised only two percent of its sales in March 1875 but by the same month in 1883 had ballooned to seventy-three percent.[4] In fact, in that year William Loring Andrews, the Met's librarian, who was an avid collector of this material, presented his own collection of nearly a hundred etchings to the Museum, well before the establishment of a Department of Prints.[5]

Etching exhibitions and clubs gained traction in American cities in the early 1880s. H. Wunderlich & Co. mounted a much-lauded exhibition of Whistler prints in New York in 1883 that duplicated the Fine Art Society's show in London from earlier that year. The New York Etching Club, a group of artists and patrons associated with the National Academy of Design, was established in 1877; it held its first exhibition, which included fifty-three American etchers, in 1882.[6] The New York Etching Club led the way for etching societies across the country. By the 1890s there were clubs in Boston, Cincinnati, Philadelphia, and San Francisco. These clubs organized exhibitions that spawned publications. From 1879 to 1881 works by members of the New York Etching Club were featured in *The American Art Review*, a periodical published under the leadership of Sylvester Rosa Koehler, a champion of etching who in 1887 became the first curator of prints at the Museum of Fine Arts, Boston.[7]

Unlike Koehler, William Ivins did not delight in the medium's recent manifestations by Whistler and his circle—in fact, in a letter to his longtime friend Paul J. Sachs, the assistant director of the Fogg Museum, Ivins drew a cartoon of a man thumbing his nose at the names Whistler and Haden.[8] Ivins considered late nineteenth-century etching pure artifice, a medium of self-expression through the manipulation of surfaces alone, devoid of greater meaning. In an article accompanying an etching show at the Museum, Ivins disapprovingly noted of the modern works: "The necessity of thinking ahead was done away with, for no matter how deep a hole one got into, one could turn [the plate] upside down, call it a mountain, and bow gracefully."[9] Art for art's sake was anathema to Ivins, who valued narrative and subject matter and sought a place for prints in the history of ideas. In this he clashed with his department's founding directive, to collect etchings that have "a distinctly artistic quality rather than those with historical, archeological, or other interests."[10]

Because of the overabundance of modern etchings in the collection in the early part of his tenure, Ivins held at least eight exhibitions on nineteenth-century etching,[11] despite his personal aversion to it.[12] With each successive show Ivins sought to place the so-called revival into historical perspective, using descriptive labels, then an innovative tool, to communicate to the public "something about the development of etching both as an artistic medium and as a graphic process."[13] In an article about a 1924 exhibition, he ventured to explain the opposing views that divided those who favored the modern artists and those who revered the old masters.

> The admirers of calligraphy in writing and of a certain technical skill in etching being interested in the how rather than in the what of the statements that are made, are perfectly justified in their preferences, but so also are the people who are primarily interested in the what rather than the how of the same statements. The dispute between them is peculiarly footless because the issue between them is not, as it is usually considered to be, of right or wrong, of good or bad taste, but between two fundamentally different temperaments.[14]

For Ivins, the disparity between the how and the what—or aesthetics versus content—was typified by the comparison of Whistler, widely celebrated as the greatest etcher of the nineteenth century, and Goya, long lauded in Europe for his draftsmanship and prowess as a storyteller but dismissed in the American market because he did not make technically good etchings.[15] Ivins and, later, Hyatt Mayor set out to correct that disregard of Goya, staging six exhibitions of his work between 1918 and 1965, publishing extensively on the artist, and enthusiastically collecting his etchings, lithographs, and drawings.[16]

Ultimately, Ivins and Mayor acquired examples of etching in its many iterations through the centuries, demonstrating the full history of the medium. And in broadening the collection from its foundational nineteenth-century etchings, which so often were regarded with a keen connoisseurial eye for variations in plate tone and states, Ivins and Mayor shifted conceptions of taste.

Jacques Callot, French (1592–1635)

Frontispiece; *Cucorongna –Pernoualla; Cap. Cerimonia – Sig. Lauinia; Smaraolo cornuto – Rarsa di Boio; Guarserro – Mestolino; Cicho Sgarra – Collo Francisco; Razullo –Cucurucu; Pasquariello Truonno – Meo Squaquara; Sig. Lucia –Trastullo; Cap. Cardoni – Maramao; Franca Trippa –Fritellino;* and *Taglia Cantoni – Fracasso*, from the Balli di Sfessania, ca. 1622

Etchings, each approximately 3 × 3¾ in. (7.5 × 9.6 cm)
Bequest of Edwin De T. Bechtel, 1957 (57.650.304[.1, .16, .23, .17, .20, .10, .4, .12, .5, .19, .6, .14])

Provenance: [C. G. Boerner, Leipzig, May 7–9, 1928, lot 291]; Purchased by The Metropolitan Museum of Art Department of Prints, Dick Fund. A duplicate etching owned by Edwin De Turck Bechtel (1880–1957), New York, was bequeathed to the Department of Prints by him in 1957. Bechtel duplicate was exchanged in 1961, and Dick Fund purchase was given credit line of Bechtel

Callot referred to these works as representations of dances, but scholars debate whether they show a theater troupe from the improvisational commedia dell'arte or, more likely, a Neapolitan song and dance associated with carnival. Mayor, with his lifelong interest in the theater and its history, interpreted them as the former, commenting that "this commedia dell'arte (skilled acting) survives best today in these etchings, which advertised the Italian comedy in France, and helped establish it there for over a century" (Mayor, undated label).

Callot employed an innovative tool known as an echoppe, a steel cylinder with an oval-shaped tip. "By twisting this slanted oval while drawing on copper, he started a line slim and then swelled it the way an engraving line swells. He swung his échoppe as freely as a quill in turning the contours of a figure" (Mayor, *Prints & People*, 456). Many of the preparatory drawings for the performers within the series exist; they mirror the flourishing lines found in the etchings. In the finished prints Callot added background figures and architecture suggesting a lively fairground.

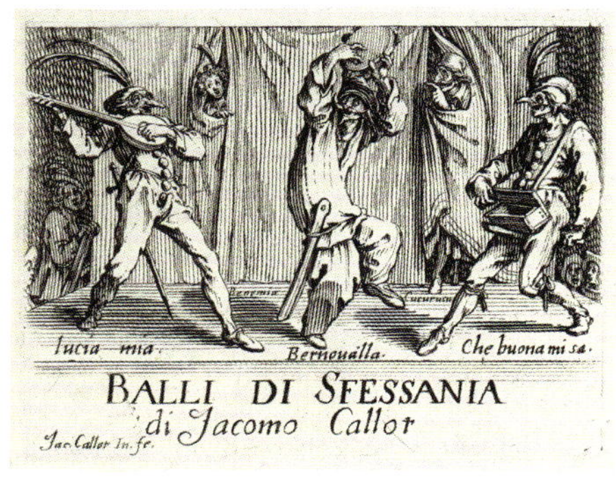

1

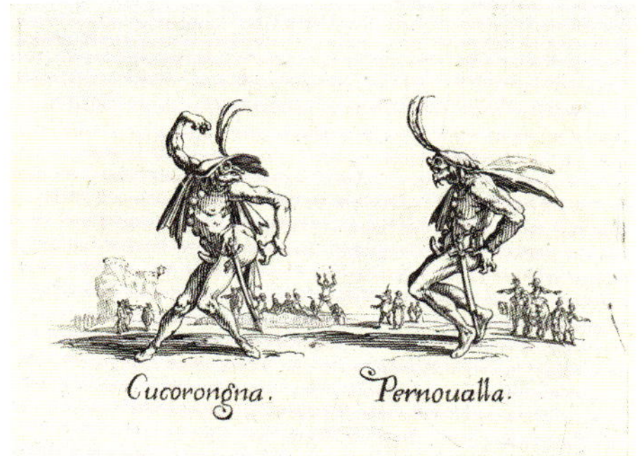

2

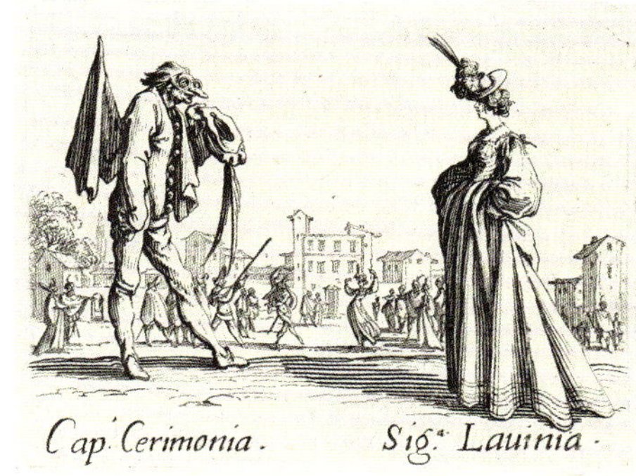

3

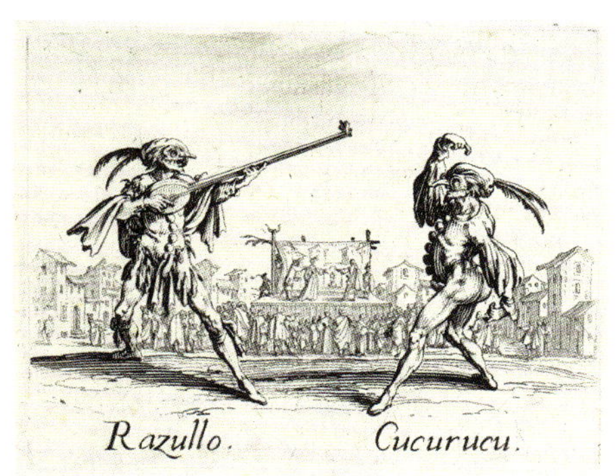

4

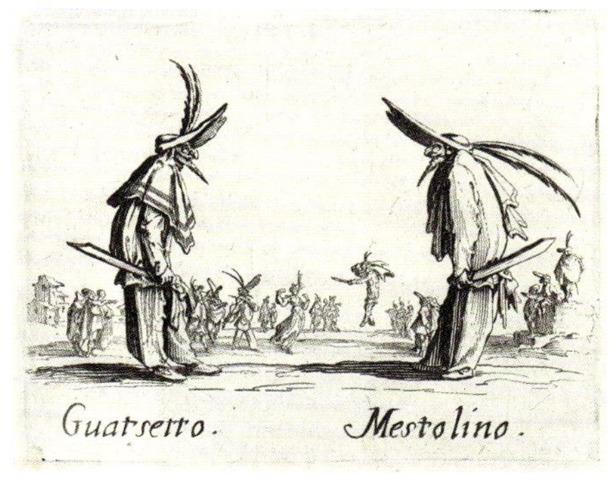

5

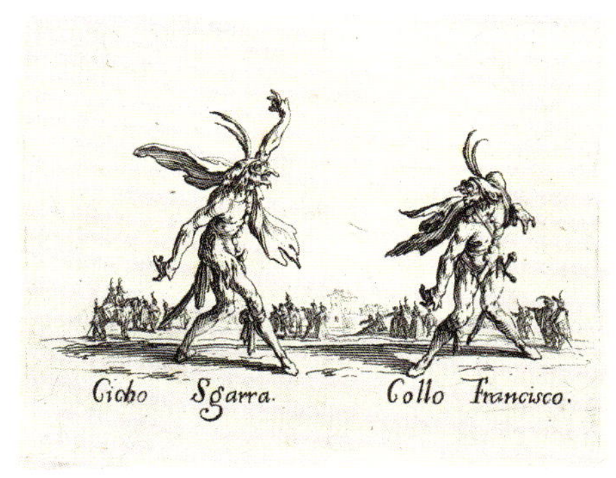

6

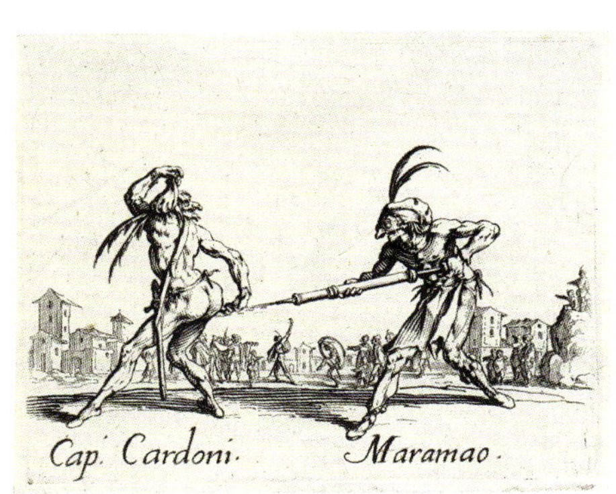

7

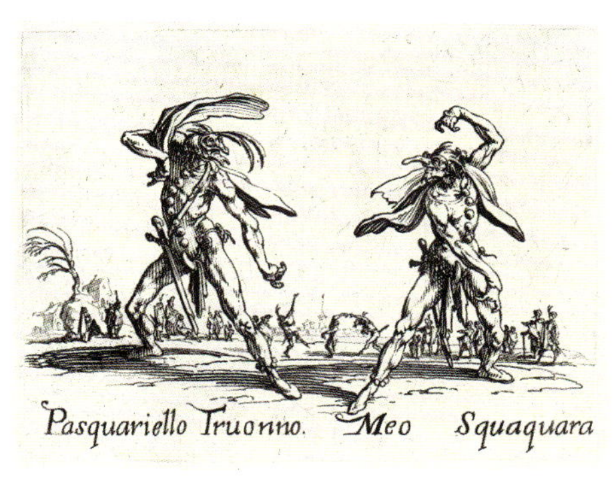

8

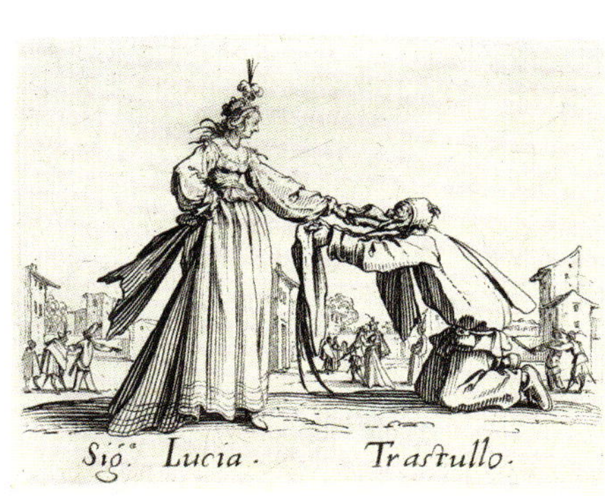

9

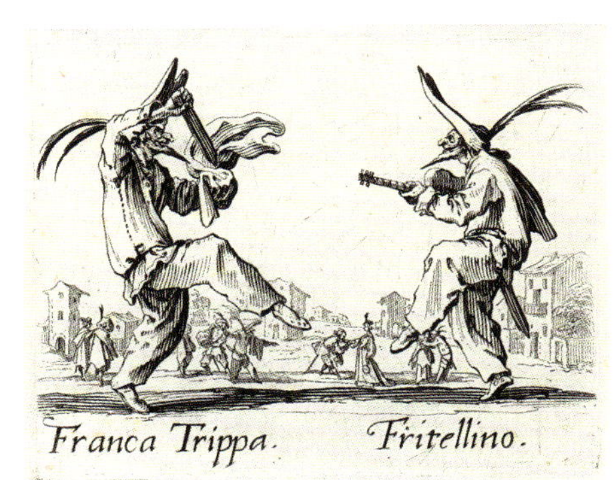

10

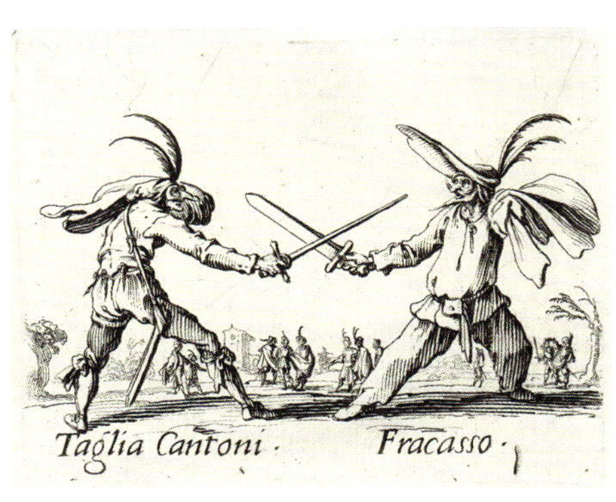

11

Taglia Cantoni.
Fracasso.

12

Jacques Callot, French (1592–1635)

The Temptation of Saint Anthony, 1635

Published in Paris by Israël Henriet
Etching, third state of five, 14¼ × 18½ in. (36.1 × 47 cm)
Bequest of Edwin De T. Bechtel, 1957 (57.650.600)

Collector's mark: Edwin De T. Bechtel (not in Lugt)

Provenance: Edwin De Turck Bechtel (1880–1957), New York; his bequest to the Department of Prints, 1957

A skilled draftsman and printmaker, Callot delighted in creating populous scenes, including fairgrounds, cityscapes, massive preparations for and enactments of war, and this religious phantasmagoria. Callot "prepared many sketches for each composition, as well as detailed pen studies for each figure, for each etched stroke. Over two thousand of his drawings still survive to show that he left nothing to chance, like an actor who rehearses most what is to seem most casual. Few artists with so strict a method have maintained such inexhaustible vivacity" (Mayor, "A Bequest of Prints by Callot and Daumier," 1958: 10–11).

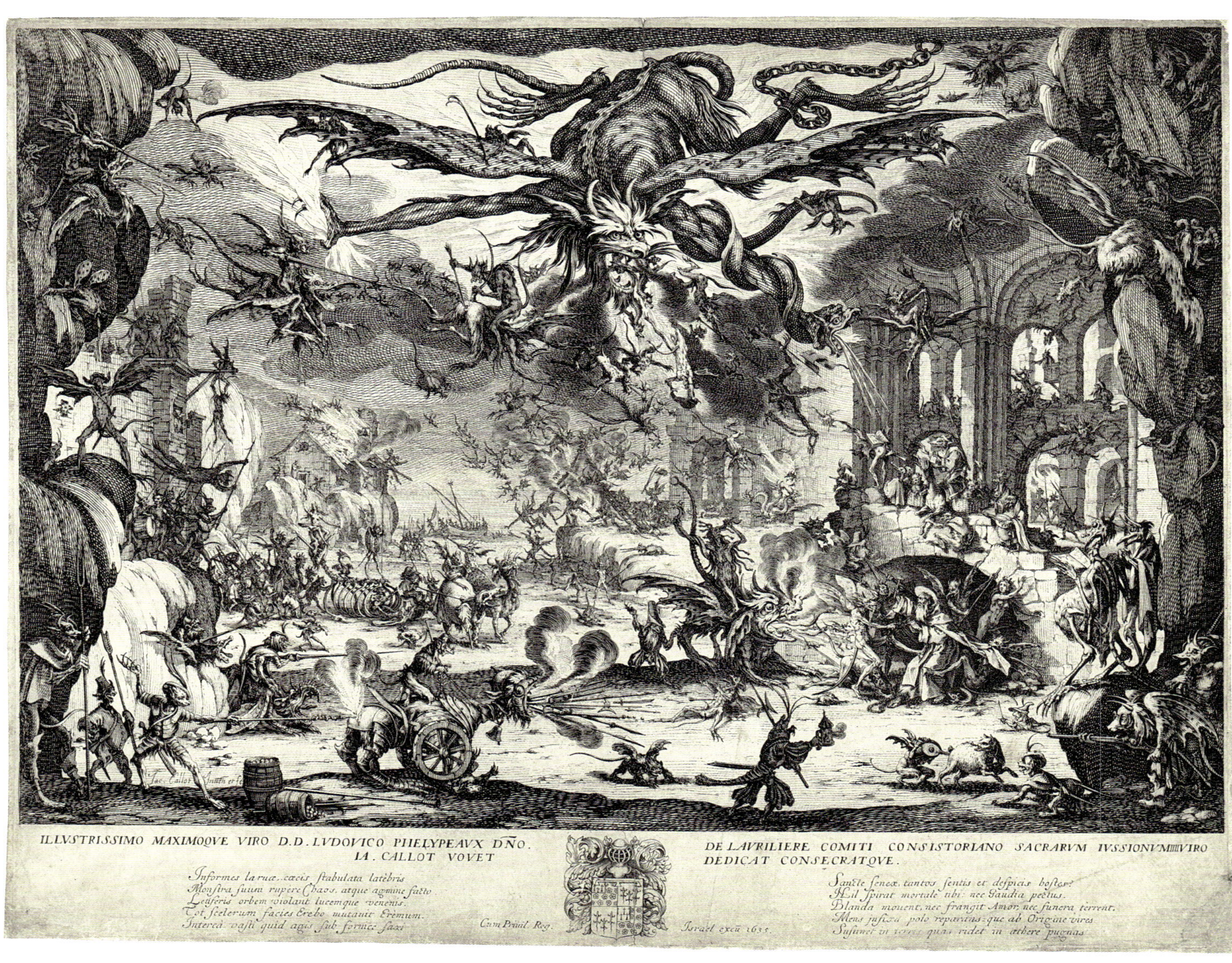

Rembrandt van Rijn, Dutch (1609–1669)

The Death of the Virgin, 1639

Etching and drypoint, third state of three, 16⅛ × 12⅜ in.
(41 × 31.4 cm)
Bequest of Ida Kammerer, in memory of her husband,
Frederic Kammerer, M.D., 1933 (33.79.14)

Watermark: Strasbourg Bend (Hinterding D'.a.a)

Provenance: Possibly in the collection of the 5th Earl of
Ayelsford (1786–1859); Frederic Kammerer (1856–1928)
and Ida Kammerer (died 1933), New York and Bern,
Switzerland; her bequest to the Department of
Prints, 1933

This print marks the first time that Rembrandt
extensively used drypoint, a technique that
allowed him to quickly rework small areas of
the copperplate that had not etched to his satisfaction. Parts of the print, notably the angels,
were created entirely with drypoint, while
many of the lower shaded areas were strengthened with it. Characteristically, Rembrandt
made little attempt to remove the traces of his
initial rapid sketch on the plate; they emerge
throughout the composition and show his
artistic process.

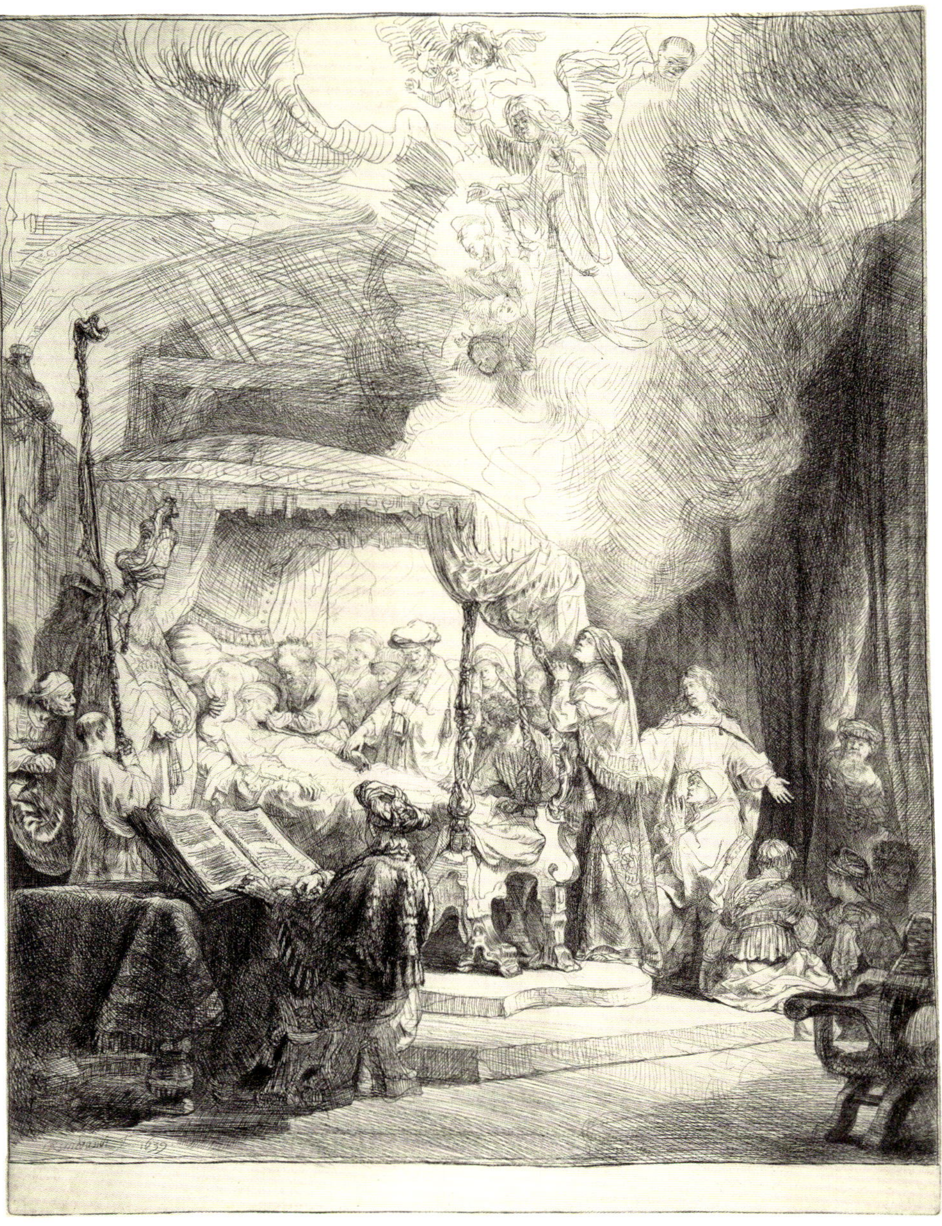

Rembrandt van Rijn, Dutch (1609–1669)

The Three Trees, 1643

Etching with drypoint and engraving, 8⅜ × 11⅛ in.
(21.3 × 28.3 cm)
H. O. Havemeyer Collection, Bequest of Mrs. H. O.
Havemeyer, 1929 (29.107.31)

Collectors' marks: unidentified collector's mark (Lugt 144);
initials of Henry Osborne Havemeyer (not in Lugt)

Provenance: Possibly Edward Cheney (1803–1884),
London; [possibly his sale, Sotheby, Wilkinson & Hodge,
London, April 29–May 3, 1885, lot 730]; Henry Osborne
Havemeyer (1847–1907), New York; Louisine Walden
Elder Havemeyer (1855–1929), New York; her bequest to
the Department of Prints, 1929

The largest and most arresting of Rembrandt's
landscape prints, *The Three Trees* "is a superb
example of the manner in which he was able
to orchestrate line into magnificent and
atmospheric light and shade, and to produce
in black and white the feeling of rich, full
color" (Ivins, *Notes on Prints*, 113). Rembrandt
produced these effects by masterfully combining drypoint, engraving, varied depths of
etched lines, and a speckled tone. The trees
dominate the composition but are offset by
the gusts of wind and the threatening storm
that approaches from the left. Beyond the
macrocosmic idea of nature in flux, the scene
is full of small incidents of human intervention: a distant city, small cottages in the nook
of a hill, a windmill, a wagon approaching an
artist sketching on the hill at right, a standing
fisherman and his wife with a lunch basket,
and an amorous couple hidden in the darkened
bushes. Ivins believed innovative prints such as
this were vastly influential, "dominat[ing] the
thought and endeavor not only of later etchers
but of many later painters" (ibid.).

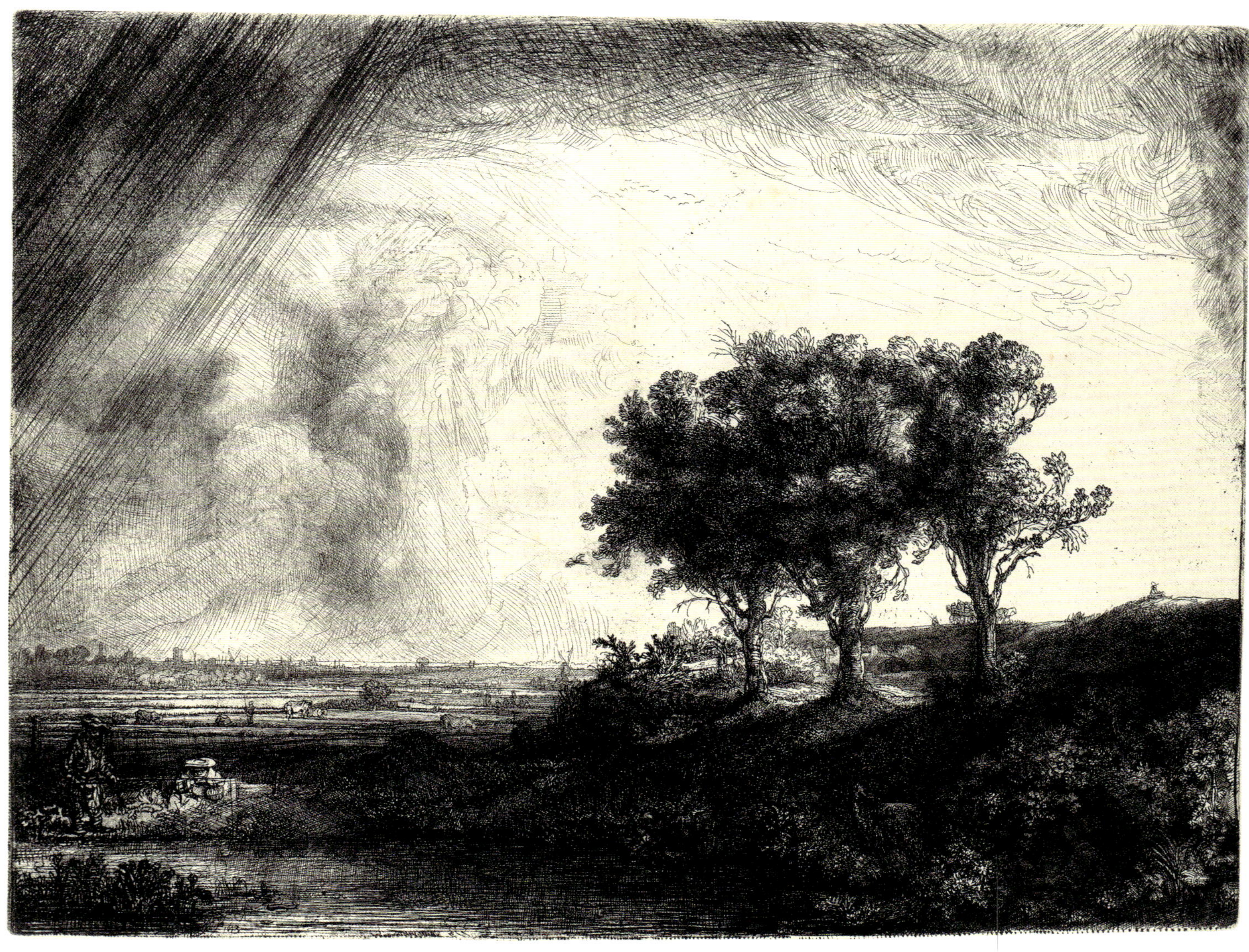

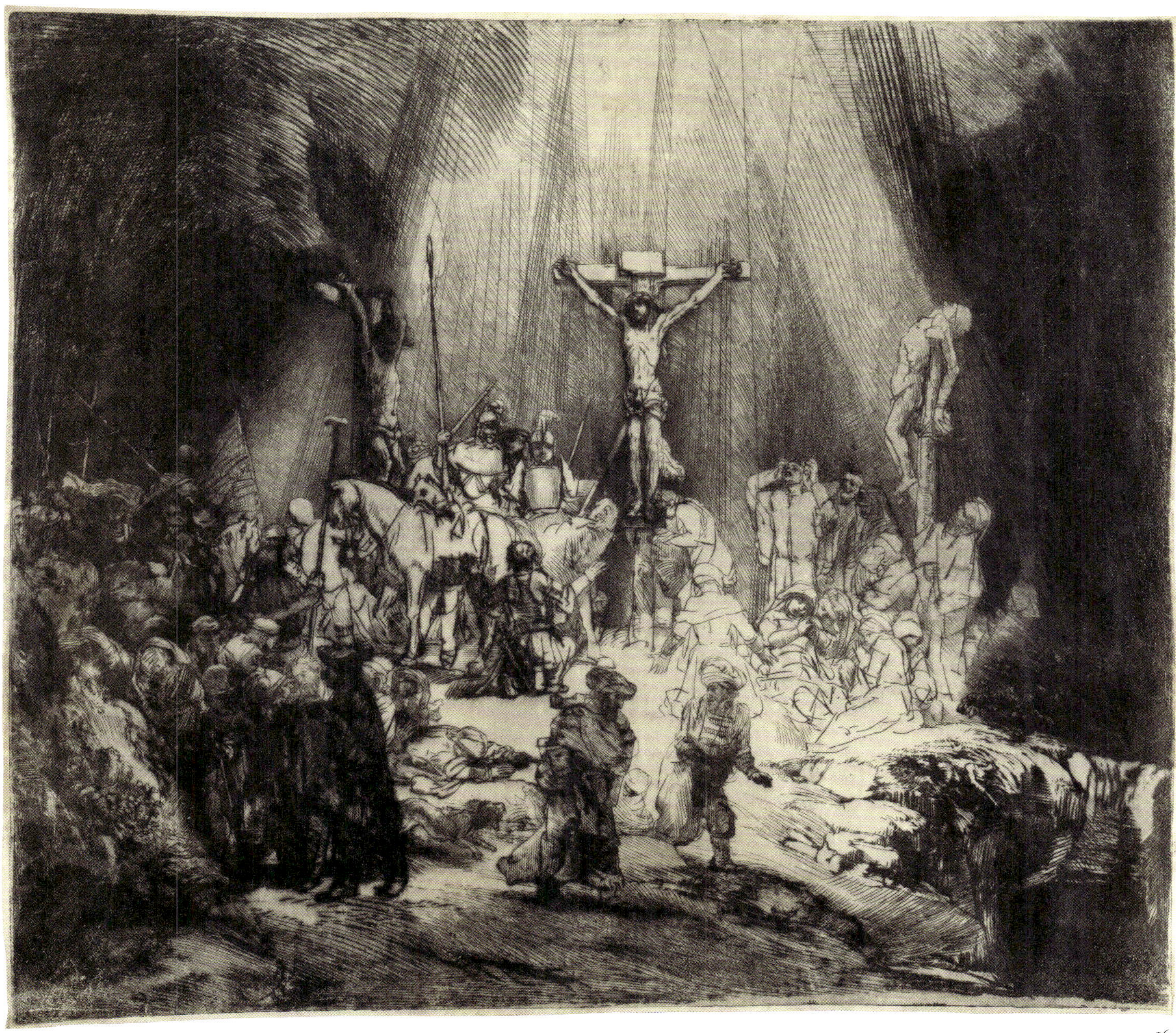

16

16–18

Rembrandt van Rijn, Dutch (1609–1669)

Christ Crucified between the Two Thieves:
The Three Crosses, 1653 [16]

Drypoint printed on vellum, first state of five,
15⅛ × 17½ in. (38.4 × 44.3 cm)

Christ Crucified between the Two Thieves:
The Three Crosses, 1653 [17]

Drypoint, third state of five, 15⅜ × 18 in. (38.9 × 45.6 cm)

Christ Crucified between the Two Thieves:
The Three Crosses, ca. 1660 [18]

Drypoint, fourth state of five, 15⅛ × 17½ in.
(38.2 × 44.4 cm)

Gift of Felix M. Warburg and his family, 1941
(41.1.31–.33)

Provenance: Felix Moritz Warburg (1871–1937), New
York; gift of Felix M. Warburg and his family to the
Department of Prints, 1941

In these spectacular works, each a different
state, or moment in the process of creation,
Rembrandt demonstrates his dexterity and
confidence with different printmaking techniques and with varied effects of tone through
wiping and scraping. As Mayor noted, "An
amateur artist hesitates to erase for fear he
may do worse next time, but the professional
shows his mastery by the ruthlessness of his

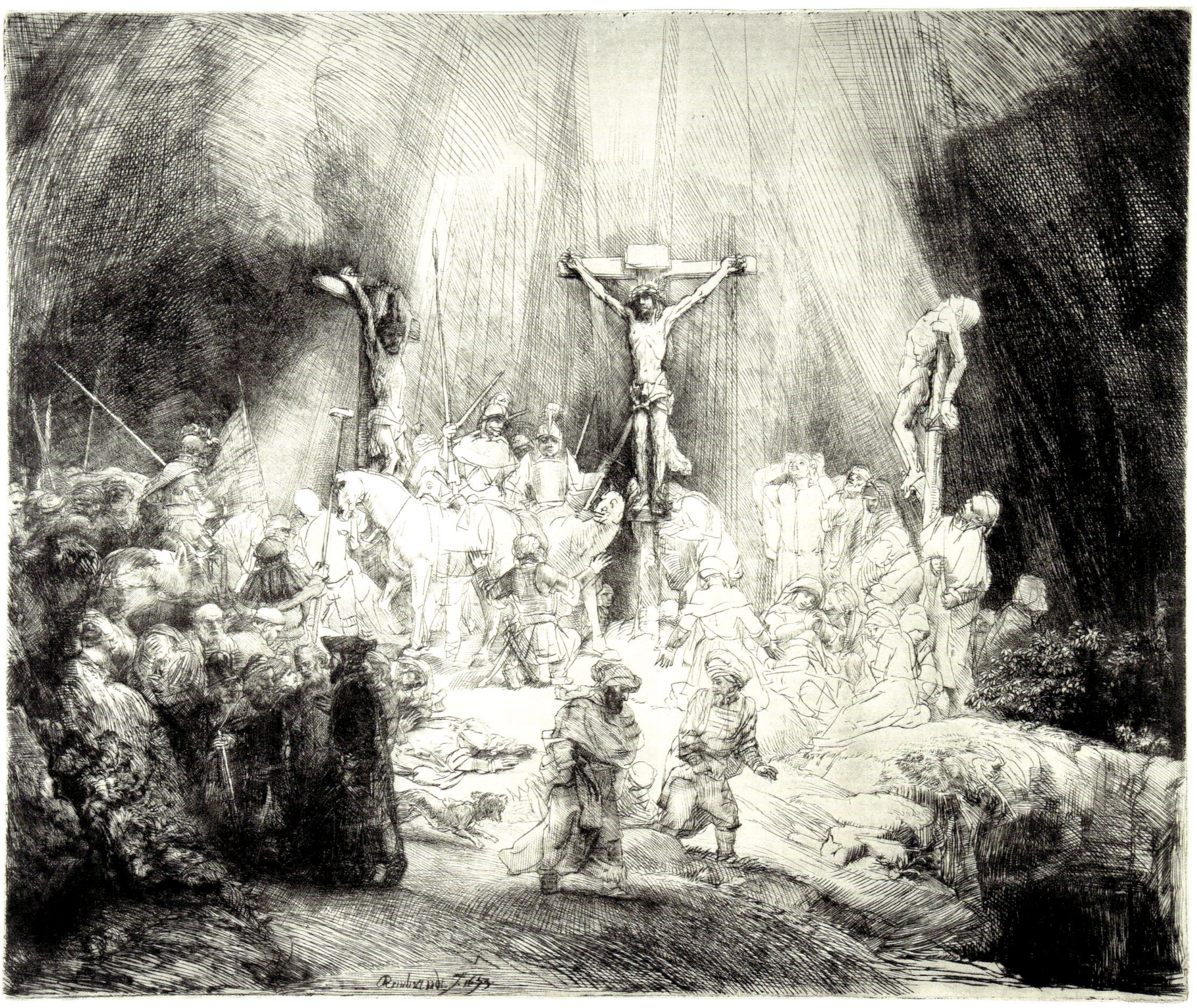

17

sacrifices. . . . He suddenly puts opera glasses to our eyes, pulling us into the void. . . . We now live inside the vision, oblivious to the calculations that went into its making . . . oblivious even to the paper and the ink" (Mayor, *Prints & People*, 489).

Rembrandt often drew from the Bible for his subject matter, "meditat[ing] all his life on episodes in which the divine penetrates the everyday to surprise ordinary people in extraordinary relationships. He returned to the Bible more often than to any other subject and expressed his preoccupation most imaginatively in his etchings" (ibid., 483). In these prints, like many of his other religious works, Rembrandt plays with the staging of the scene, variously bathing it in blinding light and cloaking it in darkness.

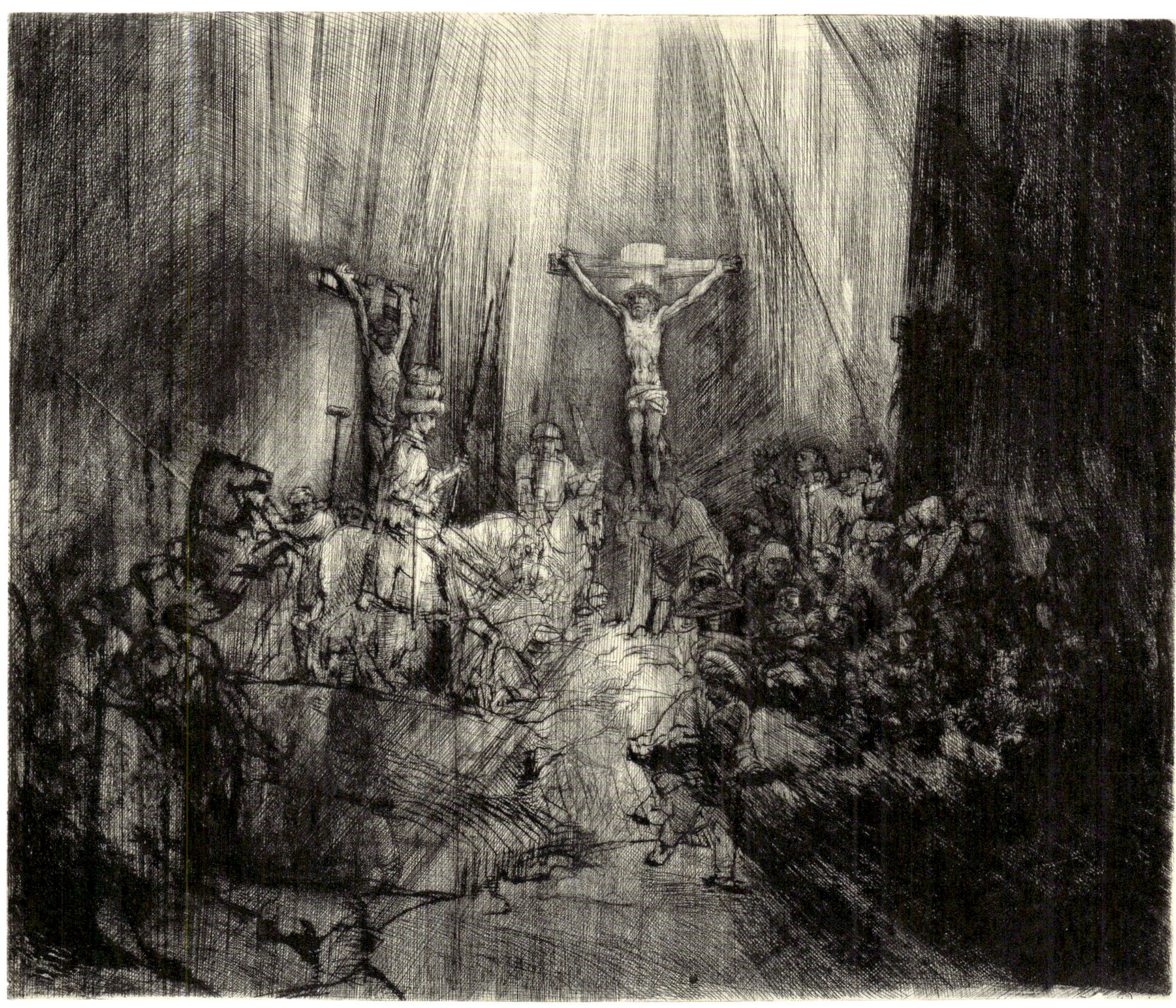

Rembrandt van Rijn, Dutch (1609–1669)

Jan Lutma, 1656

Etching and drypoint on japan paper, first state of three,
8¾ × 6⅞ in. (22.1 × 17.5 cm)
Gift of George Coe Graves, 1920 (20.46.18)

Collectors' marks: Sir Edward Astley (Lugt 2775);
handwritten signature of Chevalier I. J. de Claussin

Provenance: Sir Edward Astley (1729–1802), Norfolk,
England; Chevalier Ignace-Joseph de Claussin
(1766–1844), Paris and London; George Coe Graves
(1873–1932), Orange, N.J.; his gift to the Department of
Prints, 1920

Rembrandt's portrayal of the renowned gold-
and silversmith Jan Lutma (ca. 1584–1669)
shows him surrounded by the tools of his trade
and his own creations, including a hammer,
a vessel containing metal punches, a candle-
stick, and an ornamented drinking bowl. Ivins
observed that this deceptively simple portrait
"exemplifies the way in which Rembrandt, the
alchemist, could take any ordinary subject and
by passing it through the alembic of his mind
turn it into matter of great import. Lutma dies
and is forgotten, Rembrandt's transmutation
of his soul has immortality" (Ivins, label for
"Masterpieces, 1930–34").

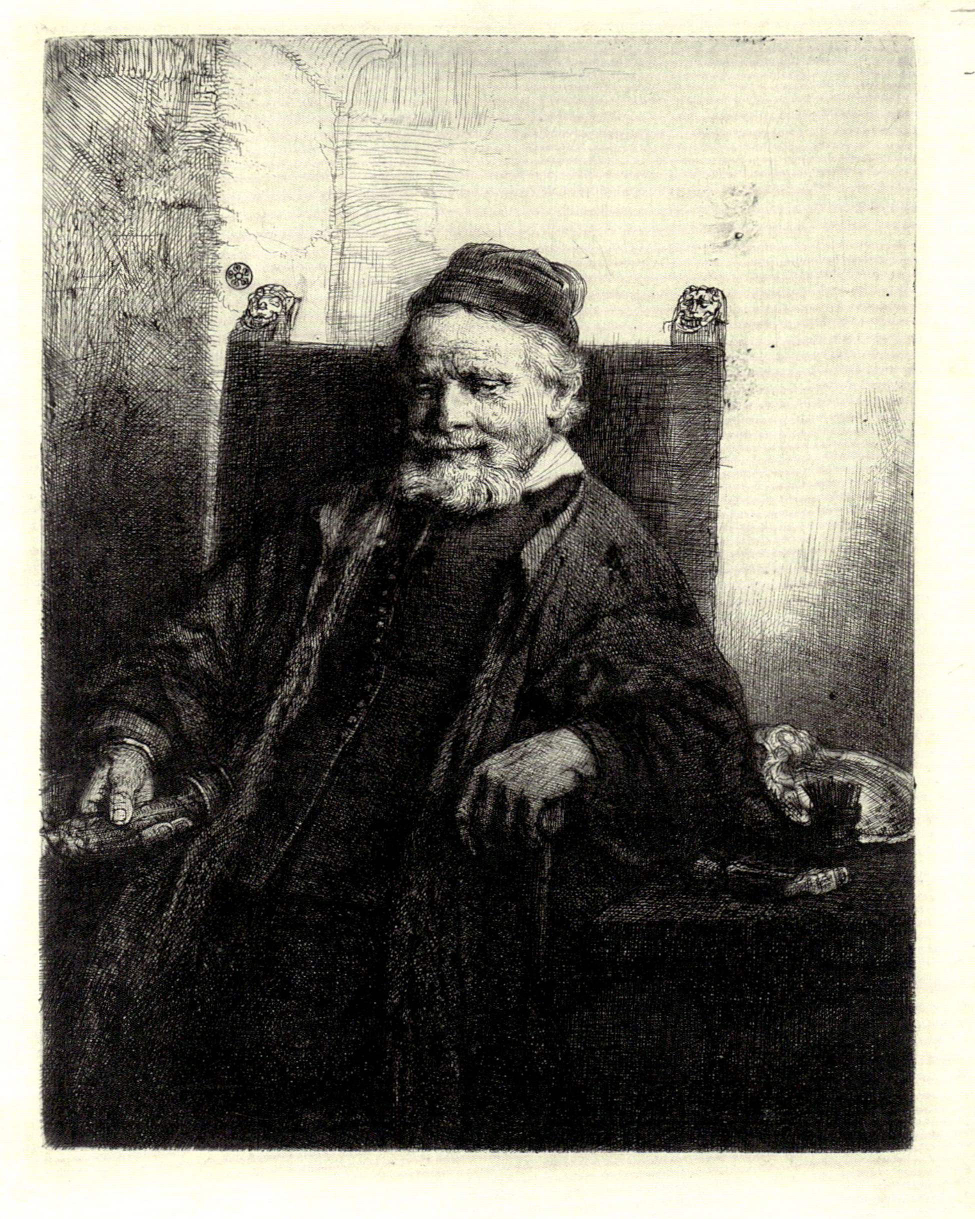

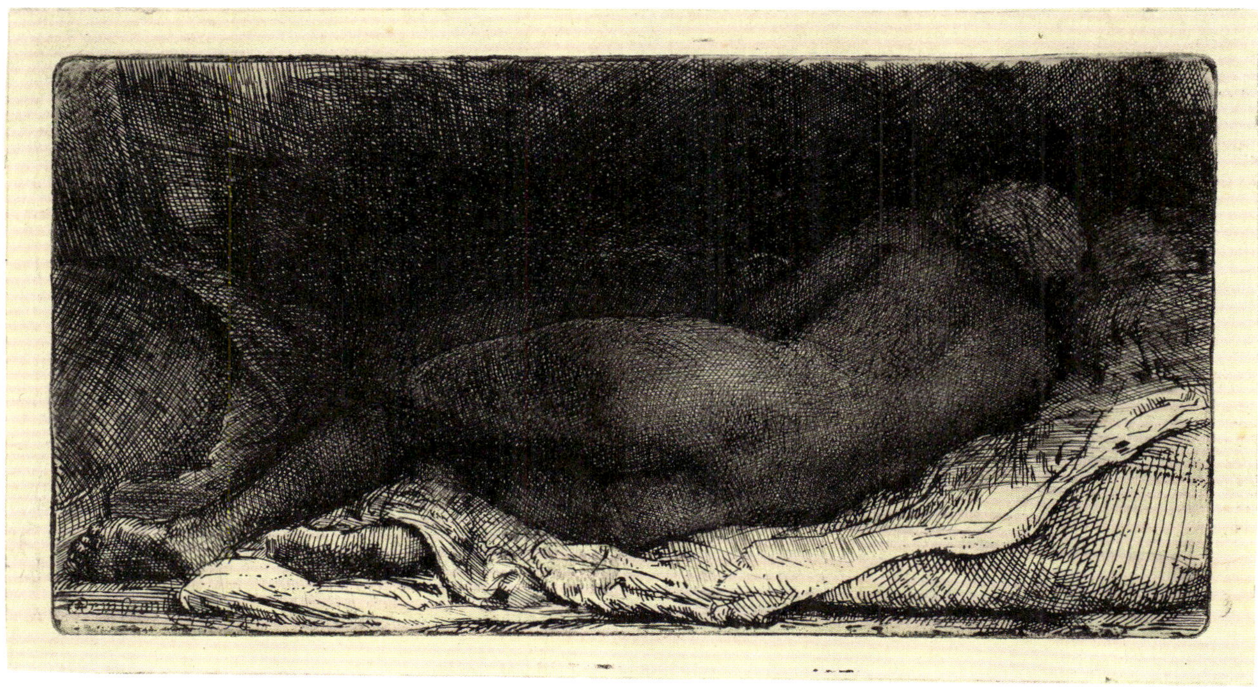

20

Reclining Female Nude, 1658

Etching, drypoint, and engraving on japan paper, second state of four, 3¾ × 6¾ in. (9.5 × 17.1 cm)
H. O. Havemeyer Collection, Bequest of Mrs. H. O. Havemeyer, 1929 (29.107.28)

Collector's mark: Sir Francis Seymour Haden (Lugt 1227)

Provenance: Sir Francis Seymour Haden (1818–1910), London; [his sale, Sotheby's, London, June 15–19, 1891, lot 465]; Henry Osborne Havemeyer (1847–1907), New York; Louisine Walden Elder Havemeyer (1855–1929), New York; her bequest to the Department of Prints, 1929

Ivins and Mayor celebrated Rembrandt not only for his technical dexterity, intelligence, and imagination but also as an artist with both feet firmly planted on the ground: a man of his time who was an astute, sensitive observer of humanity. Mayor described Rembrandt's making of this work: "While he was etching his last great landscapes, he took a copperplate to a swimming hole to sketch the bathers in the open air. He saw them like Cézanne, as bodies fractured in dappled shade or obliterated in sunlight. . . . From this noonday glimpse, Rembrandt could plunge deep into Giorgione's twilight for the so-called *Negress Lying Down*, in a Venetian dusk compacted as thick as aspic with a skill that he alone commanded. It is hard enough to draw a thing to look round, but next to impossible to embed it in a shallow, yet palpable, deposit of air. To print the magic of such drypoint, Rembrandt wiped the copperplate with a touch almost as rare as the etching itself and printed it on Oriental papers that absorbed all the warm ink into their creamy softness" (Mayor, *Prints & People*, 496).

The Garroted Man (*El Agarrotado*), ca. 1778–80

Etching printed in blue ink, 17⅛ × 12⅜ in.
(43.3 × 31.2 cm)
Rogers Fund, 1920 (20.22)

Collector's mark: George William Reid (Lugt 1210)

Provenance: George William Reid (1819–1887), London;
[Frederick Keppel & Co., New York]; Department of
Prints purchase, 1920

This unique working proof shows a man being
killed by a garrote, the standard civilian
method of execution in eighteenth-century
Spain. One of Goya's earliest etchings, this
frank representation, nuanced by the tone of
the blue ink spread across the surface, antici-
pates the inhumanity he would later depict in
The Disasters of War. This vision of cruelty
resonated with Mayor 175 years later, a time
marked by nuclear testing, the Korean War, the
Red Scare, and the Cold War. "Goya dealt
unflinchingly with such matters as despair and
death, violence and anarchy, suffering and fear.
These are the commonplace topics in our daily
press and in the literature of our times. But no
earlier artist had set them forth so pungently or
so unreservedly as did Goya. . . . [F]ew other
artists, certainly, speak to our present generation so directly and so compellingly over more
than a century of time" (Mayor, *Goya, 1746–
1828*, introduction).

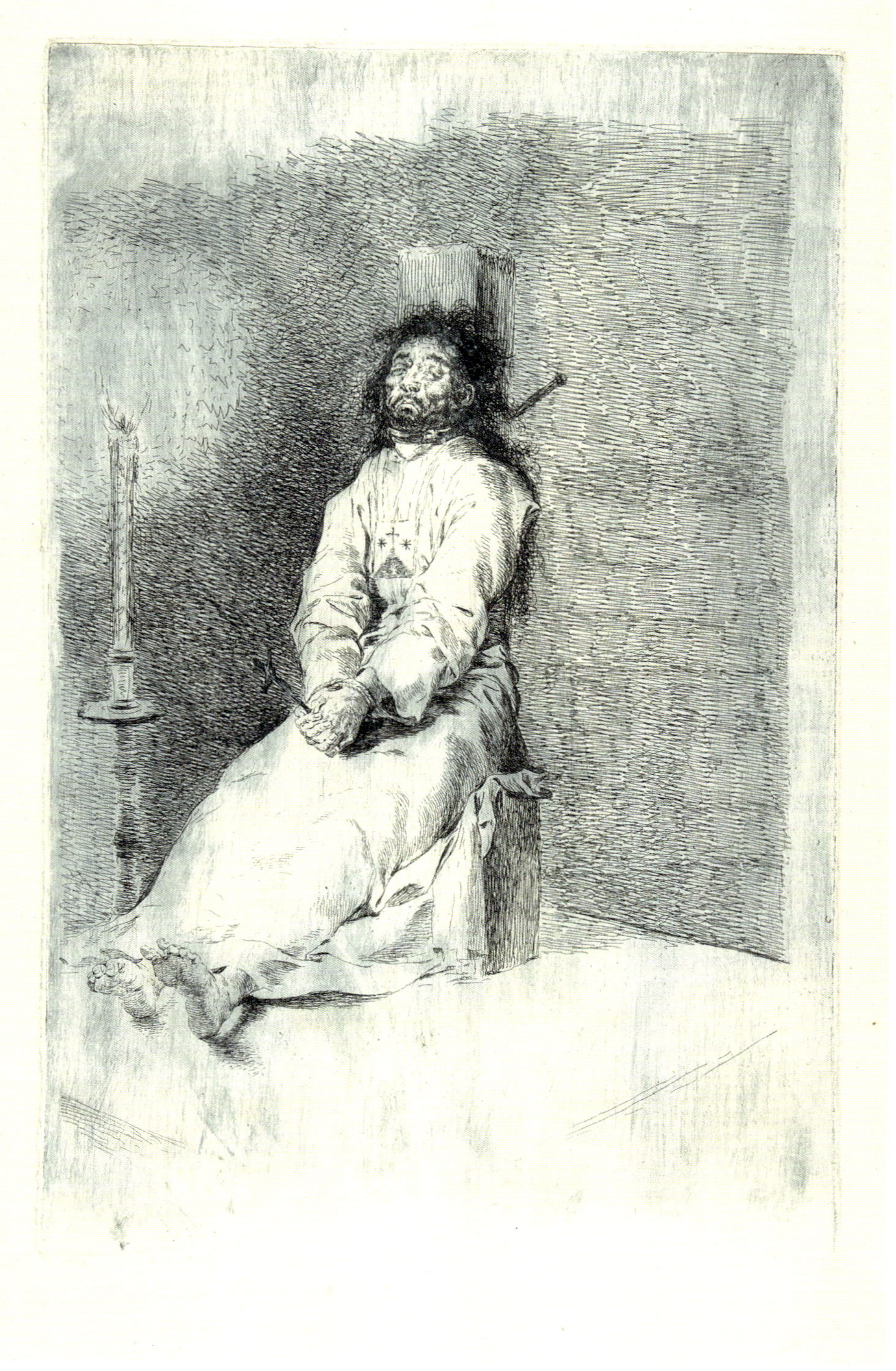

The Disasters of War (Los Desastres de
la Guerra), 1810

And There Is No Help (Y No Hai Remedio),
plate 15 [22]

Etching, drypoint, burin, and burnisher, 8⅞ × 12½ in.
(22.5 × 31.8 cm)

Bury Them and Keep Quiet (Enterrar y Callar),
plate 18 [23]

Etching, drypoint, and burin, 9⅛ × 12½ in.
(23.1 × 31.8 cm)

Ravages of War (Estragos de la Guerra),
plate 30 [24]

Etching, drypoint, burin, and burnisher, 12⅜ × 8½ in.
(31.5 × 21.6 cm)

*They Escape through the Flames
(Escapan entre las Llamas)*, plate 41 [25]

Etching and burin, 8¾ × 12¾ in. (22 × 32.3 cm)

Harris Brisbane Dick Fund, 1932 (32.62.17, .12, .5, .6)

Provenance: [XVIIIth Century Shop, New York];
Department of Prints purchase, 1932

Ivins's experience of Goya's Disasters of War
had a profound effect on his life and choice
of profession. As he described, writing about
himself in the third person: "He has never forgotten the wild excitement of the day when as a
lad of twenty, passing through Paris on his road
to the university, he found another copy of this
same 1863 edition of the Disasters of War in
Rapilly's shop on the quai; or how parting with
the sum of sixty francs he took the book with
him to Munich, where poring over it night
after night he learned far more from its pages
than from all the lectures of the Professor Doctor Rector Magnificus. . . . They were deadly
serious, they were human and masculine and
full of strong emotion, and he reacted to them
as hitherto he never had to anything but the
pistol shot from the starter's boat" (Ivins,
"Goya's Disasters of War," 1924: 222).

Ivins avidly collected Goya prints for the
Met, amassing a group of rare early, unlettered
proofs of the Disasters of War. What appealed

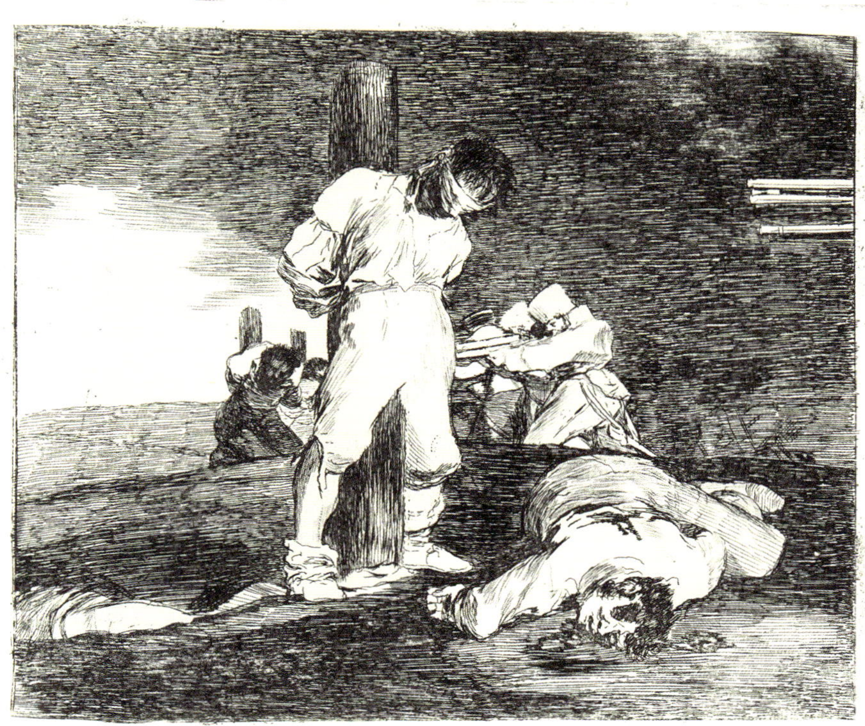

22

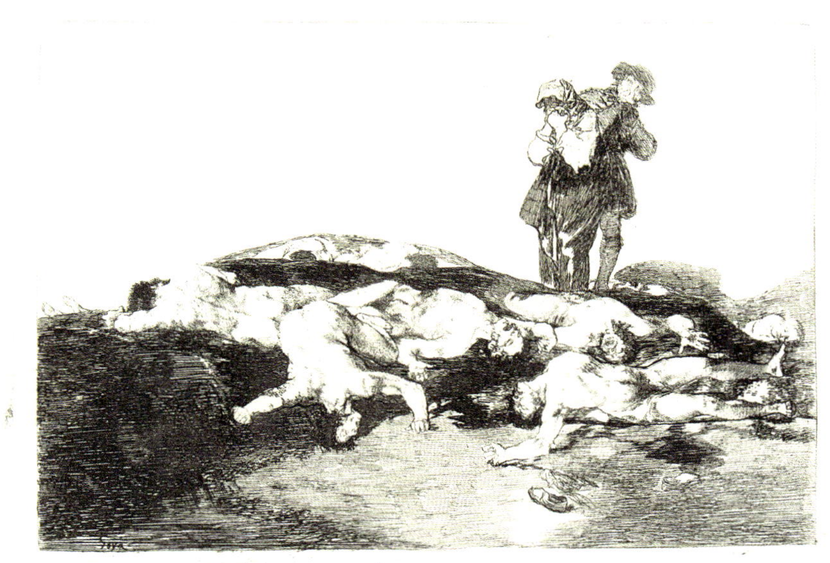

23

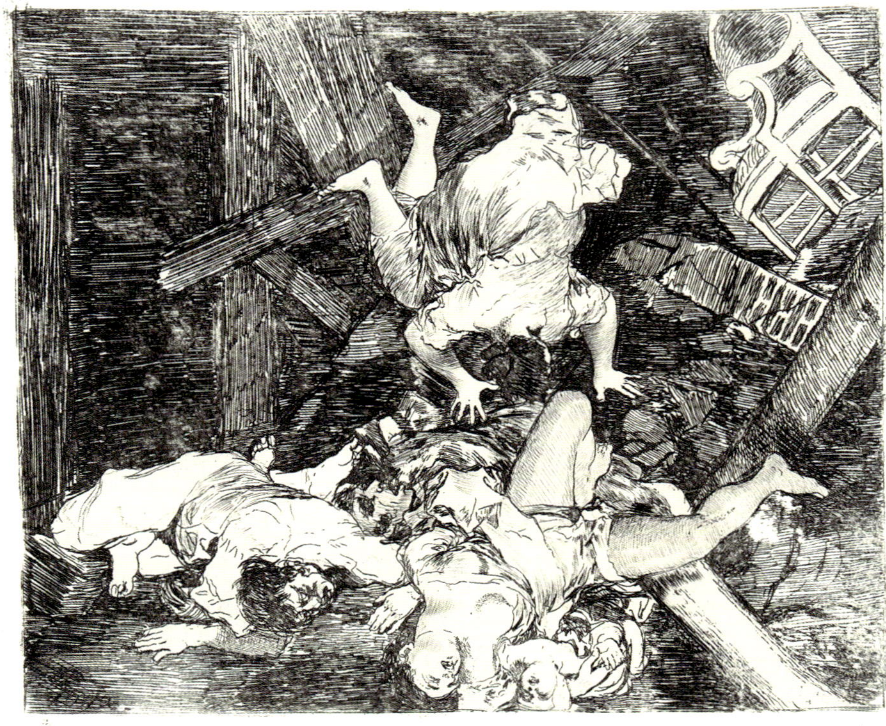

24

to Ivins and later to Mayor, who also collected, exhibited, and wrote extensively on Goya, was the artist's unflinching depiction of life's misery and the deep understanding of humanity he demonstrated in his impressions of the brutal Napoleonic invasion of Spain. Mayor noted that, in this series, Goya "saw beyond propaganda for Spain or hatred of France into the final horror; the uselessness of suffering" (Mayor, *Goya, 1746–1828,* 21).

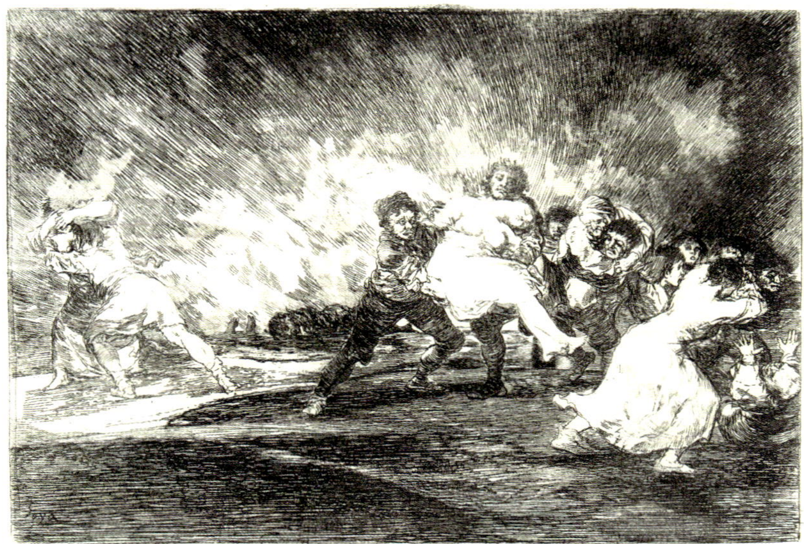

25

26

Seated Giant, by 1818

Burnished aquatint with lavis, 11¼ × 8¼ in.
(28.5 × 21 cm)
Harris Brisbane Dick Fund, 1935 (35.42)

Provenance: José Sanchez Gerona (1874–1937), Madrid;
Georges Provôt, active before 1935, Paris; [his sale, Hôtel
Drouot, Paris, April 10, 1935, lot 29]; [P. & D. Colnaghi,
London]; Department of Prints purchase, 1935

Goya meticulously executed this extremely
rare print. As Mayor described, he "first bit an
even aquatint tone all over the copper, then
scraped the half tones with a knife and burnished the high lights as though he were making a mezzotint. The fine and shallow grain
caught little ink even at the start and would
quickly have worn smooth. The print is Goya's
only experiment in the mezzotint manner.
He worked on it like a painter brushing white
over a dark canvas, and perhaps for this reason
was able to give this print a breadth he equaled
only in his greatest paintings" (Mayor, "Goya's
Giant," 1935: 154). Goya's enigmatic Giant
entranced Mayor, who wrote of the dark form
as both "looming in a dream" and the "embodi-
ment of the rousing strength" of the modern
era "that shouldered the eighteenth century
out of the road" (ibid.).

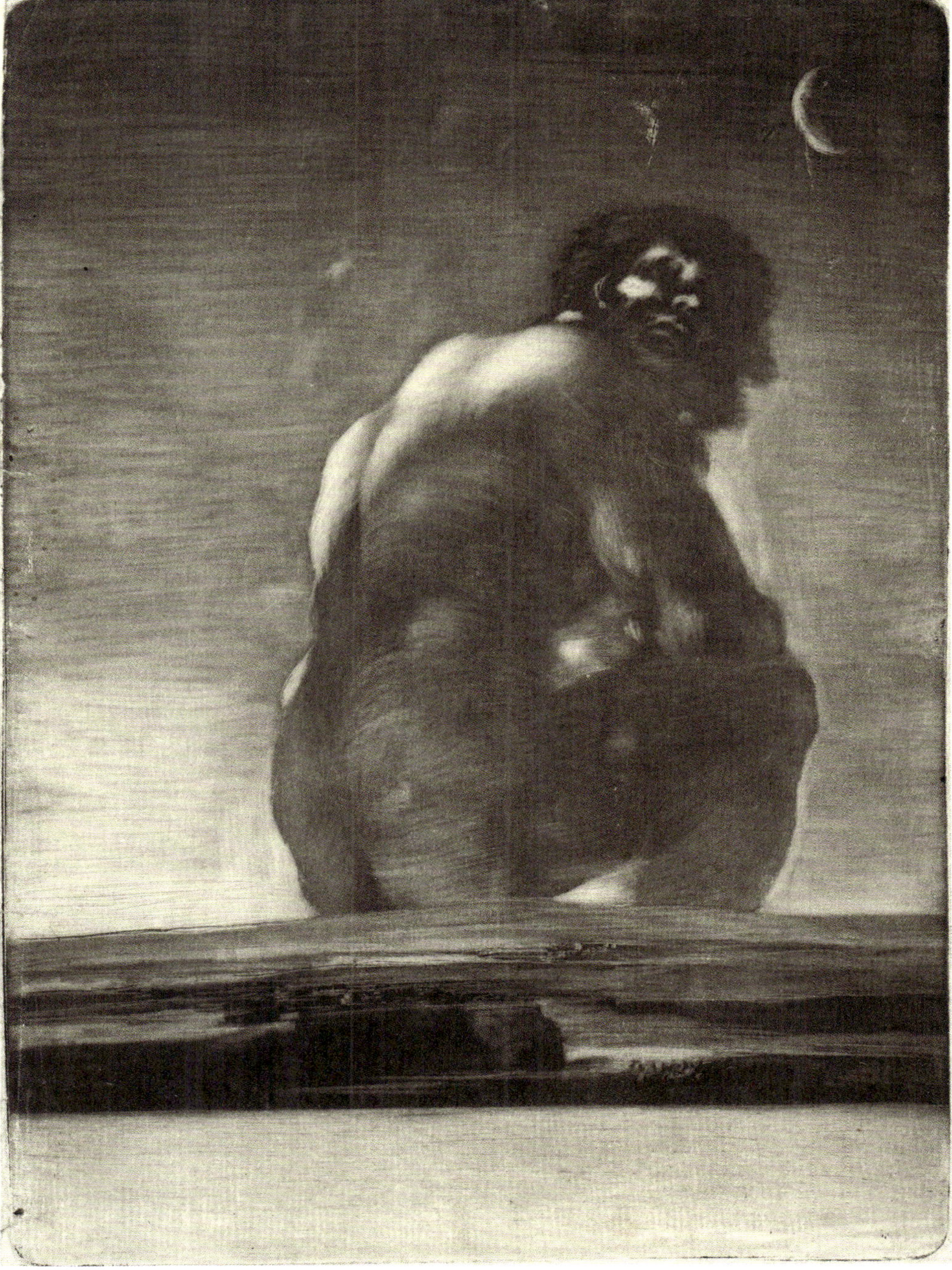

Charles Meryon, French (1821–1868)

La Rue des Toiles, Bourges, 1853

Etching with drypoint, fifth state of nine, 13¼ × 9 in.
(33.7 × 22.8 cm)
Gift of Theodore De Witt, 1917 (17.22.18)

Watermark: shield with crown, two flowers, and
crescent moon

Collector's mark: Alfred Morrison (Lugt 151)

Provenance: Alfred Morrison (1821–1897), London;
Theodore De Witt, New York; his gift to the Department
of Prints, 1917

In contrast to the technical experimentation
found in etching revival prints by such masters as Whistler and Haden, *La Rue des Toiles,
Bourges* demonstrates how Meryon thoroughly
wiped clean his plates of tone and used crisp,
dry lines to compose architectural scenes.
Meryon, who thought he was color-blind and
thus unable to be a painter, became a greatly
admired professional etcher; his technical
exactitude was often imitated. Ivins celebrated
Meryon's artistic productions but noted that
"even when working after his own drawings,
his technique is always that of the most accom-
plished maker of reproductive prints" (Ivins,
label for "Masterpieces 1930–34").

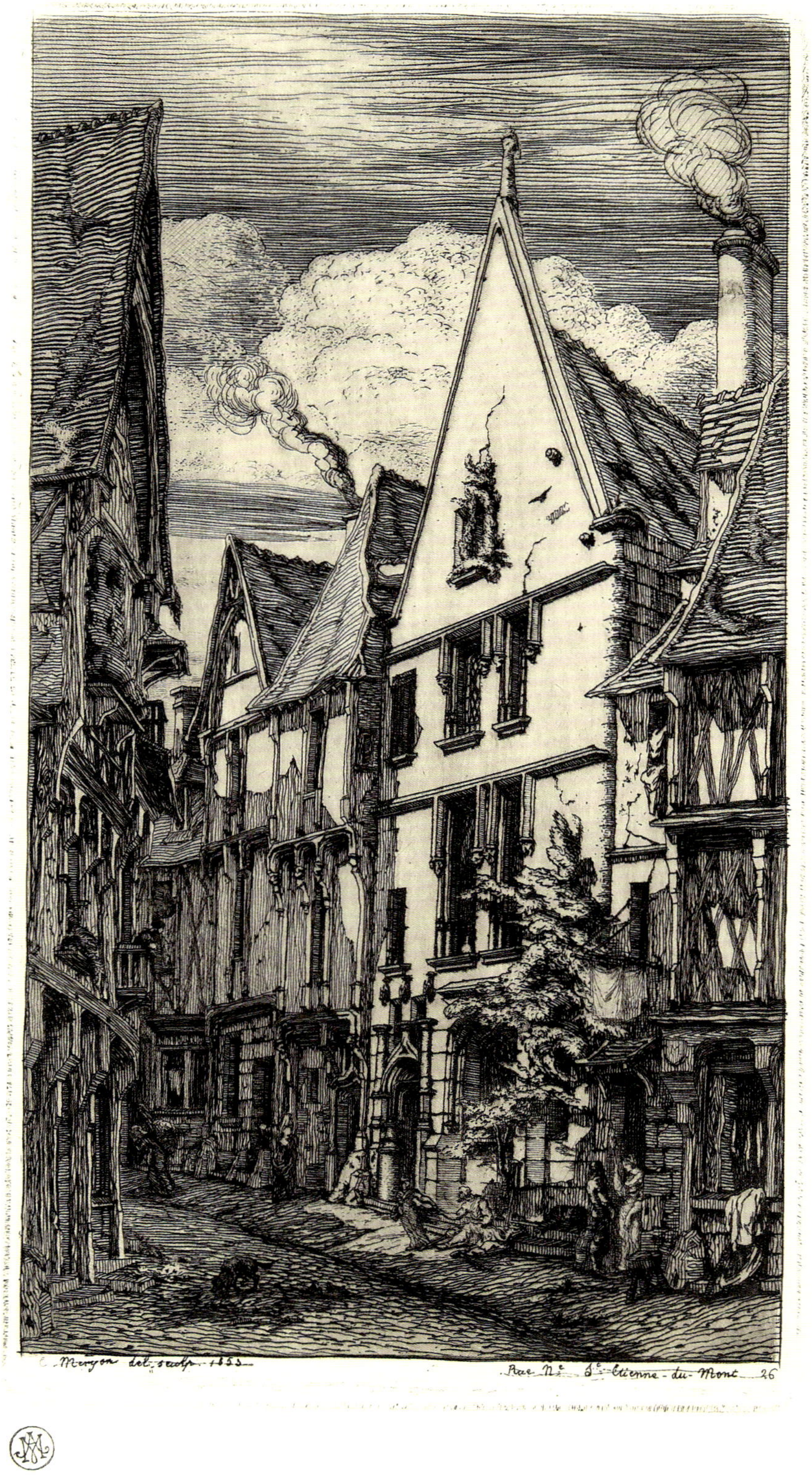

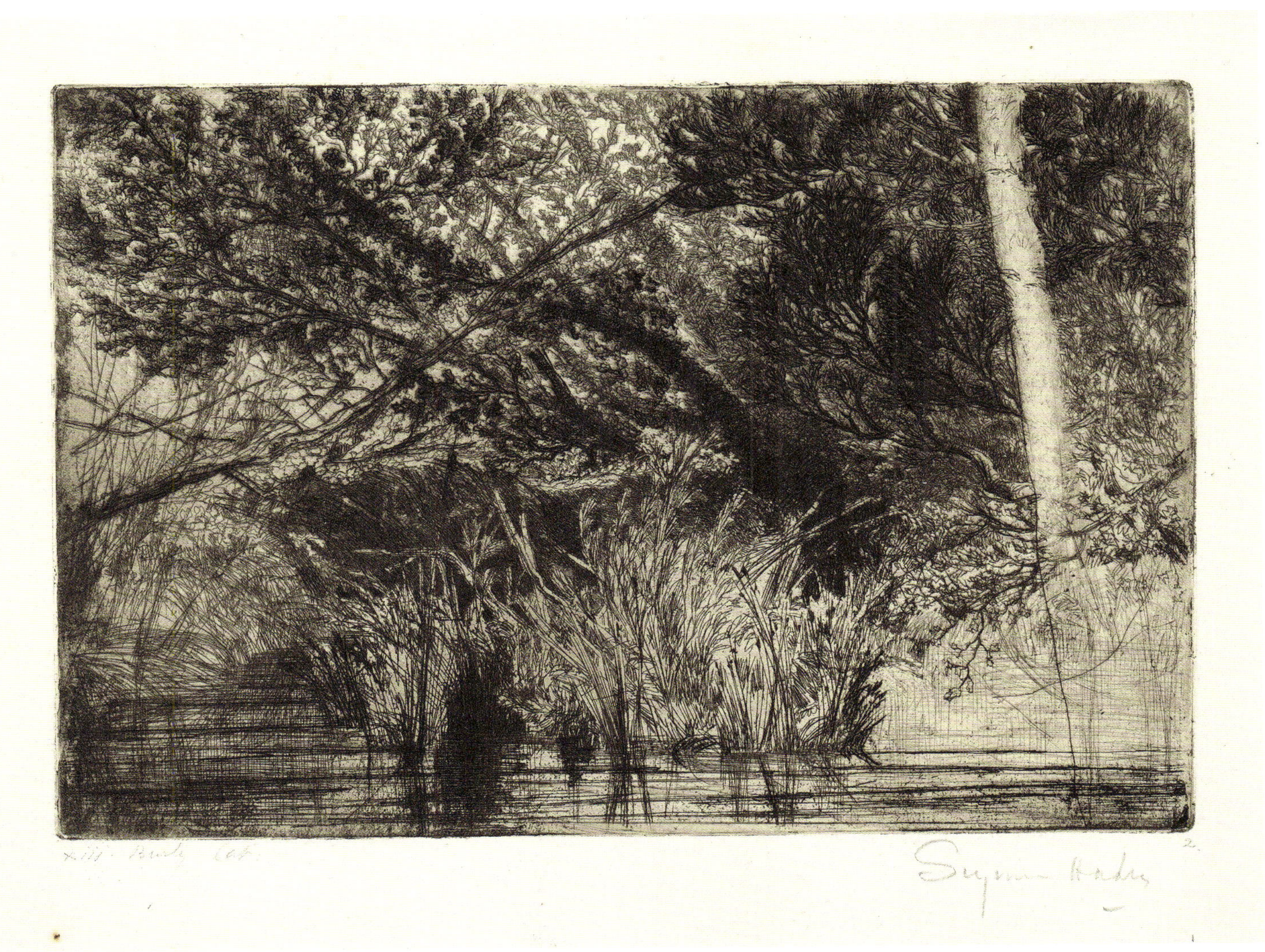

28

Sir Francis Seymour Haden, British
(1818–1910)

The Mouth of a Brook, 1859

Etching, 7¾ × 10⅛ in. (19.5 × 25.7 cm)
Harris Brisbane Dick Fund, 1917 (17.3.287)

Provenance: [Obach & Co., London]; Harris Brisbane
Dick (1855–1916), New York; Dick Estate, U.S. Trust;
Department of Prints purchase, 1917

"Seymour Haden always considered this one
of the best of his etchings," according to Ivins.
"On the back of Mr. Dick's impression of
the first state, which apparently came from
Haden's own collection, there is a rubbed pen-
cil note in his handwriting: 'The rarest and one
of the best of my plates'" (Ivins, "The Harris B.
Dick Collection of Prints," 1917: 50).

James McNeill Whistler, American
(1834–1903)

Black Lion Wharf, 1859

Etching, fourth state of four, 7⅛ × 9¾ in. (18 × 24.7 cm)
Harris Brisbane Dick Fund, 1917 (17.3.35)

Provenance: [Frederick Keppel & Co., New York]; Harris Brisbane Dick (1855–1916), New York; Dick Estate, U.S. Trust; Department of Prints purchase, 1917

As the most highly sought-after printmaker in the art market of the late nineteenth and early twentieth centuries, Whistler was enthusiastically collected by Harris Brisbane Dick. Dick amassed nearly three hundred of the artist's prints, which entered the Met with his founding gift. This etching of Black Lion Wharf in London, part of Whistler's Thames Set, shows a dangerous stretch of the river with tumbledown structures that were set to be cleared for development. Indebted to the realism of Charles Meryon's etched views of Paris, Whistler is said to have spent three weeks on each of the set's eight plates, meticulously recording the details of the barges and their cargo, as well as the wood, brick, tile, and metals of the decaying waterside buildings.

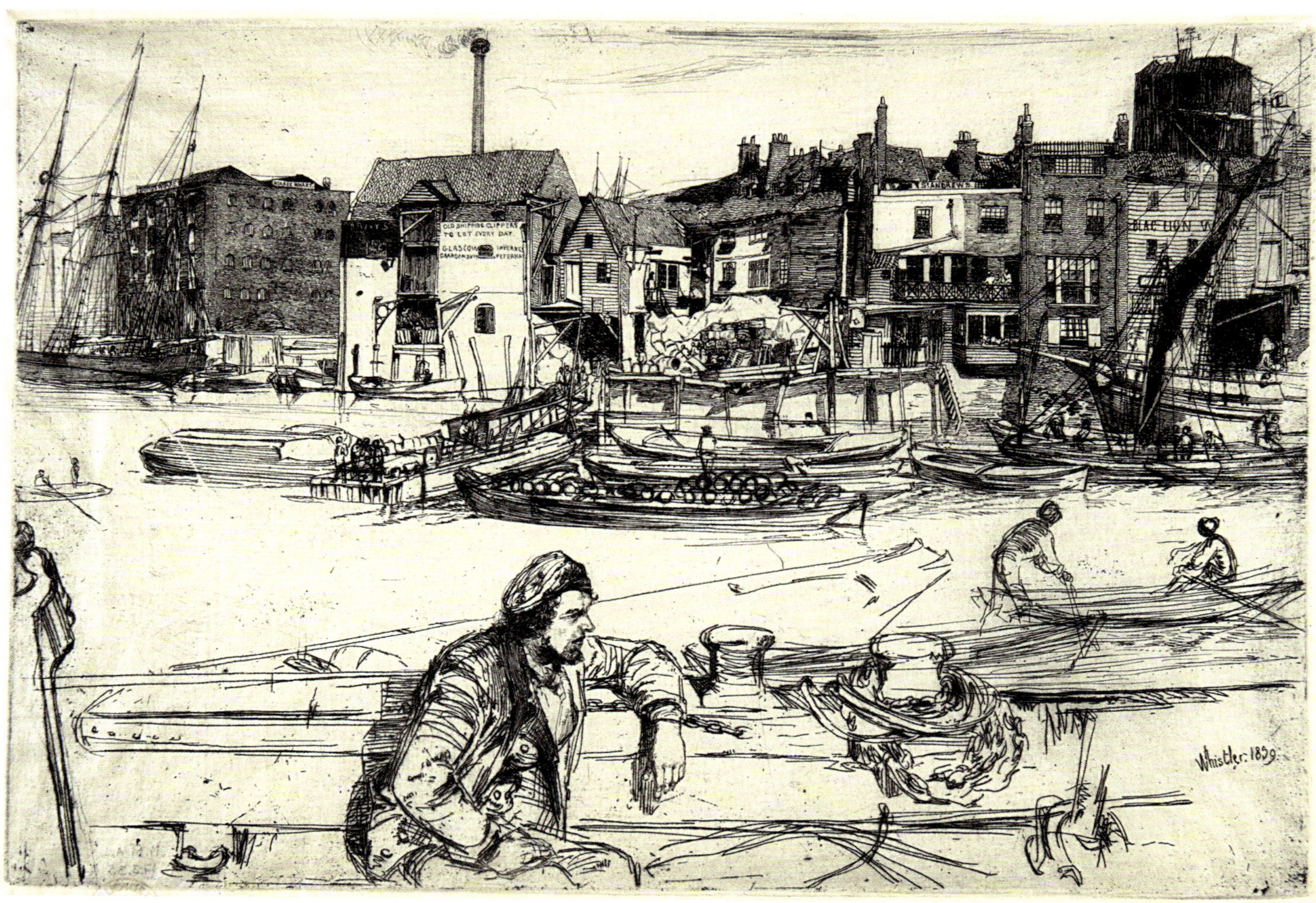

James McNeill Whistler, American
(1834–1903)

Speke Hall, No. 1, 1870

Etching and drypoint, tenth state of fourteen,
13¼ × 8 in. (33.6 × 20.3 cm)
Harris Brisbane Dick Fund, 1917 (17.3.66)

Watermark: fragment, VA

Provenance: [Obach & Co., London]; Harris Brisbane
Dick (1855–1916), New York; Dick Estate, U.S. Trust;
Department of Prints purchase, 1917

At the turn of the twentieth century Whistler
was considered the greatest etcher since
Rembrandt, and his works were coveted in
the American market. Whistler was born in
Massachusetts but had gone to France to study
art and then made his home in London. Ivins
judged the expatriate as unable to understand
or confront his own traditions and thus to
make art that reflects truth and grittiness; he
believed the exquisiteness of Whistler's etched
lines, his technical mastery, was the result of
his "dandiacal aloofness from life" (Ivins, label
for "Masterpieces 1929–30").

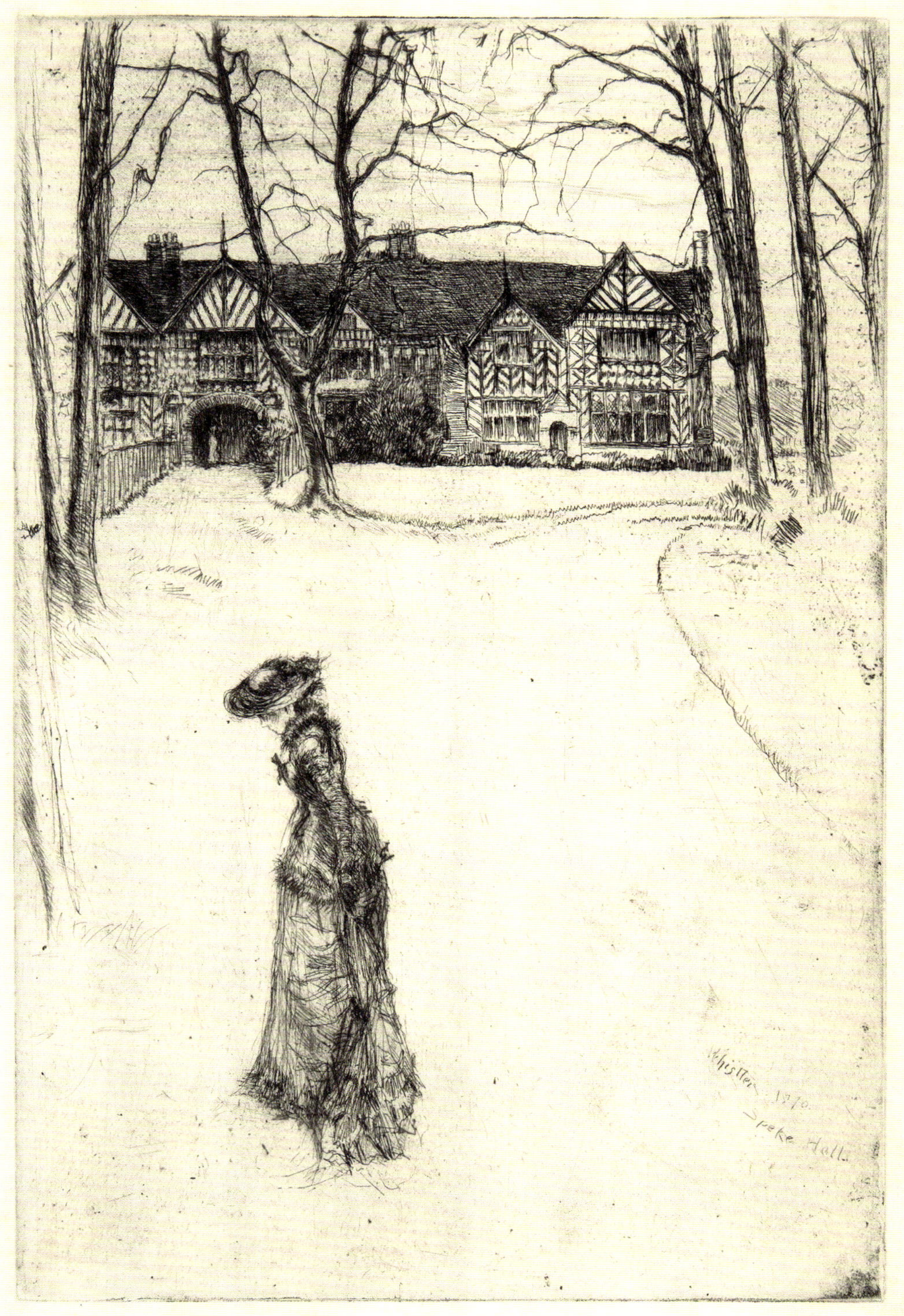

Nocturne: Palaces, 1879–80

Etching and drypoint, twelfth state of twelve,
11½ × 7⅞ in. (29.2 × 19.8 cm)
Gift of Harold K. Hochschild, 1940 (40.63.8)

Provenance: Margaret F. Everit (died 1934), Newark, N.J.;
[her sale, American Art Association, Jan. 29–31, 1917, lot
456]; Harold K. Hochschild (1892–1981), New York; his
gift to the Department of Prints, 1940

In the 1870s Whistler executed a series of
painted and printed nocturnes that embrace
simplicity and economy of expression rather
than the realism of his earlier works. Abstraction as an aesthetic device that could evoke
atmospheric effects, mood, or time of day was
a radical concept. Exemplifying Whistler's
move in this direction, *Nocturne: Palaces* shows
a darkened view of three palaces separated
by a narrow canal that is crossed by a small
bridge, where a lantern's light breaks through
the haze. Whistler manipulated the etching's
evocative nature through his delicate wiping
of the ink in the upper and lower portions of
the sheet. As Ivins noted, "[T]he distribution
of the ink on the surface of the plate [counts]
for almost everything" (Ivins, label for "Technical Show," 1927–28). This work was part of
a group that London's Fine Art Society commissioned Whistler to create during a stay in
Venice in 1879. Selected prints were published
in two groups, in 1880 and 1886, and this print
belongs to the latter, known as the Second
Venice Set.

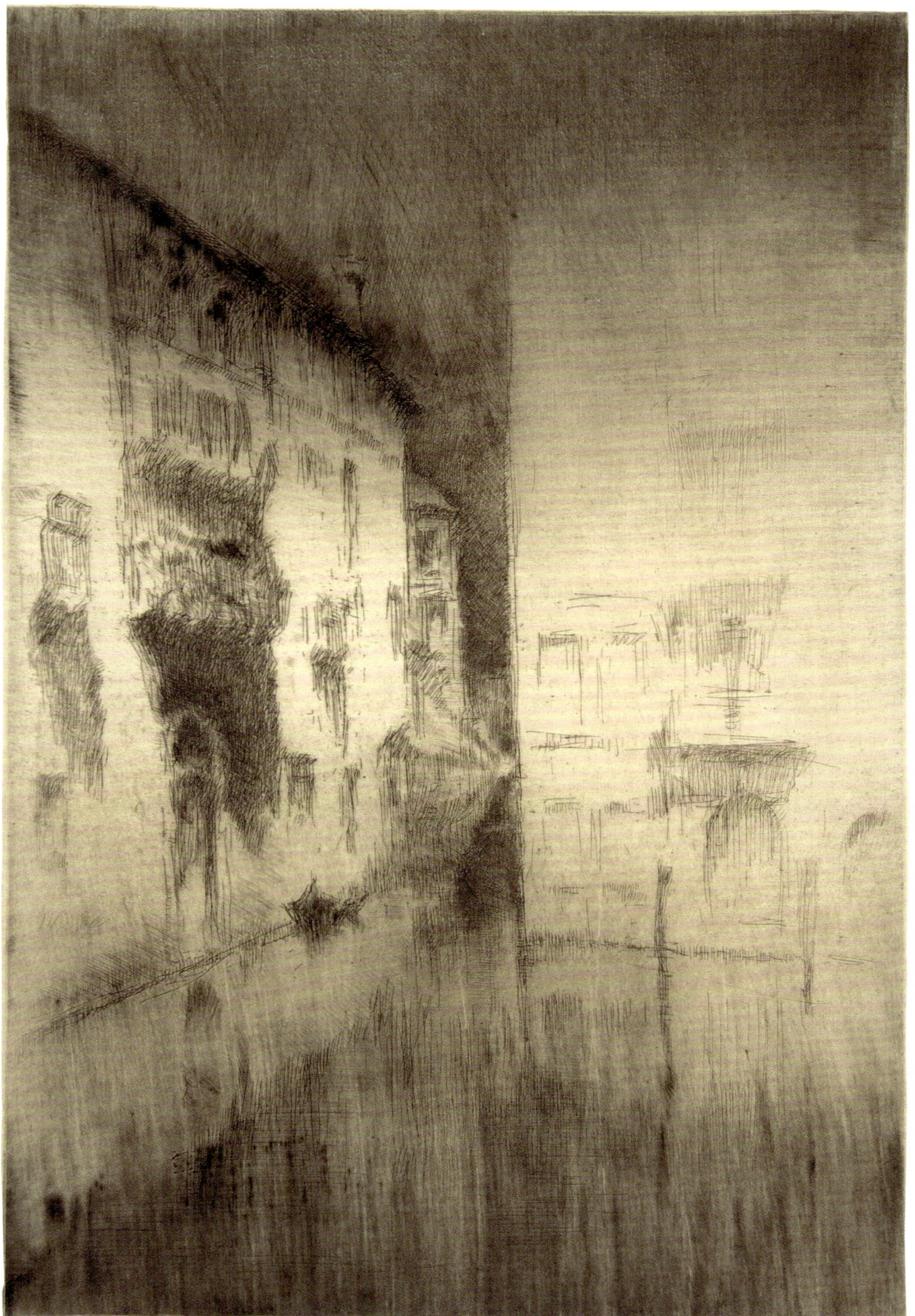

32

A Pier in England (*Une Jetée en Angleterre*),
1879

Etching, drypoint, aquatint, and roulette, second state
of eight, 16⅝ × 11⅝ in. (42.3 × 29.6 cm)
Harris Brisbane Dick Fund, 1917 (17.3.501)

Collector's mark: Félix-Hilaire Buhot (Lugt 977)

Provenance: Harris Brisbane Dick (1855–1916), New York;
Dick Estate, U.S. Trust; Department of Prints purchase,
1917

Renowned for his beautiful proofs, dramatic
state changes, and superbly inked impressions, Buhot was one of the best-known and
most collected printmakers in both his native
France and in the United States by the 1880s.
In 1888 he had his first one-man show at the
New York print dealer Frederick Keppel & Co.
His impressionistic prints exemplify the etching revival's interest in original printmaking
(especially etching), as opposed to reproductive engraving. In this second state of *A Pier in
England*, Buhot adds aquatint, roulette, and
additional drypoint to enhance the climatic
effects characteristic of his prints.

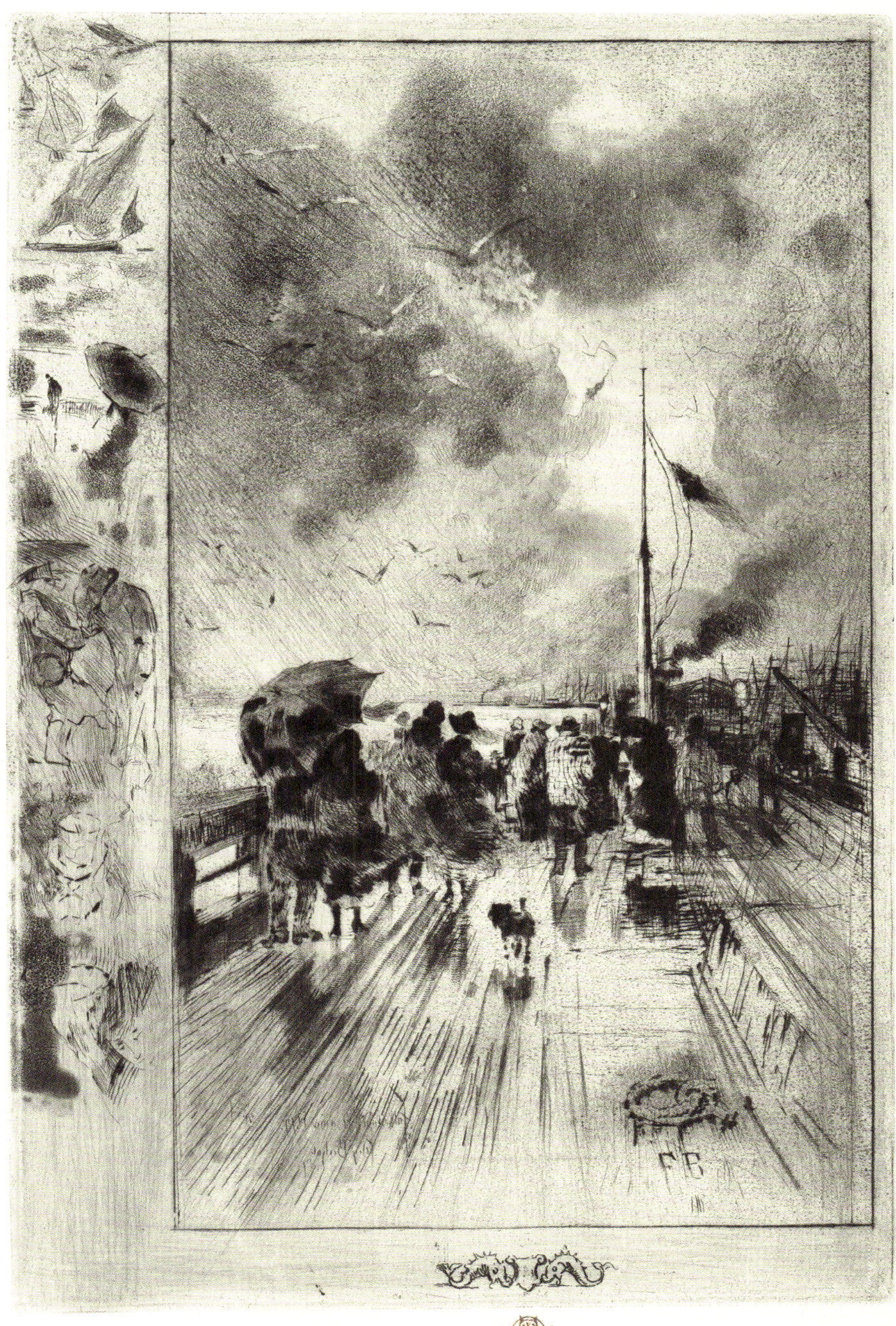

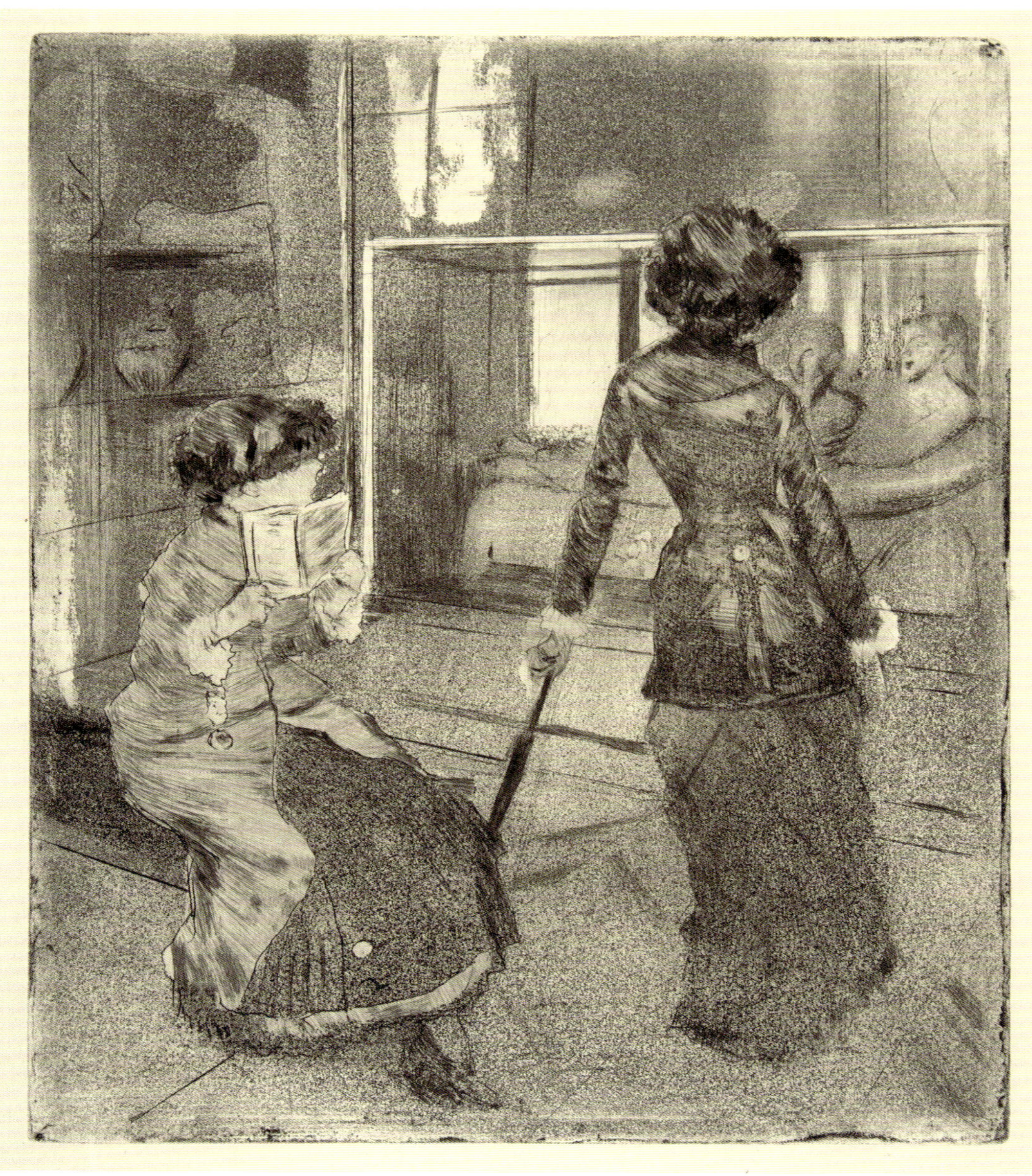

Edgar Degas, French (1834–1917)

Mary Cassatt at the Louvre: The Etruscan Gallery, 1879–80

Soft-ground etching, drypoint, aquatint, and etching, third state of nine, 17 × 12 in. (43.2 × 30.5 cm)
Rogers Fund, 1919 (19.29.2)

Collector's mark: Edgar Degas (Lugt 657)

Provenance: Edgar Degas (1834–1917), Paris; [his atelier sale, Galerie Manzi-Joyant, Paris, Nov. 22–23, 1918, possibly lot 53]; [M. Knoedler and Co., New York]; Department of Prints purchase, 1919

Degas invited Cassatt to show with the Impressionists in 1877; she was the first American to do so and became Degas's protégée. She worked closely with him on a journal about printmaking, which never materialized, and posed for him a number of times, including for this etching. Degas places her in the context of a museum, absorbed by the artwork, accompanied by her older sister Lydia. For Ivins this tour de force of printmaking, which combines etching, aquatint, and drypoint, demonstrated Degas's brilliance and artistic

pedigree: "Coming out of the classical tradition of Ingres, and enormously affected by the draughtsmanship of certain Italian primitives, the compositional invention of Utamaro and Daumier, and the studies of light made by Delacroix and Pissarro, Degas found his subject matter through Gavarni and Daumier. . . . His work may be regarded as the pictorial culmination of the mechanistic realism which conditioned most European thought and activity during the late nineteenth century" (Ivins, label for "Masterpieces 1930–34").

34

Mary Cassatt, American (1844–1926)

Portrait of George Moore, ca. 1881

Soft-ground etching, second state of two, 12½ × 9 in.
(31.8 × 22.9 cm)
Rogers Fund, 1919 (19.1.1)

Watermark: butterfly

Provenance: [Durand-Ruel Galleries, New York];
Department of Prints purchase, 1919

This soft-ground etching was carefully prepared by Cassatt, who depicted her close
friend, the eccentric Irish critic and novelist
George Moore, seated in her armchair, an
open fan held absentmindedly in one hand.
Moore, whose extensive written observations
of the Impressionists have shaped our understanding of their artistic endeavor, appears
in portraits across media, not only by Cassatt
but also by her close contemporaries Édouard
Manet and Edgar Degas.

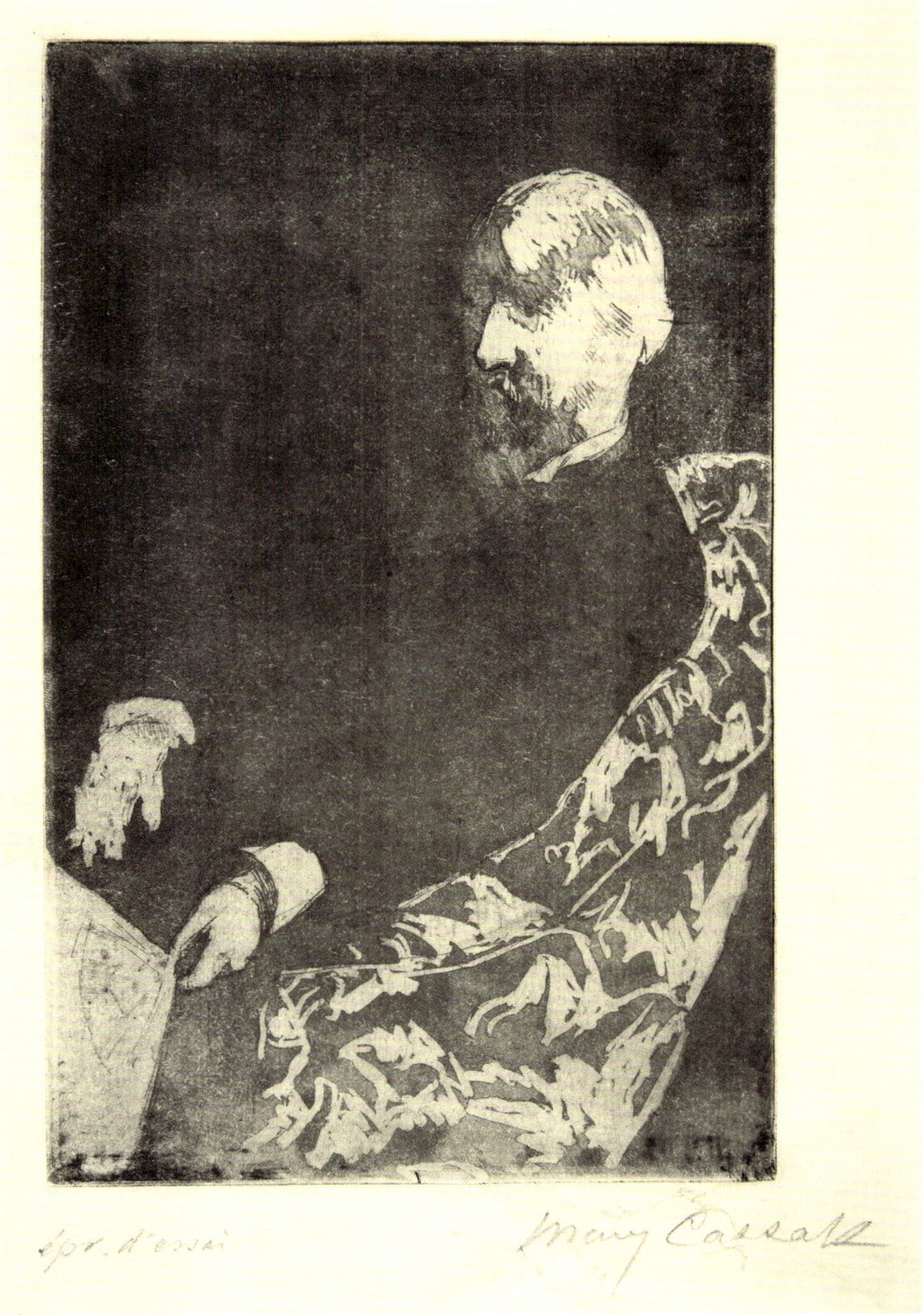

Mary Cassatt, American (1844–1926)

The Letter, 1890–91

Printed by Modeste Leroy, Paris
Drypoint, printed in black ink, first state of four,
13⅝ × 9⅛ in. (34.6 × 23.2 cm)
Inscribed in graphite by the artist: Edition de 25 série
Imprimée par l'artiste et M. Leroy/Mary Cassatt
Gift of Arthur Sachs, 1916 (16.3.2)

Collector's mark: Roger Marx (Lugt 2229)

Provenance: Roger Marx (1859–1913), Paris; possibly
Claude Roger-Marx (1888–1977), Paris; Arthur Sachs
(1880–1975), Cannes, France; his gift to the Department
of Prints, 1916

The first gifts to the Department of Prints
came directly from Ivins's circle of friends.
Paul J. Sachs, assistant director of the Fogg
Museum at Harvard University and a friend
of Ivins during his undergraduate years there,
gave ten Cassatts to the newly formed department in 1916. Sachs's brother, Arthur, who
also was friends with Ivins at Harvard, gave
an additional seven. In a letter to the director
of the Museum regarding the gift of the Cassatts, Paul noted: "I am sending these, rather
than the work of some Old Master, since I feel
that even before the Print Department gets
well under way, material of this kind may be of
interest to those who have no special interest
in the technique of prints" (Sachs to Edward
Robinson, Nov. 17, 1916; Sachs correspondence file, Office of the Secretary Records, The
Metropolitan Museum of Art Archives).

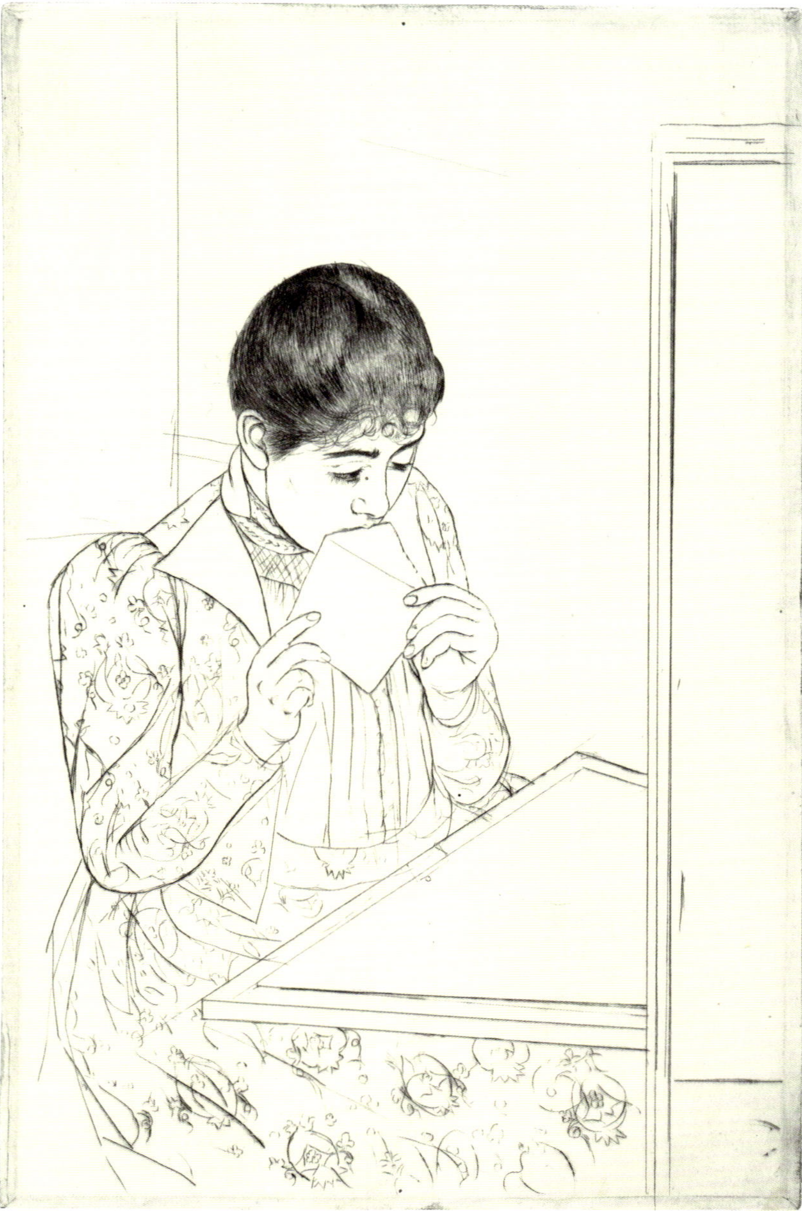

Mary Cassatt, American (1844–1926)

The Letter, 1890–91

Drypoint and aquatint, printed in color from three
plates, fourth state of four, 17 × 11¾ in. (43.2 × 29.8 cm)
Gift of Paul J. Sachs, 1916 (16.2.9)

Collectors' marks: Mary Cassatt (Lugt 604); Paul J. Sachs
(Lugt 2091)

Provenance: Paul J. Sachs (1878–1965), Cambridge, Mass.;
his gift to the Department of Prints, 1916

"After [Cassatt] and Degas had gone together
to an exhibition of Japanese prints, she consciously applied the elegance of Utamaro to the
intimacies of her dressing room, her writing
desk, her tea table, and the nursery of her baby
nieces. Through these color aquatints, as well
as her etchings and drypoints, Mary Cassatt
became one of the very few women to discover
a new vision in the abstract medium of printmaking" (Mayor, *Prints & People*, 688). In *The
Letter* Cassatt demonstrates her dexterity with
color to create an image that delights in both
pattern and the flatness of the picture plane,
two characteristics of Japanese woodcuts. The
print also conveys the importance of letter
writing to European and American women
during the late nineteenth century. Letters
were the mechanism for staying in touch with
friends and family abroad—a necessity for the
expatriate Cassatt—filling one's social calendar, and answering household inquiries.

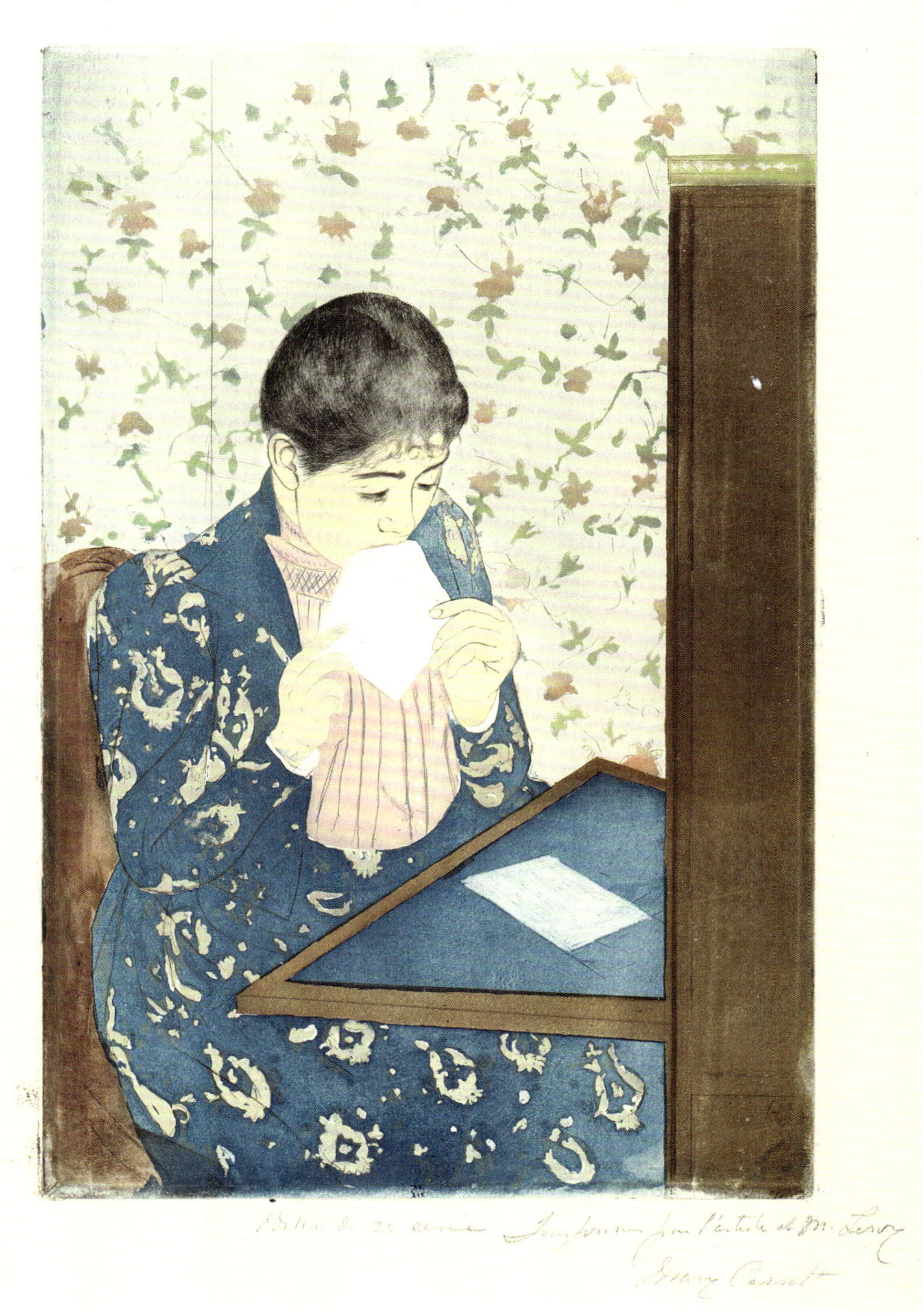

Camille Pissarro, French (1830–1903)

Impressions of Rain, Rouen, 1883

Etching, drypoint, and aquatint, second state of two,
11 × 8¾ in. (28 × 22.3 cm)
Gift of W. L. Andrews, 1917 (17.70.4)

Watermark: fragment, unreadable word

Provenance: William Loring Andrews (1837–1920),
New York; his gift to the Department of Prints, 1917

A passionate printmaker, Pissarro was
recruited by Degas to contribute to his pro-
posed journal of original prints, *Le Jour et la
Nuit*, which was to be a celebration of the ability of black-and-white media to create mood
through light and shadow. Although the journal never materialized, the project stimulated
Pissarro's interest in the technical boundaries
of etching as an inventive medium; it led him
to explore aquatint, soft ground, the use of
resins to create texture on the surface, and the
use of drypoint to create atmospheric effects.
Ivins reflected on Pissarro's etchings: "[They]
are odd in their blurriness, in their lack of
sharp definition of the kind only obtainable by
stopping and sharply focusing. But as against
this there is to be set the fact that the picture
presented by one of them is that actually seen
by any one surveying a real landscape without
fixing his eyes. Here again a great triumph
was achieved in black and white for Pissarro
succeeded in finding an adequate monochro-
matic rendering of things which offhand one
would think possible only in full color" (Ivins,
"French Black and White of the Last Half-
Century," July 1921: 154–55).

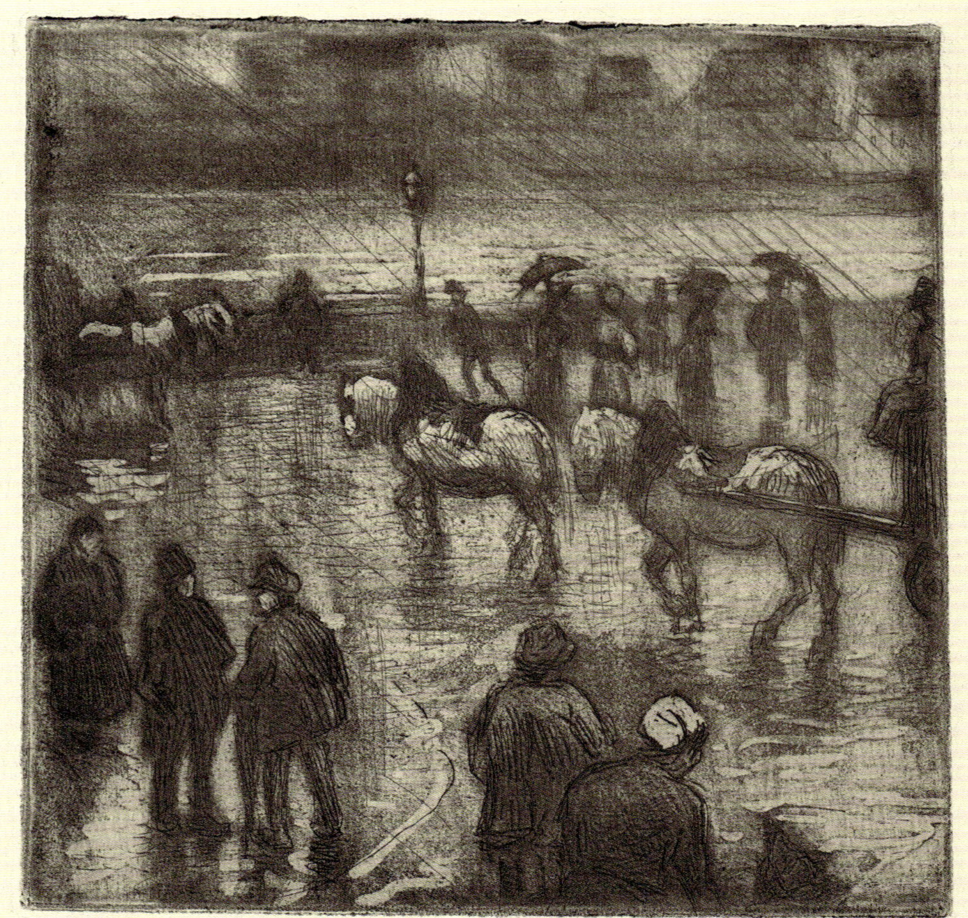

Félix Bracquemond, French (1833–1914)

Aspens on the Bank of the Seine, ca. 1884

Etching and drypoint, second state of three,
8⅞ × 10⅝ in. (22.6 × 27 cm)
Gift of Theodore De Witt, 1923 (23.65.92)

Provenance: Theodore De Witt, New York; his gift to the
Department of Prints, 1923

Bracquemond was a highly skilled etcher and a founding member of the Société des Aquafortistes Français, a group that promoted artistic printmaking during the second half of the nineteenth century. "In 700 copperplates Bracquemond experimented with all the techniques of etching and engraving. He advised and helped almost every artist who etched in Paris from Meryon to Whistler" (Mayor, label for "Cézanne and Contemporaries," 1952). This view of slender poplars on a riverbank combines etching and drypoint and relates to at least two other prints depicting fluvial subjects in the artist's oeuvre.

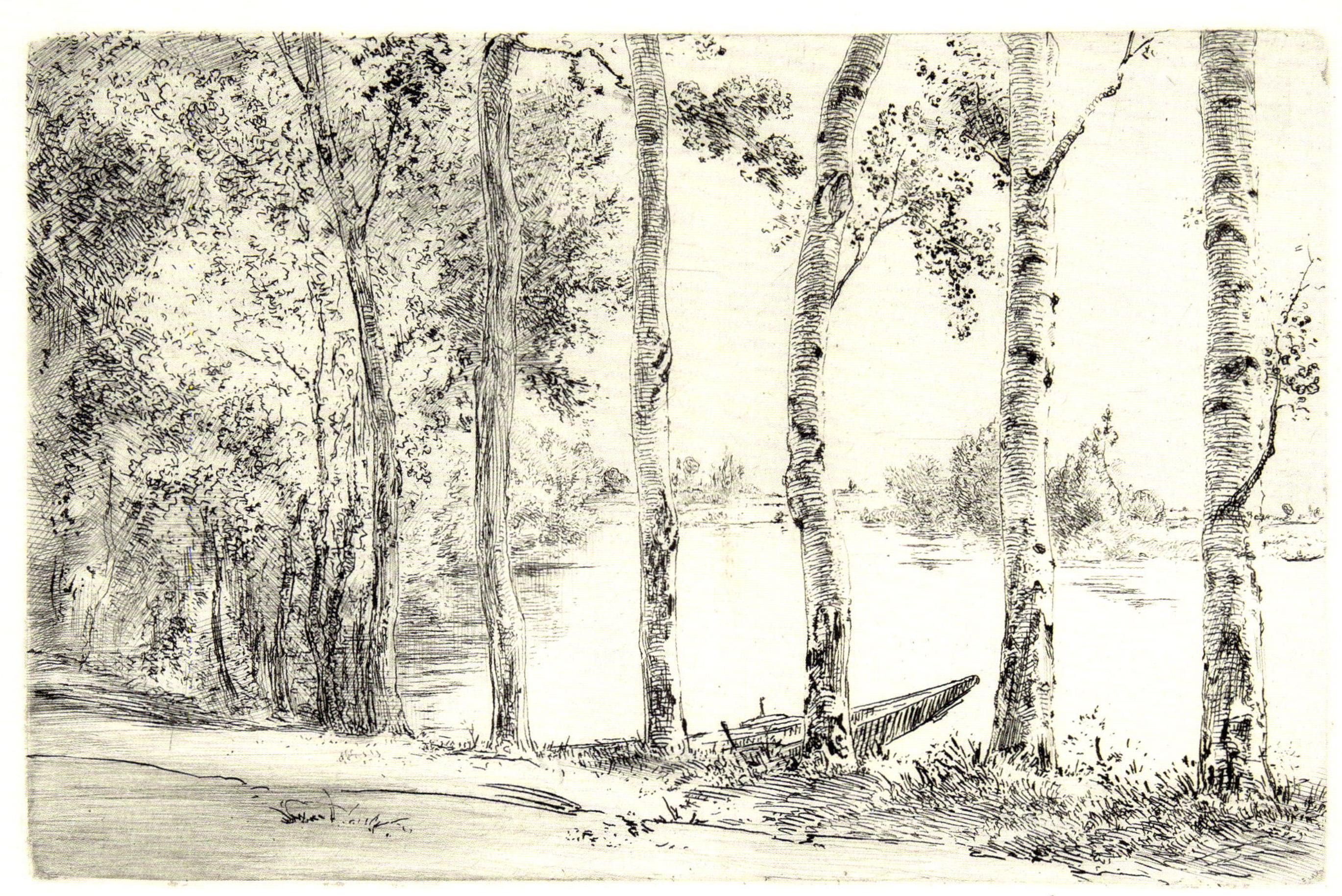

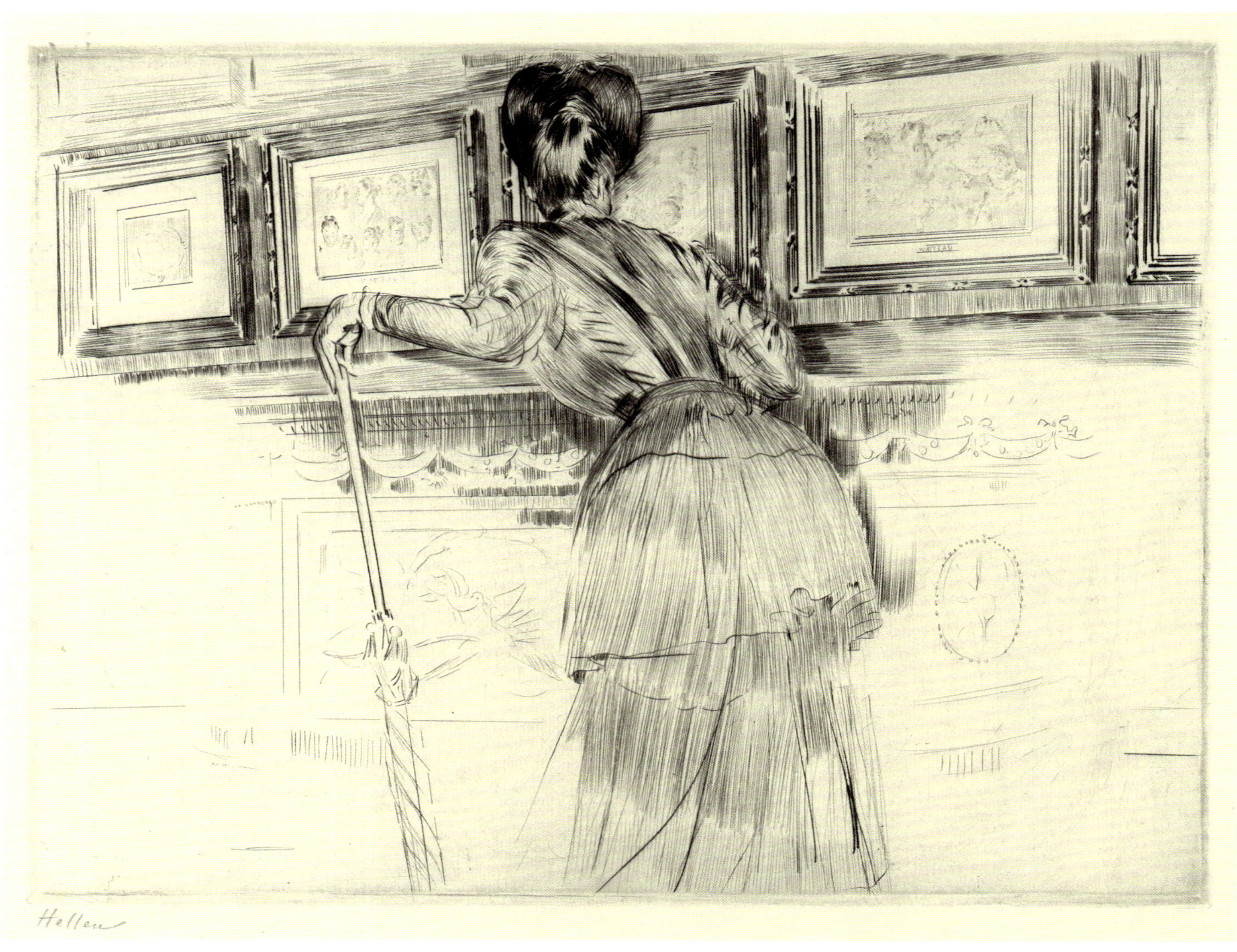

39

Paul-César Helleu, French (1859–1927)

Madame Helleu Looking at the Watteau Drawings in the Louvre, ca. 1896

Drypoint, 15¼ × 20⅛ in. (38.8 × 51 cm)
The Elisha Whittelsey Collection, The Elisha Whittelsey Fund, 1959 (59.599.19)

Watermark: Van Gelder Zonen

Provenance: [Paul Prouté, Paris]; Department of Prints purchase, 1959

Although the Met's collection was founded on Harris Brisbane Dick's vast collection of prints, mainly French and American, from the nineteenth-century etching revival, Mayor continued to selectively acquire fine examples. One such was this drypoint conveying a "triumphant femininity" (Mayor, "Prints Recently Acquired," 1960: 331). Mayor regarded Helleu as an international virtuoso of the Belle Époque. He had been celebrated during his life but by the mid-twentieth century languished as an "unjustly neglected artist" (ibid.).

40

Sir David Young Cameron, British
(1865–1945)

Two Bridges, from the North Italian Set,
1896

Etching, 9¾ × 12⅜ in. (24.7 × 31.4 cm)
Harris Brisbane Dick Fund, 1917 (17.3.2209)

Provenance: Harris Brisbane Dick (1855–1916), New York;
Dick Estate, U.S. Trust; Department of Prints purchase,
1917

Cameron was a leader of the Scottish etching
revival and a member of the Royal Society of
Painters-Etchers from 1889 to 1902. Though
he frequently traveled to cities in Europe and
often depicted architecture, he was greatly
inspired by vast and beautiful landscapes, such
as those surrounding his home in Kippen, a
village in the Scottish Highlands with expansive views of Ben Ledi. In this bird's-eye view
of a turn in a river, Cameron creates a highly
symbolic landscape with a dramatic arch-
shaped shadow whirling, almost like an eddy,
around the light emanating from the center of
the work.

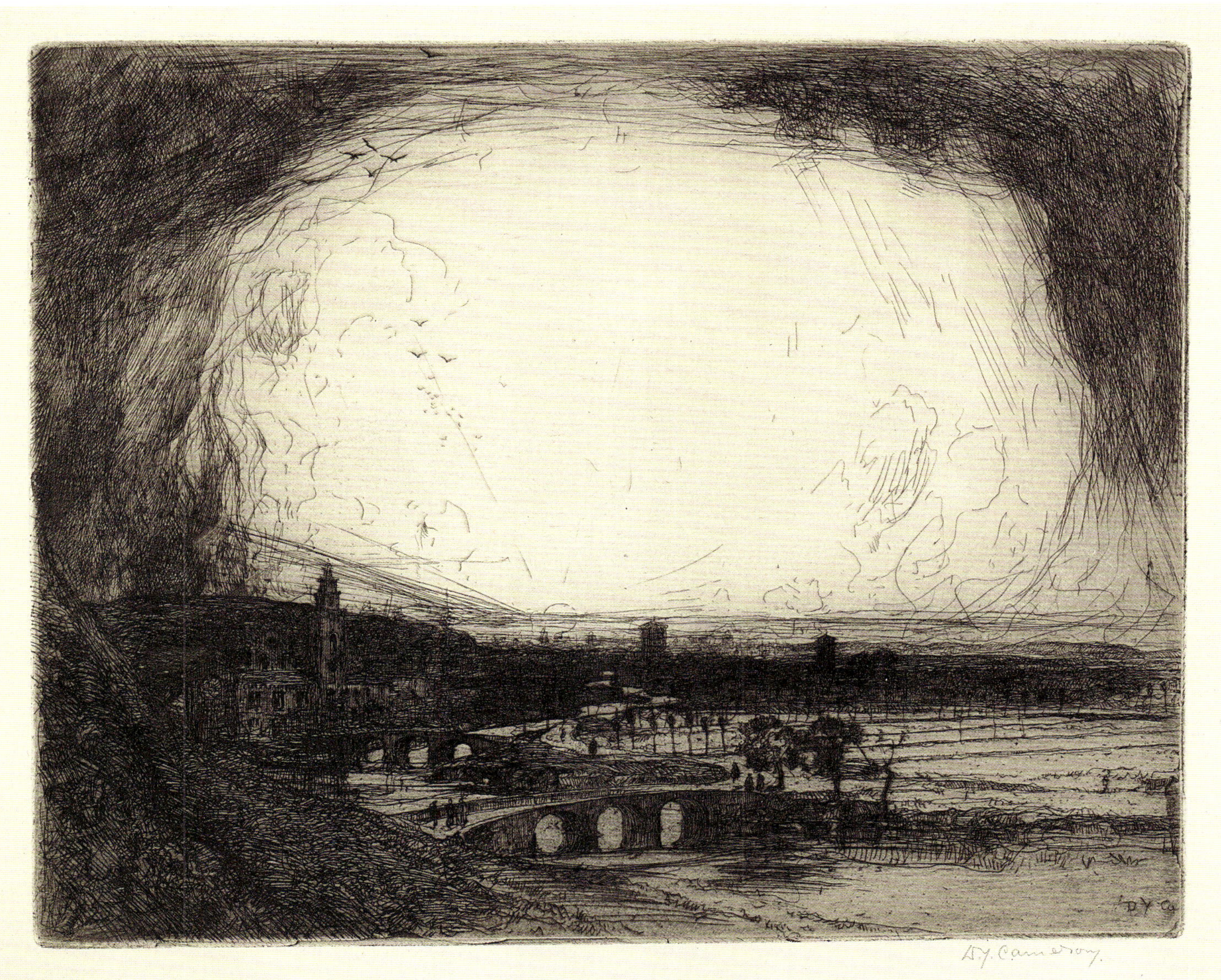

Joseph Pennell, American (1857–1926)

Rainy Night, Charing Cross Shops, 1903

Etching, 12½ × 8⅜ in. (31.8 × 21.3 cm)
Harris Brisbane Dick Fund, 1917 (17.3.505)

Provenance: [Frederick Keppel & Co., New York]; Harris Brisbane Dick (1855–1916), New York; Dick Estate, U.S. Trust; Department of Prints purchase, 1917

A powerful proponent of experiments with the etching medium and of the work of James McNeill Whistler, Pennell "emphasized in writing and speech . . . the pictorial unimportance of subject matter as compared with artistry in handling and workmanship" (Ivins, "Joseph Pennell," 1926: 254). In this print, torrents of rain obscure the artist's beloved London, which like his native New York was one of the "most astonishing artificial landscape[s] in the world, [a] gateway of stone and iron and water . . . impersonal as some great force of nature" (ibid.).

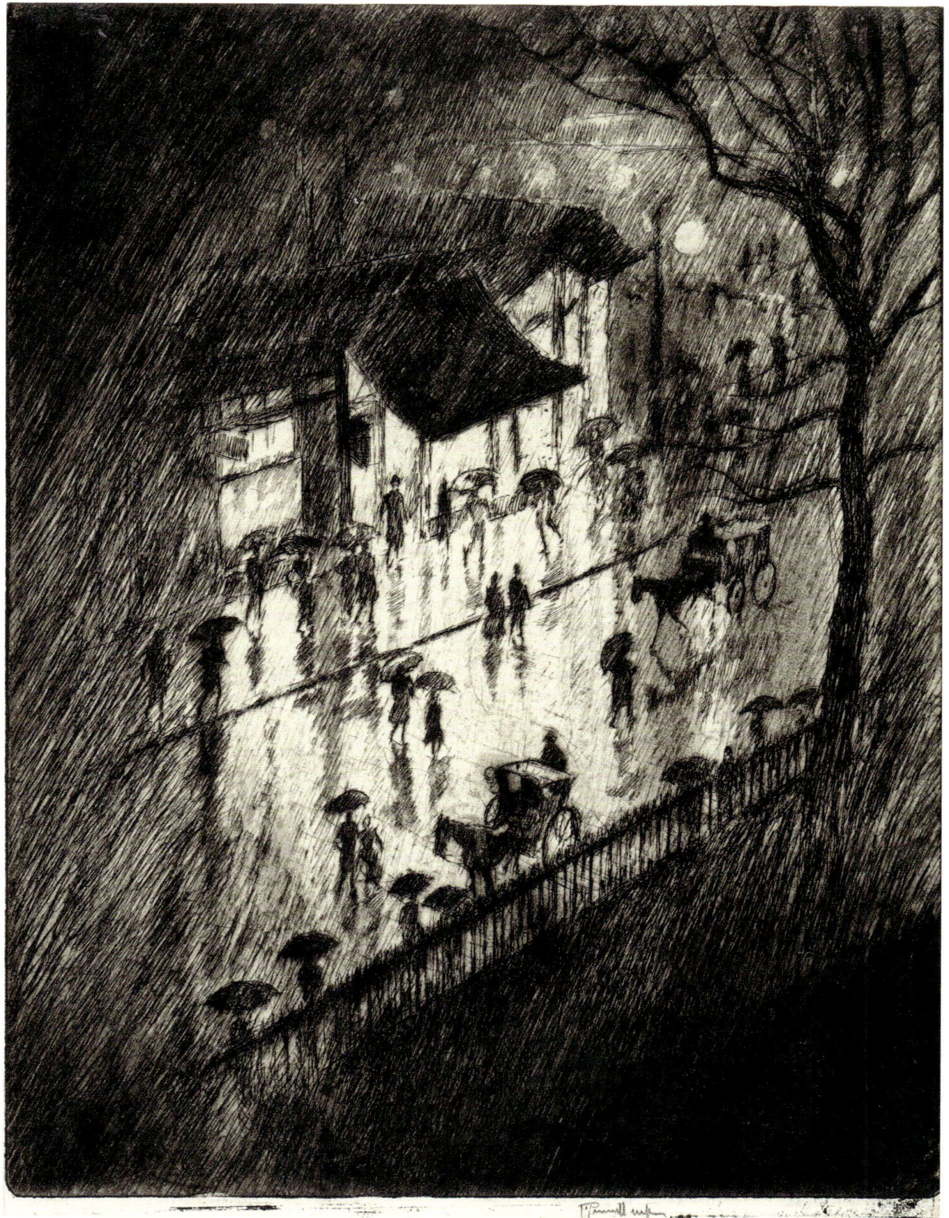

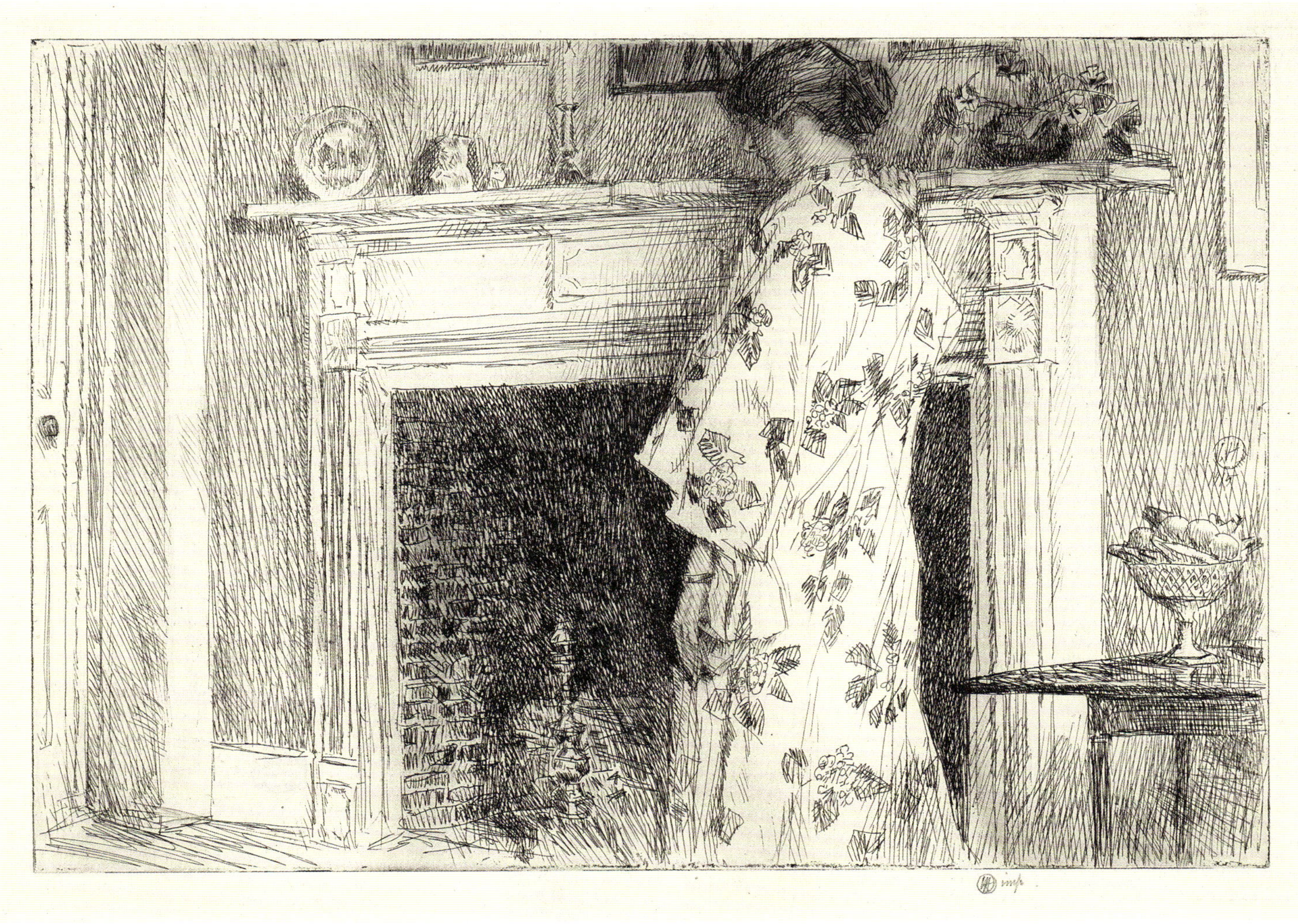

42

The White Kimono, 1915

Etching and drypoint, 10⅛ × 14 in. (25.5 × 35.5 cm)
Harris Brisbane Dick Fund, 1917 (17.3.494)

Watermark: MBM

Provenance: [Frederick Keppel & Co., New York]; Harris Brisbane Dick (1855–1916), New York; Dick Estate, U.S. Trust; Department of Prints purchase, 1917

Though Hassam "objected, and quite rightly, to being called the American Claude Monet," *The White Kimono* is among the finest American Impressionist prints (Mayor, "Childe Hassam," 1940: 138–39). Both Monet and Hassam "saw with the eye of their time, an eye that refused to look at [Jacques Louis] David's sharp-edged solids in a vacuum, but saw the world as an ever-shifting shimmer of surfaces" (ibid.). Mayor compared Hassam to another American artist, the writer Henry James, who was only a few years older: "Their impressions of New England are so similar as to be like words and pictures put forth by a single mind" (ibid.). Hassam, a New England native who often turned to the region's landscape, architecture, and history for subjects, approached his prints as if they were paintings, bringing keen attention to the diffusion of light and the precision of the draftsmanship. In this print he shows a beautifully sculpted woman standing before the hearth of a venerable boardinghouse in Cos Cob, Connecticut, a waterfront community where New Yorkers often summered.

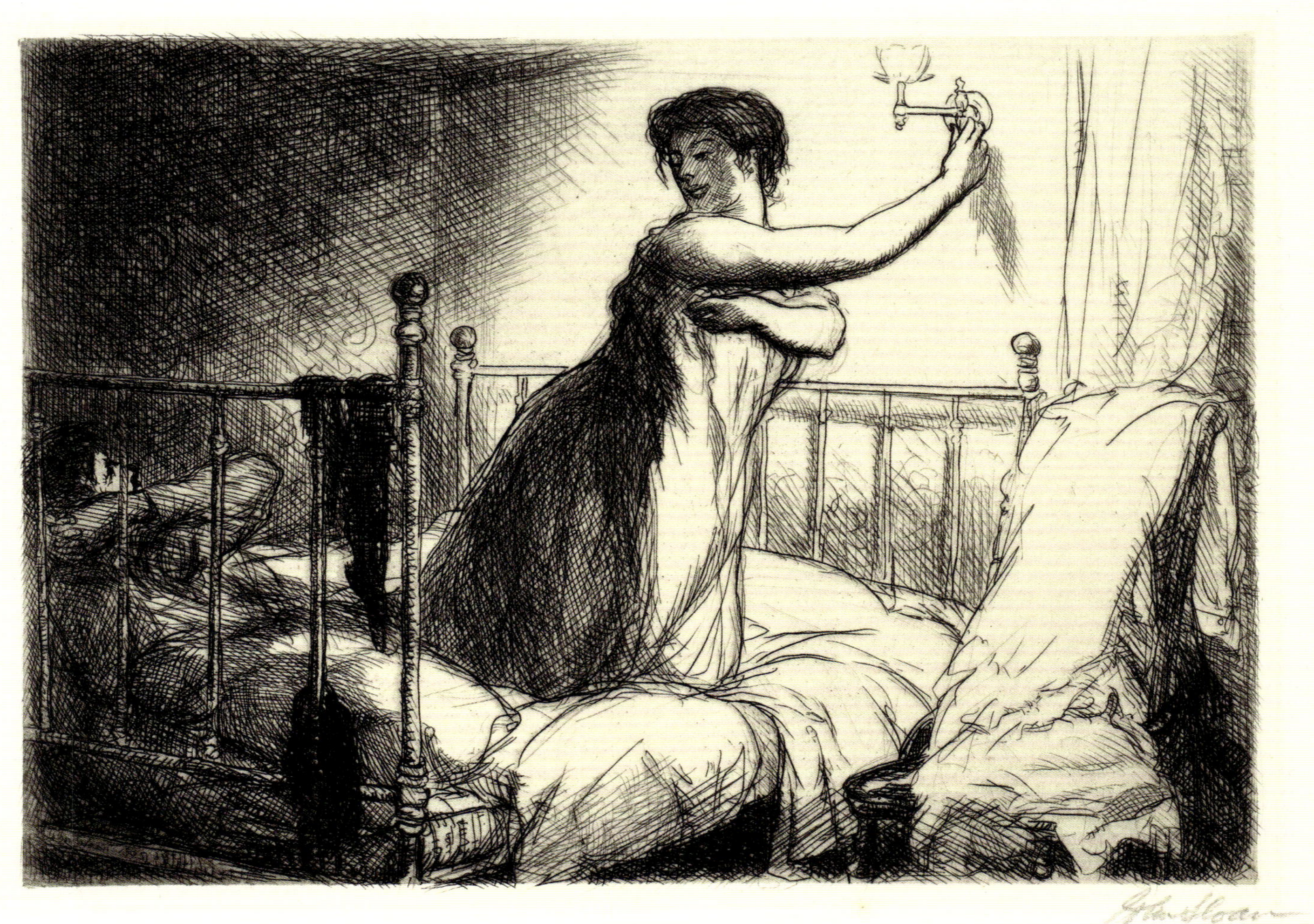

43

John Sloan, American (1871–1951)

Turning out the Light, from New York City
Life, 1905

Etching, 9⅝ × 12¼ in. (24.4 × 30.9 cm)
Gift of Mrs. Harry Payne Whitney, 1926 (26.30.16)

Watermark: arches

Provenance: Mrs. Harry Payne Whitney (Gertrude
Vanderbilt Whitney) (1875–1942), New York; her gift to
the Department of Prints, 1917

The sculptor and patron of the arts Gertrude
Vanderbilt Whitney, who would later open her
own museum in support of living artists in
America, gave to the nascent Department of
Prints more than 160 etchings by John Sloan.
Turning out the Light is part of Sloan's series
New York City Life, which Ivins described as
"cheerful, casual, jolly, understanding pictures
of you and me . . . [that] probably constitute
the best existing pictorial commentary on life"
in the city (Ivins, "A Gift of Etchings by John
Sloan," 1926: 219).

44

Early, 1914

Etching, 16¾ × 12⅞ in. (42.4 × 32.6 cm)
Harris Brisbane Dick Fund, 1917 (17.3.685)

Watermark: Van Gelder Zonen

Provenance: [Frederick Keppel & Co., New York]; Harris
Brisbane Dick (1855–1916), New York; Dick Estate, U.S.
Trust; Department of Prints purchase, 1917

Zorn was a Swedish wunderkind, a painter,
sculptor, and printmaker who spent most of
his artistic life wandering England, France,
and Spain. From the start, his virtuosic etchings were highly praised and much in demand.
Ivins noted that "his prints with their remarkable brilliance of light and shade, and their
division into spots of indefinitely contoured
color, are the immediate reflection of his technique with the [paint]brush" (Ivins, "Legros,
Lepère, and Zorn," 1921: 232). Although
Zorn's style of making lines on the etching
plate suggested Parisian Impressionist painting, his boldness of vision, with its "photographic lack of reticence" that could be "quite
ruthless about the human body," recalls the
work of Rembrandt (ibid.).

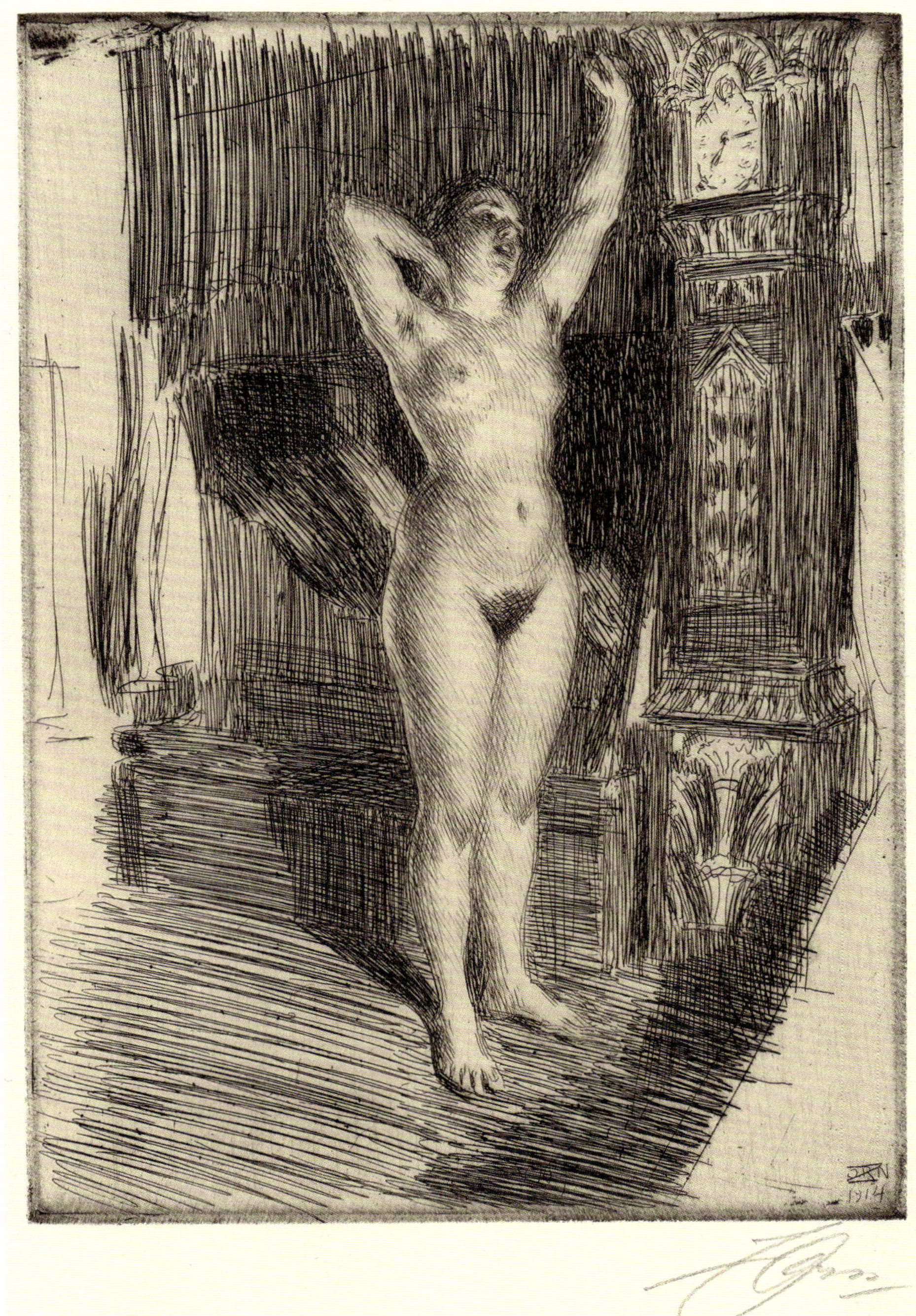

45

Night Shadows, 1921

Etching, 13¼ × 14½ in. (33.5 × 36.6 cm)
Harris Brisbane Dick Fund, 1925 (25.31.2)

Provenance: [E. P. "Ned" Jennings, White Plains, N.Y.];
Department of Prints purchase, 1925

This bird's-eye view of a darkened street corner could be understood as any ordinary street in any city across the United States, although it represents an actual place in downtown New York; Hopper also featured the site in his painting *Corner Saloon* (1913). This mysterious etching, with its dramatic lines and lighting, evokes a sense of the loneliness in the city at night. From 1915 to 1923 Hopper focused on printmaking, making etchings and drypoints while he supported himself as a commercial artist and illustrator. Unlike many of his etchings, *Night Shadows* was steel-faced so that it could be printed in a large edition of several hundred images; it was published in the December 1924 issue of the politically progressive magazine *The New Republic*.

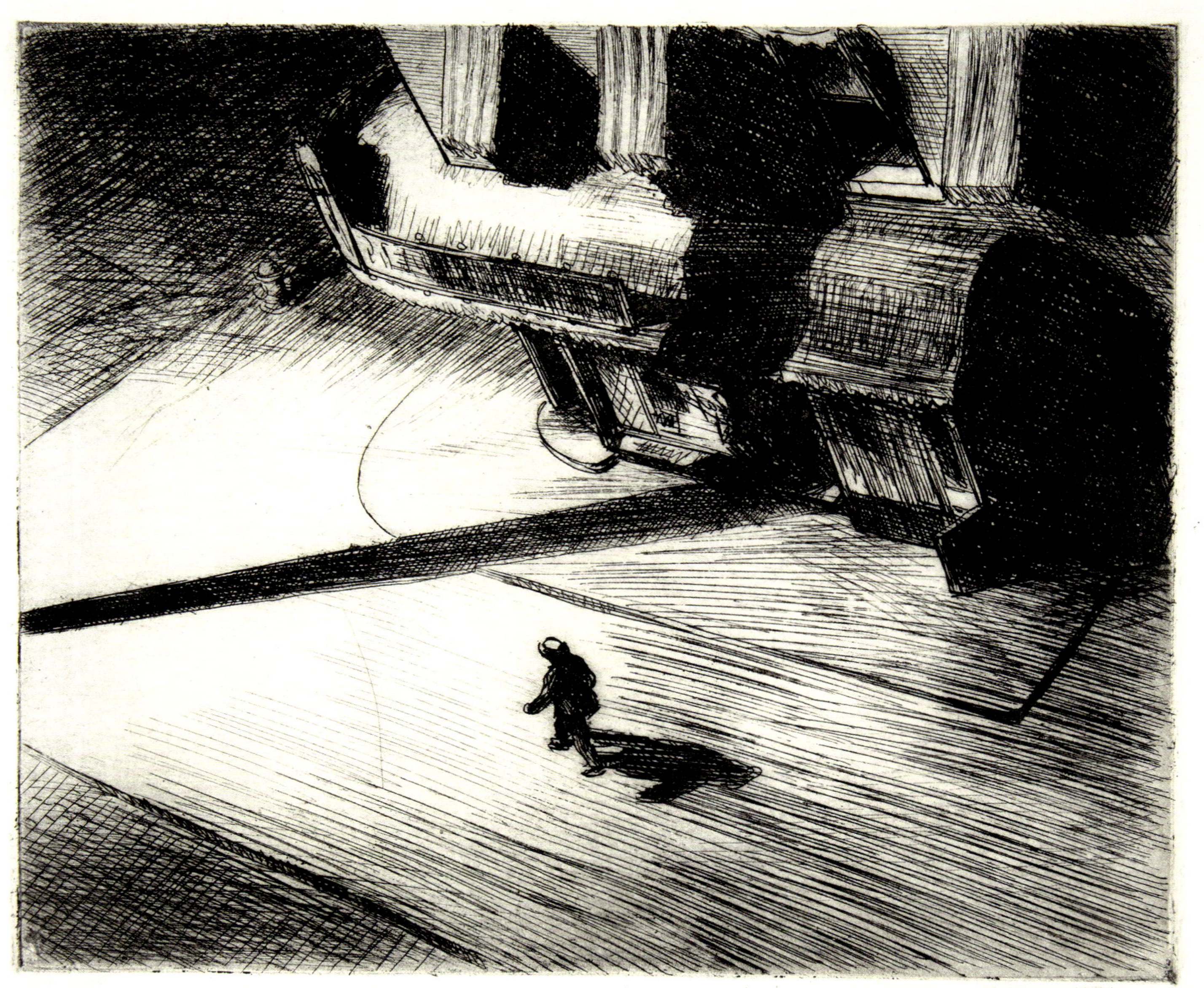

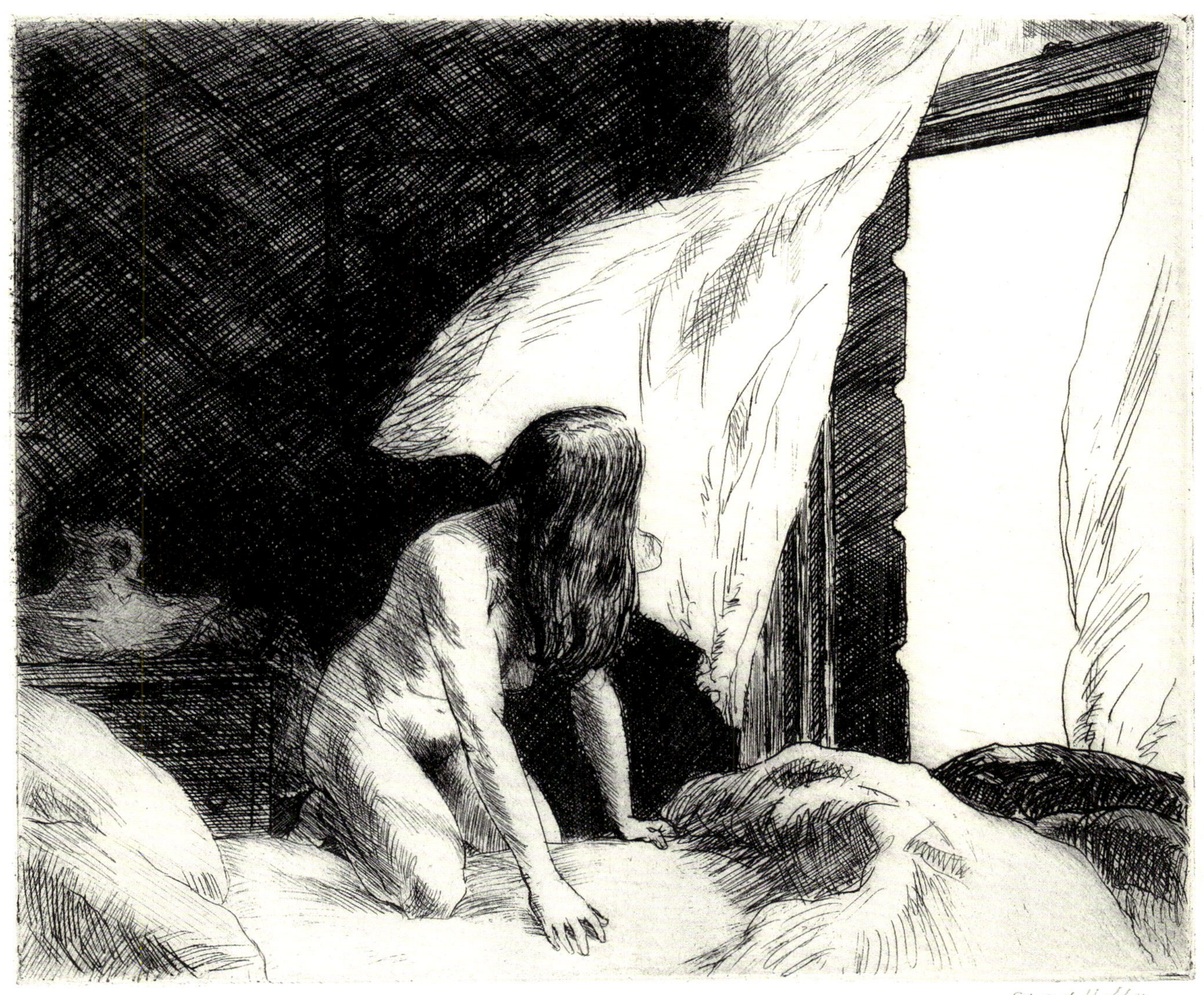

46

Evening Wind, 1921

Etching, 9½ × 10⅝ in. (24 × 27 cm)
Harris Brisbane Dick Fund, 1925 (25.31.7)

Provenance: [E. P. "Ned" Jennings, White Plains, N.Y.];
Department of Prints purchase, 1925

Ivins worked closely with contemporary artists
and their patrons. He bought *Evening Wind*
and *Night Shadows* in a group of fifteen etchings
from Hopper's dealer, Ned Jennings. After selling the Met these works—the first by Hopper
in the collection—Jennings went abroad and
sold a large group to the British Museum, London, whose department of prints and drawings
was founded in 1808 and served as a model for
Ivins in collection building.

Martin Lewis, American, born Australia
(1881–1962)

Relics (Speakeasy Corner), 1928

Drypoint, 17¾ × 14 in. (45.1 × 35.6 cm)
Harris Brisbane Dick Fund, 1929 (29.7.1)

Watermark: Etruria, Italy

Provenance: Martin Lewis (1881–1962), New York;
Department of Prints purchase, 1929

Lewis's skills as a master printmaker were
widely recognized by his contemporaries.
After a series of prints about Japan, in 1927 the
Australian-born artist turned his attention to
his new home, New York City. *Relics*, executed
in 1928, was avidly collected, and the edition
sold out quickly. This impression came directly
from Lewis and is indicative of Ivins's desire to
collect contemporary art. Both Lewis's subject
matter—the city at night—and his refined
etching technique greatly influenced Edward
Hopper, who studied printmaking with Lewis
beginning in 1917, while working as a freelance
commercial artist.

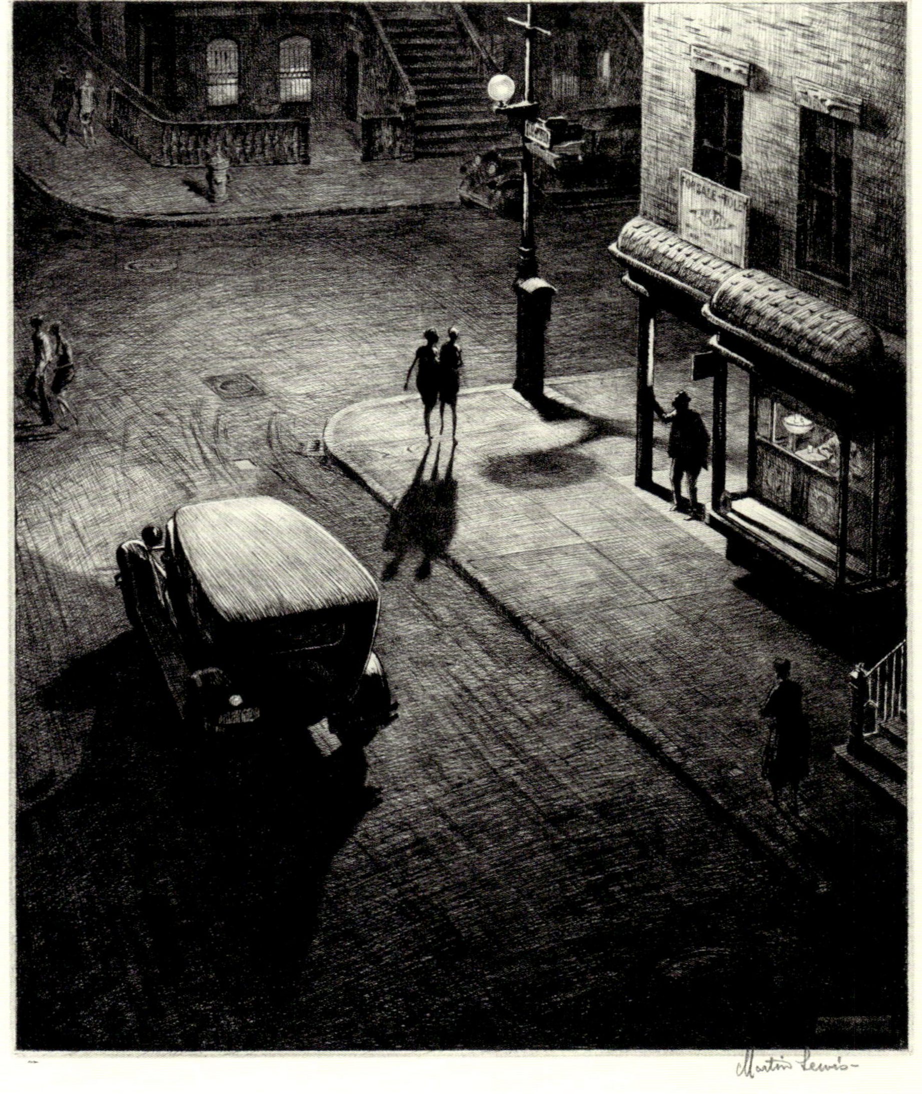

Tombs Prison, 1929

Etching, touched proof, 8½ × 10⅞ in. (21.4 × 27.7 cm)
Gift of the Honorable William Benton and Mrs. Felicia
Meyer Marsh, 1956 (56.508.8)

Provenance: Felicia Meyer Marsh (1912–1978); gift of
the Honorable William Benton and Mrs. Felicia Meyer
Marsh to the Department of Prints, 1956

This etching demonstrates Marsh's penchant
for revising his plates, thereby revealing his
process. Mayor recounted how Marsh would
start "the copper with only so much as he felt
sure of, printing a proof or two to see what
he had done, then a few more strokes on the
plate, another proof, until at last, in a rush of
confidence he would fill in a whole sky with
clouds or smoke. But still he had not done,
for he would again pull a proof, add a touch or
two, then another proof, and so on until the
print looked easy and spontaneous" (Mayor,

Reginald Marsh Etchings, vii–viii). Marsh often
described himself as a man of the sixteenth
century, when the technique of etching on
copper was invented. "His allegiance to the
greatness of the late renaissance gave him
something of the melancholy, even morose
distinction of an exile from a grander time. His
real home, after all, was not 14th street, but
the Piazza della Signoria" (ibid.). The etching
was given to the Met by Marsh's wife and his
lifelong friend and patron Senator William
Benton.

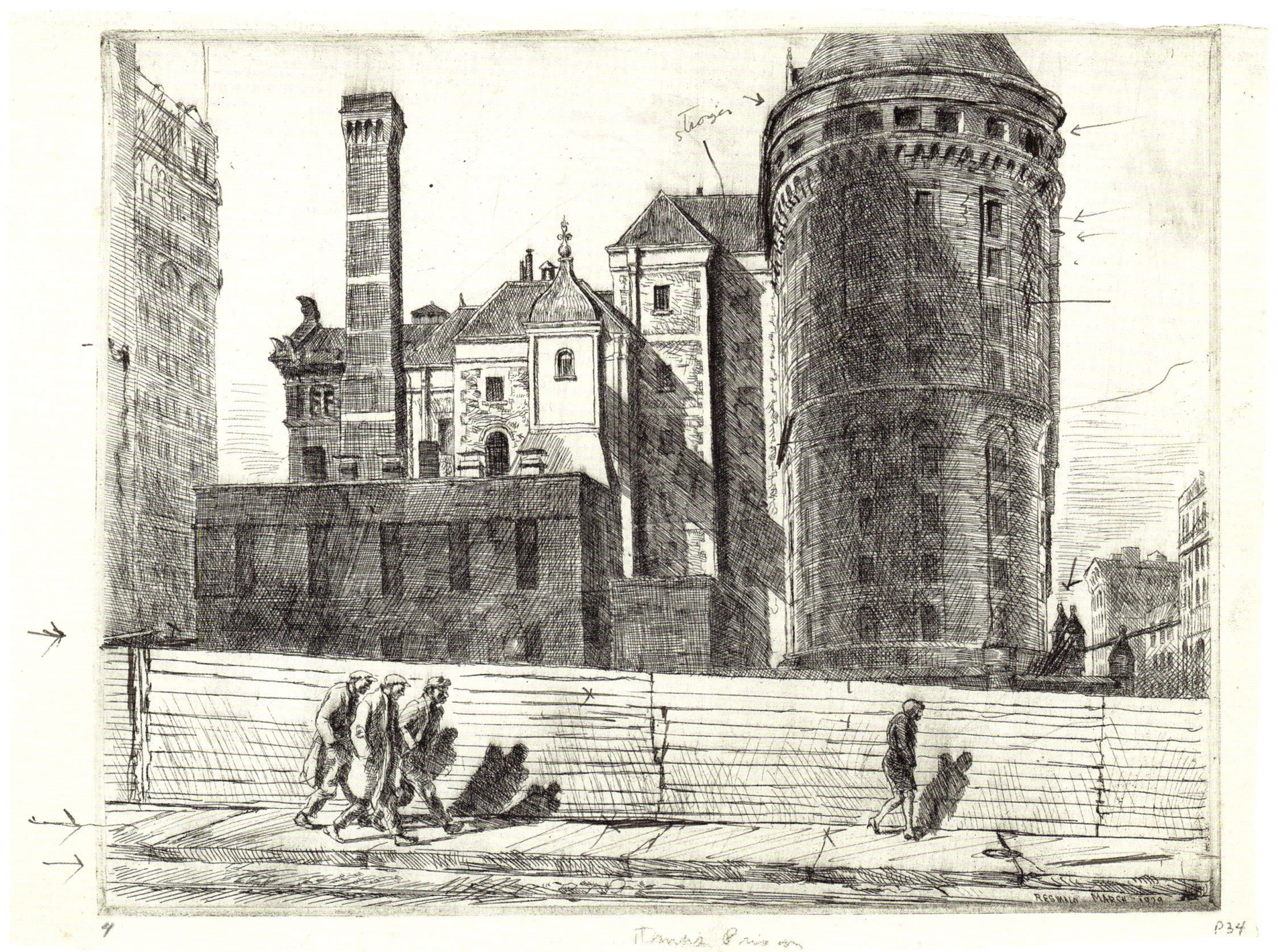

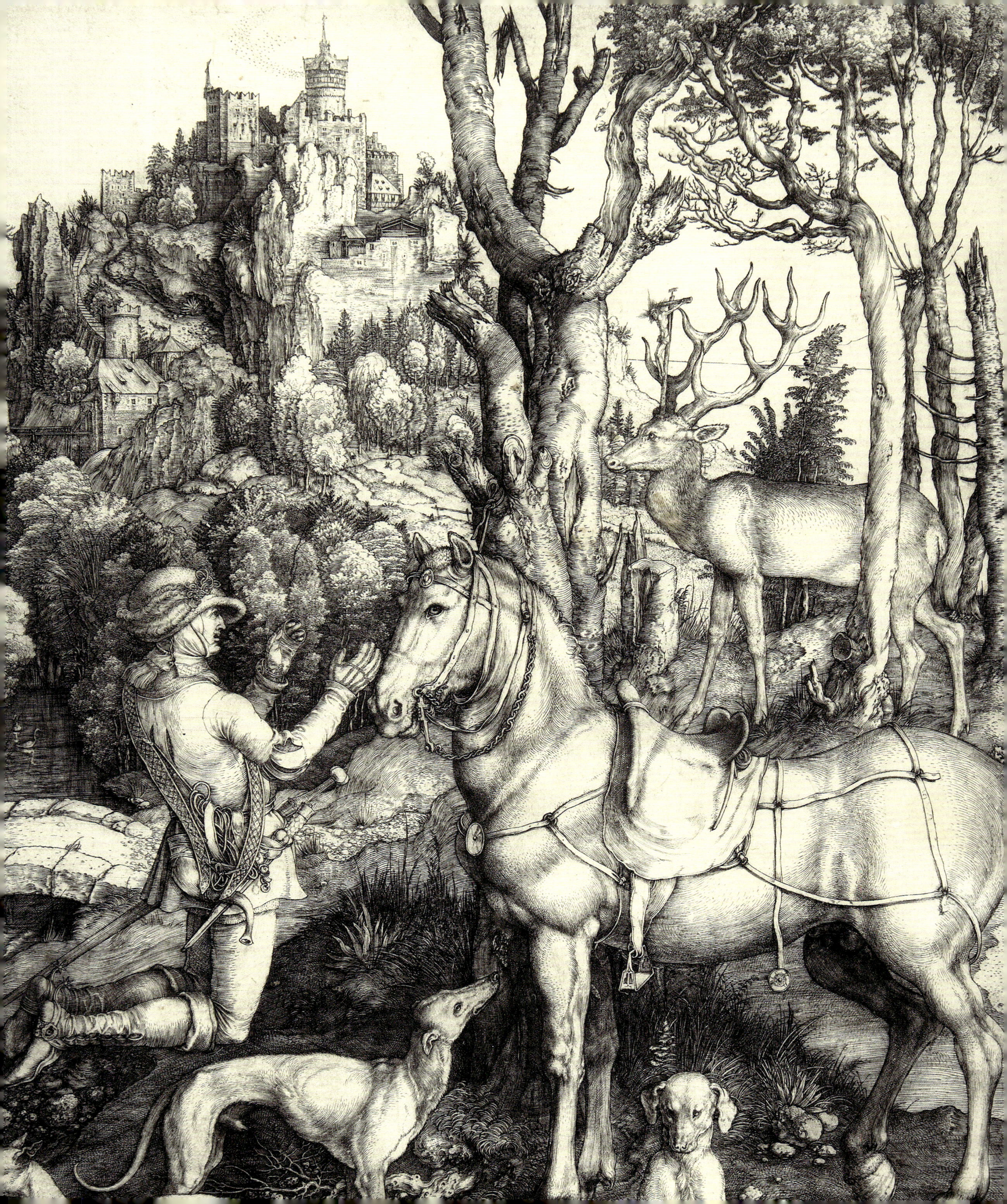

Engravings

"IN SPITE OF all the changes of fashion among collectors of prints, the engravings by [Andrea Mantegna, Marcantonio Raimondi, Albrecht Dürer, and Lucas van Leyden] have never been out of favor since they were made,"[1] William Ivins observed. While interest in etchings and woodcuts had fluctuated over the years, works by the likes of these Renaissance masters, especially Dürer, had remained widely celebrated. In a 1916 letter to the Museum's director, Edward Robinson, Ivins recalled how Dürer had ignited what would be his lifelong passion for prints.

> As an undergraduate [at Harvard] Dürer came to me as a revelation, and when I went abroad after graduation one of the very few books I took with me was Koehler's remarkable Grolier Club catalogue of Dürer's engraved work. In Munich, where I matriculated, I devoted most of my time during the two semesters I was in residence, to the study of Dürer and his contemporaries.[2]

Six years after returning from Munich, in 1908, Ivins arranged a catalogue on Dürer's graphic work for the New York dealer Frederick Keppel & Co.[3] He would continue to collect Dürer and to ponder and write about the artist's accomplishments and failures throughout his career—a sustained attention that Dürer justified perhaps because, as Ivins perceived, his art and theory "seem always to be working at some conundrum which, like the squaring of the circle, is incapable of solution."[4]

Although Ivins's collecting policy for the Museum was to "[spread] the butter thin on as much bread as possible," seeking to show variety among techniques and schools, in Dürer's case he set out to acquire an almost comprehensive collection of the artist's engravings and woodcuts.[5] In 1919 Ivins negotiated Junius Spencer Morgan's gift of his remarkable and extensive Dürer woodcut collection and the purchase of Morgan's Dürer engravings.[6] Though Dürer was the focal point of Ivins's Renaissance collection and a constant preoccupation, the curator also recognized the importance of representing the evolution of engraving north and south of the Alps, which reached its peak in the early sixteenth century with Marcantonio's fluid and easily reproducible engraving style. Ivins's models for collecting were the British Museum in London and Berlin's Kupferstichkabinett, both of which had extensive collections of Renaissance engravings by artists including Dürer and his northern contemporaries, as well as by Italian engravers like Antonio Pollaiuolo.[7]

Ivins prized the prints of these trained draftsmen; to him their prints conveyed intelligence and disseminated information. Although Mantegna's engravings fail on the technical side because his lines merely ape his pen lines and wear quickly, Ivins observed, they are extraordinary compositions, stellar examples of draftsmanship, and "simplicity itself."[8] Narrative and subject matter were paramount to Ivins, but his analytic mind and keen eye could not help but focus also on the making of the engravings, the grammar or syntax of the lines that make the whole readable. Each artist created an engraving in a distinctive manner, laid down lines differently, and grouped them in particular ways to describe objects and figures in space, as Ivins summarized.

> Pollaiuolo and Mantegna drew firm carefully considered outlines, and shaded by using almost parallel lines running tilted from right to left without regard to the direction of the outlines. . . . In Germany the artists, true to their calligraphic habit of drawing, shaded with lines that had a tendency to follow the shapes, as can be seen in the prints of the Master E.S., Schongauer, and Dürer. . . . Taking elements from Dürer's two different linear systems, that for his woodcuts and that for his engravings, Marc Antonio devised a kind of shading that represented not the play of light across the surface, and not the series of local textures, but the bosses and hollows made in a surface by what is under it. . . . With the curious Italian logic of his time he reduced this to a sort of rudimentary grammatical or syntactical system. Lucas van Leyden, fascinated by this, ceased to be an inspired teller of fairy tales and became a great theoretical grammarian of the engraved line.[9]

Marcantonio's engraving technique, a comprehensive linear syntax that harmonized and systematized elements of Dürer's technique, was endlessly copied. As Hyatt Mayor phrased it: "If Dürer created the new doctrine of printmaking, Marcantonio was the Saint Paul who gave it currency."[10] Marcantonio was also the first important printmaker whose work largely copied paintings and drawings—notably by Raphael, his contemporary—giving rise to the so-called reproductive print. His became the language used by reproductive engravers from the late sixteenth to the eighteenth century.

In 1931 Ivins held an unprecedented exhibition of reproductive engravings that followed from Marcantonio's systematic syntax. Ivins endeavored to challenge the prejudice against these works that had crept up in the mid-nineteenth century with the advent of photography and the veneration of etching. Arguing against the claim that reproductive prints were merely derivative, he wrote: "[T]he line between the original and reproductive in print making is extremely difficult to draw. The two things are divided not by any sharp line, but by an exceedingly broad penumbra, in which some of the greatest and most important prints that have ever been made are to be found."[11] Indeed, Marcantonio's prints, which are largely based on other artists' compositions but, like many other artists' reproductive engravings, incorporate his own ideas and style, were collected as exemplars of Renaissance engraving throughout the centuries. Mayor defended reproductive engraving by writing about Marcantonio's art: "Reproduction is hardly the word for an engraver who had the ability to invent harmonious draperies for Raphael's nudes and to blend his groups into landscapes adapted from Dürer and Lucas of Leiden. The French accurately call this 'interpretive engraving.'"[12]

During Ivins's tenure no collections of reproductive engravings came on the market. But Mayor jumped at the chance to buy large groups of reproductive engravings when the renowned and expansive art collection of the Princes of Liechtenstein became available, beginning in 1949. Over the next thirteen years Mayor made several sizable purchases of Liechtenstein engravings.[13]

> I got the reproductive prints of the Italian schools, of the German schools; I got the theatre prints, a wonderful lot of those, marvelous; and varied things like that. It was a great purchase because they are not collector's prints. They are not prints you ever show on the walls, they're not works of art; but they're the prints that answer questions. And there's no collection like them outside the very, very old collections like—well, like Paris or Vienna. There aren't too many of them in the British Museum. But they were the collections that were the pre-photographic approach to works of art, you see, when you got engravings of things for lack of any better picture of them.[14]

Mayor further capitalized on postwar Europe's poor economy by purchasing large lots of Italian and Flemish reproductive engravings from the Albertina in Vienna, which had and still has a large collection of that kind of material.[15] Mayor never felt compelled to write exclusively on the subject of reproductive engravings or hold an exhibition to promote their acceptance; however, by reintegrating them into the larger story of printmaking, as he did in *Prints & People*, he transformed how they were collected, exhibited, and considered by scholars in the field as well as by the public.

49

Battle of Nude Men, ca. 1465

Engraving, 15⅛ × 23¼ in. (38.4 × 58.9 cm)
Purchase, Joseph Pulitzer Bequest, 1917 (17.50.99)

Provenance: The Earls of Pembroke and Montgomery,
Wilton House, Wiltshire; [sale of Reginald Herbert
(1880–1960), 15th Earl of Pembroke and 12th Earl of
Montgomery, Sotheby, Wilkinson & Hodge, London,
July 5–6, 1917, lot 119]; [P. & D. Colnaghi & Co.,
London]; Department of Prints purchase, 1917

In this, the only engraving by Pollaiuolo,
the Florentine painter "deliberately surveyed
the whole equipment of muscles to provide a
syllabus for teaching. He dissected to uncover
man with the eagerness of the navigators who
were then exploring the shores of the expand-
ing world" (Mayor, "Artists as Anatomists,"
1964: 204). Ivins and Mayor recognized that
prints were fundamental to the discoveries of
the Renaissance, "used not for amusement or
moral edification but for the propagation of
knowledge" (ibid.).

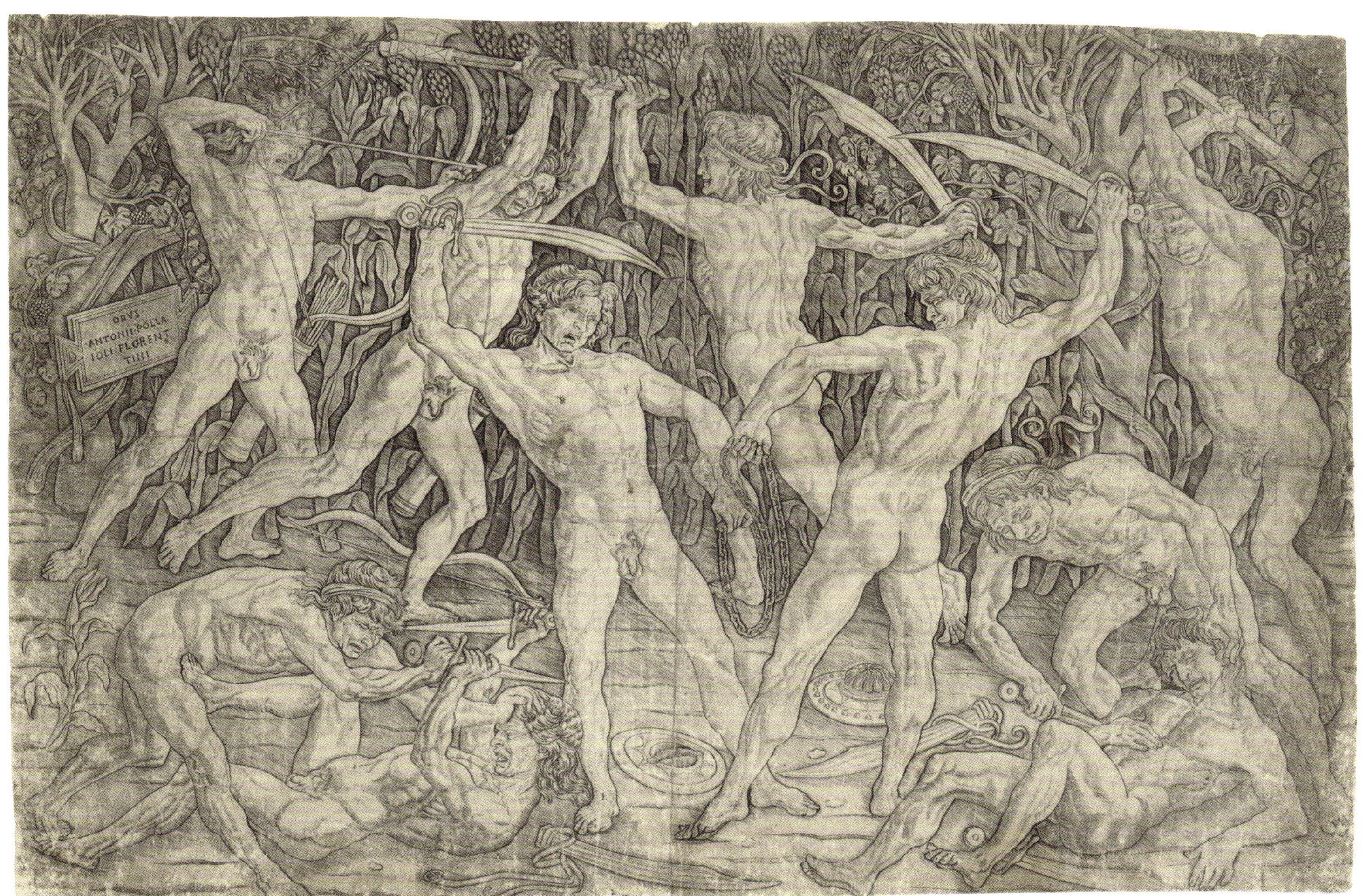

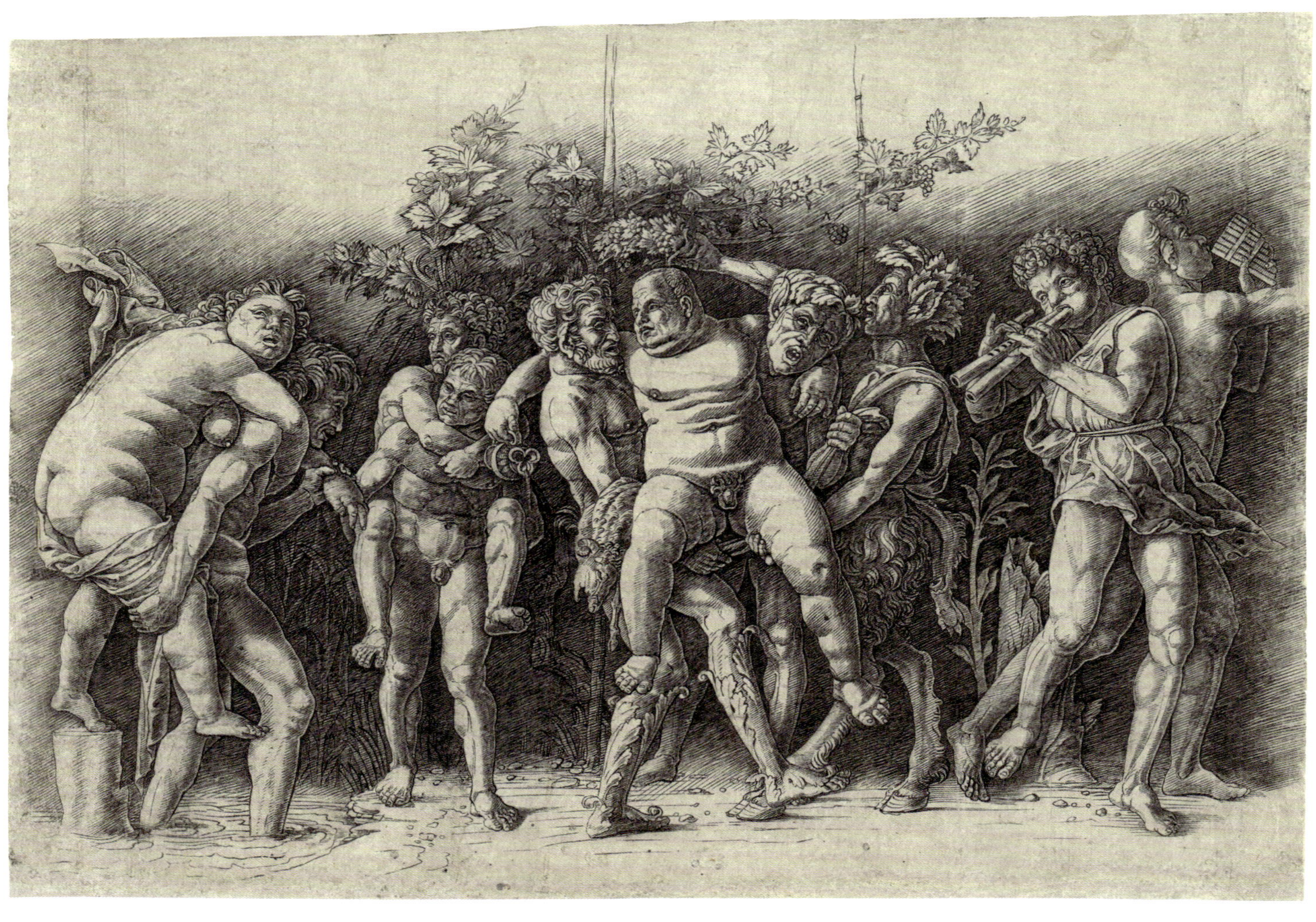

50

Andrea Mantegna, Italian (1430/31–1506)

Bacchanal with Silenus, early 1470s

Engraving with drypoint, 12 × 17¼ in. (30.5 × 43.8 cm)
Anonymous gift, 1929 (29.44.15)

Provenance: Private collector, New York; her anonymous gift to the Department of Prints, 1929

Mantegna created this monumental engraving while working in Mantua, the city of the poet Virgil's birth. It depicts the tale Virgil recounts in the sixth piece in his *Eclogues*: how Silenus, the tutor of Bacchus known for his wisdom as well as his drunkenness, is roused from inebriated sleep by two satyrs and a nymph, bound with his own garlands, and forced to sing. His song of cosmic creation and the relationship between man and nature incites the fauns and wild beasts to dance, which can be seen in Mantegna's print.

Mantegna's bold engravings of mythological and religious subjects mark a watershed in the history of prints. Although Mantegna's was a nascent medium, Ivins regarded prints such as the *Bacchanal* as fully developed works of art: "In [Mantegna's] prints there is a sense of volume and bigness of form, in detail as well as in organization of composition, and an ease and certainty of handling, which combine to produce such a feeling of ordered freedom and strength as is not to be met with again in black and white until the coming of Rembrandt in the seventeenth century" (Ivins, "Early Prints Acquired by the Museum," 1929: 168).

51

*The Risen Christ between Saint Andrew and
Saint Longinus*, ca. 1472

Engraving, 12⅜ × 11⅜ in. (31.5 × 28.9 cm)
Rogers Fund, 1921 (21.28)

Collectors' marks: P. von Baldinger-Seidenberg (Lugt 212);
Paul Davidsohn (Lugt 654)

Provenance: P. von Baldinger-Seidenberg (died 1911),
Stuttgart; Paul Davidsohn (1839–1931), Berlin; [his sale,
C. G. Boerner, Leipzig, Nov. 22–26, 1920, lot 1225];
[P. & D. Colnaghi & Co., London]; Department of Prints
purchase, 1921

Ivins once remarked that *The Risen Christ* was
the most important work to enter the collection during his tenure. Mantegna's work "is
one of the epoch-making prints, as it showed
that in the hands of a major artist engraving
was capable of producing pictures with as great
and as serene emotional power and life as any
other artistic medium. . . . It is a marvelous
example of the way in which true personality
breaks through all the bounds of tradition and
theory" (Ivins, *Notes on Prints*, 51). Mantegna
laid the lines on the plate in the same way he
rendered his pen drawings, creating rich effects
of tone and modeling through parallel diag-
onal hatching, so finely rendered in this print
that the lines appear to dissolve.

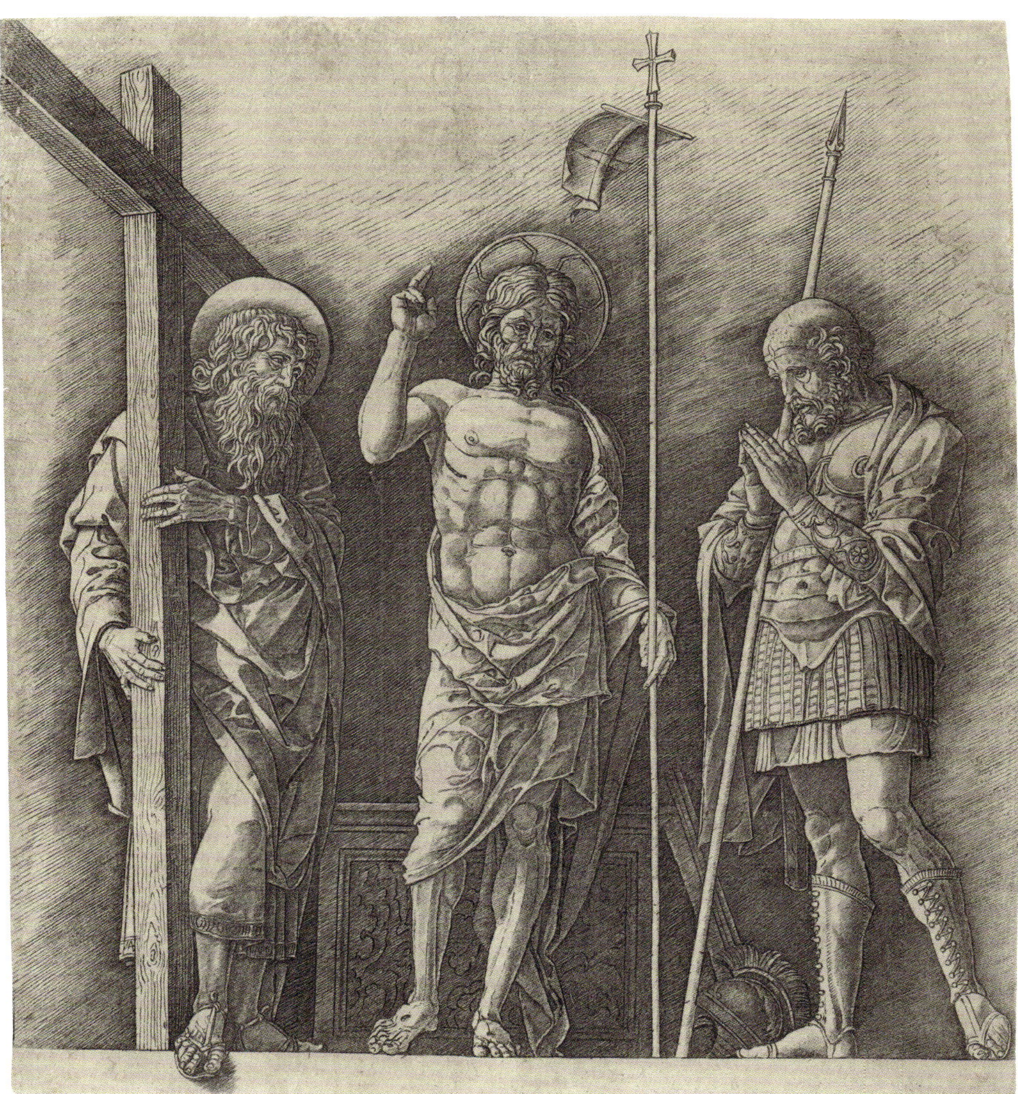

Giovanni Antonio da Brescia,
Italian (active ca. 1490–ca. 1525), and
Giovanni Pietro da Birago, Italian
(active 1470–1513)

A Satyr Holding a Violin; A Nereid and Two
Children Playing Musical Instruments; and
A Triton and Two Infant Satyrs, from Twelve
Ornamental Panels, ca. 1490–1515

Engravings, each 22 × 3¾ in. (55.7 × 9.3 cm)
Harris Brisbane Dick Fund, 1923 (23.39.10, .2, .4)

Provenance: Giuseppe Storck (1766–1836), Milan;
[W. G. Russell, Boston]; Department of Prints purchase,
1923

Collected at the height of Ivins's interest in
ornament prints, these three vertical engravings are part of a series of twelve believed to
have been jointly made by the Milanese printmaker and miniature painter Giovanni Pietro
da Birago and Giovanni Antonio da Brescia, an
engraver who worked in the circle of Andrea
Mantegna. With their superabundance of
sphinxes, putti, mermaids, cornucopias, vases,
and jewels, as well as arms, mottoes, *imprese*,
portraits, and political allegories, the prints
are fine examples of an Italianate style of ornament that can also be found in Birago's manuscript illuminations for the Sforza court (1490,
1491–94). The style was inspired by ancient
grotesques on frescoes in the Golden House
of Nero, which was unearthed in Rome in the
late 1480s. The mural decorations were quickly
translated into prints, which were instantly
popular, widely disseminated north and south
of the Alps, and profoundly influential.

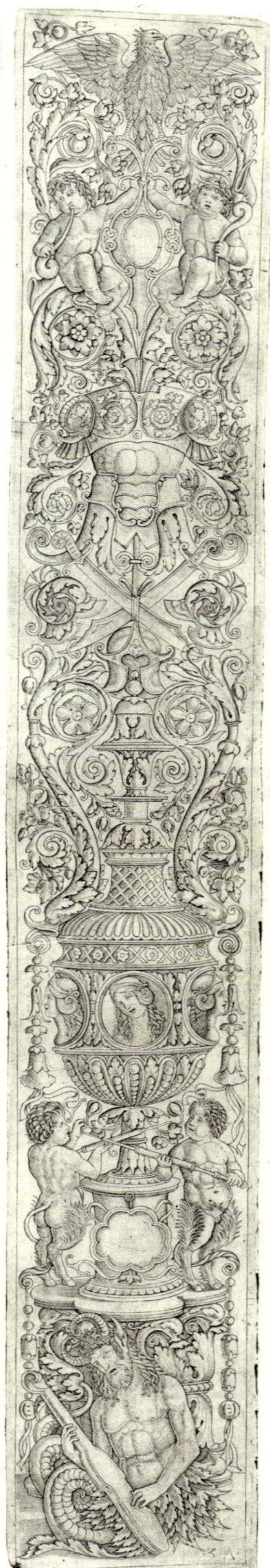
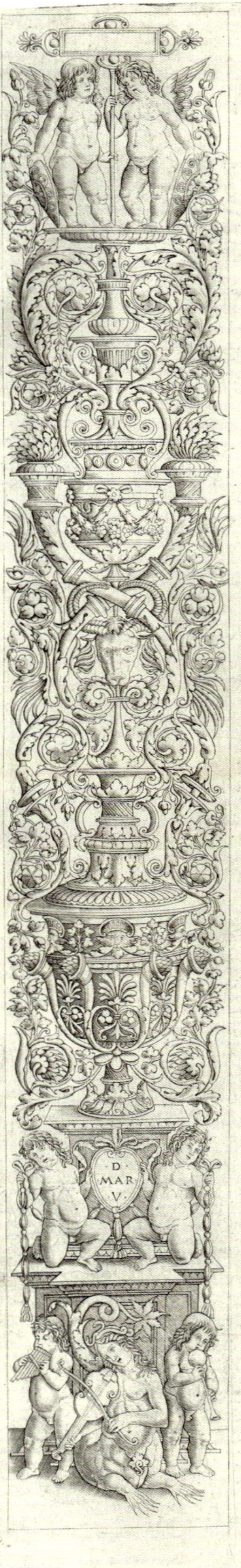
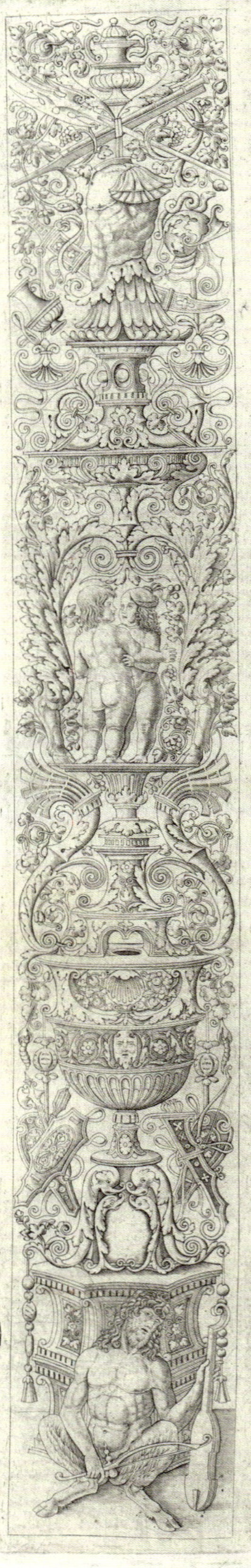

55

Albrecht Dürer, German (1471–1528)

Saint Eustace, ca. 1501

Engraving, 13¾ × 10¼ in. (35 × 25.9 cm)
Fletcher Fund, 1919 (19.73.65)

Watermark: high crown (Piccard 53437)

Provenance: Junius Spencer Morgan (1867–1932), New York and Paris; Department of Prints purchase, 1919

Dürer's largest engraving depicts the moment of conversion of the Roman general Placidus. While hunting, he was confronted by a stag with a crucifix miraculously between its antlers who spoke in the name of Christ. Placidus fell from his horse and became a Christian, baptized with the name Eustace. The eye delights in the delicate luminosity of the scene, created through subtle gradations in tone, and in Dürer's characteristic attention to the animals. Dürer is exploring the ideal of mathematically precise proportion in the horse, the stag, and the five identical dogs, who are seen from a variety of angles, placed almost as scientific specimens. This virtuosic pattern sheet served as a model for artists into the next century.

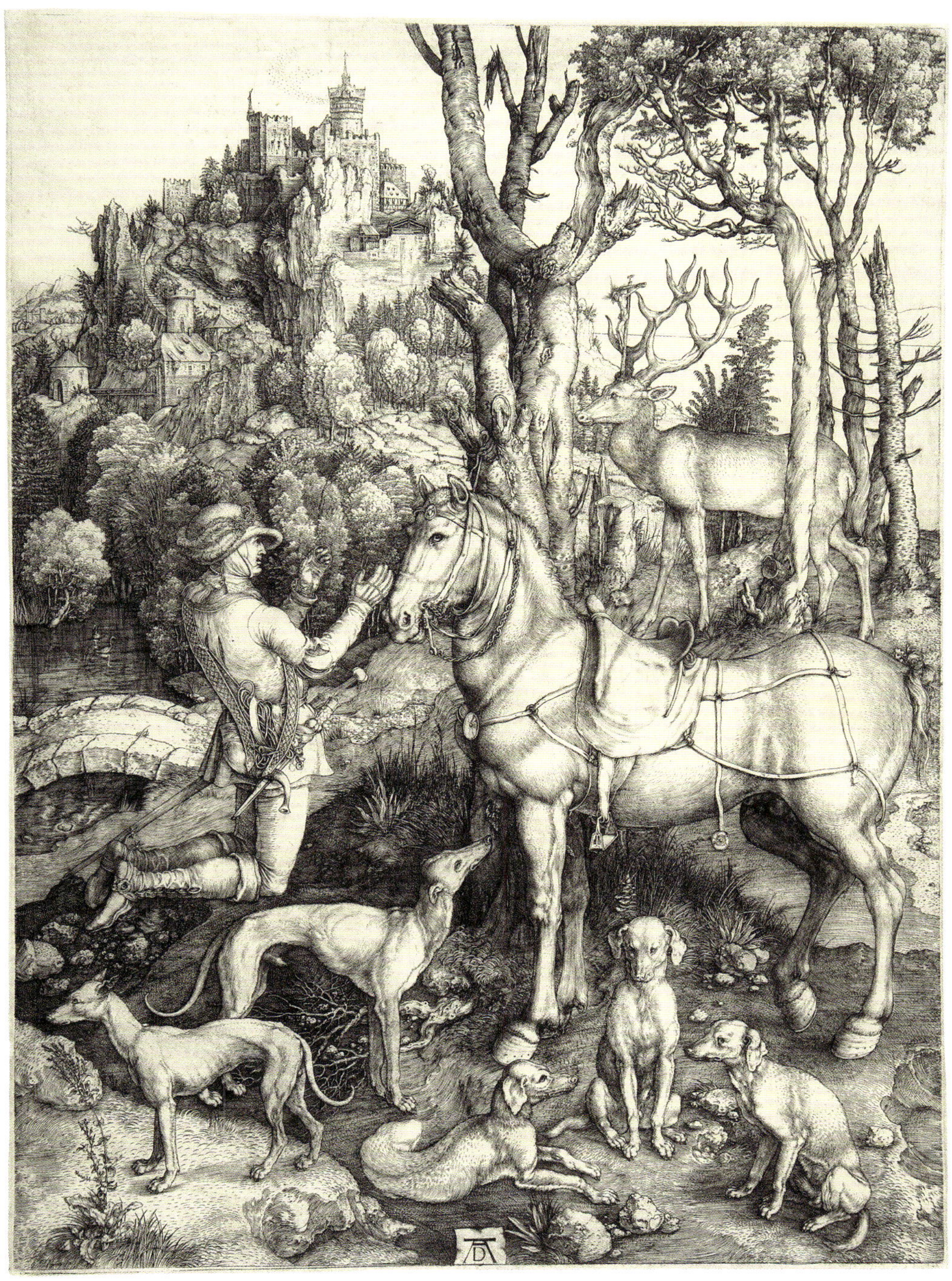

Albrecht Dürer, German (1471–1528)

Nemesis (The Great Fortune), 1501–2

Engraving, second state of two, 13⅛ × 9⅛ in.
(33.3 × 23.1 cm)
Fletcher Fund, 1919 (19.73.89)

Watermark: high crown (Piccard 53437)

Collectors' marks: François Debois (Lugt 985); Henry
Brodhurst (Lugt 1296); Adalbert Freiherr von Lanna
(Lugt 2773)

Provenance: M. Rossi; François Debois (ca. 1845), Paris;
[his sale, P. Defer, Paris, April 25, 1843, lot 256]; Henry
Brodhurst (ca. 1860), Mansfield, England; Adalbert
Freiherr von Lanna (1836–1909), Prague; [his sale, H. G.
Gutekunst, Stuttgart, part 1, May 11–22, 1909, lot 1455];
Junius Spencer Morgan (1867–1932), New York and
Paris; Department of Prints purchase, 1919

In this early feat of engraving, Dürer depicts
the goddess of fate, the magnificently winged
figure of Nemesis, towering over her domin-
ion, a mountainous landscape with buildings
nestled in the bend of a river. The meticulously
rendered town has been identified as Klausen
im Eisacktal, a village in the southern Alps
that Dürer passed on his way to Venice. This
work is part of the near-comprehensive collection of Dürer engravings and woodcuts Ivins
was thrilled to acquire in 1919. The collection,
he described, "contains at least one very fine
impression from each plate now generally
considered by students to have been made by
Dürer himself, and either originals or copies
of almost all the other engravings which at
one time or another have been attributed to
him. . . . What with the engravings and woodcuts which had already entered the Museum
through gift and purchase, its collection now,
doubtless, contains the fullest and finest representation of Dürer's prints on this side of
the Atlantic Ocean. . . . So far as concerns the
engravings, etchings, and dry points . . . there
cannot be more than two or three other places
[in the world] where the engraved 'oeuvre' is
so uniformly high in quality, or in which so
many of what the trade calls 'the finest impression we have ever seen' are to be found" (Ivins,
"Engravings and Woodcuts by Albert Dürer,"
1920: 33).

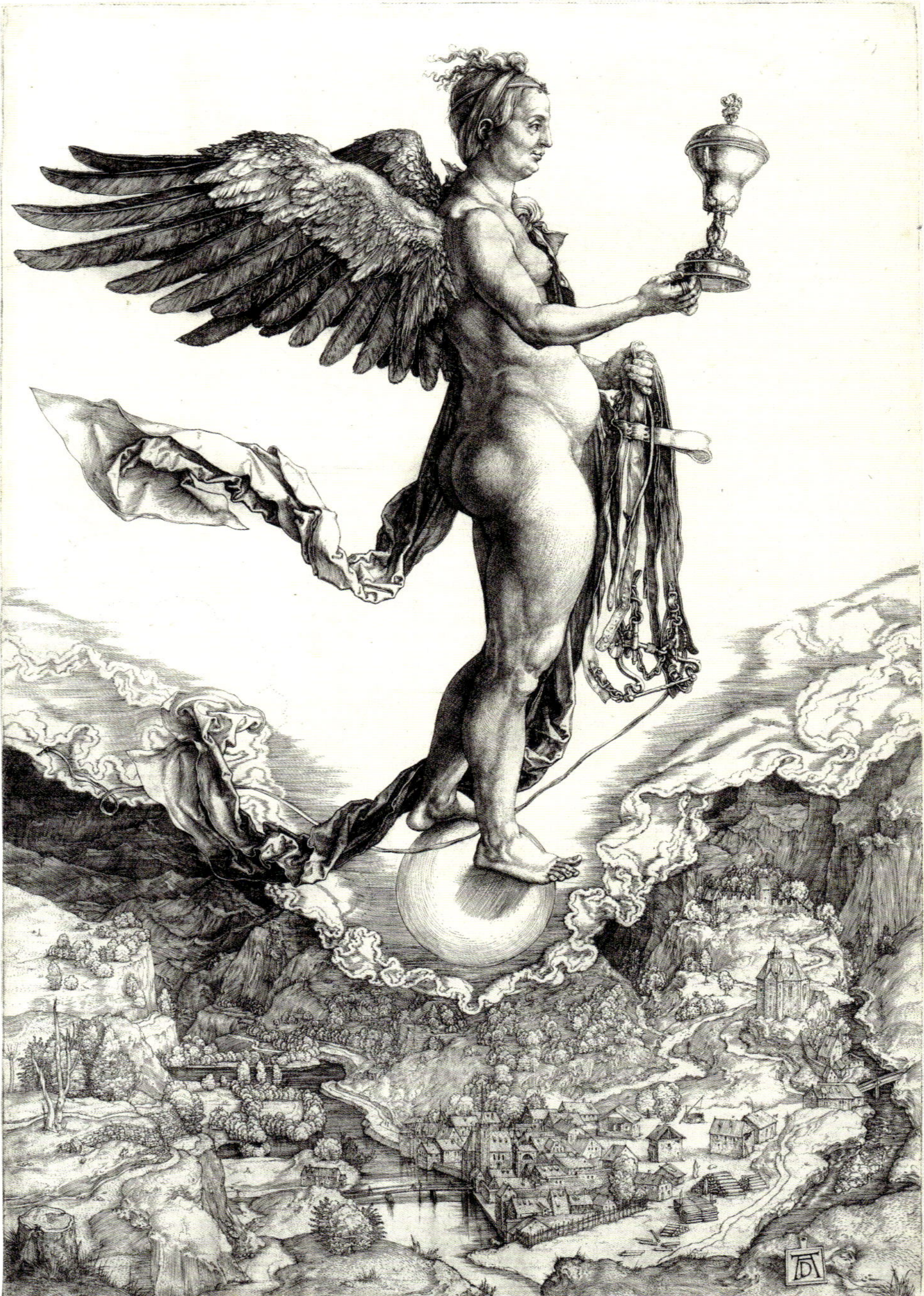

Albrecht Dürer, German (1471–1528)

Coat of Arms with a Skull, 1503

Engraving, 9⅝ × 7 in. (24.3 × 17.9 cm)
Fletcher Fund, 1919 (19.73.113)

Watermark: high crown (Piccard 53437)

Provenance: Junius Spencer Morgan (1867–1932), New York and Paris; Department of Prints purchase, 1919

Dürer's stunning engraving is a brilliantly unusual take on the memento mori. A patrician woman dressed in a stylish contemporary costume and identified by her crown as a bride is embraced by a wild man, symbolic of Germany's mythic past. This traditional figure from German folklore is often present at depictions of weddings, but the surface of his shield, which faces outward toward the viewer, reveals him to be a harbinger of the bride's death.

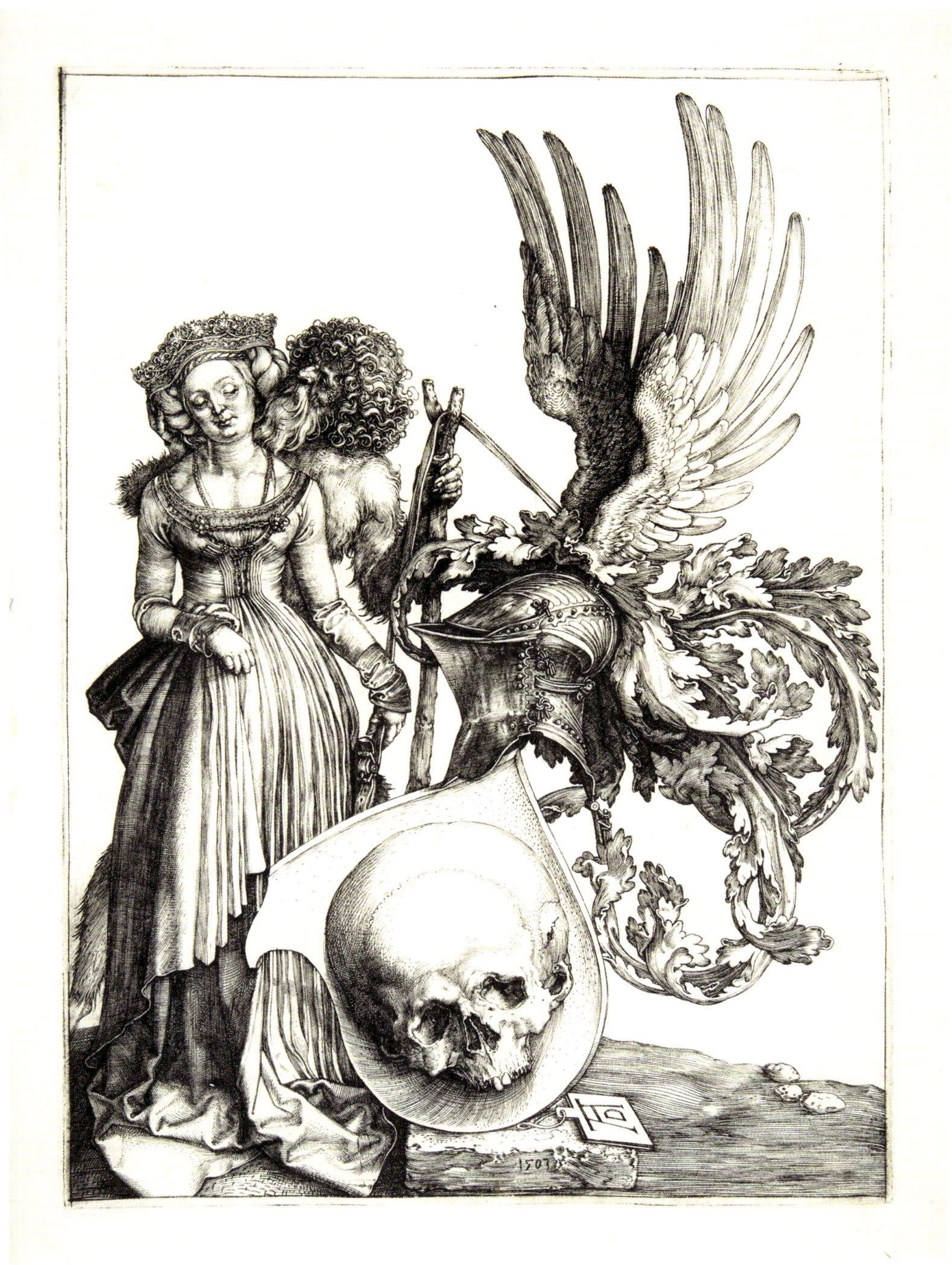

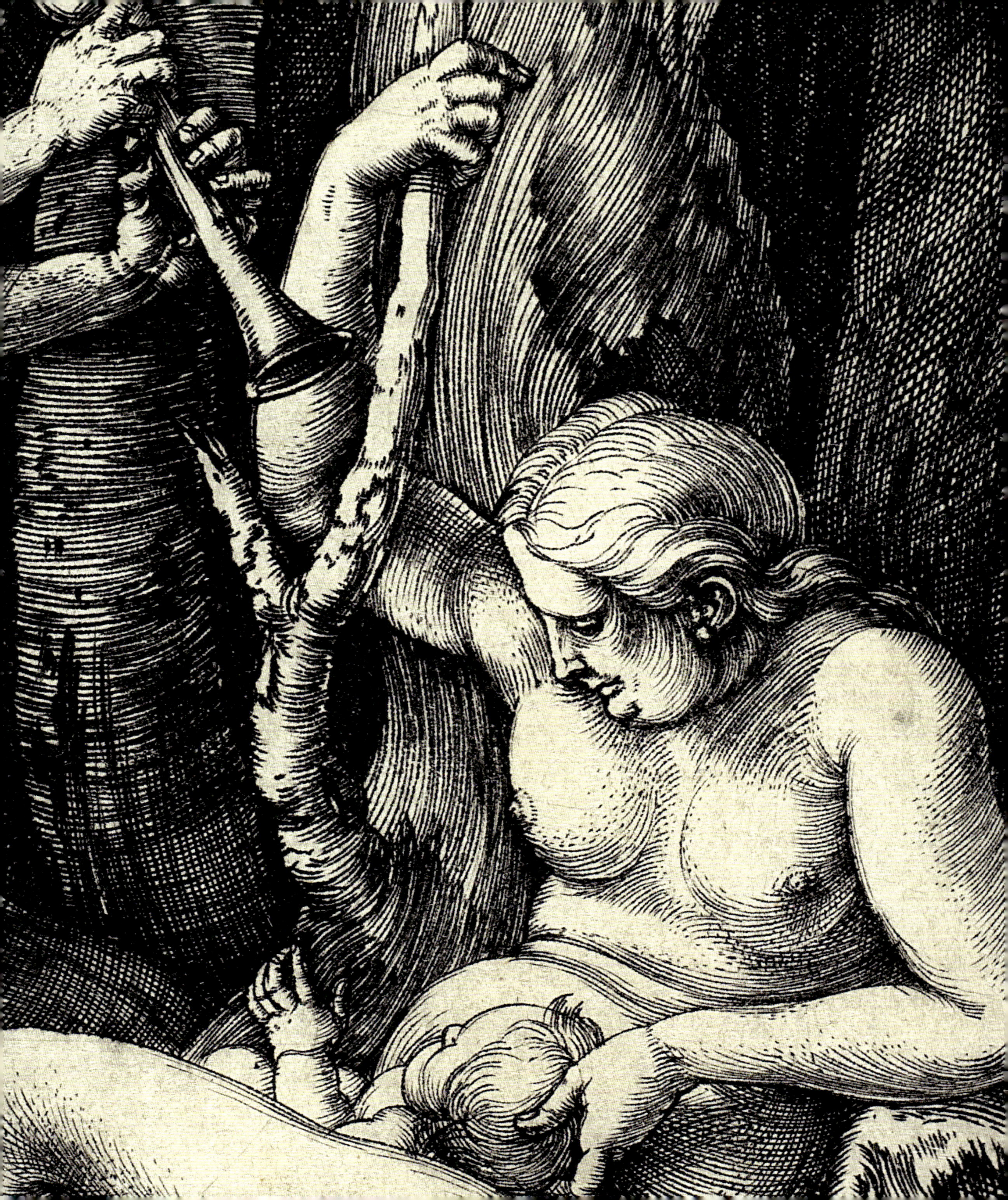

58

Satyr Family, 1505

Engraving, 4½ × 2⅞ in. (11.4 × 7.1 cm)
Fletcher Fund, 1919 (19.73.77)

Collector's mark: Henry Studdy Theobald (Lugt 1375)

Provenance: Henry Studdy Theobald (1847–1934), London; [his sale, H. G. Gutekunst, Stuttgart, May 12–14, 1910, lot 231]; Junius Spencer Morgan (1867–1932), New York and Paris; Department of Prints purchase, 1919

Although Ivins's collecting philosophy tended to favor a small sampling by a great many artists, he made an exception for Dürer, "by common consent the greatest of [all] German artists" and "one of the very artists who cannot be adequately represented by a small selection of his work" (Ivins, *Notes on Prints*, 23). Ivins acquired a near-comprehensive collection of Dürer's engravings, among them this rich, velvety impression of the *Satyr Family*. One of several extraordinary prints created just after 1500, as Dürer began to experiment with the medium of engraving, it sets an intimate family scene within a small clearing in a dense forest. The satyr plays a rustic cornemuse, or bagpipe, while his human bride gently holds their child on her lap. German humanists of the early sixteenth century understood the forest—a wilderness filled with mythic satyrs, wild men, and even Druid priests—as a stage for a distinctly German nationalism, as opposed to Italianate classicism.

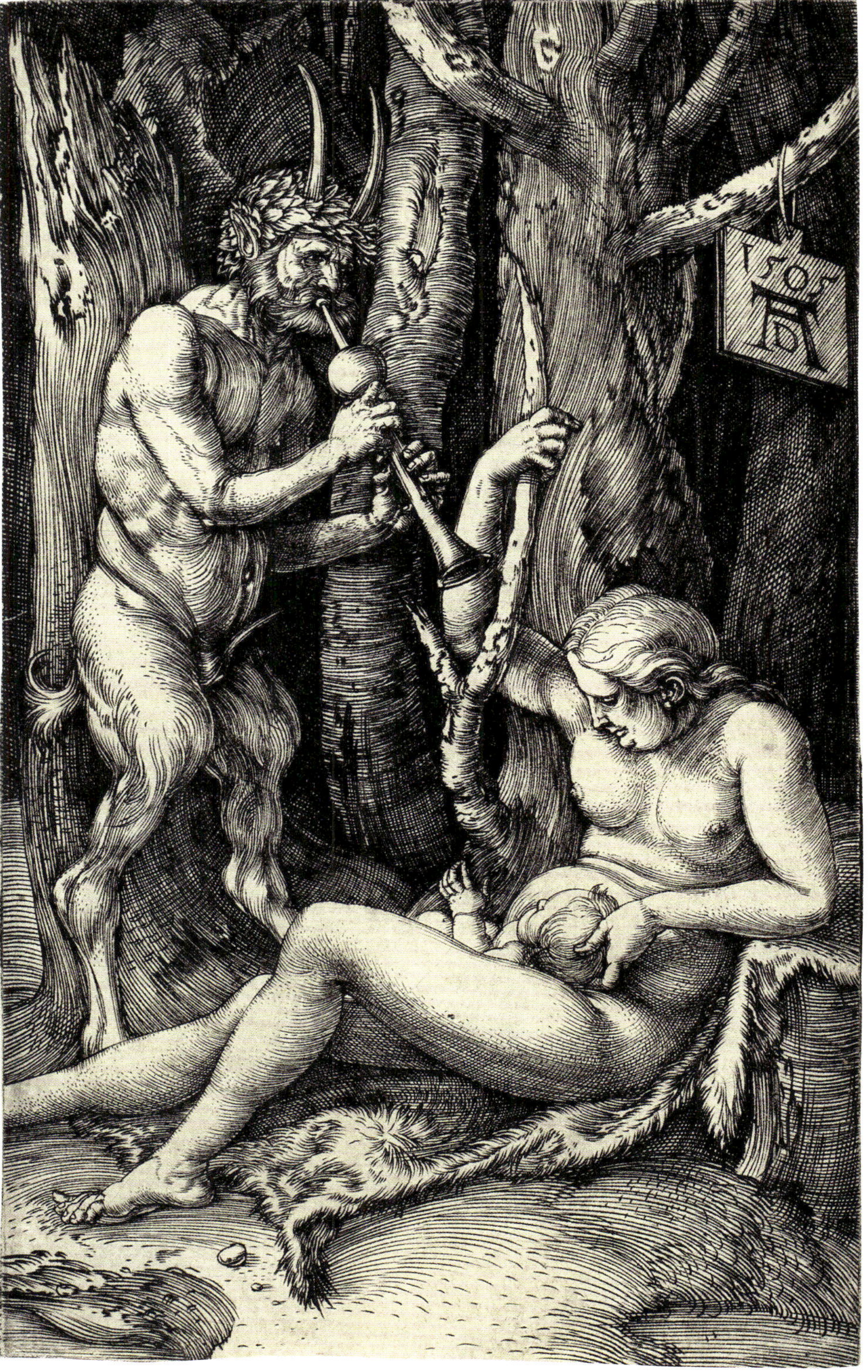

59

Adam and Eve, 1504

Engraving, 9⅞ × 7⅞ in. (25.1 × 20 cm)
Fletcher Fund, 1919 (19.73.1)

Watermark: bull's head (Piccard 66308)

Collectors' marks: Ernst Theodor Rodenacker (Lugt 2438);
Junius S. Morgan (Lugt 1536)

Provenance: Ernst Theodor Rodenacker (ca. 1840–before
1894), Gdansk; Junius Spencer Morgan (1867–1932),
New York and Paris; Department of Prints purchase,
1919

Dürer was obsessed with creating a perfect
human form that corresponded to a system of
proportion and measurements. Early in his
search for the ideal nude, he engraved Adam
and Eve, "God's own personally made patterns
of beauty," as Mayor put it (Mayor, *Prints &
People*, 277–78). The result was not wholly successful, Mayor explained: "He engraved [them]
with such caution—one might say trepida-
tion—that he finished the entire background
before he got the courage to sneak up on the
figures, around which he reserved an aura of
blank to allow him to fatten them if need be.
He may have known the saying of Polycletus,
that beauty depends on adjustments the thick-
ness of a fingernail. Though Dürer modeled
the flesh with a powdering of dots and flicks
of a delicacy never seen before, however often
attempted since, the engraving fails to satisfy
because he was striving too tensely to achieve
his masterpiece. Details steal the show, like the
mouse playing by the cat's claws in the closing
instant of the world's innocence" (ibid.).

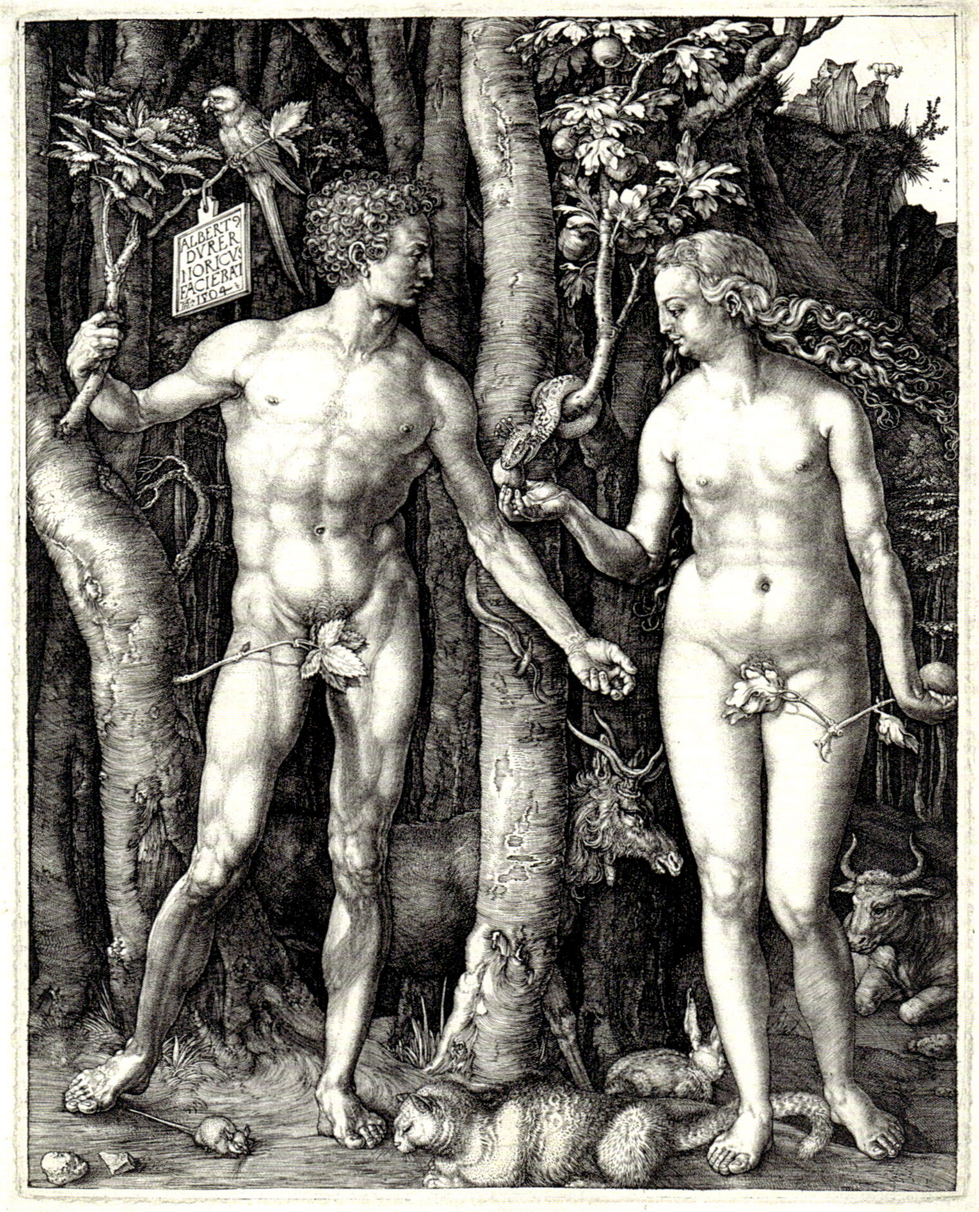

60

Apollo and Hyacinth and Amor, 1506

Engraving, 11¼ × 8⅞ in. (28.6 × 22.5 cm)
Gift of Felix M. Warburg and his family, 1941 (41.1.2)

Collectors' marks: James Reiss (Lugt 1522 and 1523);
possibly Junius Spencer Morgan (Lugt 1536)

Provenance: James Reiss (1812–1899), London; possibly
Junius Spencer Morgan (1867–1932), New York and
Paris; Richard Ederheimer (1878–1959), New York; Felix
Moritz Warburg (1871–1937), New York; gift of Felix M.
Warburg and his family to the Department of Prints,
1941

In this early work Marcantonio skillfully imi-
tates the engraved style and compositional
arrangement of Dürer's 1504 *Adam and Eve*.
He may also have worked from an intermediary drawing by Raphael, been influenced by
the style of Mantegna or Francesco Francia,
or even worked directly from an ancient
sculptural group then visible in Rome. What is
remarkable is how Marcantonio integrates all
of these threads of influence to create an original composition. It depicts a mythological love
story that came to an abrupt end with the tragic
death of young Hyacinth.

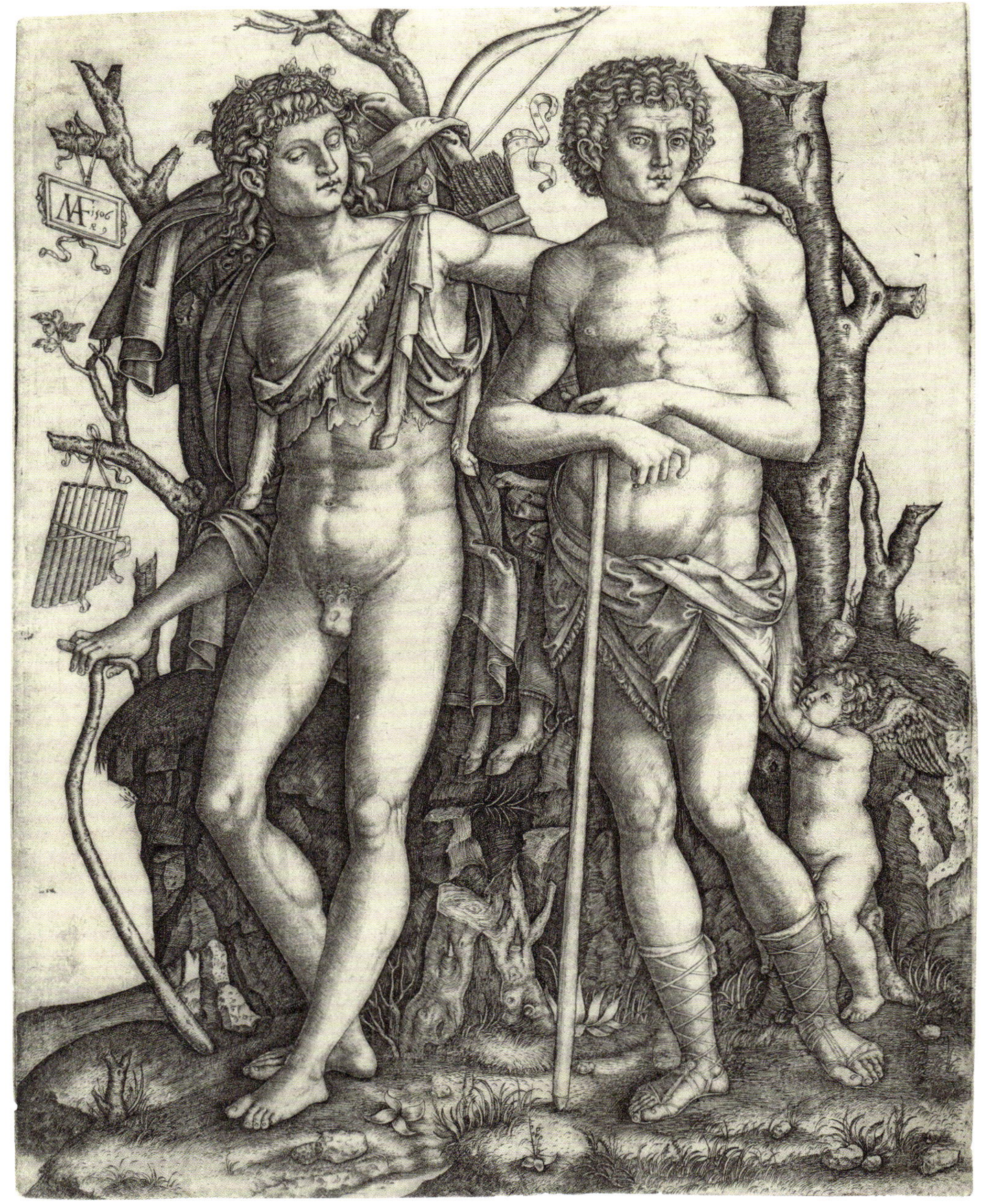

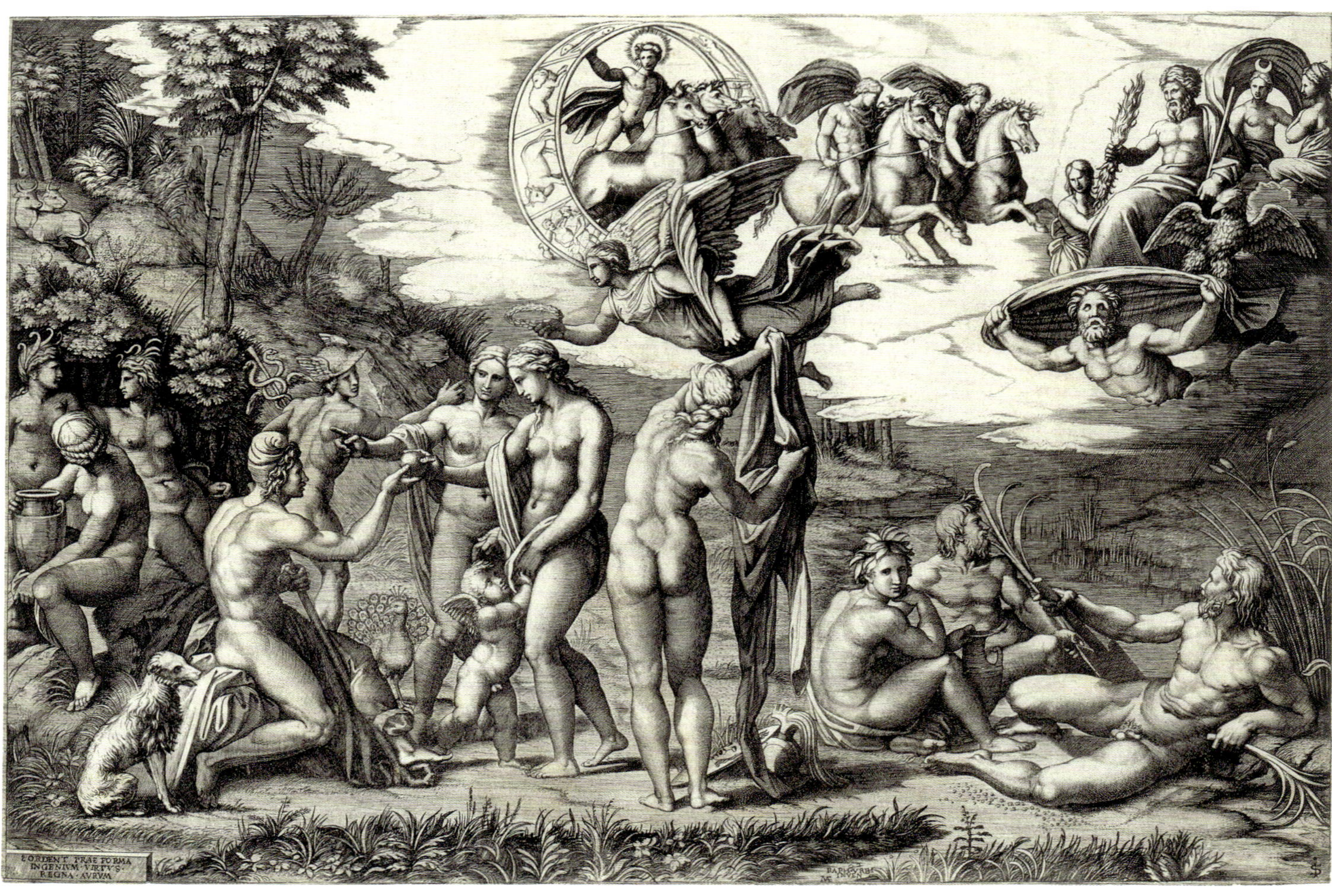

61

After Raphael, Italian (1483–1520)

The Judgment of Paris, ca. 1510–20

Engraving, 11½ × 17¼ in. (29.1 × 43.7 cm)
Rogers Fund, 1919 (19.74.1)

Collector's mark: John Spencer (Lugt 1532)

Provenance: John Spencer (1708–1746), Althorp,
Northamptonshire, England; [P. & D. Colnaghi & Co.,
London]; Department of Prints purchase, 1922

Although Ivins did not systematically collect
reproductive engravings (engravings that
imitate and disseminate the ideas, styles, and
compositions of others), he was intrigued by
their role in the development of taste and the
history of printmaking. He noted that Marcantonio "[started] in Bologna as an amusing
but second-rate original engraver, [but] went
to Rome where, working for Raphael, he
became the progenitor of the most important
line of reproductive engravers the world has
ever known. From this time on Italian painters
in large measure ceased to make engravings
and contented themselves with turning their
drawings over to professional engravers for
reproduction and publication" (Ivins, *Notes on
Prints*, 63).

Lucas van Leyden, Netherlandish
(ca. 1494–1533)

Mohammed and the Monk Sergius, 1508

Engraving, first state of three, 11¼ × 8½ in.
(28.6 × 21.5 cm)
Rogers Fund, 1921 (21.3.3)

Watermark: serpent (Piccard 43266)

Collectors' marks: Alfred Morrison (Lugt 151); Peter
Gellatly (Lugt 1185); Paul J. Sachs (Lugt 2091)

Provenance: Alfred Morrison (1821–1897), London;
Peter Gellatly (1831–1912), London; [his sale with C. E.
Baxter, H. G. Gutekunst, Stuttgart, May 13–18, 1911,
lot 669]; Paul J. Sachs (1878–1965), Cambridge, Mass.;
Department of Prints purchase, 1921

The earliest dated engraving by Lucas van
Leyden, this print was executed when the artist
was a mere fourteen-year-old. It displays a styl-
istic affinity with two engravers, the fifteenth-
century Netherlandish Master IAM of Zwolle
and the more prolific and widely disseminated
German Renaissance artist Albrecht Dürer.
Mayor noted the influence of Dürer, "whose
virtuosity [Lucas] simplified, and whom he
followed by signing his prints with his L and
the date on the tablet" (Mayor, *Prints & People*,
330). This print of a rarely illustrated episode
from the popular medieval book *The Travels
of Sir John Mandeville* showed "such mastery
that the landscape was copied two years later
in Rome when Marcantonio needed a background for figures from Michelangelo's cartoon of the Battle of [Cascina]" (ibid.).

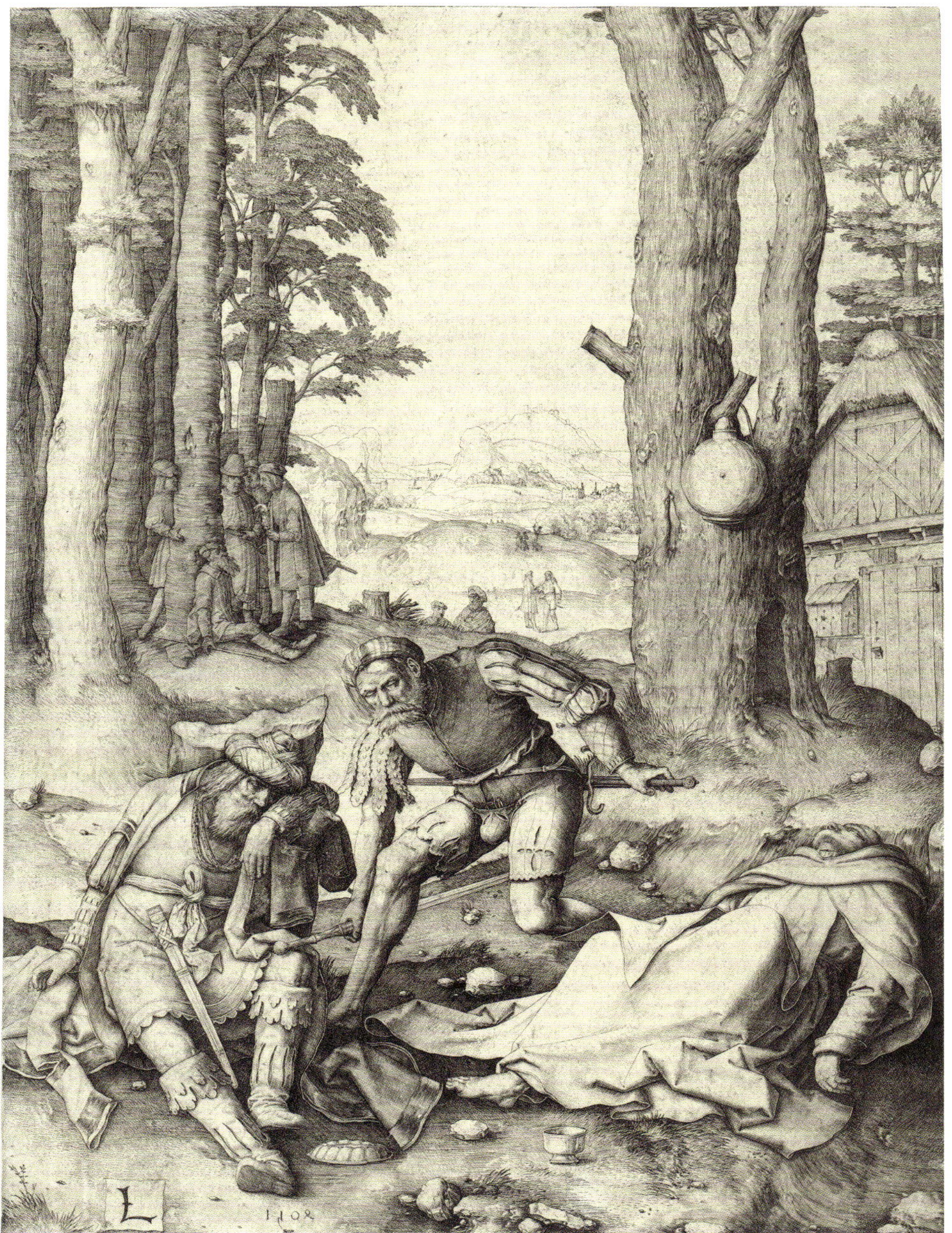

63

The Flagellation, from the Circular Passion,
1509

Engraving, Diam. 11⅛ in. (28.3 cm)
Purchase, Joseph Pulitzer Bequest, 1940 (40.41.5)

Watermark: serpent (Piccard 43266)

Provenance: [M. Knoedler & Co., New York];
Department of Prints purchase, 1940

Lucas is said to have designed the inventive
engravings from his Circular Passion as models for stained-glass windows. "In [Lucas's]
earliest and best liked prints, like this one, he
showed an amazing originality, both in his
delicate style of engraving and in his poetical
feeling and imagination" (Ivins, label for "Old
and Modern Prints No. 1," 1943). The ornamental frame for the Flagellation of Christ,
with its vines and putti, is from a separate plate
and was reused for the eight other prints in
the series.

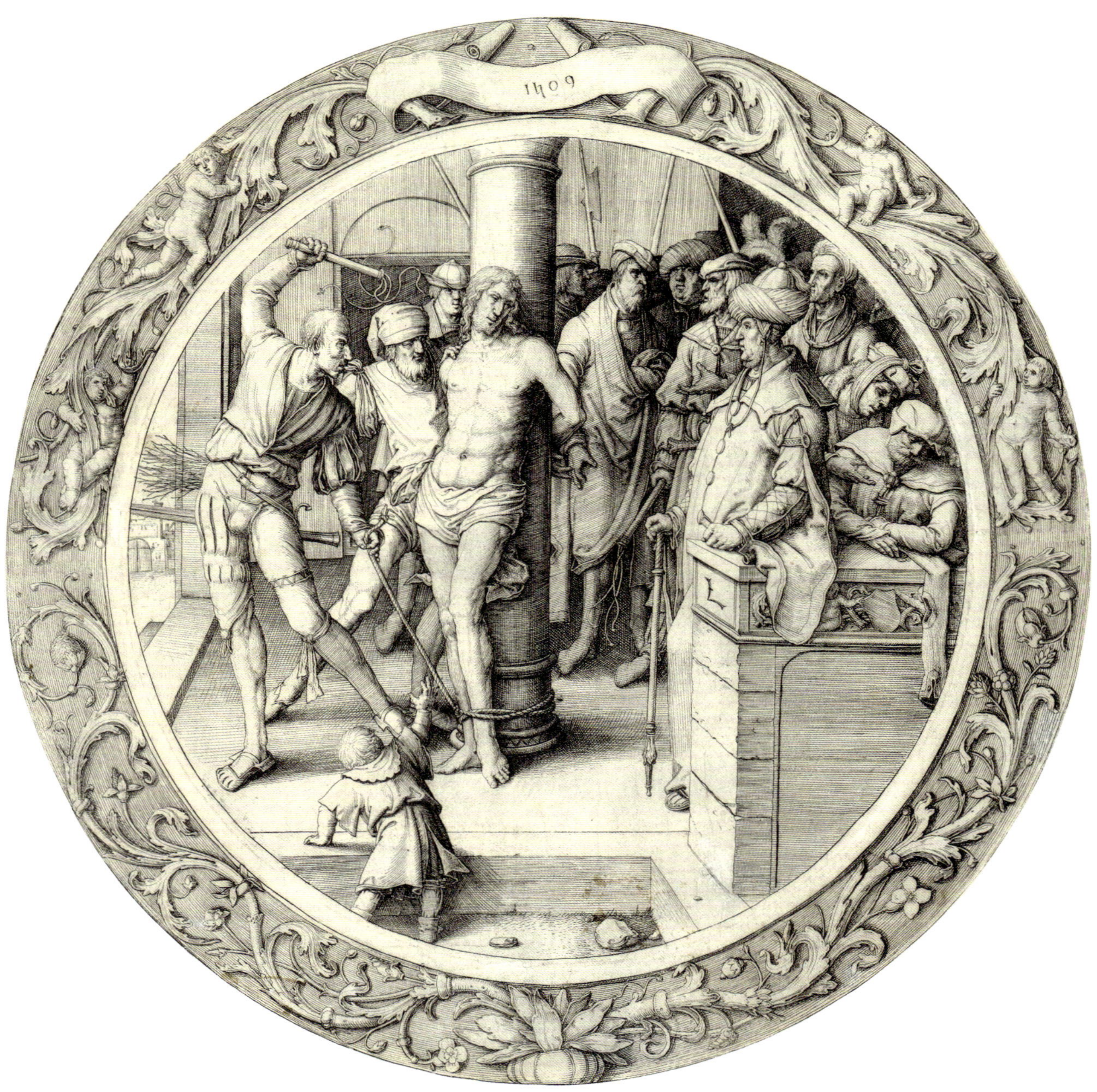

Lucas van Leyden, Netherlandish
(ca. 1494–1533)

The Dance of the Magdalene, 1519

Engraving, 11⅛ × 15⅝ in. (29 × 39.7 cm)
Gift of Felix M. Warburg and his family, 1941 (41.1.30)

Watermark: Gothic "P" (Piccard 106856)

Collector's mark: Junius S. Morgan (Lugt 1536a)

Provenance: Junius Spencer Morgan (1867–1932), New York and Paris; Felix Moritz Warburg (1871–1937), New York; gift of Felix M. Warburg and his family to the Department of Prints, 1941

Lucas depicts Mary Magdalen in her worldly life as a courtesan, prior to her conversion to Christianity—a portrayal unusual in the visual arts that sometimes appeared in contemporary Netherlandish mystery plays. Mary is shown dancing to the music of a piper and drummer among lovers under a canopy of trees; the main scene could be understood as a sixteenth-century love garden. Lucas was a masterful storyteller, able to render difficult narratives and a variety of visages with ease and wit, which Ivins credited to his familiarity with the world around him. "The single requisite to an understanding of Lucas's subject matter is smiling, sympathetic observation of your fellow men. To succeed in it you have only to waste your time sitting or standing around watching and listening to people and swapping nonsense and boasts with them. You need no notebooks or long verbal memory, but you do need the ability to recall vividly how Tom looked at Sue and the silly little gestures he made with his hands when she fell and hurt herself, the expressions on men's faces when they throw their weight into what they are doing, and the way the stuffed shirts strut and purse their lips and scowl" (Ivins, "Engravings by Four Renaissance Masters," 1944: 296).

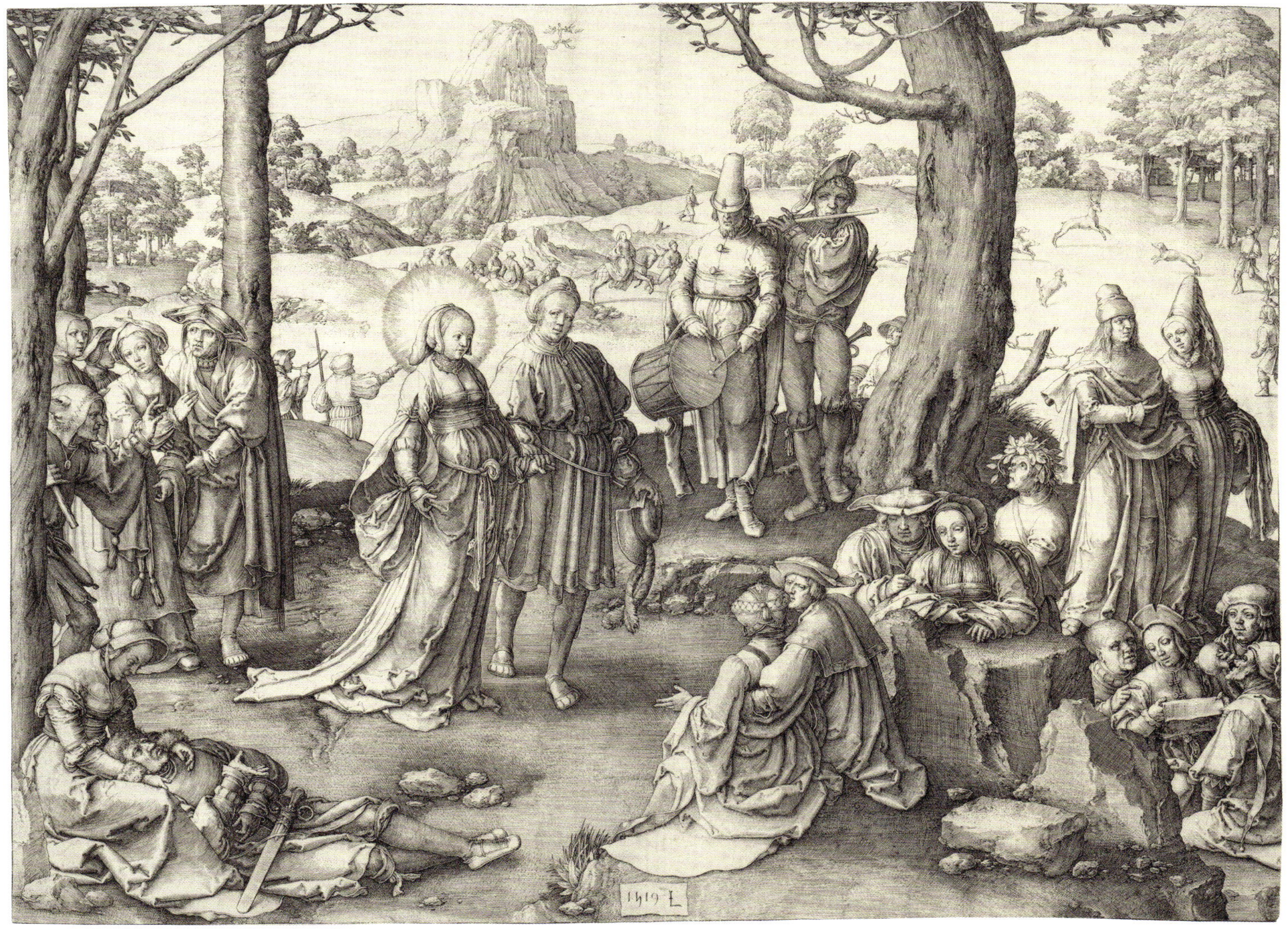

65

Panel of Ornament with Two Sirens, 1528

Engraving, 4¾ × 3⅛ in. (12 × 8 cm)
Harris Brisbane Dick Fund, 1933 (33.56.18)

Collector's mark: Pierre Mariette II (C. F. Lugt 1788–90)

Provenance: Pierre Mariette II (1634–1716), Paris;
[P. & D. Colnaghi & Co., London]; Department of
Prints purchase, 1933

This engraving demonstrates the impact of
the Italianate style of ornament, which was
circulating north of the Alps in prints by Marcantonio, Agostino Veneziano, and Giovanni
Antonio da Brescia. Ivins observed that Lucas,
"in his later work [like this one] . . . came under
the influence of Marc Antonio, who had in turn
learned much from him. In this period of his
work, which is not much savored today, Lucas
took the first steps towards that codification
of engraving practice which later in the hands
of Goltzius became the standardized type of
Northern engraving for a long time" (Ivins,
Notes on Prints, 31).

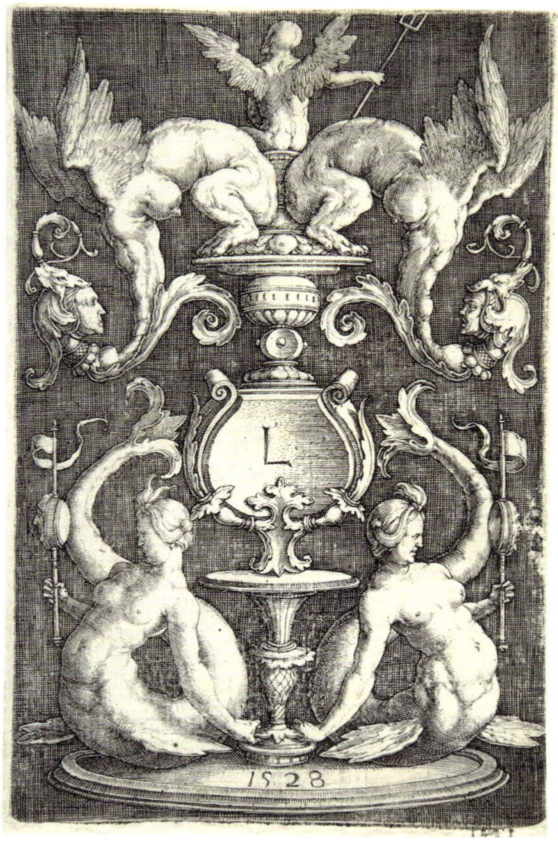

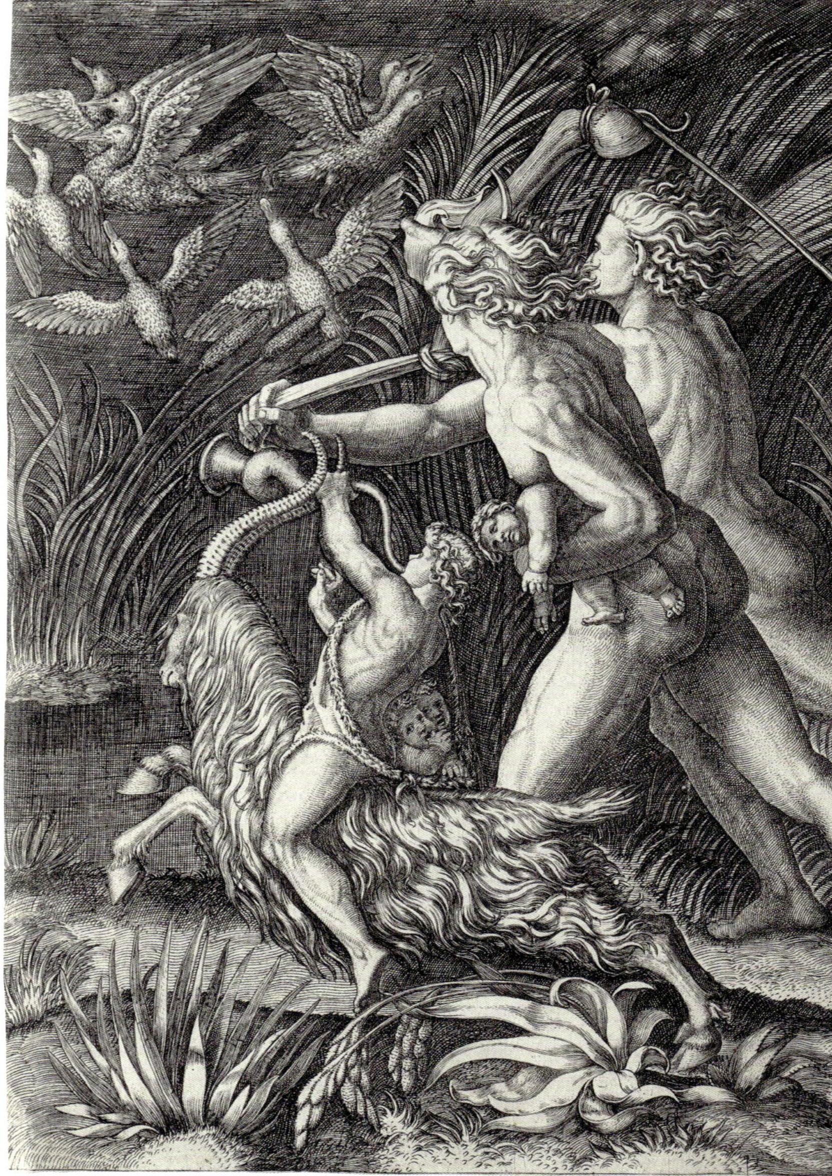

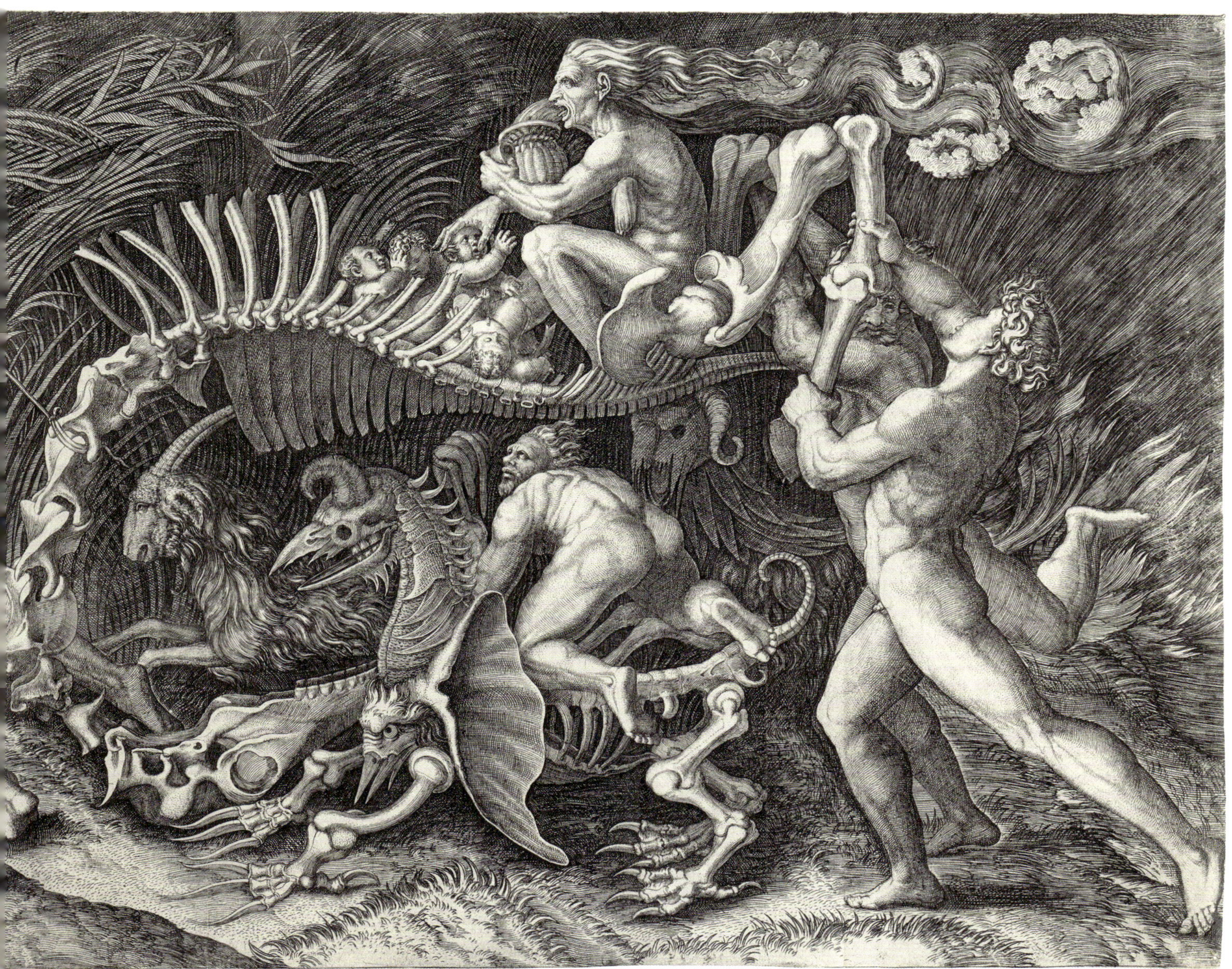

66

Lo Stregozzo (*The Witch's Procession*),
ca. 1515–25

Engraving, first state before engraver's initials,
11⅞ × 24½ in. (30 × 62.3 cm)
The Elisha Whittelsey Collection, The Elisha Whittelsey
Fund, 1949 (49.97.146)

Provenance: Albertina, Vienna; Department of Prints
purchase, 1949

This dramatic, mysterious print of a strange
and menacing procession through a dark
underworld was engraved by Agostino
Veneziano, but it was based on an original
design by another artist whose identity is
still open to debate. Veneziano was a student of Marcantonio, who may have begun
the engraved composition that Veneziano
completed.

Giovanni Jacopo Caraglio, Italian
(ca. 1500/1505–1565)

After Raphael, Italian (1483–1520)

*Aeneas Rescuing Anchises with a Young Boy
Carrying a Lantern at Left*, ca. 1525

Engraving, 8⅛ × 7⅜ in. (20.7 × 18.8 cm)
The Elisha Whittelsey Collection, The Elisha Whittelsey
Fund, 1949 (49.97.253)

Collector's mark: Albertina (Lugt 5h)

Provenance: Albertina, Vienna; Department of Prints
purchase, 1949

This engraving is based on one of Raphael's
preliminary drawings for *The Fire in the Borgo*
in the Vatican, a fresco for which Raphael
likewise drew on existing models. Among
them was an ancient Roman coin that
depicted the pious Aeneas rescuing his father,
Anchises, from fallen Troy. Caraglio was part
of Marcantonio's engraver's workshop, which
"perfected a system of collaboration that
spread uninterruptedly until about 1875, when
reproductive printmaking began to give way to
the cheaper and more accurate photomechani-
cal processes" (Mayor, *Prints & People*, 657).

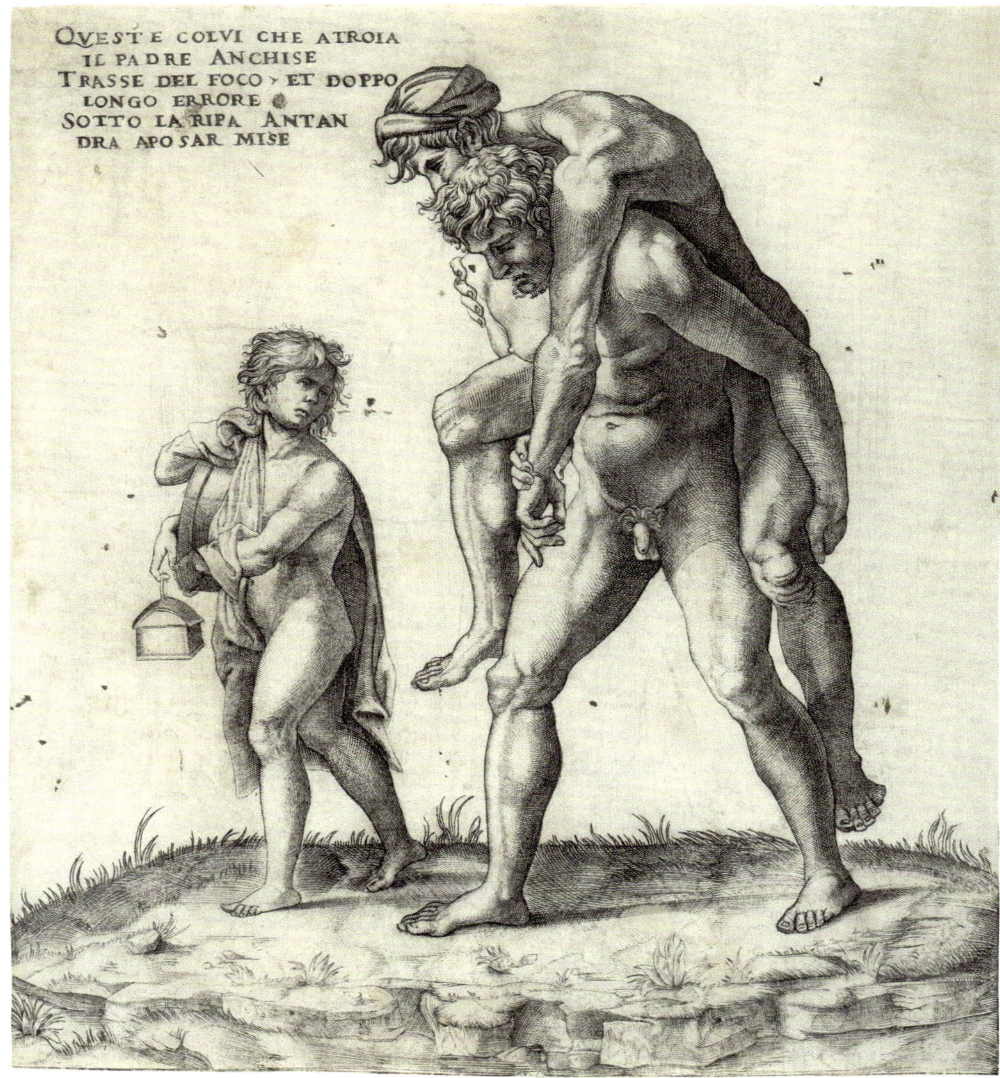

Master of the Die, Italian
(active ca. 1530–60)

After Giovanni da Udine, Italian
(1487–1564)

After Raphael, Italian (1483–1520)

Three Putti Playing with an Ostrich,
ca. 1530–40

Engraving, first state of two, 8¼ × 11 in. (21 × 28 cm)
The Elisha Whittelsey Collection, The Elisha Whittelsey
Fund, 1949 (49.97.332)

Collectors' marks: Pierre Mariette II (C. F. Lugt 1788–90);
Albertina (Lugt 5h)

Provenance: Pierre Mariette II (1634–1716), Paris;
Albertina, Vienna; Department of Prints purchase, 1949

This is one of four engravings after a set of tapestries about the games of putti that was woven
for Pope Leo X in Flanders in about 1521. It is
likely based on Giovanni da Udine's designs
for the tapestries, which in turn depended on
Raphael's work. This striking impression is a
first state before the addition of the name of
the Roman publisher, Antonio Lafreri, and the
indication that Raphael invented the designs.
Mayor acquired the set of four engravings from
Vienna's illustrious graphics collection, the
Albertina, during its sales of duplicates after
World War II.

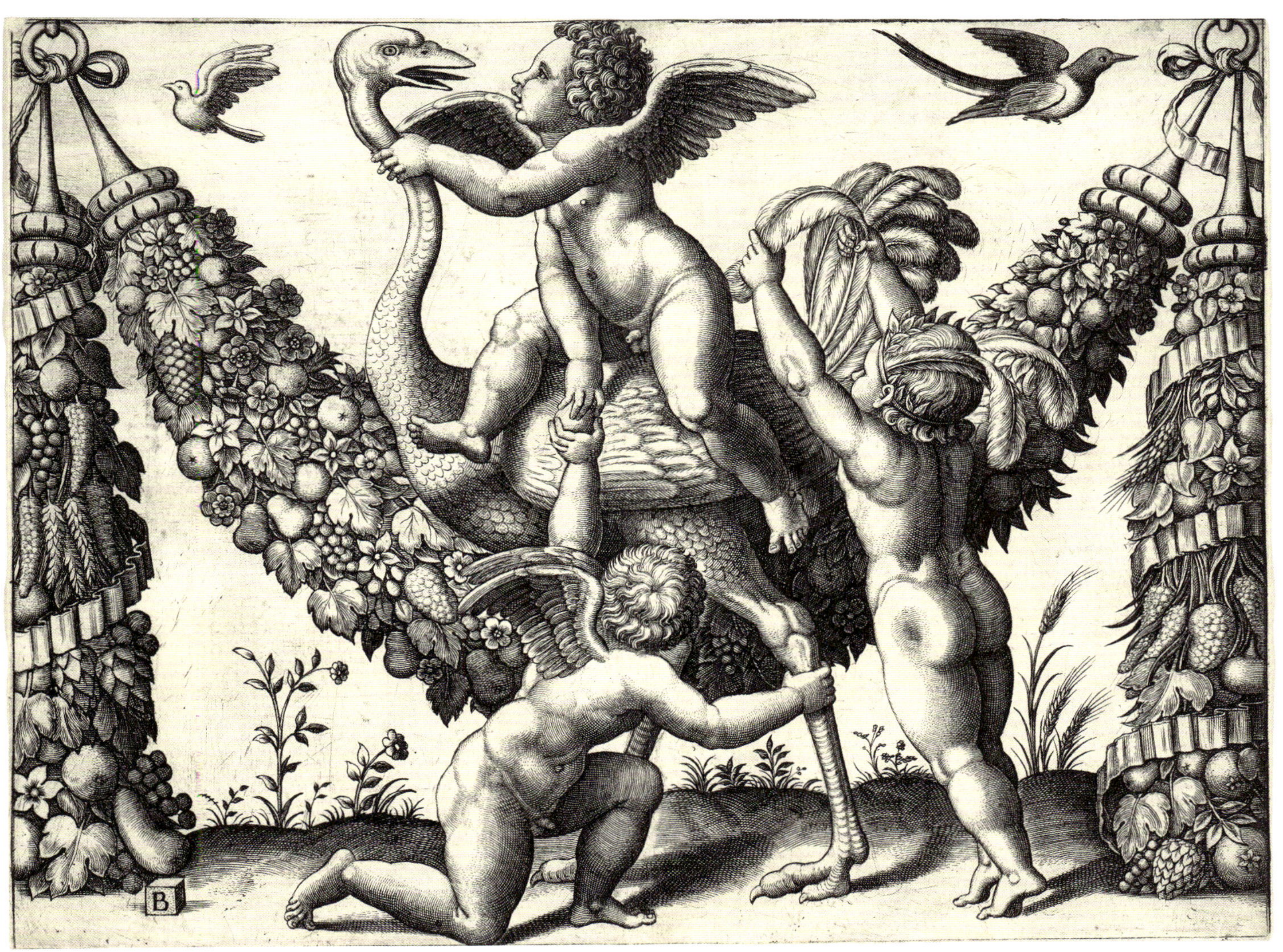

Allegory of the Power of Love, before 1535

Engraving, 11⁷⁄₈ × 11¹⁄₈ in. (30 × 28.3 cm)
Anonymous gift, 1929 (29.44.20)

Provenance: Private collector, New York; her anonymous gift to the Department of Prints, 1929

This vision of putti and nudes wrapped in vines and billowing sashes in a rocky landscape owes its visual vocabulary to Il Robetta's Italian contemporaries, but the lively web of engraved lines recalls the style of the leading northern engravers, Martin Schongauer and Albrecht Dürer. The meaning of the learned allegory that the engraving depicts is elusive, which may be why Ivins reacted emotionally to it:

"In some ways the most curiously and hauntingly beautiful print . . . [it] had certain *other* quality that to me was very wonderful—just strange enough and artificial enough and clumsy enough done to emphasize the very real poetry of it—as though the man had had a vision" (Ivins to Paul J. Sachs, April 14, 1915; Harvard Art Museums Archives).

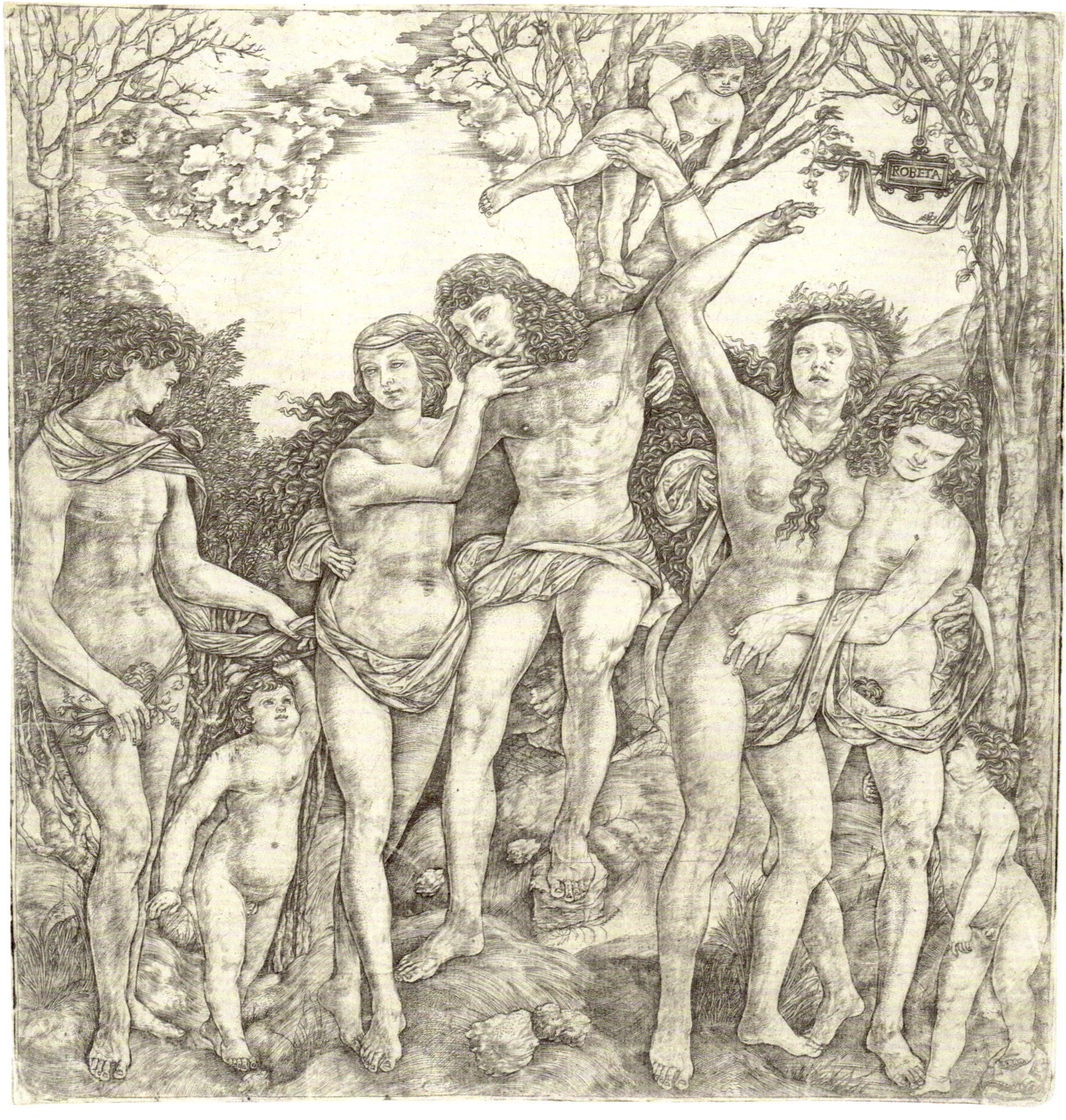

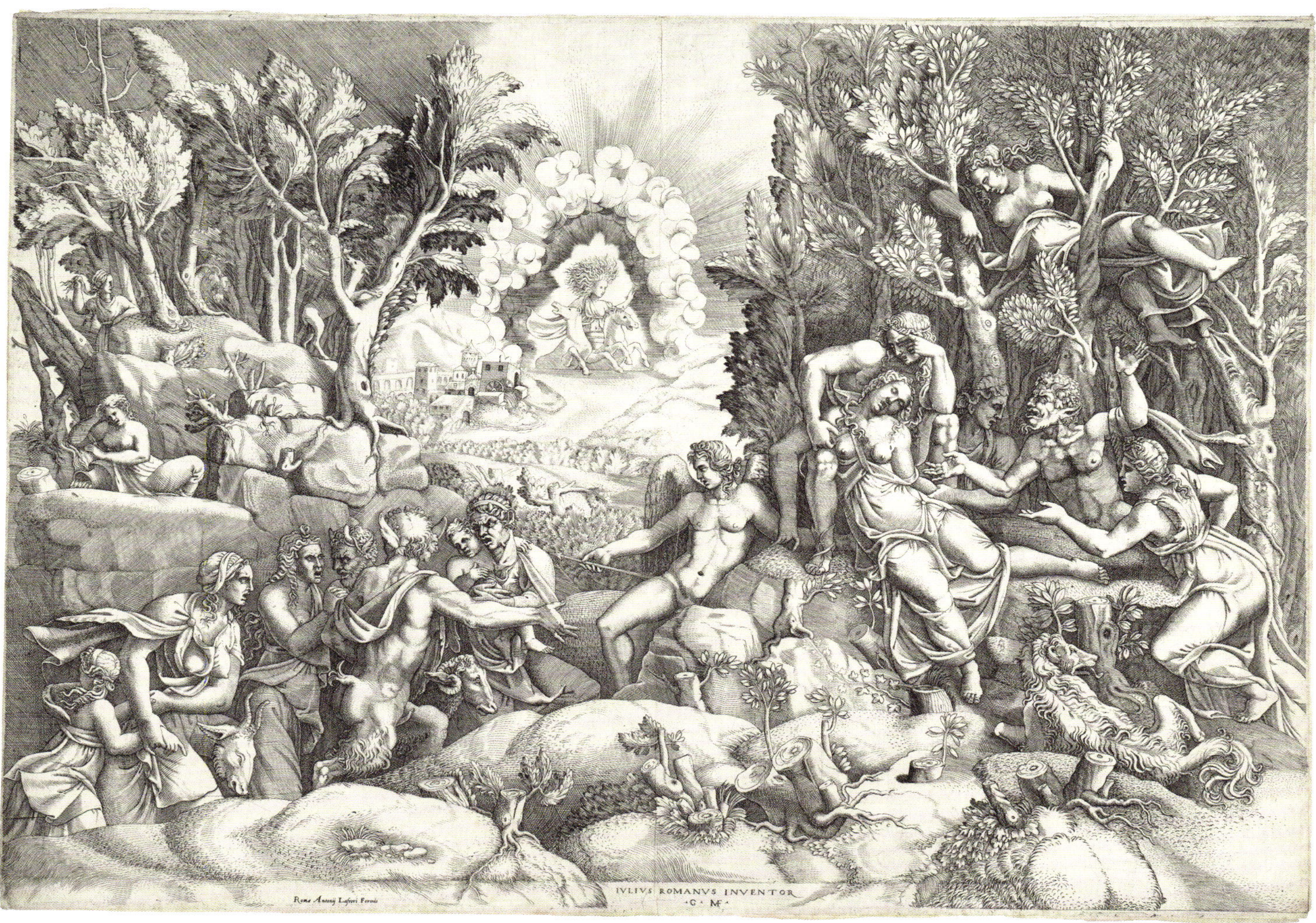

70

Giorgio Ghisi, Italian (ca. 1520–1582)

After Giulio Romano, Italian (ca. 1499–1546)

The Death of Procris, ca. 1540

Engraving, 15½ × 22¼ in. (39.4 × 56.5 cm)
The Elisha Whittelsey Collection, The Elisha Whittelsey
Fund, 1951 (51.501.7109)

Provenance: Princes of Liechtenstein, Vaduz and Vienna;
[P. & D. Colnaghi, London]; Department of Prints
purchase, 1951

The story of Cephalus and his wife, Procris,
from Ovid's *Metamorphosis* (Book VII), is a
tale of a mistaken infidelity that ends with
the death of Procris during a hunt. This print
reproduces in reverse a drawing by Giulio
Romano that is now in the Städelsches Kunst-
institut, Frankfurt. Three other Ovidian
scenes in the same scale were produced at
about the same time by various etchers from
the Fontainebleau School. The drawings for
the compositions may have been designs for a
series of tapestries for Giulio's patron Federico
Gonzaga.

Domenico del Barbiere, Italian
(1506–1565)

Écorchés and Skeletons, ca. 1540–45

Engraving, 9½ × 13¼ in. (24.1 × 33.6 cm)
The Elisha Whittelsey Collection, The Elisha Whittelsey
Fund, 1949 (49.95.181)

Provenance: Princes of Liechtenstein, Vaduz and Vienna;
[P. & D. Colnaghi, London]; Department of Prints
purchase, 1949

A noted sculptor and engraver, Domenico del
Barbiere was born in Florence but spent most
of his career in France, both in the prosperous
city of Troyes and at the court of Fontainebleau, where many Italian artists enjoyed the
patronage of Francis I. This engraving may
reproduce a now-lost composition by Rosso
Fiorentino for a book on anatomy that was
never published. However, Domenico signed
only his own name, and some scholars have
suggested that the design might be his invention. The engraving depicts two skeletons,
each paired with an écorché, or flayed man; the
figures in each grouping assume a similar pose,
which is shown from front and back, under-
scoring the artist's understanding of anatomical complexities.

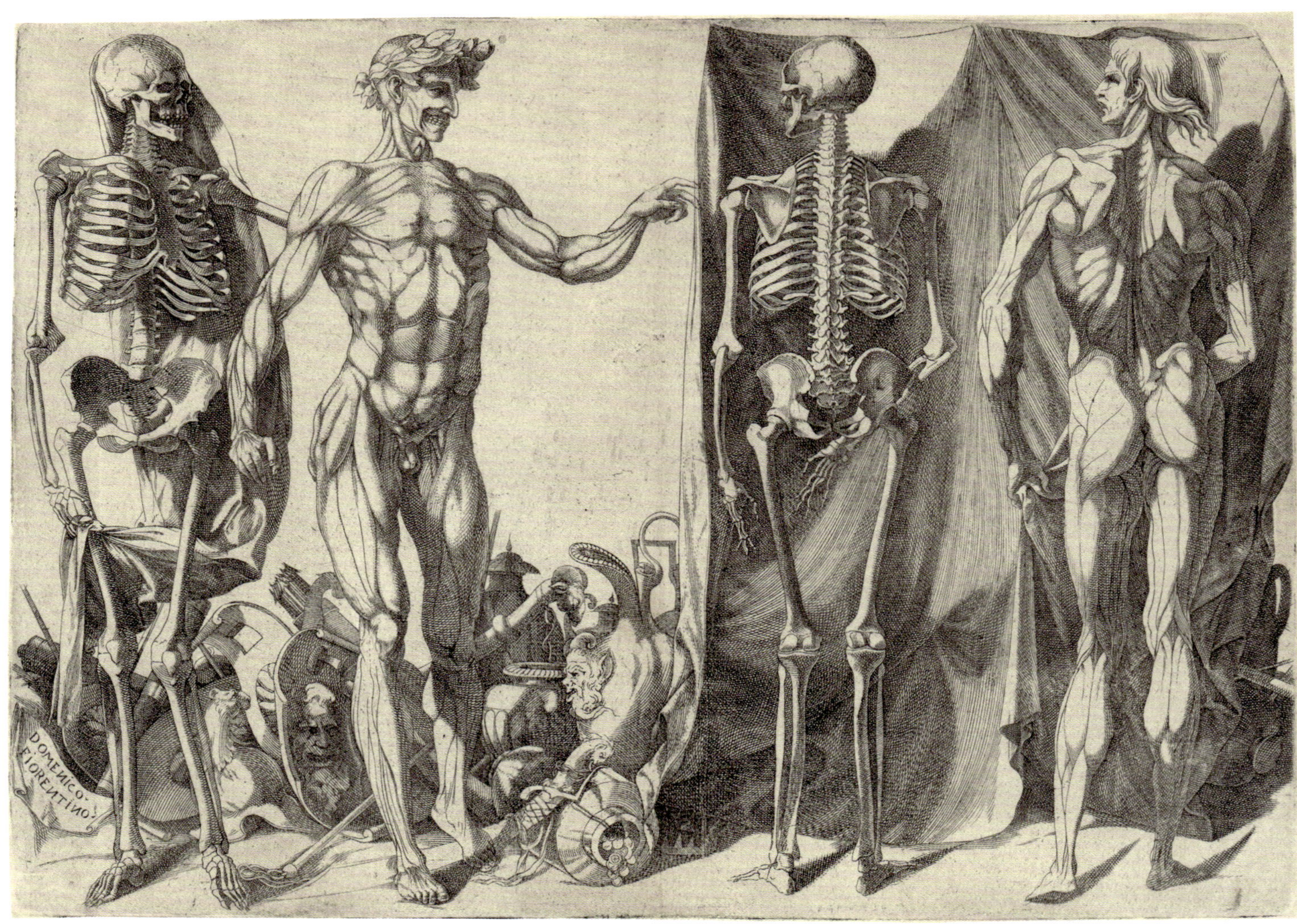

Cornelis Cort, Netherlandish
(ca. 1533–1578)

After Jan van der Straet (called Stradanus),
Netherlandish (1523–1605)

The Practitioners of the Visual Arts, 1578

Engraving, 16⅞ × 11¼ in. (42.8 × 28.6 cm)
Harris Brisbane Dick Fund, 1953 (53.600.509)

Provenance: Princes of Liechtenstein, Vaduz and Vienna;
[P. & D. Colnaghi, London]; Department of Prints
purchase, 1953

Cort's engraving brings together in an imagi-
nary and very busy studio setting the various
practitioners of the visual arts: a sculptor,
painter, printmaker, and architect. In the lower
left, a group of boys eager to learn the principles of figure drawing studies a skeleton and
an animated corpse that is strung up on pul-
leys. Cort created this spectacular example of
the reproductive engravings Mayor esteemed
by transferring or reproducing a design by fellow Netherlander Stradanus onto an engraved
plate while both were working in Rome.

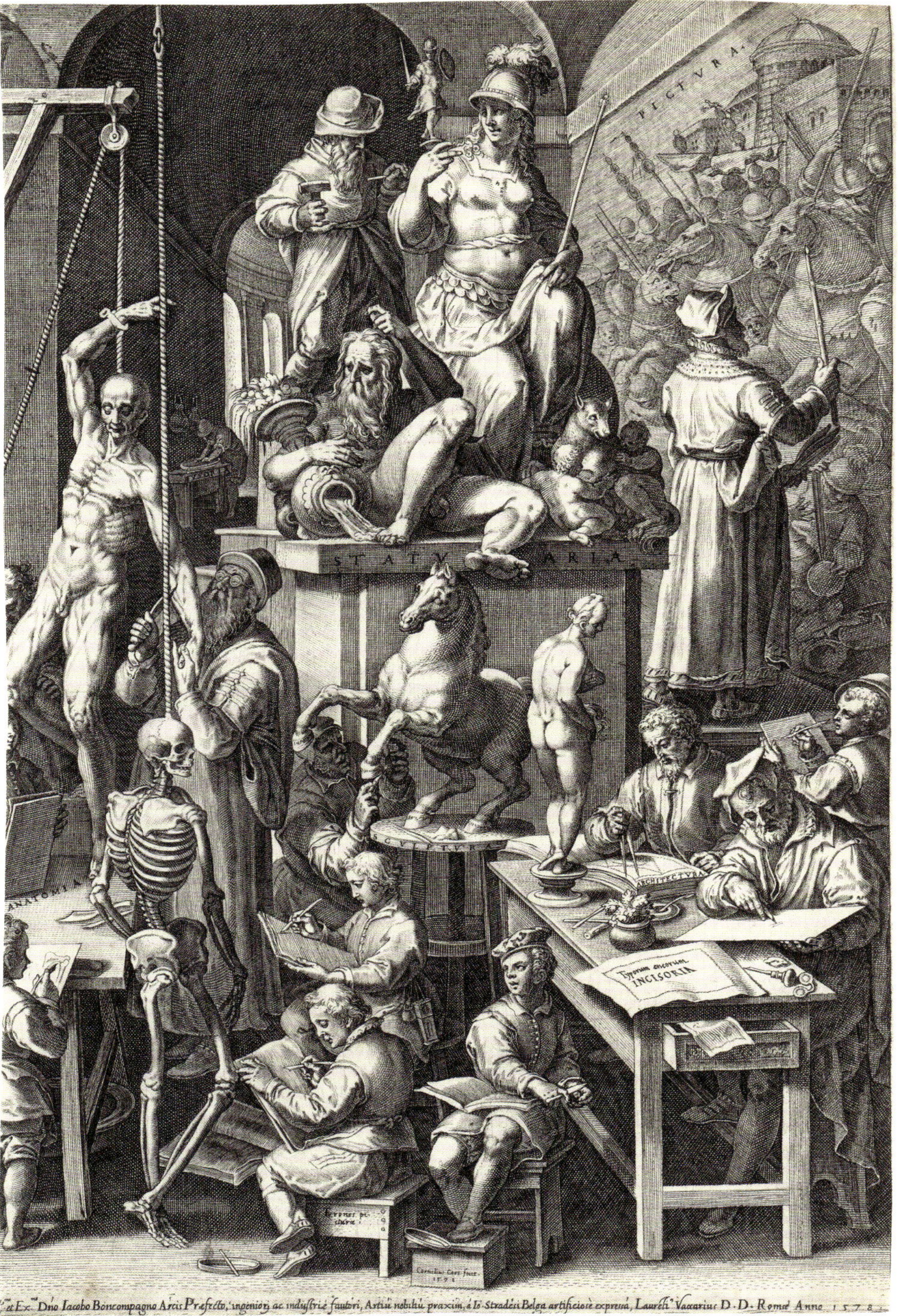

73

Jacob Matham, Netherlandish
(1571–1631)

After Hendrick Goltzius, Netherlandish
(1558–1617)

The Four Elements, 1588

Engraving, 11¾ × 8¼ in. (29.8 × 20.8 cm)
The Elisha Whittelsey Collection, The Elisha Whittelsey
Fund, 1951 (51.501.77)

Provenance: Princes of Liechtenstein, Vaduz and Vienna;
[P. & D. Colnaghi, London]; Department of Prints
purchase, 1951

Matham was a prolific printmaker. He executed more than three hundred prints after
drawings and paintings by Goltzius, who was
his stepfather, and other artists, both northern
and Italian. This complicated composition
is based on a sketch by Goltzius now in the
Prentenkabinet Universiteit Leiden. In addition to a few subtle lines, some gray wash, and
white heightening to strengthen the scene's
dramatic effect, Goltzius included notations
about the figures, which are borne out in
Matham's print. In his representations of the
four elements, Goltzius eschews a generic personification of water, which was characteristic
of allegorical prints of the period; instead,
he depicts the goddess Thetis, a Nereid and
mother of Achilles, resplendent in the lower
center. She is offset by the personification of
Earth, shown from the back and in shadow,
with his huge vegetal crown.

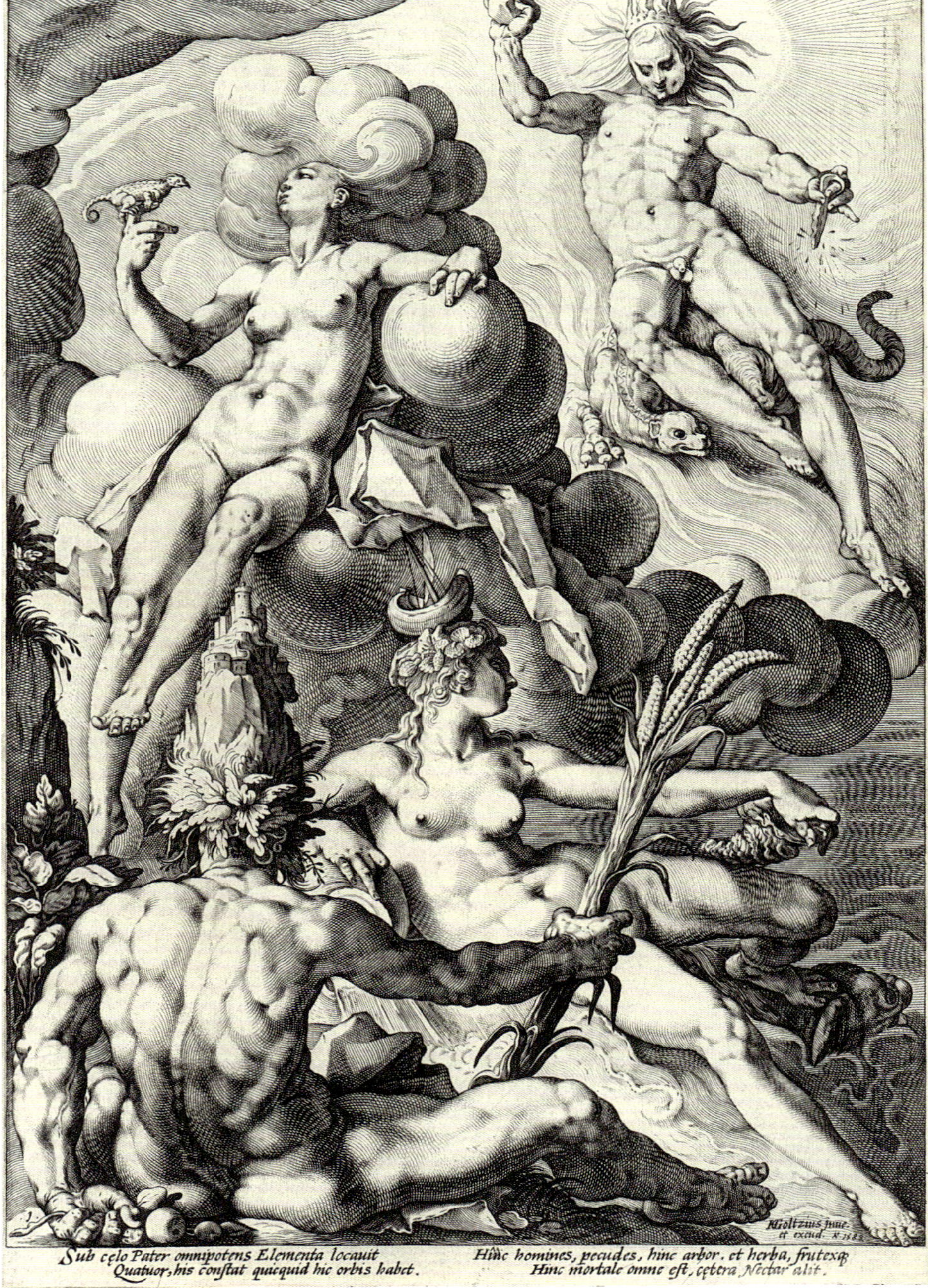

Hendrick Goltzius, Netherlandish
(1558–1617)

The Great Hercules, 1589

Engraving, first state of two, 21⅞ × 15⅞ in.
(55.5 × 40.4 cm)
Harris Brisbane Dick Fund, 1946 (46.140.28)

Watermark: shield with the letter "P" (Piccard 116036)

Collector's mark: Emanuel Levy (Lugt 876)

Provenance: Emanuel Levy (20th century), New York;
Elizabeth B. Levy, Larchmont, N.Y.; [her sale, the
American Art Association, New York, March 29, 1916,
lot 216]; [Holman's Book Shop, Boston]; Department of
Prints purchase, 1946

Goltzius was a student of anatomy. He owned
a collection of plaster écorchés, small sculptures of figures with their skin removed to
show musculature, and attended a dissection in
the anatomical theater in Leiden. An impression of this remarkable and artful engraving
once hung in that anatomical theater, though
it has little to do with scientific realism. In his
signature "bulbous" style, Goltzius shows a
monumental Hercules with every exagger-
ated muscle tensed. His Hercules is a symbol
of Dutch strength; thought to be after the
Hercules in Federico Zuccaro's frescoes for
the Palazzo Farnese in Caprarola, it far sur-
passes the strength and physicality of its Italian
model. The sense of power is echoed in the size
of the engraving, the largest plate known to be
used in this period, and in Goltzius's deftness
with the medium.

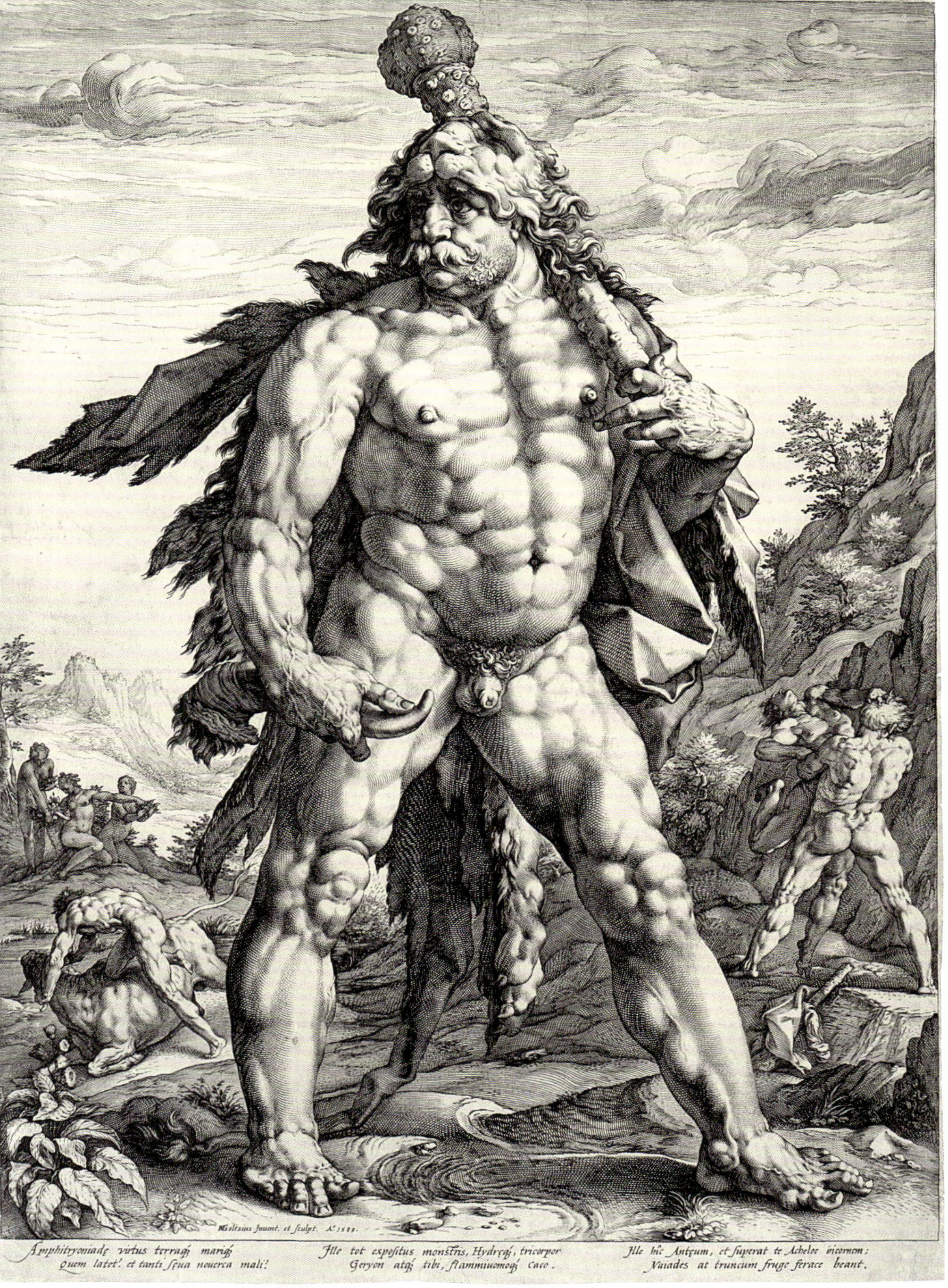

THEORICA ECLIPSIS LVNARIS.

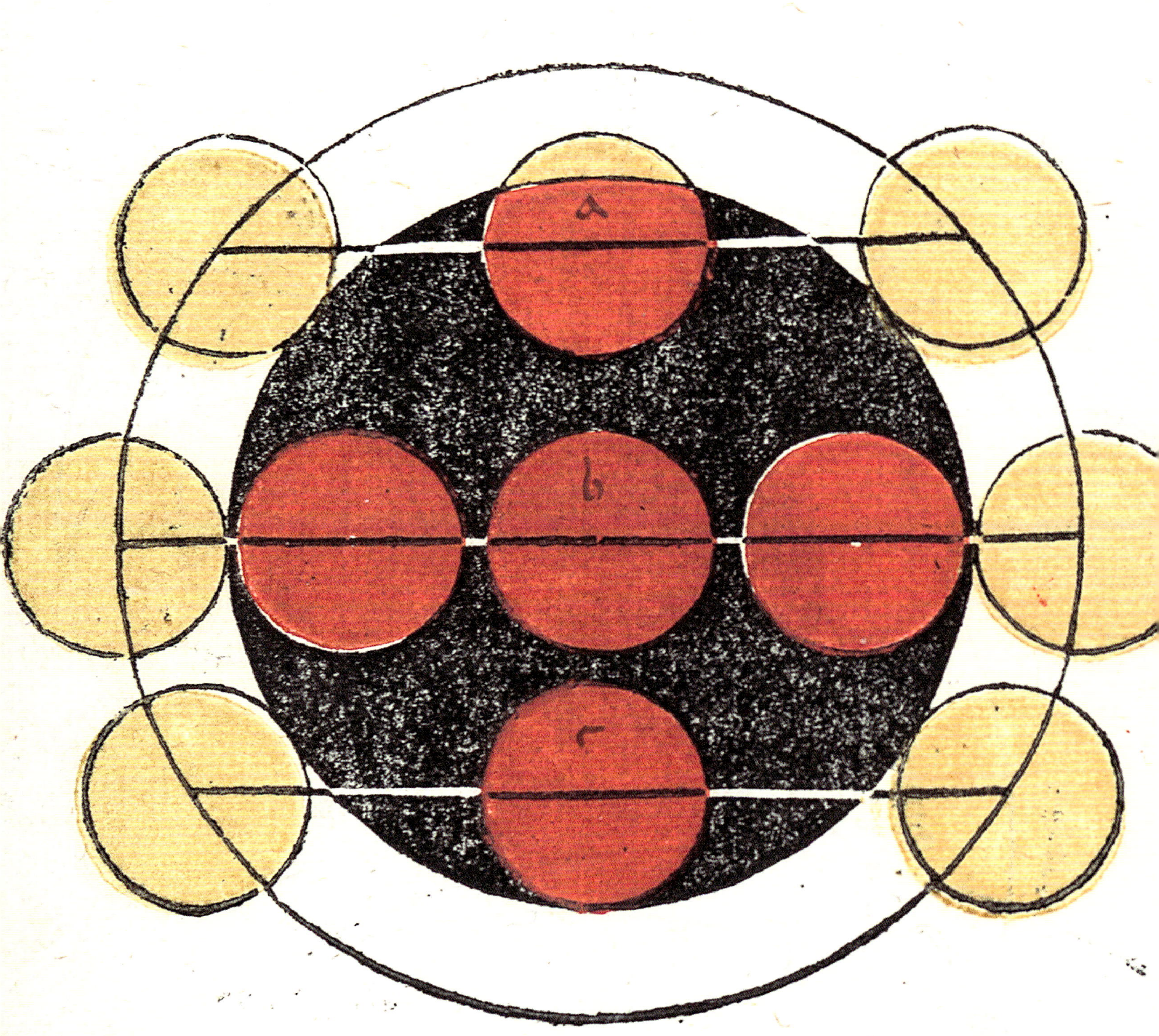

Woodcuts

"NEXT TO A HUMAN BEING the most precious thing in the world was a book,"[1] William Ivins once remarked. Books had riveted him ever since his youth, when he traveled to South America with his father and a group of engineers. Arriving in a new locale, the men would always ask for the addresses of the best bookstores in town because, as they told him, "You can tell more in less time about a community by the kinds of books it owns and reads than in any other known way."[2] From then on, Ivins was drawn to books—and the woodcuts that illustrated them—not only as beautiful physical objects but also as purveyors of knowledge. He considered them "living things with character and a mysterious force which not only transmits thought and emotion of every kind but which actually forces men to action."[3]

Fittingly, Ivins's inaugural exhibition at the Met in 1917 celebrated single-sheet woodcuts and some of the earliest illustrated books, whose texts were accompanied by woodcuts. It was the first large-scale exhibition of its kind in the United States. Carl Zigrosser, then a print dealer at Frederick Keppel & Co., rejoiced at the attention being given to this "rather discredited medium."[4] Fifteenth- and early sixteenth-century woodcuts, often made by anonymous masters and meant for a wide public, had lost their appeal for collectors of prints, Zigrosser suggested, as the taste for more finely made "artistic" etchings flourished in the nineteenth century. Woodcuts had continued to be coveted, however, by book collectors.

Illustrated books and exhibitions featuring them had enjoyed widespread popularity in the mid- to late nineteenth century in Europe and the United States. During that period, book exhibitions most often took place outside of museums: at learned societies, world's fairs, clubs, galleries, and libraries. Nevertheless, in 1851, to coincide with the Great Universal Exposition at the Crystal Palace in London's Hyde Park, Anthony Panizzi, the Keeper of Printed Books at the British Museum Library, organized two concurrent five-month shows that displayed nearly 250 of its early printed books. In 1877 the South Kensington Museum, now the Victoria and Albert Museum, staged a sizable exhibition celebrating the four hundredth anniversary of the first printed book in England, William Caxton's *The Dictes and Notable Wise Sayings of the Philosophers*. Curated by the book printer and biographer William Blades, the exhibition included a staggering number of items—more than 4,700—and was accompanied by an extensive catalogue.

Ivins from the start endeavored to bring illustrated books back into the province of the art museum and to spur a reevaluation of their role, and that of single-sheet woodcuts, in the larger history of printmaking. He had been involved in a small show of printed books, "Revival of the Woodcut," at the Grolier Club in 1914, but mounting an exhibition of Italian Renaissance woodcuts in the galleries of a prestigious public art museum three years later was, as Zigrosser noted, a breakthrough.[5] Although systematic catalogues on the subject predate Ivins's exhibition,[6] he for the first time chronicled the history of the woodcut, explaining its value as a relatively inexpensive medium that could be used for copious reproductions and the dissemination of information. The exhibition included some of the earliest known illustrated books, such as Juan de Torquemada's *Meditationes* (second edition, 1473), Roberto Valturio and Matteo de' Pasti's *De re militari* (first edition, 1472), and Johannes de Sacrobosco's *Sphaera Mundi* (second edition, 1485).[7] The innovative *Sphaera Mundi* (opposite; see cat. 79), printed in Venice by the German publisher Erhard Ratdolt, contains simple astronomical diagrams printed in red and yellow—taking what Ivins called the first steps "toward that development of the printed picture in color with which our bill-boards and our magazines are flooded at the present time."[8] Ivins's comment was an early signal of his recognition of the woodcut's significance both as a means of communication and as a forerunner of contemporary mass media. As Ivins later expressed in his canonical text *Prints and Visual Communication*, the woodcut enabled prints to "pervade the life and thought of western Europe,"[9] by providing a deliberate and exactly repeatable means of conveying information. Perfectly complementing the text it accompanied and serving as its near-equivalent in printed symbols, the woodcut became a catalyst for significant intellectual developments. In a 1937 article about Italian prints and illustrated books, Ivins rhapsodized, "The Italian printed picture was the central aqueduct that gathered together the waters of the artistic and intellectual Renaissance and put them into world circulation."[10]

Previous scholars had been concerned with the technicalities of printing books and with details such as the names of the designer, binder, and printer; Ivins identified the woodcuts contained within as our entrée to the information age. Unlike etching, which developed into a medium of pure aestheticism in the nineteenth century, with print runs limited to ensure fineness of texture, the woodcut had a populist and utilitarian function: to convey information clearly and inexpensively. As Ivins explained, woodcut

> was made for a specific purpose and in response to a definite economic demand. Having, therefore, an immediate and practical raison d'être of a kind lacking to most modern "fine prints". . . they "work," and they were meant to "work," were contrived and executed to fill needs. Open of line and, on occasion, rough of texture as they are, they almost without exception have that essential character which marks every truly functional thing. In great part made by anonymous artists for the pleasure of the anonymous public, these woodcuts are among the most delightful manifestations of "popular art."[11]

Roberto Valturio, Italian (1405–1475)

Illuminated initials and woodcuts attributed to
Matteo de' Pasti, Italian (ca. 1420–after 1467)

De Re Militari (*On the Military Arts*), 1472

Published in Verona by Johannes ex Verona
Harris Brisbane Dick Fund, 1926 (26.71.4)

Collector's marks: British Museum, the Department of
Prints and Drawings (Lugt 305 and variant of Lugt 296)

Provenance: British Museum, London [Bernard Quaritch,
Ltd., London]; Department of Prints purchase, 1926

The woodcuts in this early military treatise,
the first book to be published in Verona, were
printed separately from the text. "They are
hand-stamped in blanks left in the text, for the
Veronese printer had not heard that you can
print a woodblock along with metal type after
this had been done 5 years before in Rome, and
over 10 years before in Bamberg" (Mayor, label
for "Illustrated Books," 1965). Valturio's text
is illustrated with more than eighty woodcuts,
printed in a slightly thinner black ink, that
show weapons, war chariots, siege engines,
cannons, flags, water floats, bridges, and
pontoons, among other devices for warfare.
"These are the first how-to-do-it prints" (ibid.).
Ivins called the volume "the deliberate communication of information and ideas" about the
uses of the machinery of war (Ivins, *Prints and
Visual Communication*, 31).

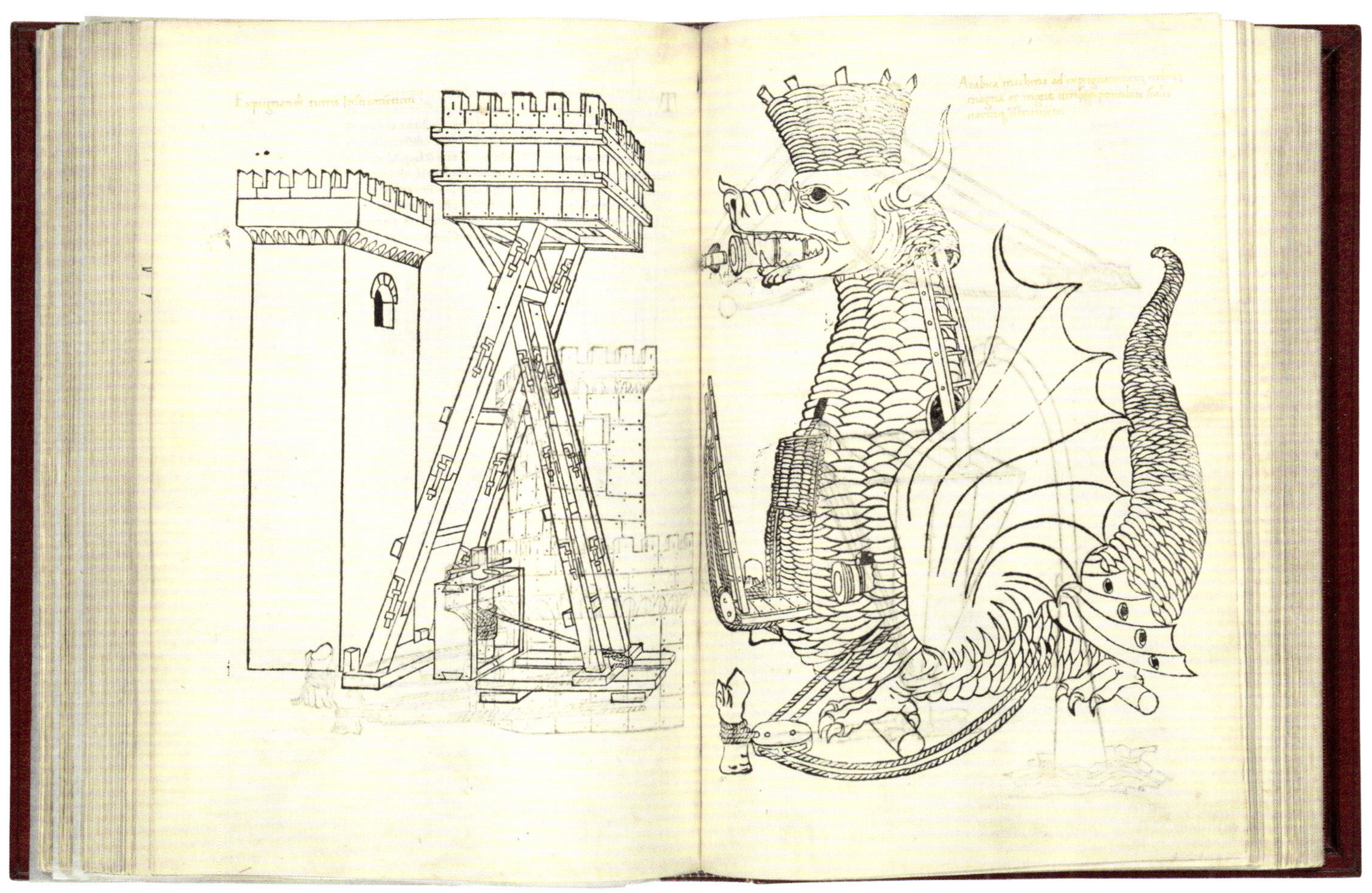

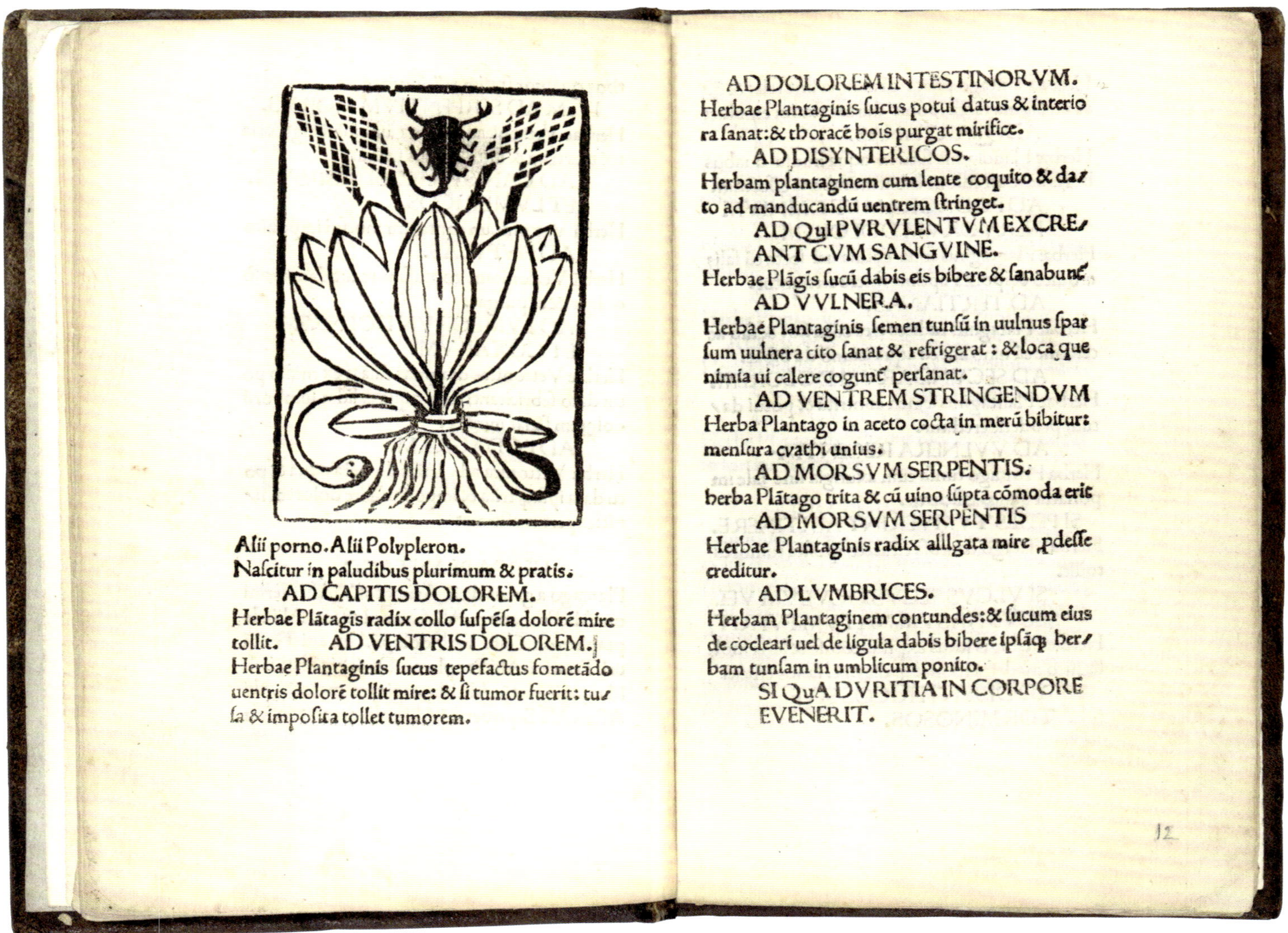

76

Attributed to Pseudo-Apuleius
Platonicus, North African (?) (active 4th
century)

Woodcutter unknown

Herbarium, 1483–84

Published in Rome by Johannes Philippus de Lignamine
The Elisha Whittelsey Collection, The Elisha Whittelsey
Fund, 1944 (44.7.1)

Provenance: [Lathrop Harper (1867–1950), New York];
Department of Prints purchase, 1944

Ivins was fascinated by the seemingly rapid development of herbals like this volume, whose illustrations merely copy a classical manuscript without reference to nature, into books with scientifically accurate renderings. That advancement framed his theory of the role of prints in the dissemination of knowledge during the Renaissance. The Pseudo-Apuleius herbarium is the first printed book on botany to contain illustrations of any kind, though Ivins warned that the "copyist in copying a picture of something that he has not seen is unable to determine whether wiggles in lines are due to nervousness or other incapacity of the original draughtsman or actually represent the characteristics of the object represented" (Ivins, "À Propos of the *Fabrica* of Vesalius," 1943: 578–79).

77

German Almanac, 1484

Published in Augsburg by Hans Schönsperger the Elder
Harris Brisbane Dick Fund, 1926 (26.56.1)

Provenance: [Emil Hirsch (1866–1954), Munich];
Department of Prints purchase, 1926

The woodcuts in this volume, which is likely
Germany's first printed almanac, delighted
Mayor. Examples such as a man warming
himself at the fire and a woman spinning
"illustrate contemporary life with intimate
charm" (Mayor, label for "Illustrated Books,"
1965). Just as later almanacs provided astronomical and meteorological data for a given
year, this early woodcut shows the astrological
signs variously positioned on a human figure,
reflecting the belief of medieval astrologers
that the stars' movements influenced much
on Earth, from the weather and the growth of
crops to children's personalities and the body's
inner workings.

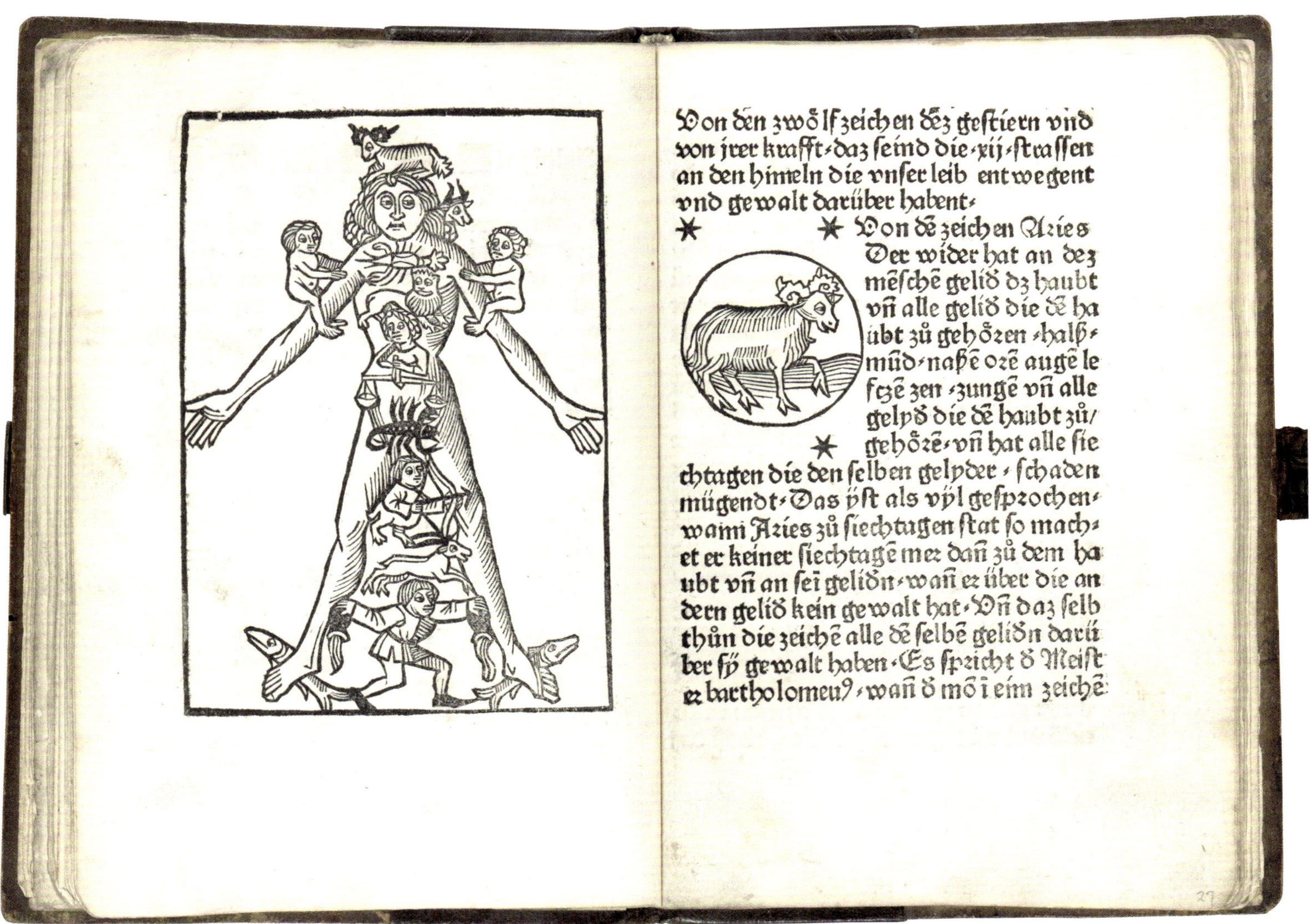

Attributed to Johannes von Cuba, German (died 1503–4)

Frontispiece possibly by Erhard Reuwich, Netherlandish, active in Germany (ca. 1455–ca. 1490); woodcutter unknown

Gart der Gesundheit (*Garden of Health*), 1485

Published in Mainz by Peter Schöffer the Elder
The Elisha Whittelsey Collection, The Elisha Whittelsey Fund, 1944 (44.7.15)

Provenance: [Lathrop Harper (1867–1950), New York]; Department of Prints purchase, 1944

This innovative German botanical, which contains some of the first woodcuts made after the direct observation of nature, helped transform the field. Responding to the serious scientific intentions expressed in the book's introduction, written for the first time in the vernacular rather than in Latin, Ivins wrote: "This is thus the first printed and illustrated account of the results of a trip undertaken for scientific purposes. It is also the first statement that I have met with to the effect that a writer or artist refused to have his book illustrated from hearsay instead of from actual acquaintance with the objects represented. In its funny way it is a milestone in the history of the intellectual development of Western Europe" (Ivins, "What about the *Fabrica* of Vesalius?," 1952: 53–54). The volume was most likely commissioned by the bishop of Mainz, Bernhard von Breydenbach, and published by an apprentice of Johannes Gutenberg. Its woodcuts were copied repeatedly by printers eager to produce botanicals, which were widely sought after in the late fifteenth and early sixteenth centuries.

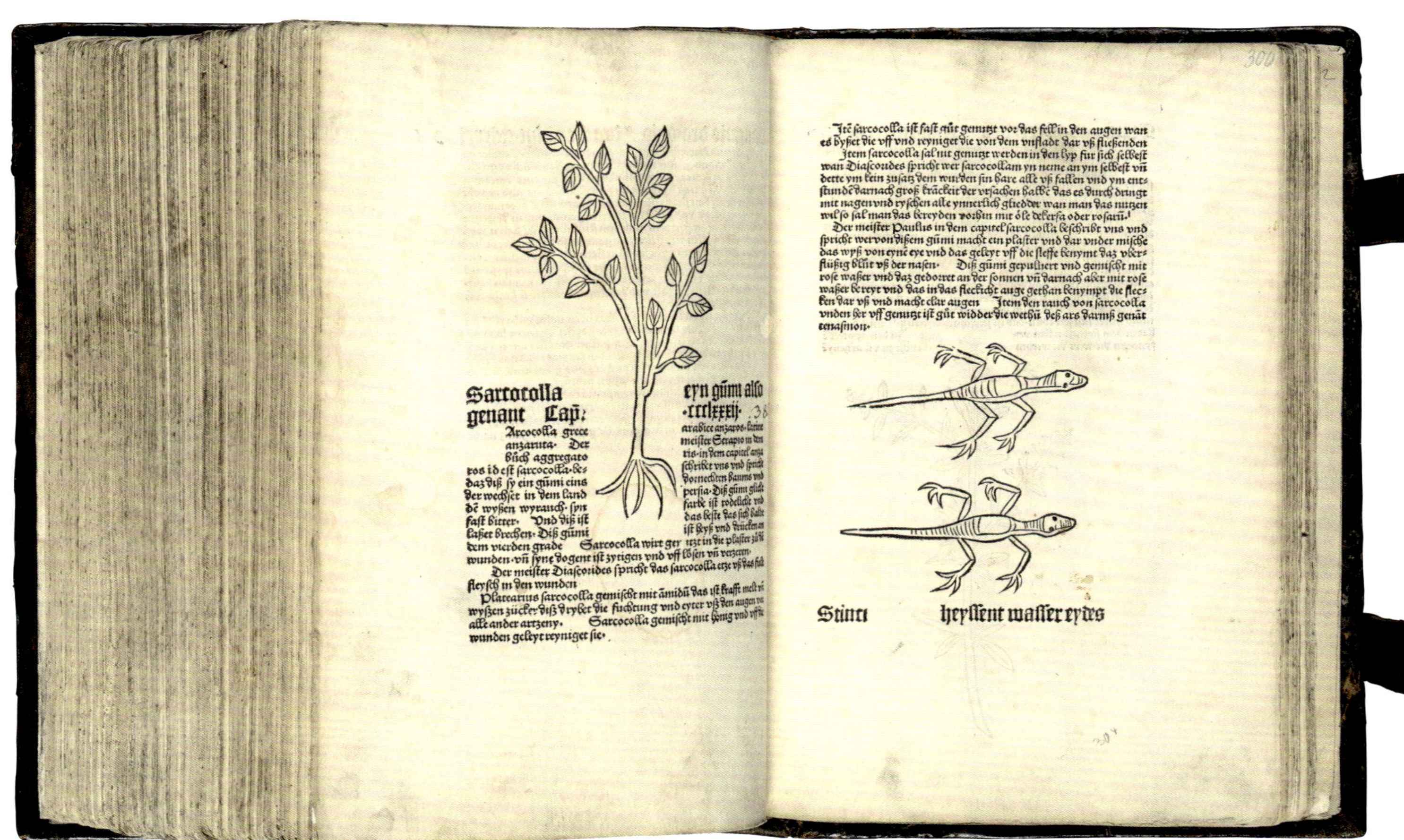

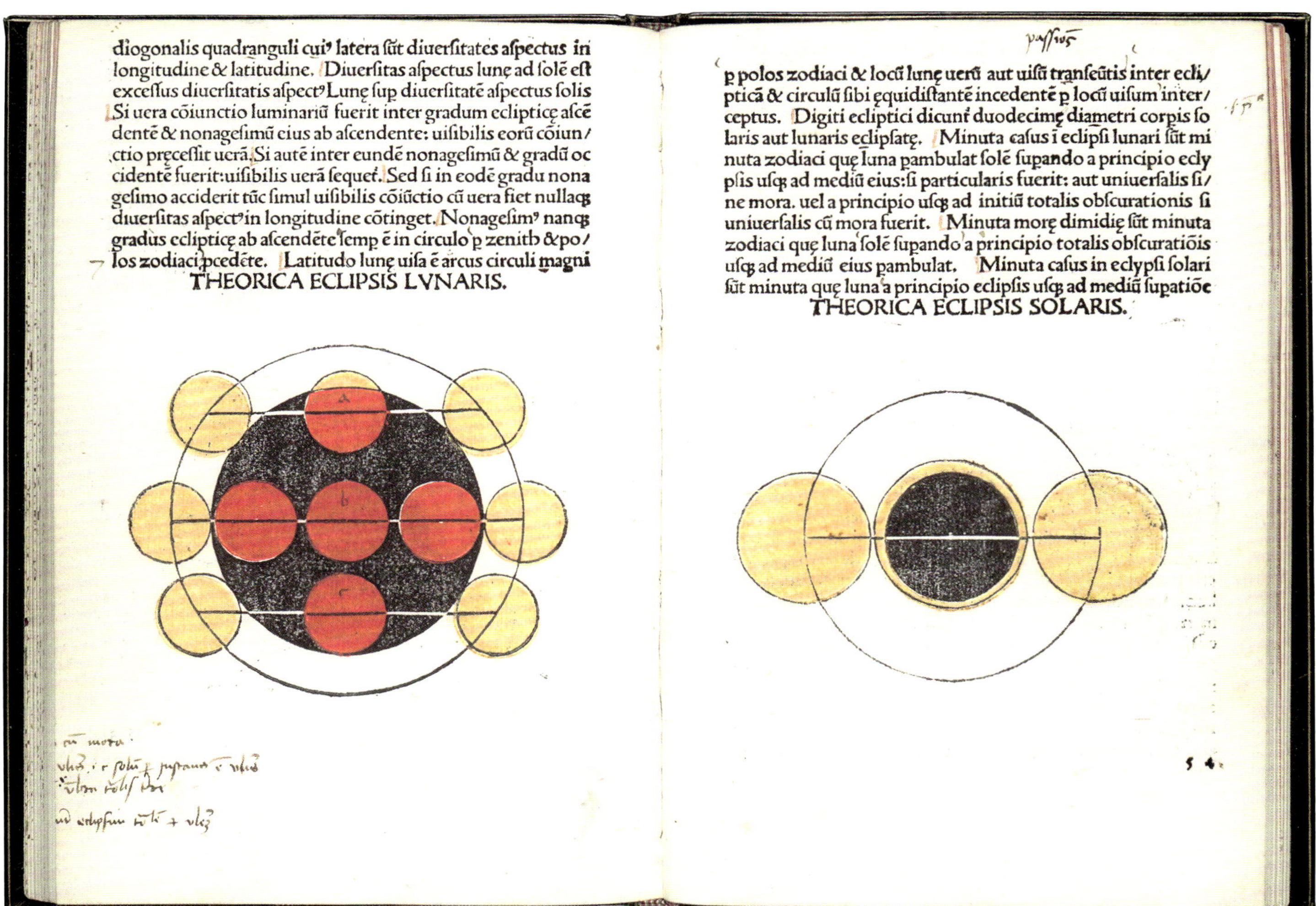

79

Johannes de Sacrobosco (a.k.a. John Holybush), British (?) (active in Paris ca. 1220–ca. 1256), George von Puerbach, Austrian (1423–1461), and Johann Regiomontanus, German (1436–1476)

Woodcutter unknown

Sphaera Mundi (*Sphere of the World*), 1485

Published in Venice by Erhard Ratdolt
Gift of Paul J. Sachs, 1917 (17.45)

Provenance: Paul J. Sachs (1878–1965), Cambridge, Mass.; his gift to the Department of Prints, 1917

The printer Erhard Ratdolt left his native Augsburg in 1475 and by the following year was at work in Venice, where his publications were among the most inventive to come off the press. Ratdolt had particular interests in astronomy and mathematics and in exploiting printed images to elucidate those subjects. This astronomical treatise is a compendium of texts by earlier authors, including the thirteenth-century astronomer and mathematician John Holybush (Sacrobosco in Italian), who spent most of his life teaching at the University of Paris. In these remarkable woodcuts showing lunar and solar eclipses Ratdolt printed in different colors using separate woodblocks. The book is "the earliest recorded example of European color printing. An historical moment of great importance" (Ivins, Gift Papers, Oct. 15, 1917, in the Met's Department of Drawings and Prints Files). In addition to this volume, Ratdolt published an edition of Regiomontanus's *Calendarium* in 1476 and the first printed edition of Euclid's *Elements* in 1482.

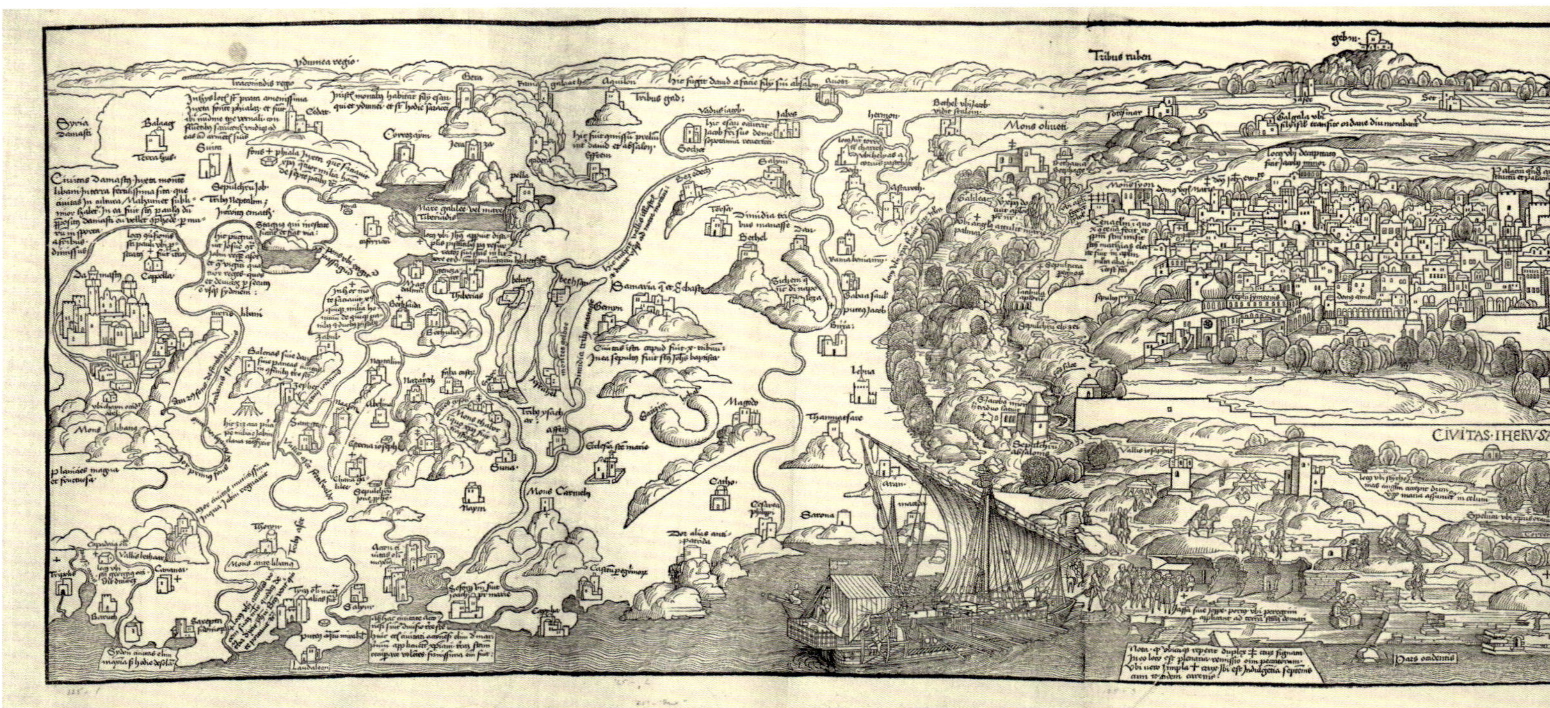

80

Bernhard von Breydenbach, German
(ca. 1440–ca. 1497)

Woodcuts by Erhard Reuwich, Netherlandish,
active in Germany (ca. 1455–ca. 1490)

Peregrinatio in Terram Sanctam
(*Journey to the Holy Land*), 1486

Published in Mainz by Peter Schöffer the Elder
Rogers Fund, 1919 (19.49.3)

Provenance: George Wilbraham (1779–1852), Chester,
England; [Bernard Quaritch, Ltd., London];
Department of Prints purchase, 1919

Breydenbach's account of his pilgrimage from
Venice to the Holy Land revolutionized book
publishing when it appeared in 1486. It was the
first book to contain oversized woodcuts that
fold out, examples of animals seen on the journey, and topographically correct views of cities,
notably a detailed map and view of Jerusalem.
The woodcuts are also the first signed by the
artist, Erhard Reuwich of Utrecht. "Reuwich's
travel book published views of seven cities,
seen from a hilltop or a ship's crow's nest,
as well as studies of Near Eastern costume

and the first exotic alphabet printed in the
West," Mayor wrote (*Prints & People*, 43–44).
"Over some 30 years his book appeared in 13
illustrated editions, his original blocks being
shipped for the printings at Lyons, Speyer,
and Zaragoza. Seven years after their first
appearance, Reuwich's blocks were adapted in
the Nuremberg Chronicle" (ibid.), a groundbreaking encyclopedia of world history (see
cat. 82).

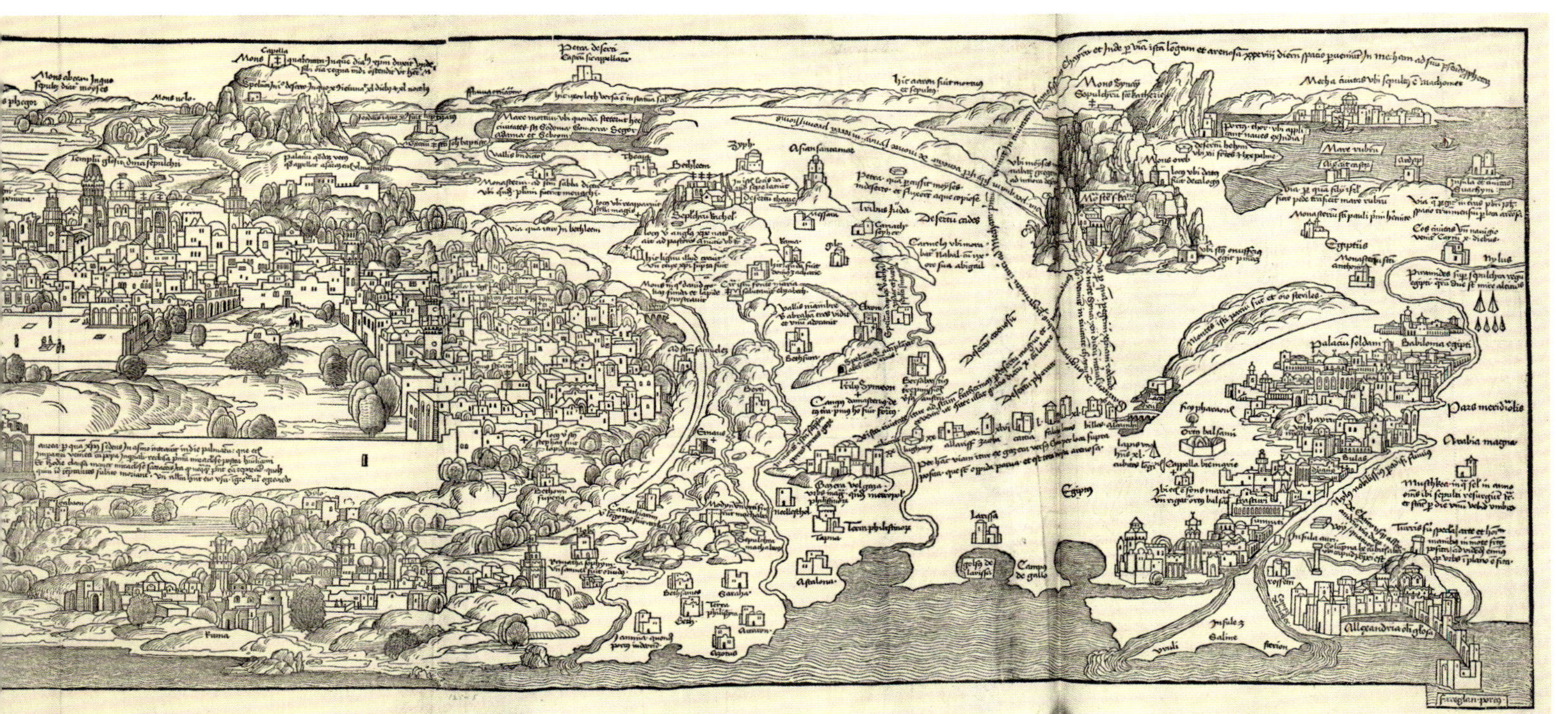

81

Filippo Calandri, Italian (active late 15th century)

Woodcutter unknown

De Aritmetica (*Arithmetic*), 1491

Published in Florence by Lorenzo Morgiani and Johannes Petri
Rogers Fund, 1919 (19.24)

Provenance: Richard Bright (1789–1858), London; [Bernard Quaritch, Ltd., London]; Department of Prints purchase, 1919

The first illustrated book on mathematics written in Italian rather than Latin, this book is also notable for two other firsts. It was the first book to present the modern form of long division and the first to depict the hand signs for numbers, which were used for centuries to signal bids across noisy auctions and exchanges. A small volume with great commercial utility, it could fit into the pocket of one of the many merchants and craftsmen who prospered in Florence during the 1490s.

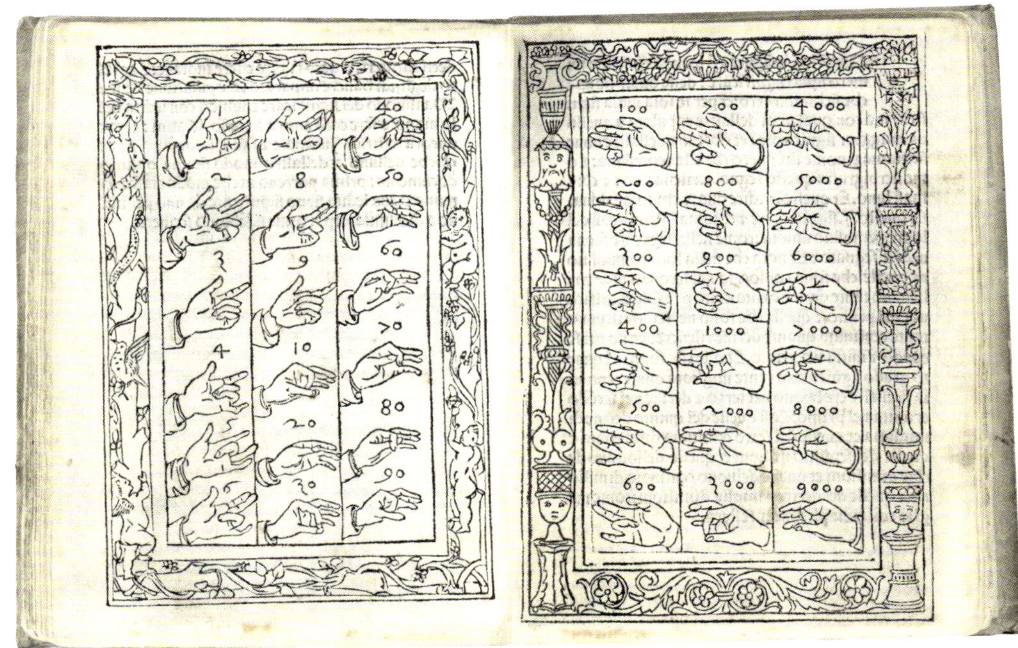

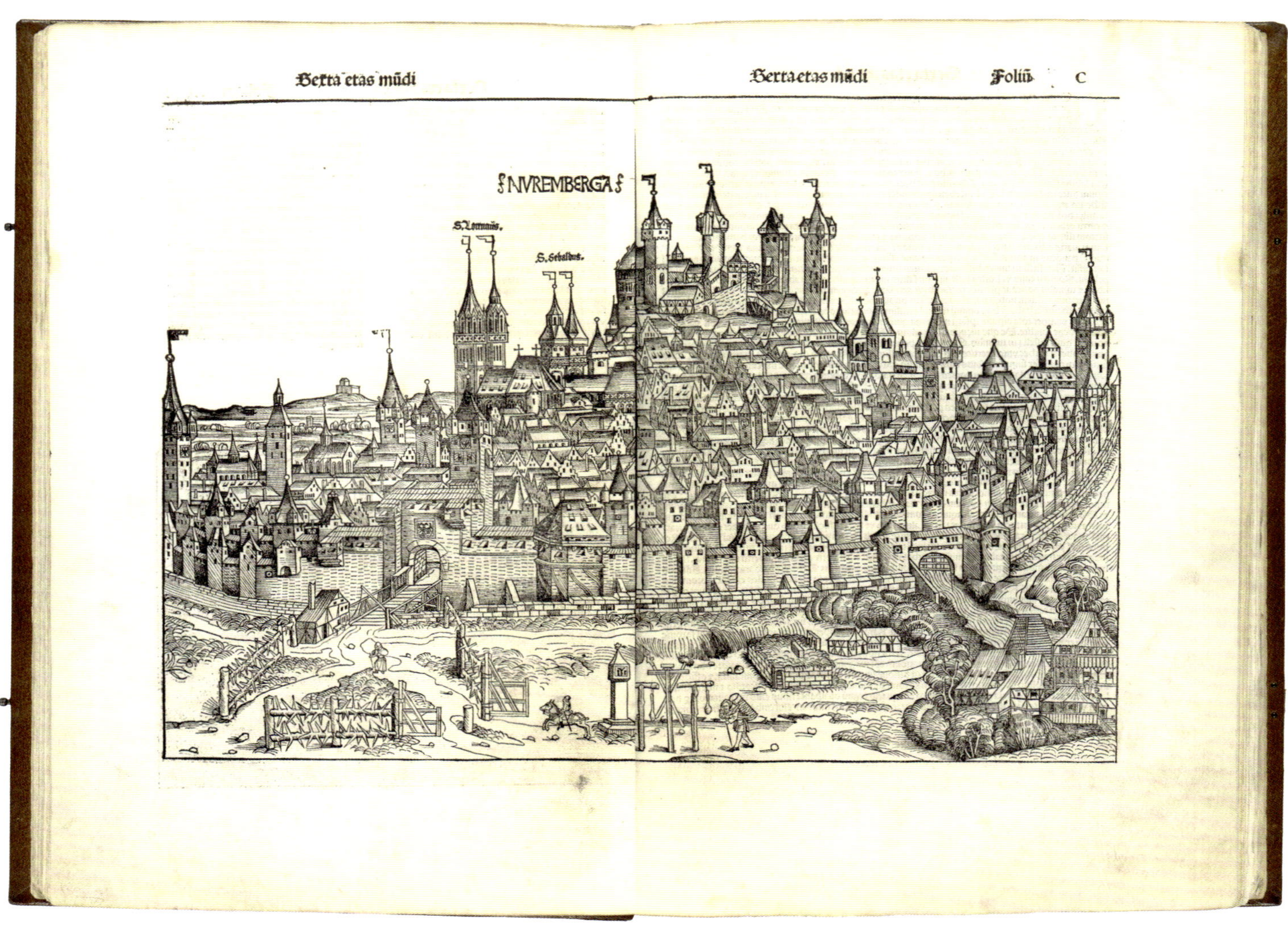

82

Woodcuts by Wilhelm Pleydenwurff, German
(ca. 1460–1494), and Michael Wolgemut,
German (1434–1519)

Liber Chronicarum (*Nuremberg Chronicle*), 1493

Published in Nuremberg by Anton Koberger
Rogers Fund, transferred from the Library (21.36.145)

Provenance: Dominican Convent, Augsburg; Franciscan
Monastery of St. Anna, Munich; F. Stiglmeier,
Straubing, Germany (1850); Museum Accession,
transferred from the Library to the Department of
Prints, 1921

Compiled by the physician, humanist, and
cartographer Hartmann Schedel, this book
describes in text and images the world from
its creation until Schedel's own late medieval
time. The most profusely illustrated book of
the fifteenth century, "[this] pioneer encyclopedia of world history and geography
assembles mythical scenes, foreign peoples,
and famous cities in 1809 illustrations printed
from 645 blocks. The illustrators copied more
or less truthful views of half a dozen foreign
cities and made use of unpublished drawings of some 20 Germanic towns, but had to
represent many places by a stock cut of roofs
inside a wall, repeated up to 11 times to indicate that 'here you can read a city.' The artists
were Michael Wolgemut, his more talented
stepson, Wilhelm Pleydenwurff, and possibly
their teen-age apprentice Albrecht Dürer, who
worked in their shop from 1486 to 89" (Mayor,
Prints & People, 44).

83

Fasciculo di Medicina (Pamphlet on Medicine),
1494

Published in Venice by Giovanni and Gregorio
de' Gregori
Harris Brisbane Dick Fund, 1938 (38.52)

Provenance: [Gabriel Wells, New York]; Department
of Prints purchase, 1938

Once associated with the obscure author
Johannes de Ketham, the *Fasciculo* is a compilation of ancient and medieval medical knowledge. This opening shows *The Anatomy Lesson*,
added in the second edition, which serves
as a frontispiece to an anatomical treatise
by Mondino de' Liuzzi (active circa 1316). It
depicts a traditional operating theater, where
the surgeon-barber conducts the dissection
while the physician sits at a remove from the
menial act; stenciled colors accentuate the
bishop's throne where he sits and the cloaks
and caps characteristic of fifteenth-century students. The division of labor and the problems
caused by separating theory from practice were
about to be transformed by Andreas Vesalius's
1543 *De humani corporis fabrica* (see cat. 93).

Ivins remarked that, looking at this woodcut,
"one has the feeling of being on a magic car-
pet of some kind that takes one hurtling back
across the ages through the amazing histories
of education, medicine, philosophy, law, and
theology, from the Venice that Dürer knew
to the time of the Platonic Academy. It would
hardly be overstating the mark to say that if
one had to pick a single work of art from which
to work backward across the general history
of thought and intellectual achievement for
the two thousand years preceding it, one could
make no better choice than this; for its every
detail raises a series of questions pregnant in
the development of civilization" (Ivins, "The
Ketham of 1493," 1939: 47).

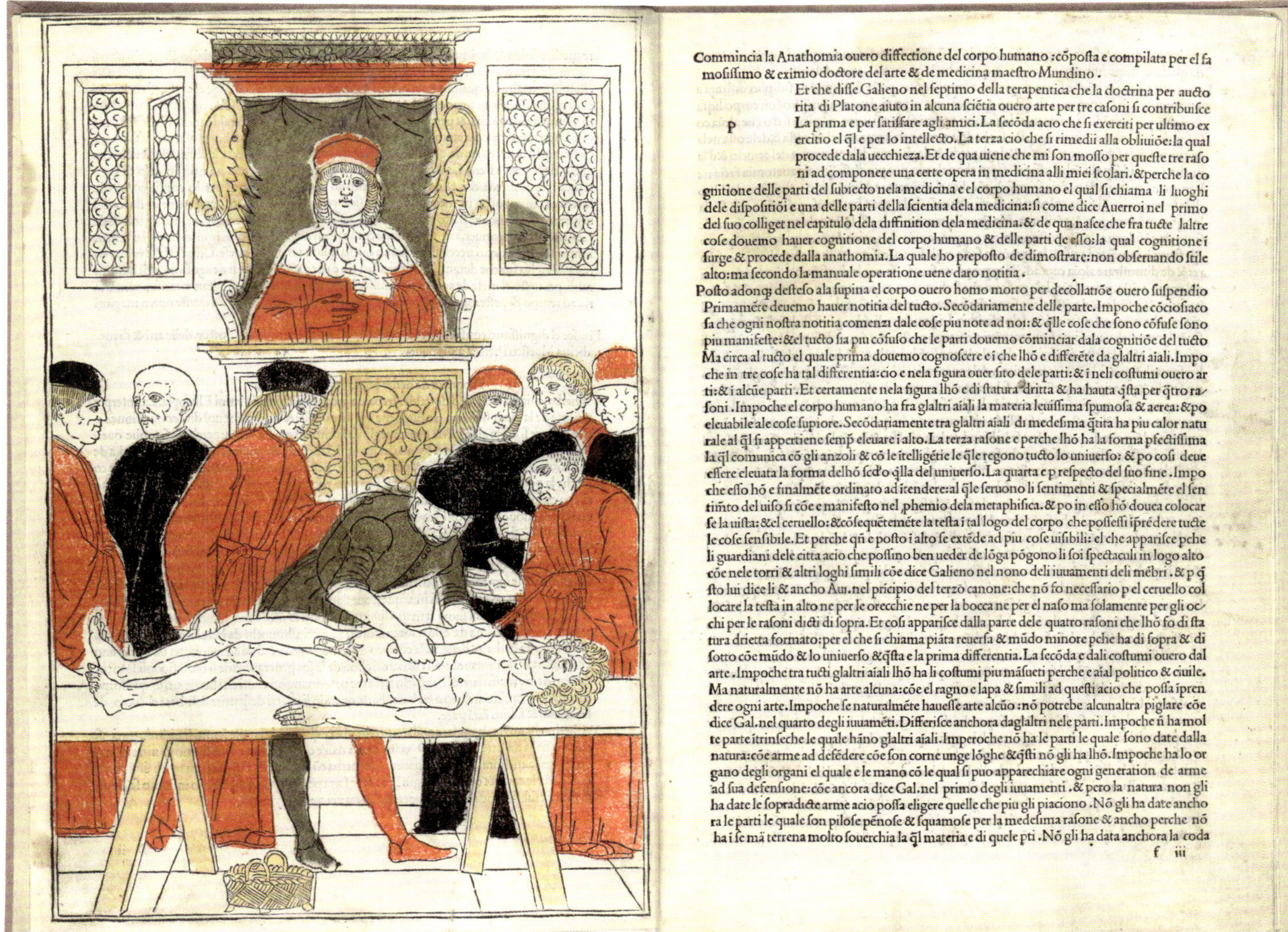

Marcus Pollio Vitruvius, Roman
(active late 1st century B.C.)

Woodcuts and annotations by Fra Giovanni
Giocondo da Verona, Italian (1433–1515)

De Architectura (*On Architecture*), 1511

Published in Venice by Giovanni Taccuino
Bequest of W. Gedney Beatty, 1941 (41.100.325)

Provenance: W. Gedney Beatty (1869–1941), New York;
his bequest to the Department of Prints, 1941

The profusion of Renaissance books on architecture and the impact they had on the study, design, and proliferation of ancient forms fascinated Ivins, who wrote extensively on the dissemination of knowledge through early illustrated books. These books combined the architectural forms of surviving classical monuments with the ancient text of Vitruvius and theoretical writing and illustrations by contemporary architects like Sebastiano Serlio, Andrea Palladio, and Jacopo Barozzi da Vignola. "The result was the creation of an academic grammar and vocabulary of forms which for centuries has dominated the architecture of Italy, France, England, and this country. Perhaps no other so small a group of texts and pictures has had a greater or more concrete effect upon the arts and cultures of the western European peoples" (Ivins, "Renaissance Books on Architecture," 1942: 152).

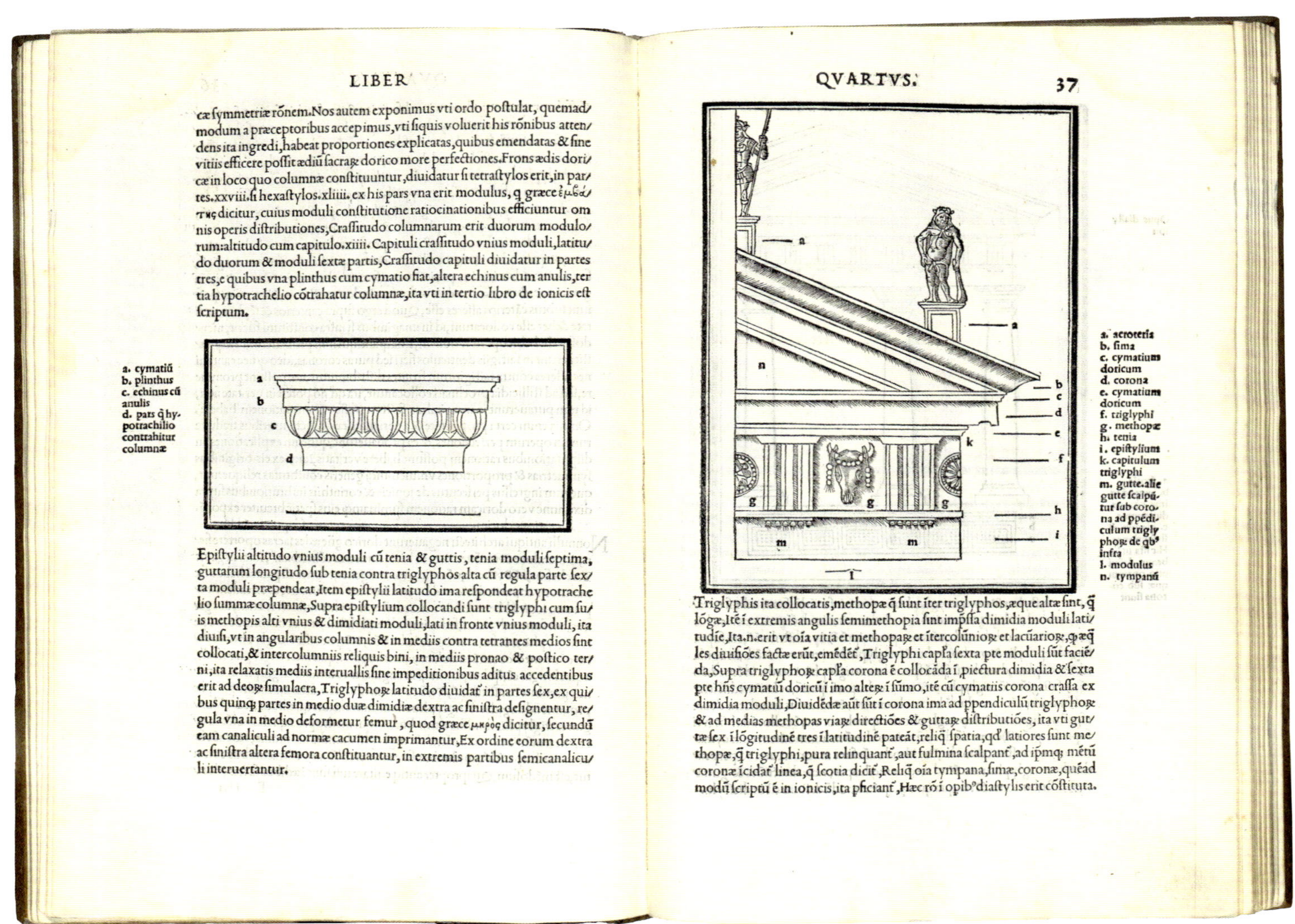

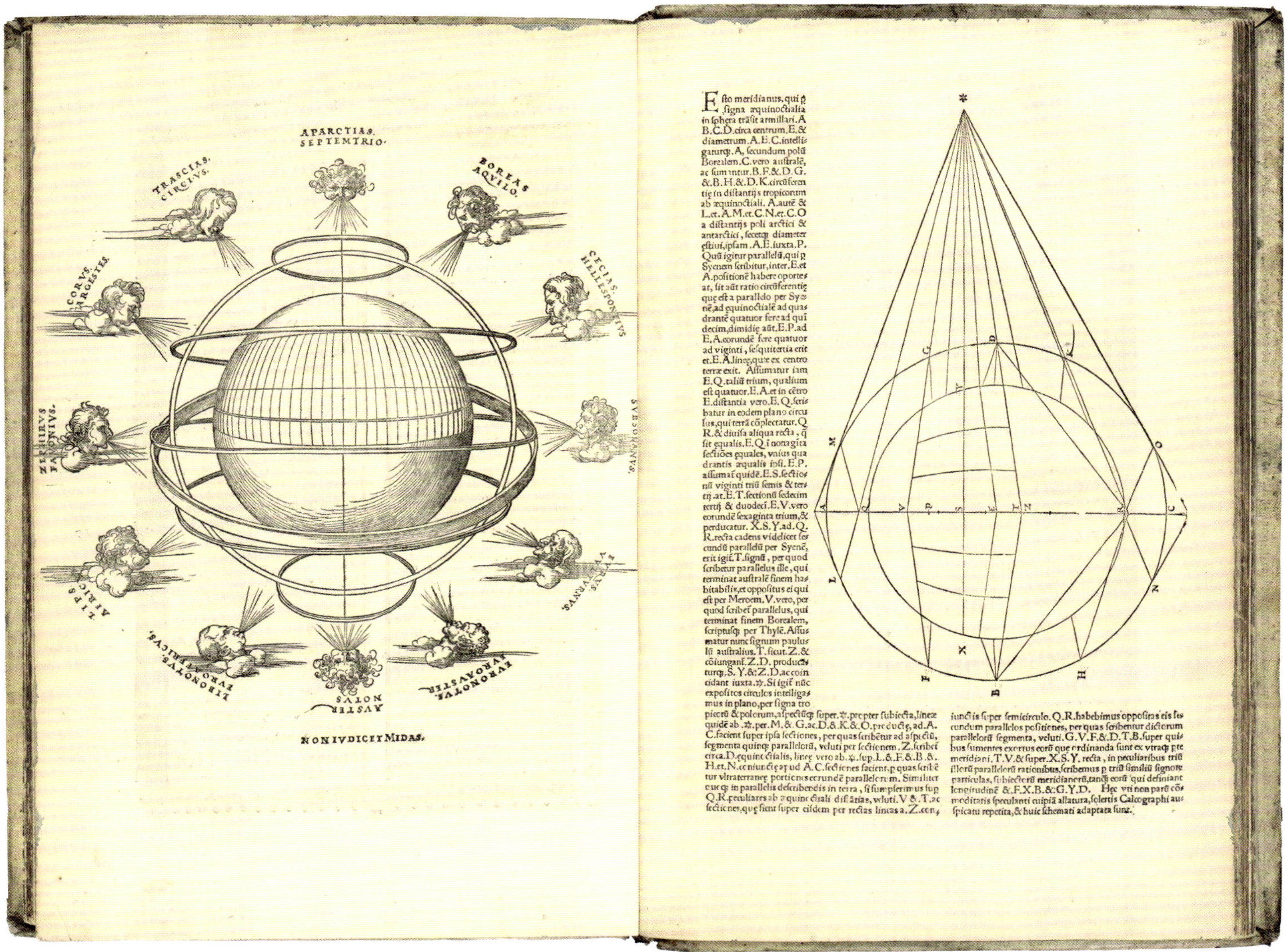

85

Claudius Ptolemaeus, Greek
(A.D. 2nd century)

Woodcuts by Albrecht Dürer, German (1471–
1528), and unknown woodcutter, some works
after Daniel Hopfer, German (1471–1536)

Geographiacae Enarrationis Libri Octo
(*Eight Books on Geographical Exposition*), 1525

Edited and translated by Willibald Pirckheimer, German
(1470–1530)
Published in Strasbourg by Johannes Grüninger
Rogers Fund, 1920 (20.83)

Provenance: Library of Count of Salm-Krautheim, most
likely Joseph zu Salm-Reifferscheidt-Dyck (1773–1861),
Germany; [P. D. Colnaghi & Co., London]; Department
of Prints purchase, 1920

Dürer created the woodcut at left for a Latin
translation of Ptolemy's *Geography* by his closest friend, the humanist Willibald Pirckheimer.
Ptolemy's book investigates the method of
mapping the inhabited regions of Earth, which
Dürer's emphatic but limited parallel lines and
grid give dimension. Earth hovers within the
armillary sphere, which, lacking a stand, looks
less like a scientific instrument than like a
floating framework for the schematized world.
Despite the complexity of Ptolemy's text about
a so-called third projection, the woodcut's simple and clear rendition of the armillary sphere
is extremely legible.

Woodcuts by Hans Weiditz the Younger,
German (1500–ca. 1536)

Herbarum Vivae Eicones
(*Living Pictures of Plants*), 1530

Published in Strasbourg by Johann Schott
Gift of Mortimer L. Schiff, 1918 (18.57.6)

Provenance: King George III of Great Britain and Ireland
(1738–1820); Thomas Kerrich (1748–1828), Cambridge;
Betram Fulke Hartshorne (1844–1921), Oxfordshire;
Charles Fairfax Murray (1849–1919), London; [his sale,
Christie, Manson & Woods, London, Dec. 10–12, 1917,
lot 210]; [Bernard Quaritch, Ltd., London]; Mortimer L.
Schiff (1877–1931), New York; his gift to the Department
of Prints, 1918

Brunfels's text relies on medieval predecessors, but Weiditz's woodcuts, which revolutionized the field of botany, are drawn from the direct observation of nature, as is evident in their attention to detail and the display of each individual plant in all of its particularities. These intricate depictions upended previous botanicals, even Schöffer's 1485 *Gart der Gesundheit* (see cat. 78), whose woodcuts are more schematic and generalized. Ivins observed: "The history of botanical illustration when coupled with the history of the processes of representation shows how men's thinking is limited by their techniques of picture making—Oscar Wilde's witty paradox that nature copies art becomes basically true and of the most profound import. Until Hans Weiditz illustrated Brunfels Herbal of 1530 there was no cheap and easily communicable accurate pictures of flowers and plants. The innovation was so startling that Brunfels has been called 'the restorer of the science [of botany] in Europe'—for those who used his book gave him the credit that belonged to another man" (Ivins, "Plants, Patterns, and Knowledge," 1933: 141).

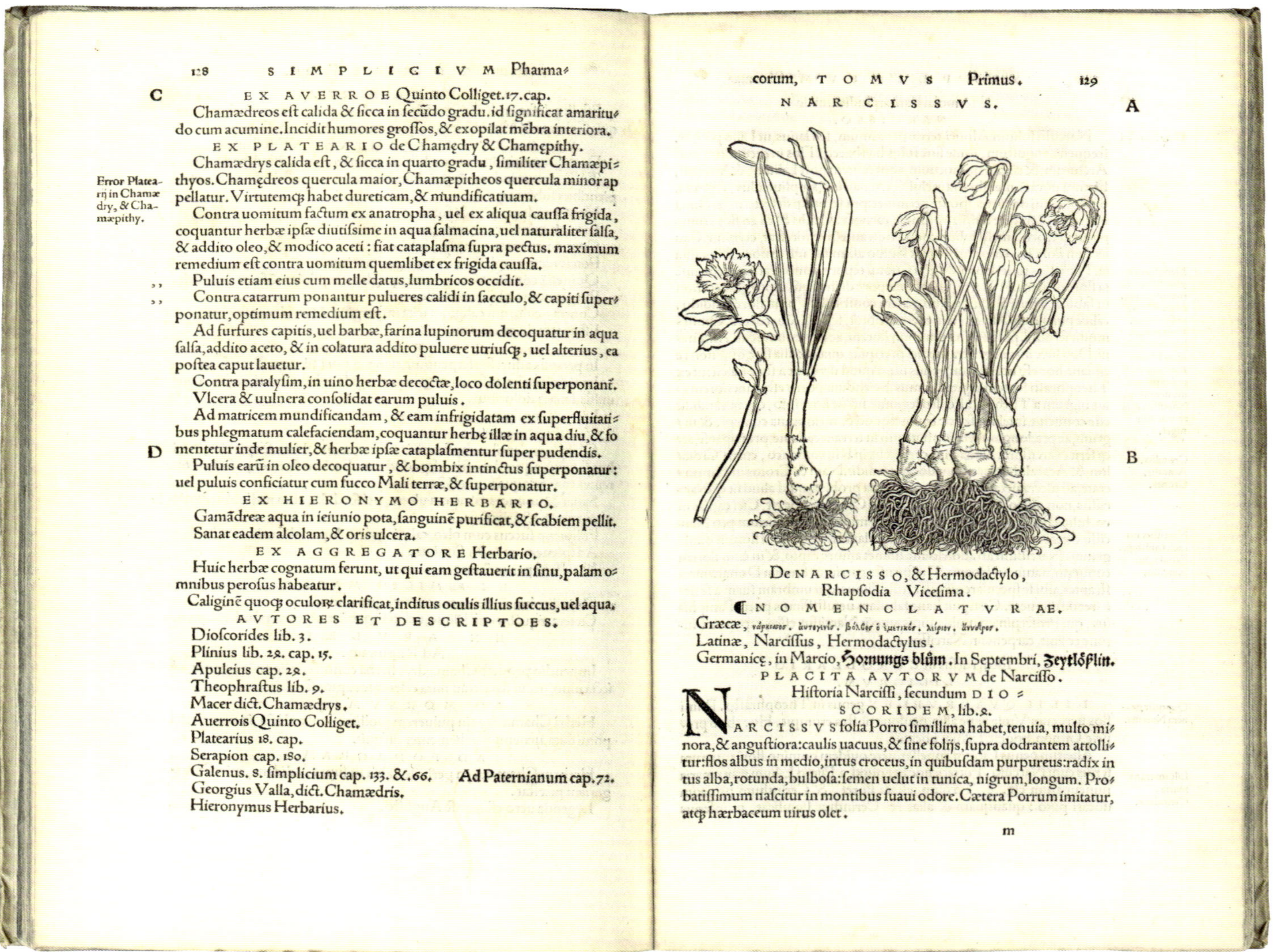

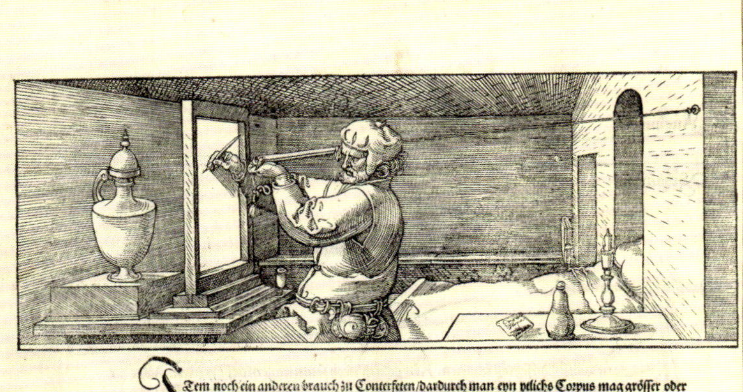

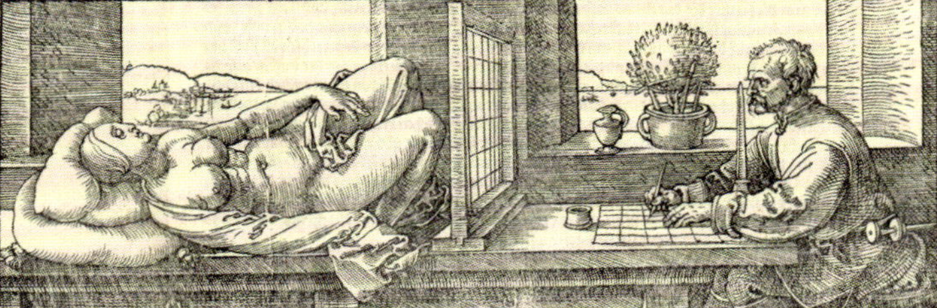

87

Albrecht Dürer, German (1471–1528)

Die Befestigungslehre (*Treatise on Fortifications*), 1527

Die Proportionslehre (*Treatise on Proportion*), books 1 and 2 of 4, 1528

Underweysung der Messung (*Instruction on Measurement*), 1538

All three published in Nuremberg by Hieronymus Andreae
Gift of Felix M. Warburg, 1918 (18.58.3)

Provenance: Charles Fairfax Murray (1849–1919), London; [his sale, Christie, Manson & Woods, London, Dec. 10–12, 1917, lot 161]; Felix Mortiz Warburg (1871–1937); his gift to the Department of Prints, 1918

This volume combines Dürer's treatise on fortifications, two of his four books concerned with human proportion, and a revised edition of his 1525 manual of geometric theory for students, which includes the first scientific treatment of perspective by a Northern European artist. Dürer describes his theory of linear perspective and, in his woodcuts, gives instructions for making mechanical drawing aids to help the artist depict objects and figures—like this resplendent woman—with correct foreshortening. Dürer's book on perspective intrigued Ivins, who admitted that he almost obsessively "pursued . . . the notion that the most important thing that happened during the Renaissance was the emergence of the ideas that led to the rationalization of sight" (Ivins, *On the Rationalization of Sight*, 7).

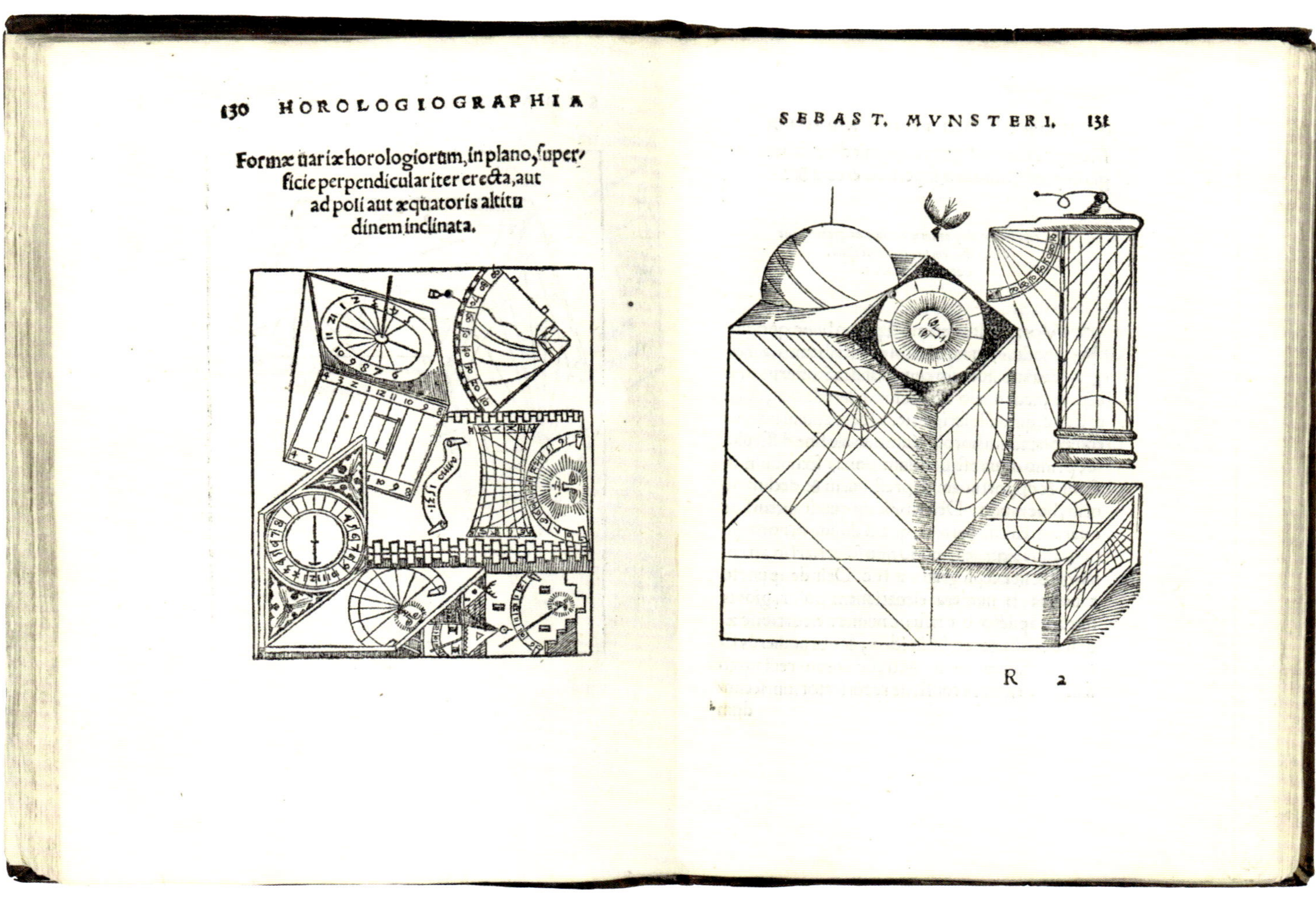

88

Sebastian Münster, German (1488–1552)

Woodcuts by Hans Holbein the Younger,
German (1497/98–1543)

Horologiographia (*Sundials*), 1533

Published in Basel by Heinrich Petri
Harris Brisbane Dick Fund, 1934 (34.85)

Provenance: George Shirley (died 1622),
Northamptonshire, England; Washington Sewallis
Shirley, 9th Earl of Ferrers (1822–1859), England;
[William Robinson, London]; Department of Prints
purchase, 1934

Münster, a German cartographer, cosmog-
rapher, and Hebrew scholar, published three
books on the design and use of sundials. This
genre became popular after Dürer's pioneering
Underweysung der Messung (*Instruction on Measurement*; 1525), which contained the first illustrated directions for constructing a sundial.
Münster's ideas were not revolutionary, and he
often combined classical knowledge with his
own experiments; his great accomplishment
was integrating and organizing information,
marrying it with images, and publishing it
widely for a broad audience. The woodcuts in
this volume are by Holbein, who often worked
with astronomers illustrating and sometimes
designing scientific instruments. Some of his
woodcuts transmit practical knowledge about
how to construct and use the sundials, while
others were intended as models but were too
imprecise to use.

Jean Pélerin (called Viator), French
(ca. 1435/40–1524)

Woodcutter unknown, after woodcuts in
Pélerin's 1505 French edition of *De artificiali
perspectiva*

Von der Kunst Perspectiva
(*On the Art of Perspective*), 1540

Published in Nuremberg by Albrecht Glockendon
Purchase, Jacob H. Schiff Bequest, 1922 (22.66.4)

Provenance: Charles Fairfax Murray (1849–1919),
London; [his sale, Christie, Manson & Woods, London,
Dec. 10–12, 1917, lot 335]; [Bernard Quaritch, Ltd.,
London]; Department of Prints purchase, 1922

This remarkable book comes from the collection of the English connoisseur, painter, and art dealer Charles Fairfax Murray. Initially a collector of works by the Pre-Raphaelite painters with whom he collaborated, Murray turned to early printed books and illuminated manuscripts after retiring in 1903. Ivins avidly sought books from Murray's collection and had acquired nearly twenty by 1922. Ivins noted in his book on perspective the following about this first book on the subject: "To anyone who is familiar with fifteenth-century and early sixteenth-century pictures, and especially with the book illustration of that time, the first sight of a copy of the *De artificiali perspectiva*, in either the original Toul edition of 1505 or [this] Nuremberg piracy, comes with a sort of a shock. The many pictures of known buildings with which Viator exemplified his perspective method are so clear, so reasonable, so just, that they are wholly out of tune with anything that had been done before them or that was done for a long time afterwards. Such a sudden step across the centuries into a completely modern system of pictorial organization and point of view can hardly have happened on any other occasion" (Ivins, *On the Rationalization of Sight*, 30).

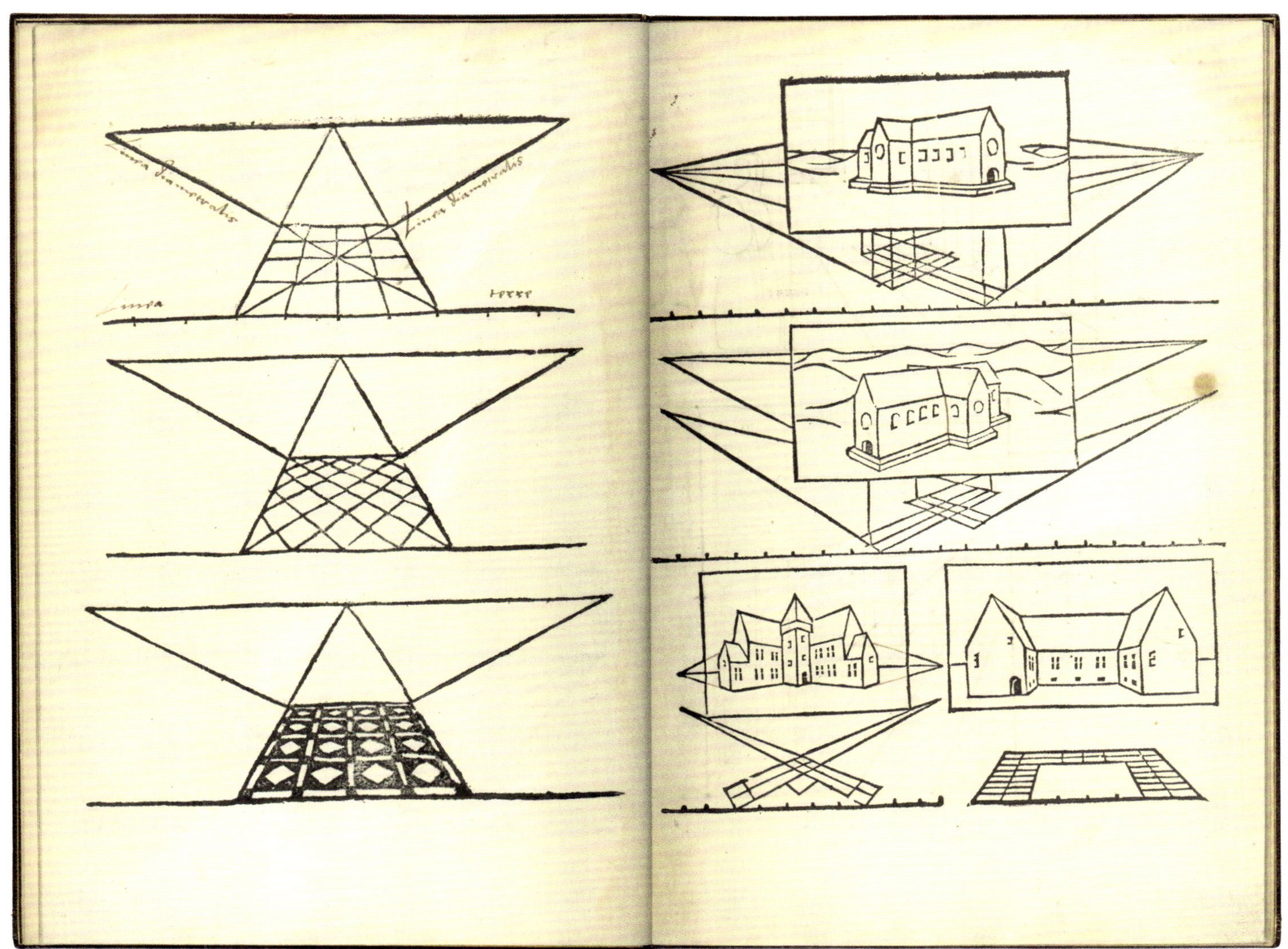

Hippocrates, Greek (460–370 B.C.),
Galen, Greek (130–200), and Oribasius,
Greek (ca. 320–403)

Woodcutter unknown, many works
probably after Francesco Salviati (1510–1563)
or Francesco Primaticcio (1504–1570)

Chirurgia (*Surgery*), 1544

Translated into Latin by Guido Guidi, Italian
(1509–1569)
Published in Paris by Pierre Gaultier
Harris Brisbane Dick Fund, 1947 (47.21)

Provenance: [Herbert Reichner, New York]; Department
of Prints purchase, 1947

Guidi's *Chirurgia* is derived from a tenth-
century Byzantine manuscript of a work by
Hippocrates, Galen, and Oribasius about
surgical procedures for fractures and disloca-
tions. In 1542 Guidi presented a copy of that
manuscript, along with his own illustrated
Latin translation, to Francis I of France, for
whom he served as a court physician until the
king's death in 1547. The authorship of the
illustrations for Guidi's manuscript, which
are preserved in the Bibliothèque Nationale
de France, has long been the subject of debate.
Whether or not they are after drawings by

Salviati or Primaticcio, Mayor considered the
woodcuts for this printed edition "the greatest
series of woodcuts by any of the Italians who
brought the Renaissance to France" (Mayor,
label for "Recent Accessions," 1948). Gaultier
printed this text at the Paris home of the artist
and writer Benvenuto Cellini, where Guidi also
resided when he was in that city.

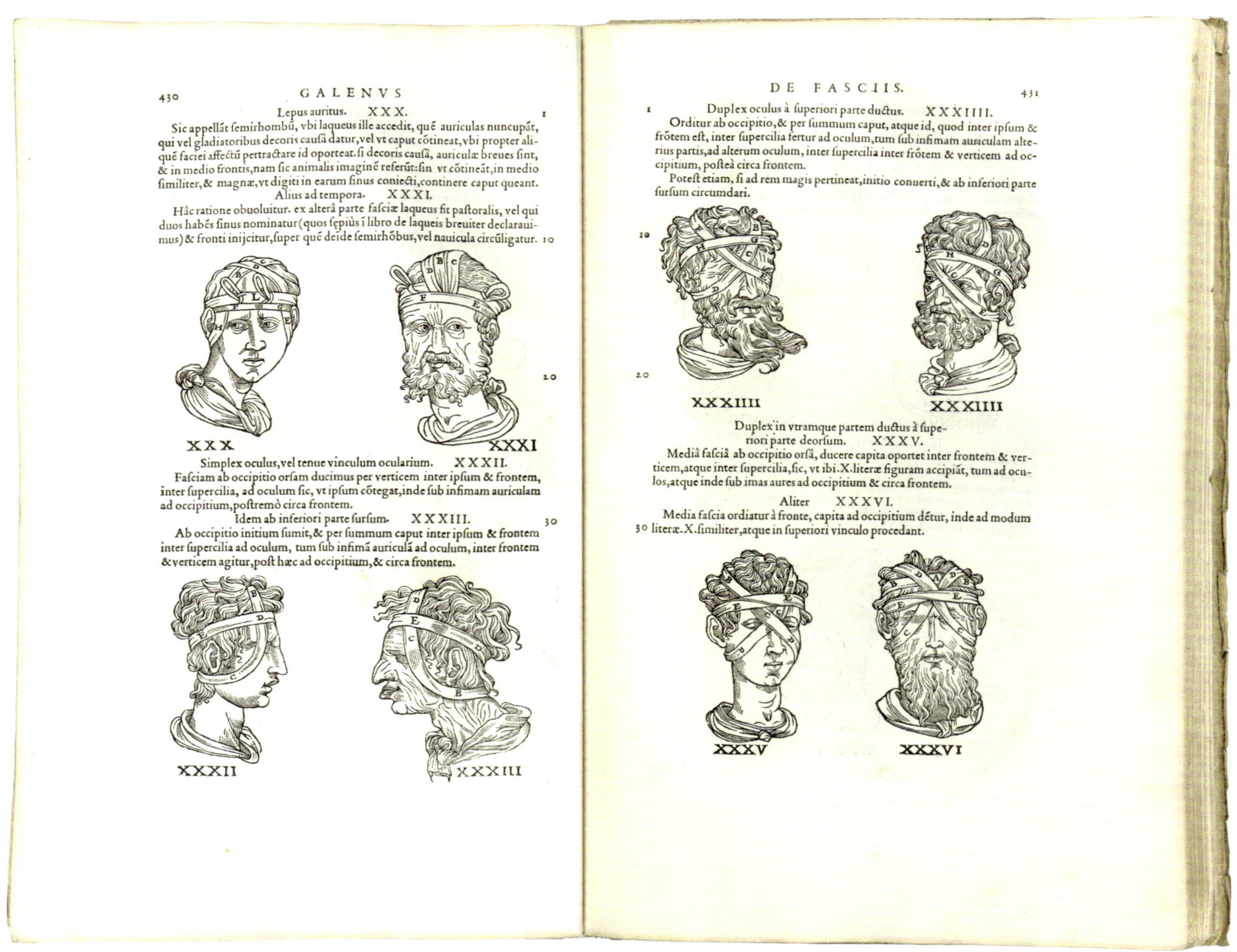

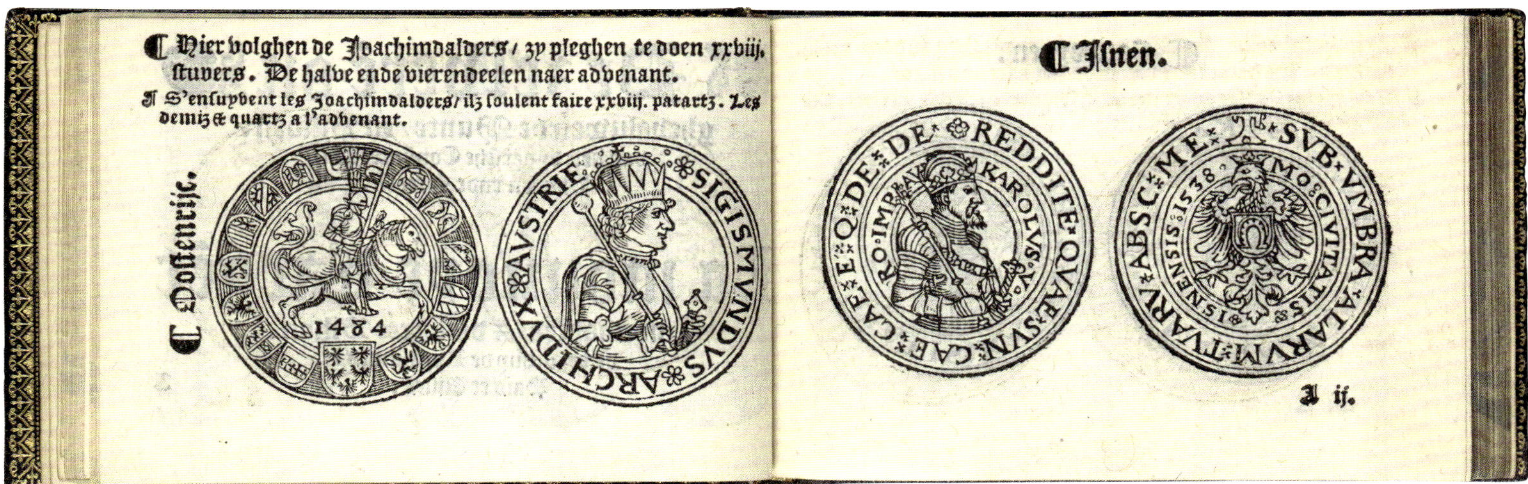

91

Les Monnoyes d'Or & d'Argent
(*Gold and Silver Coins*), 1544

Published in Ghent by Josse Lambert
Harris Brisbane Dick Fund, 1932 (32.94.1)

Provenance: [B. Galanti, Paris]; Department of Prints
purchase, 1932

The Ghent printer Josse Lambert published
both religious and secular books. This pocket-
sized book, meant to be readily referenced
by a merchant or tradesman, shows the form
and details of many different types of currency. Mayor noted that the nearby port city
of Antwerp, where "South American gold and
silver changed the base of Europe's economy
from land to cash, . . . became the first great
international money market. Money chang-
ers protected themselves against counterfeits
by pocketing booklets with woodcuts of the
world's coins and their values in Flanders"
(Mayor, label for "Illustrated Books," 1965).

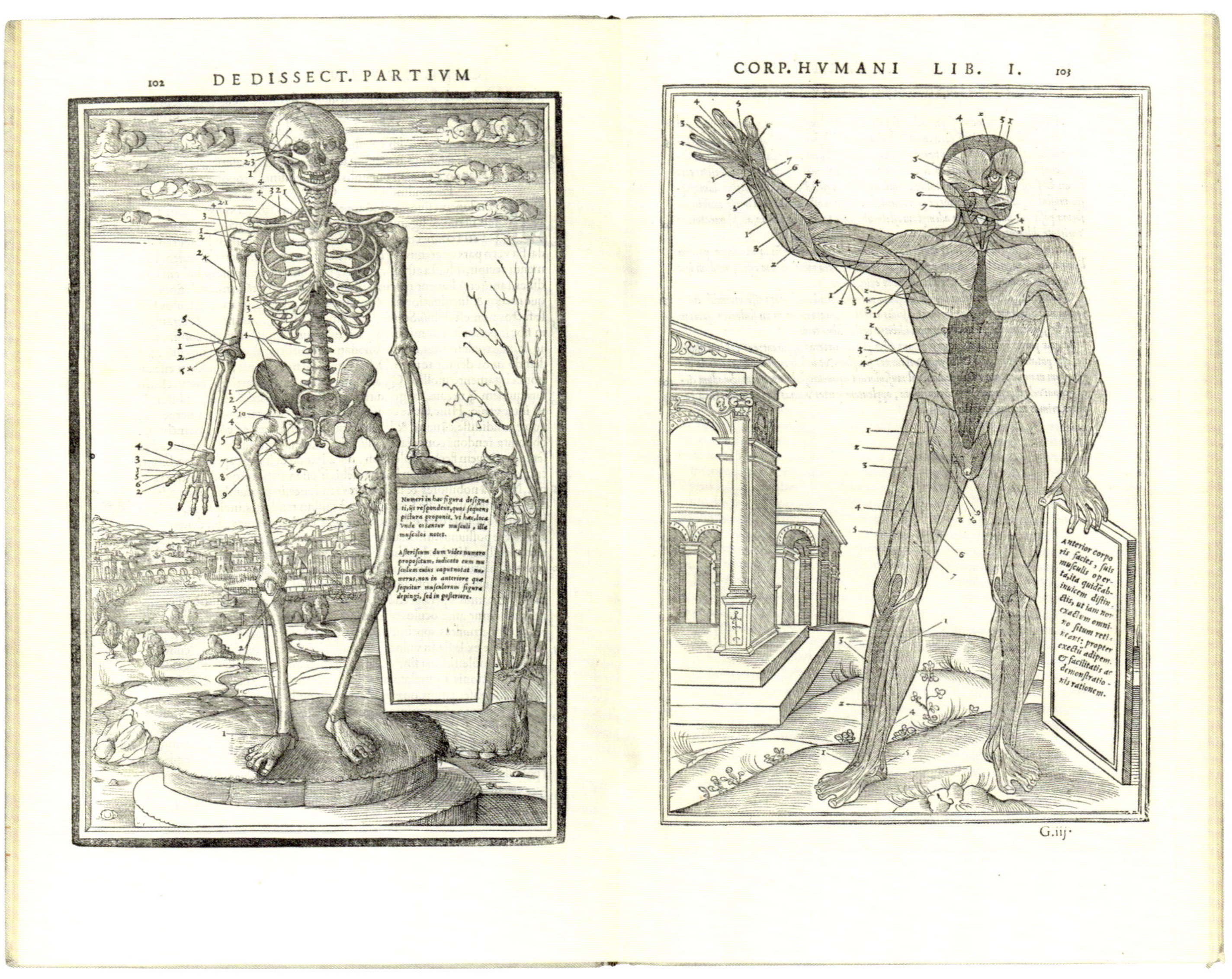

92

Woodcuts attributed to Jean Jollat, French (ca. 1490–ca. 1550), Estienne de la Rivière, French (died 1569), workshop of Geoffroy Tory, French (1480–1533), in certain instances after Perino del Vaga, Italian (1501–1547), and Rosso Fiorentino, Italian (1494–1540)

De Dissectione Partium Corporis Humani Libri Tres (*On the Dissection of the Parts of the Human Body*), 1545

Published in Paris by Simon de Colines
Harris Brisbane Dick Fund, 1942 (42.138)

Provenance: [Herbert Reichner, New York]; Department of Prints purchase, 1942

Estienne belonged to a famous French family of printers and was a classmate of Andreas Vesalius in a course of anatomical studies under Jacobus Sylvius in Paris in 1535. Estienne completed his monumental anatomical text in 1539, but it was not published until 1545 owing to a legal dispute; it thus is considered a pre-Vesalian work, even though it came out after Vesalius's 1543 first edition of *De humani corporis fabrica*. Unlike Vesalius's scientific illustrations, which "required a long partnership between an artist and an anatomist," many of Estienne's woodcuts are stiff and lifeless or are copies of compositions in erotic prints after drawings by the Italian artists Perino del Vaga and Rosso Fiorentino (Mayor, *Artists and Anatomists*, 94). While Vesalius's epic volume transformed the study of the human body, Estienne still delivered some noteworthy discoveries, including illustrations of the entire external venous and nervous systems.

Andreas Vesalius, Flemish (1514–1564)

Woodcutter unknown

De Humani Corporis Fabrica
(*On the Fabric of the Human Body*), 1555

Published in Basel by Johann Oporinus
Gift of Dr. Alfred E. Cohn, in honor of William M.
Ivins Jr., 1953 (53.682)

Provenance: possibly Philip Yorke (1690–1794), London;
most likely Alexander Buchan, M.D., England; Samuel
Lane (1780–1859), London; Francis Turner, England;
H. W. Turner, Surrey, England; Sir D'Arcy Power (1855–
1941), London; Harold and Frida Laski (1893–1950 and
1884–1977), London; Dr. Alfred E. Cohn (1879–1957),
New York; his gift to the Department of Prints, 1953

Vesalius's visual and textual account of the human body contains eighty-three woodcuts showing detailed views of the muscles, skeleton, and viscera, as well as of the circulatory, nervous, and reproductive systems. For Ivins, the volume represented the perfect fusion of text and exactly repeatable images (then thought to be by Jan Stephan van Calcar) that allowed for the explosion of knowledge in the descriptive sciences during the Renaissance. As Ivins explained, the anatomist Vesalius's partnership with a draftsman for a book on anatomy produced "a binocular report of that kind—a statement so remarkable that it recast and reformed a lore as old as the human race and transformed it into a scientific study and knowledge. . . . The first time that the verbal and visual media of statement were conjoined in a communicable form to the end of the conveyance of new information about concrete things was thus an event in the history of thought of the most incalculable importance" (Ivins, "The Woodcuts to Vesalius," 1936: 141–42).

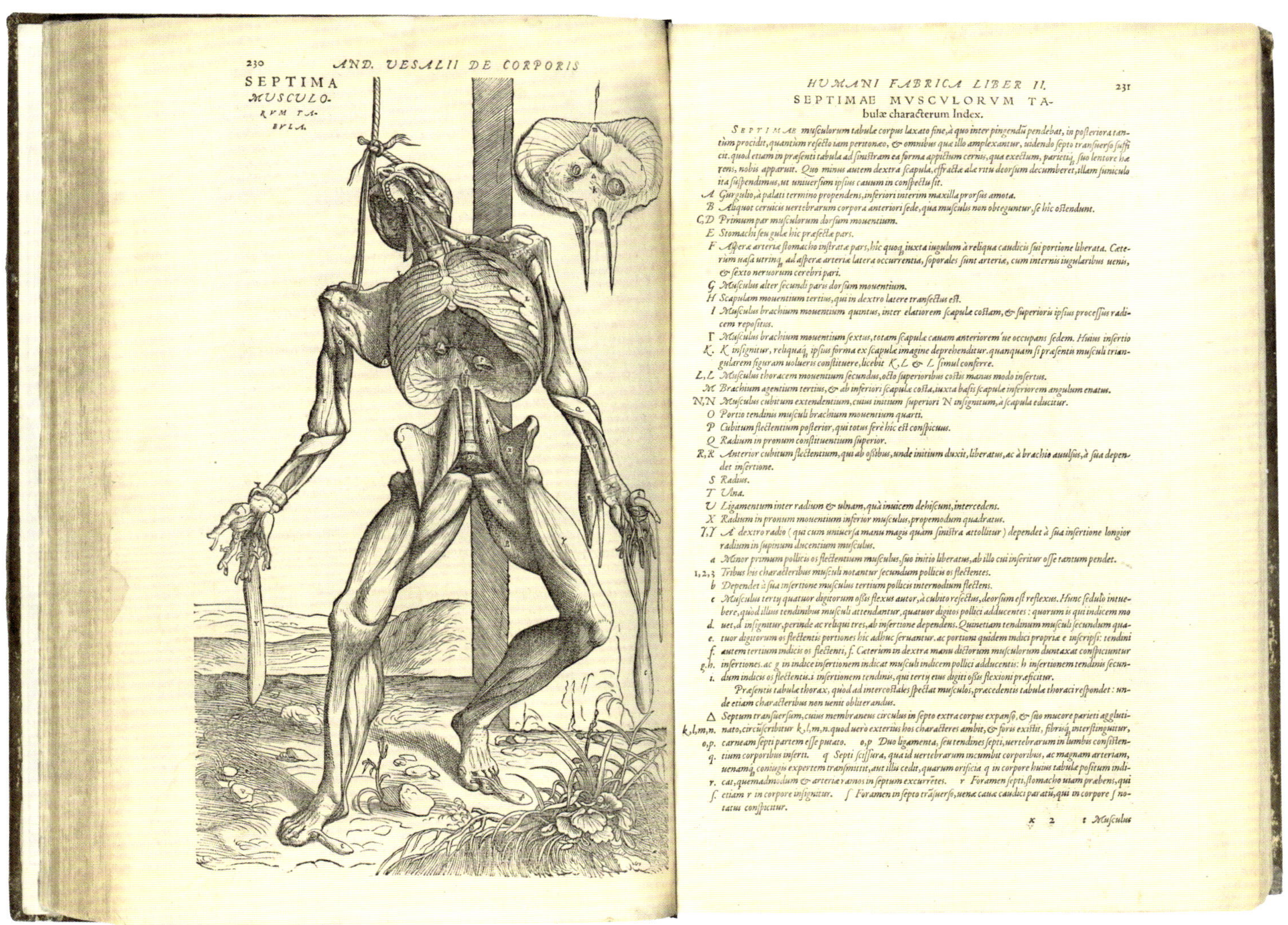

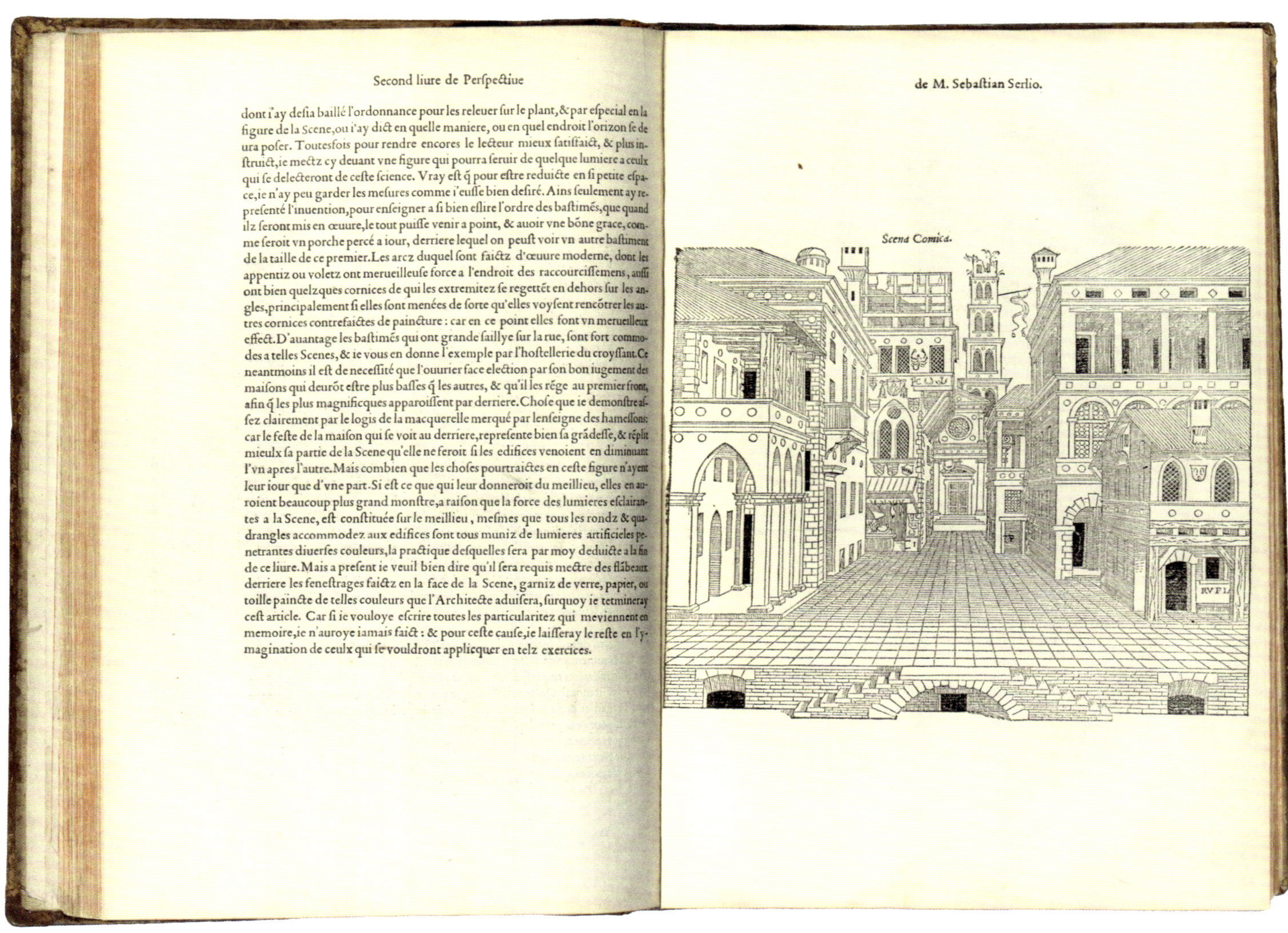

dont i'ay desia baillé l'ordonnance pour les releuer sur le plant, & par especial en la figure de la Scene, ou i'ay dict en quelle maniere, ou en quel endroit l'orizon se deura poser. Toutesfois pour rendre encores le lecteur mieux satisfaict, & plus instruict, ie meetz cy deuant vne figure qui pourra seruir de quelque lumiere a ceulx qui se delecteront de ceste science. Vray est q̃ pour estre reduicte en si petite espace, ie n'ay peu garder les mesures comme i'eusse bien desiré. Ains seulement ay representé l'inuention, pour enseigner a si bien eslire l'ordre des bastimés, que quand ilz seront mis en œuure, le tout puisse venir a point, & auoir vne bône grace, comme seroit vn porche percé a iour, derriere lequel on peust voir vn autre bastiment de la taille de ce premier. Les arcz duquel sont faictz d'œuure moderne, dont les appentiz ou voletz ont merueilleuse force a l'endroit des raccourcissemens, aussi ont bien quelzques cornices de qui les extremitez se regettét en dehors sur les angles, principalement si elles sont menées de sorte qu'elles voysent rencôtrer les autres cornices contrefaictes de painĉture : car en ce point elles font vn merueilleux effect. D'auantage les bastimés qui ont grande saillye sur la rue, sont fort commodes a telles Scenes, & ie vous en donne l'exemple par l'hostellerie du croyssant. Ce neantmoins il est de necessité que l'ouurier face election par son bon iugement des maisons qui deurót estre plus basses q̃ les autres, & qu'il les rege au premier front, afin q̃ les plus magnificques apparoissent par derriere. Chose que ie demonstre assez clairement par le logis de la macquerelle merqué par lenseigne des hamessons: car le feste de la maison qui se voit au derriere, represente bien sa grâdesse, & réplit mieulx sa partie de la Scene qu'elle ne feroit si les edifices venoient en diminuant l'vn apres l'autre. Mais combien que les choses pourtraictes en ceste figure n'ayent leur iour que d'vne part. Si est ce que qui leur donneroit du meillieu, elles en auroient beaucoup plus grand monstre, a raison que la force des lumieres esclairantes a la Scene, est constituée sur le meillieu, mesmes que tous les rondz & quadrangles accommodez aux edifices sont tous muniz de lumieres artificieles penetrantes diuerses couleurs, la practique desquelles sera par moy deduicte a la fin de ce liure. Mais a present ie veuil bien dire qu'il sera requis meĉtre des flâbeaux derriere les fenestrages faictz en la face de la Scene, garniz de verre, papier, ou toille painĉte de telles couleurs que l'Architecte aduisera, surquoy ie tetmineray cest article. Car si ie vouloye escrire toutes les particularitez qui meviennent en memoire, ie n'auroye iamais faict : & pour ceste cause, ie laisseray le reste en l'ymagination de ceulx qui se vouldront applicquer en telz exercices.

94

Sebastiano Serlio, Italian (1475–1554)

Compendium of Architectural Books by Sebastiano Serlio (Books I–V)

Books I–II and V translated by Jean Martin, French (died 1553)
Books I–II printed in Paris in 1545 by Jean Barbé; Books III–IV printed in Venice in 1544 by Francesco Marcolini da Forli; Book V printed in Paris in 1547 by Michel de Vascosan
Harris Brisbane Dick Fund, 1937 (37.56.2[1–5])

Provenance: Hugh Cecil Lowther, 5th Earl of Lonsdale, British (1857–1944); [Davis and Orioli, London]; Department of Prints purchase, 1937

Mayor enjoyed a lifelong fascination with the theater and with books and prints on the subject. The art and architecture of theater design was codified during the Renaissance in books such as Serlio's, which was featured in an exhibition on Italian theatrical design that Mayor mounted in 1951. In an earlier exhibition on stagecraft Mayor noted that "Serlio wrote the first book on stage design ever printed with illustrations. When he first tried to follow Vitruvius (1st century B.C.) whose manuscript texts are unillustrated, the resulting stage designs were more medieval than classical. This woodcut shows 'houses' . . . which Serlio has telescoped in perspective" to create a design for a comic scene (Mayor, label for "Carpentry and Candlelight in the Theater," 1943).

95

François Desprez, French
(active 16th century)

Woodcutter unknown, many works after Enea
Vico, Italian (1523–1567)

Recueil de la Diversité des Habits (*Treatise on
Costume*), 1562

Published in Paris by Richard Breton
Harris Brisbane Dick Fund, 1940 (40.129)

Provenance: [Herbert Reichner, New York]; Department
of Prints purchase, 1940

Desprez's *Recueil* is a very early example of
a costume book, the first that was widely
published. It also exemplifies the new ethno-
graphic impulse to create a taxonomy of the
world's peoples—including Cyclopes and the
so-called noble savages—based on the clothing
that ornaments their bodies. In this opening
Desprez pairs the Savage Scotswoman, dressed
in pelts to stave off the cold, and the Savage
Captain, carrying weapons, which the author
suggests were used to cause trouble for the
English. During a new age of worldwide trade,
exploration, and discovery, Desprez's text and
its images helped define and differentiate cultures. Many of the woodcuts depend on prints
by the Italian engraver Enea Vico, which were
never published as a volume and remain only
as loose plates.

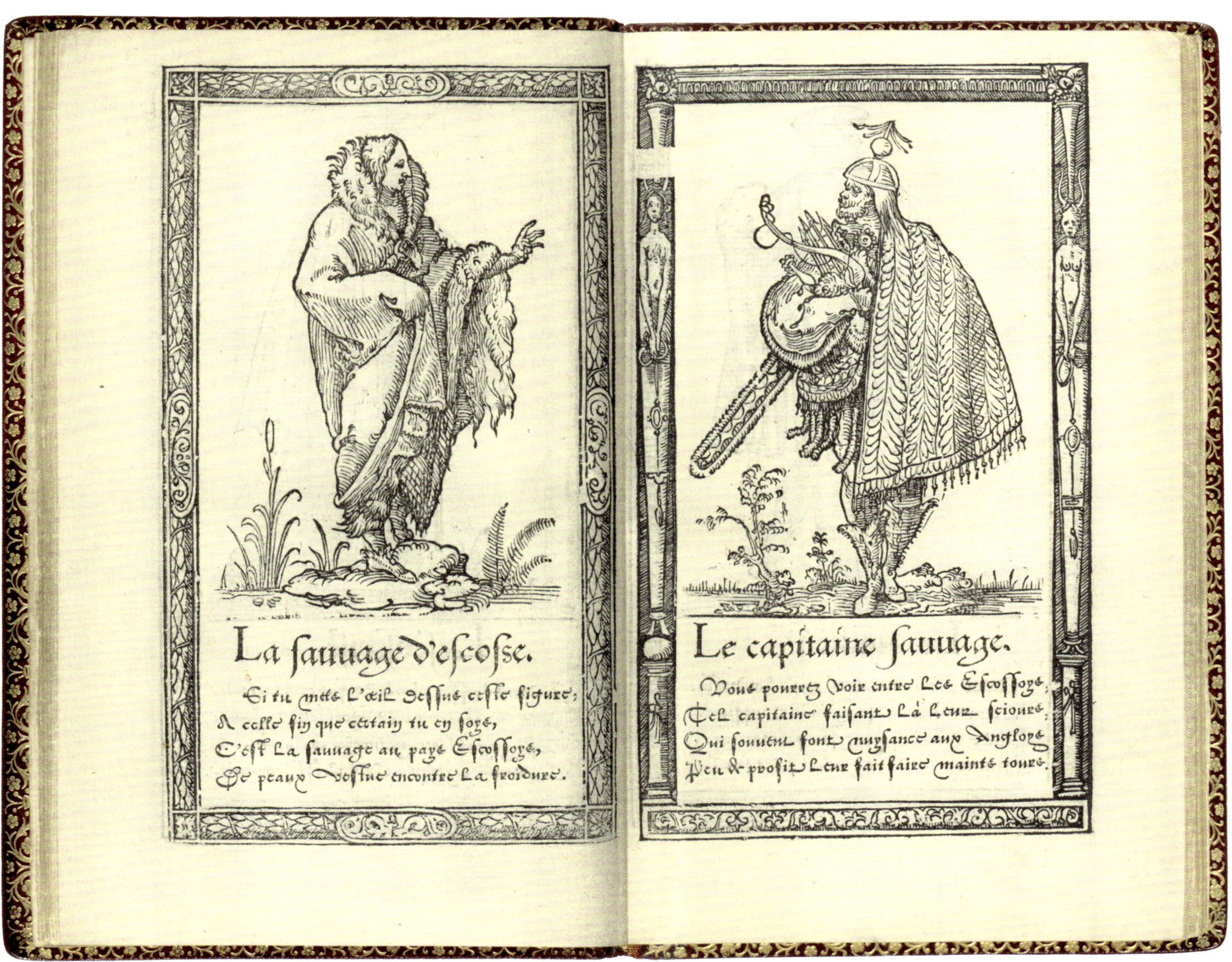

Juan de Alcega, Spanish (active 16th century)

Woodcutter unknown

Libro de Geometría, Práctica y Traça (*Geometry, Practice, and Patterns*), 1589

Published in Madrid by Guillermo Drouy
Harris Brisbane Dick Fund, 1941 (41.7)

Provenance: [Herbert Reichner, New York]; Department of Prints purchase, 1941

At a time when Spanish fashions dominated European dress, the first book on tailoring was published in Madrid. Alcega noted in the introduction that this kind of book, which included tailoring patterns for men and women and cutting layouts, was quite new in Spain; he hoped it would have "life and permanence in the world." The text and images were meant to be used by readers in the making of clothes. Although very few garments survive, Alcega's designs provide critical information about tailoring of the period.

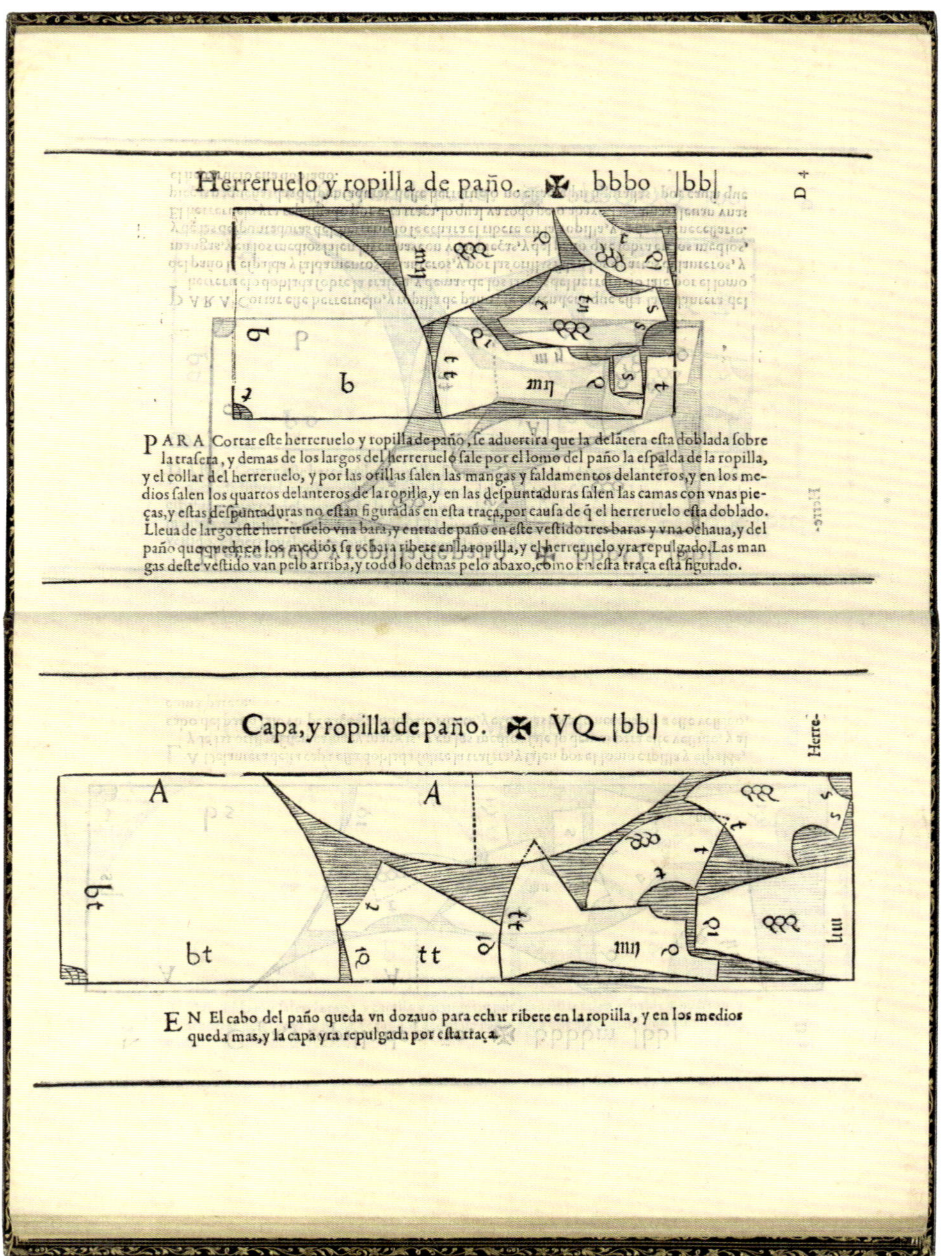

97

Woodcuts by Christoph Krieger, German
(died ca. 1590)

*De gli Habiti Antichi et Moderni di Diversi
Parti del Mondo, Libri Due . . . (Of Ancient and
Modern Dress of Diverse Parts of the World in
Two Books . . .)*, 1590

Published in Venice by Damiano Zenaro
Rogers Fund, 1906, transferred from the Library
(21.36.146)

Vecellio's ambitions to map the diversity of
dress across the globe mirrored contemporary
cartographers' efforts to create world atlases.
His popular book marks the culmination of a
trend that began in the mid-sixteenth century
with Enea Vico's series of costume engravings,
which were made into woodcuts and used in
François Desprez's 1562 *Treatise on Costume*
(see cat. 95). It contains 420 illustrations of
costumes; the first section covers European
dress, including that of Ottoman Turkey, and
the short section on Africa and Asia includes
the apparel of Persians, Moors, and Arabs. This
opening shows the dress of two noble Venetian
brides, one after her wedding and the other at
the Feast of the Ascension.

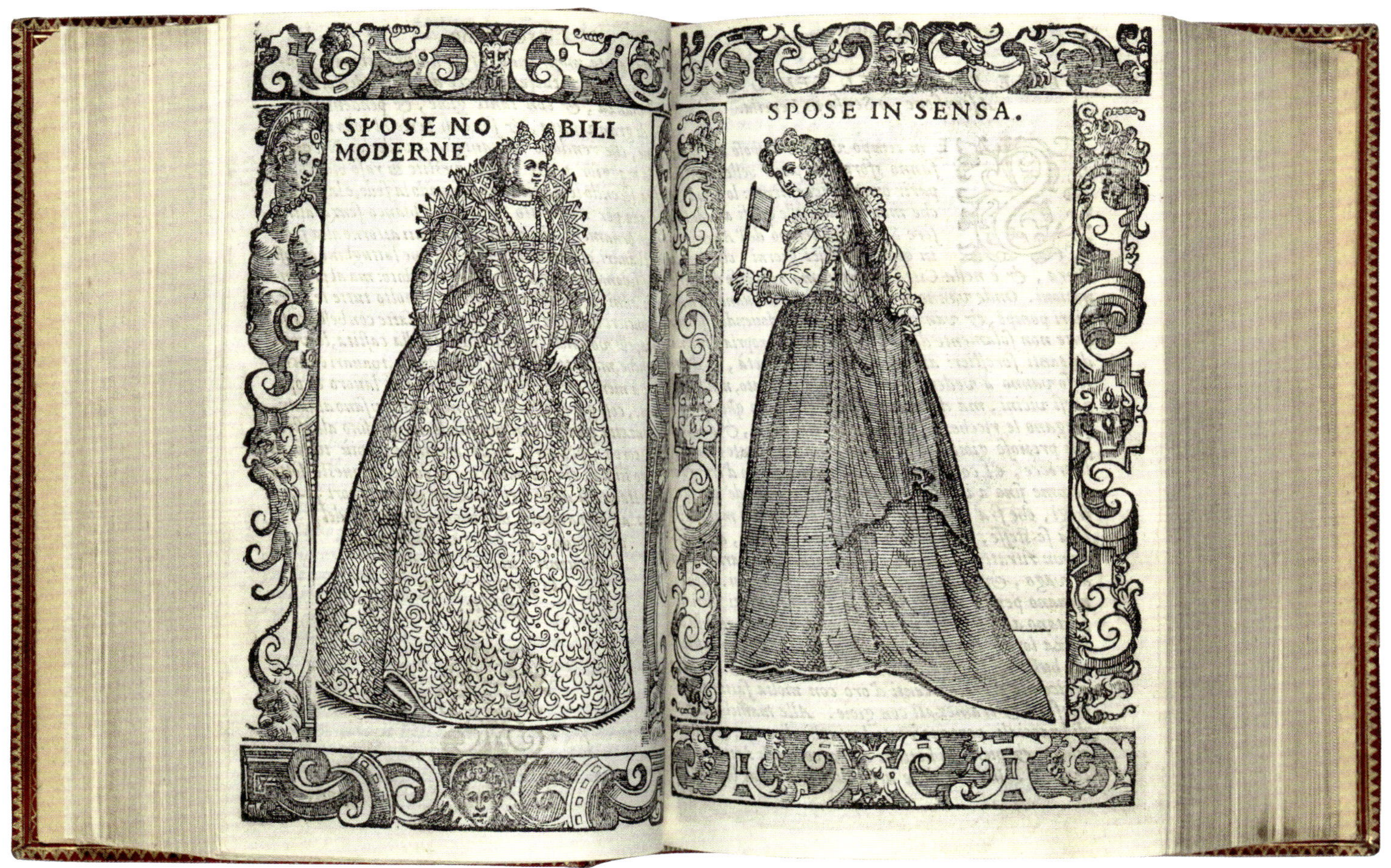

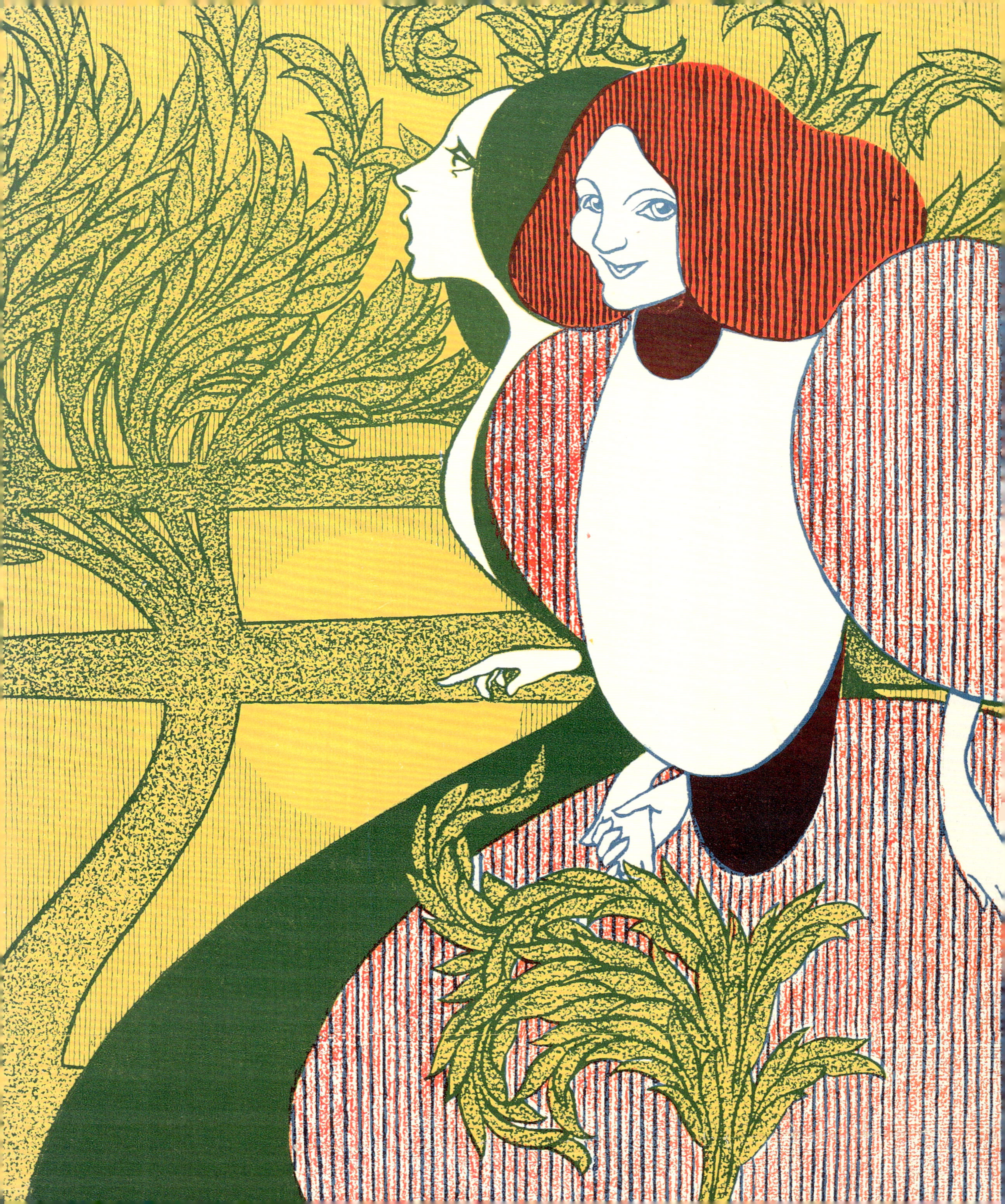

Lithographs

T HE HISTORY OF lithography is short relative to those of etching, engraving, and woodcut. It was developed in the last years of the eighteenth century by the German dramatist Alois Senefelder as a means of printing his own plays and songs. Lithography has always been a medium of advertising; in Senefelder's case, he was promoting himself and his work. By the nineteenth century lithography had been widely adopted for more commercial means. It became *the* medium used to promote an artist; an avant-garde style; a political, social, or religious ideology or critique; a product; an industry; a romanticized ideal; a foreign land; or a new technology. At the same time, publishers like Currier & Ives in New York began to mass-produce inexpensive lithographs, with a range of subject matter meant to appeal to every type of market. Lithography's durability and versatility, combined with technological advances both in printing and with presses, made it a democratic medium, one that brings art within everyone's reach. Ivins noted that color lithographic reproductions of masterpieces in European museums, many produced by the American publisher Louis Prang, powerfully and influentially spread fine art to the masses and perhaps leveled ideas of taste.[1]

Although lithography was employed as a commercial medium from the start, many nineteenth-century artists, including Whistler, Degas, and Delacroix, also explored the possibilities of lithographic printmaking. A seemingly straightforward technique, in which the artist freely draws with a greasy crayon on a treated stone surface, resulted in what Mayor called an "authentically 'original'" print, identical to a drawing but produced in multiples.[2] Lithographs were not widely collected, but those that were typically were of the type celebrated for their artistry—for example, works by Whistler and the now-forgotten French printmaker Georges William Thornley, which came into The Metropolitan Museum of Art with Harris Brisbane Dick's founding gift.[3]

William Ivins and Hyatt Mayor maintained that focus on artistic lithography for some years before Mayor began collecting more popular, ephemeral forms in earnest in the early 1940s. An early exhibition by Ivins in 1923 showcased artistic lithographs—masterpieces, no less—from the medium's inception in the late eighteenth century to the late nineteenth century.[4] Mayor's 1948 exhibition "Lithographs 1798–1948" likewise focused on works by named artists; it made the case that artistic lithography should be celebrated, studied, and collected because it simply reproduces an artist's sketch, without the mediation of a specialized craftsperson like an engraver or woodcutter, thus communicating an intimacy with the maker.[5] In that, Mayor was repeating the arguments made by artists, curators, and critics since lithography's inception. For example, in 1918 Frank Weitenkampf, the founding curator of the New York Public Library's prints department, definitively labeled lithography a painter's art, stating that lithographs represented "the artist's touch absolutely, giving a straight reproduction of his drawing without the intervention of an engraver-translator."[6]

Running parallel to this narrative of painters making lithographs as drawings on stone was the myth, reiterated by Ivins, that making a lithograph required no special technical education except the knowledge of draftsmanship.[7] As Antony Griffiths points out, printing a lithograph successfully is a "matter of considerable professional expertise, and almost all artists have been happy to resign this business to a friendly printer."[8] In his writings on the medium, the artist Joseph Pennell underscored the need for artists to draw, etch, and print their own lithographs.[9] However, Pennell and other prominent members of London's Senefelder Club (which promoted lithographic art) relied on the printing firm of Vincent Brooks, Day & Son when it came to their own lithographs.[10] The printer thus played a crucial role in the history of the medium, sometimes acting as publisher as well. The professionalization of the craft and the speed and efficiency of the process led to the exploitation of lithography as a medium for reproduction to an extent that was impossible in other printed media.

One artist who fully capitalized on the lithographic process was Honoré Daumier, who readily translated his reactions to current events into art that reached the masses. Working for the radical French newspaper *La Caricature* and its milder satirical offshoot *Le Charivari*, Daumier and editor Charles Philipon fought the monarchy and its policies with six to eight lithographs a month for nearly three decades. Daumier took up lithography because of his need for paying work, not for love of the medium. That proved to have certain advantages. As Mayor recounted, Daumier pursued "shape and expression regardless of, and even against, a medium [that] saved him from the professional print-maker's finicky technicalities, while the brute recklessness of his despair drove him to invent more than any French artist of his century."[11] As an artist who so skillfully expressed the political and social complexities of nineteenth-century France and reveled in the medium's ability to reach the widest possible audience, Daumier made the ideal subject for Mayor's only monographic exhibition on a lithographer.[12]

Mayor widely and avidly collected in the field of lithography. His acquisitions included large collections of French and American posters produced in the mid- to late nineteenth century by the likes of Jules Chéret, Henri de Toulouse-Lautrec, William Henry Bradley, and Edward Penfield. He sought out not just so-called artistic prints but hundreds of thousands of works that were considered popular, commercial, and sometimes merely ephemeral.[13] As a social historian, Mayor valued the window that such lithographs opened on to everyday life; he wrote in 1952 with great sentiment about Currier & Ives lithographs, in which "we read the stories of our grandparents," "our American family past."[14] His book

Popular Prints of the Americas not only addressed the broad phenomenon of popular prints from Brazil and Mexico to the northeastern United States but also recounted detailed stories of lithography's westward movement and flowering around California's shipping industry, resulting in a profusion of posters, pamphlets, and trade cards.[15]

From America's emergence from the Civil War and into the tumultuous twentieth century, lithography recorded "the most dramatic moments of the century-long explosion that transformed the continent convulsively, drastically, irresistibly, and at breakneck speed," Mayor observed.[16] Thus he collected lithographs used for advertising, which accounted for more than half of America's popular prints and ephemera; he also collected contemporary lithographs dating from the Great Depression and World War II, including lithographs by the preeminent Works Progress Administration artists and posters, pamphlets, and magazine images, sometimes by anonymous designers, that related to the war at home and abroad.[17] Lithographic imagery was emblazoned on billboards, posters, handbills, fans, trade cards, calendars, and paper dolls; it appeared within newspapers, magazines, and in numerous other forms. To Mayor, such works were our "encyclopedias of social history," and there could be no clearer inventory of the range of interests of a given time and place.[18] Perceiving the value of such common forms of printed matter, Mayor built a collection that masterfully integrates them with the most exceptional works. He was an "aristocratic popularizer," as his longtime friend Lincoln Kirstein observed. "The everyday was his caviar."[19]

Honoré Daumier, French (1808–1879)

Rue Transnonain, le 15 Avril, 1834, plate 24, published in *L'Association mensuelle lithographique*, July 1834

Printed by Delaunois, Paris
Lithograph, 14³⁄₈ × 21³⁄₄ in. (36.4 × 55.1 cm)
Rogers Fund, 1920 (20.23)

Collector's mark: N. A. Hazard (Lugt 1975)

Provenance: N. A. Hazard (1834–1913), Orrouy, France; [Weyhe Gallery, New York]; Department of Prints purchase, 1920

Daumier was a careful observer and often a bitter critic of daily life; Ivins and Mayor treasured him as the exemplar of an artist entrenched in his own time. Mayor described this large-scale lithograph, in which the artist illustrates the French government's brutal repression following an uprising: "In 1834 Daumier made his most famous though not his greatest picture, which represents the bedroom of a working-class family shot by soldiers during a riot in the Rue Transnonain. The still disorder of the furniture and the bodies littering the moonlit floor—'trivial and terrible,' as Baudelaire called it—is an astonishing achievement for an artist of twenty-six. The lithograph attracted queues of spectators, was seized by the police and probably hastened the passing of the stringent laws of censorship. . . . The Rue Transnonain is Daumier's parting shot in his first skirmish against the French government" (Mayor, "A Bequest of Prints by Callot and Daumier," 1958: 13–14).

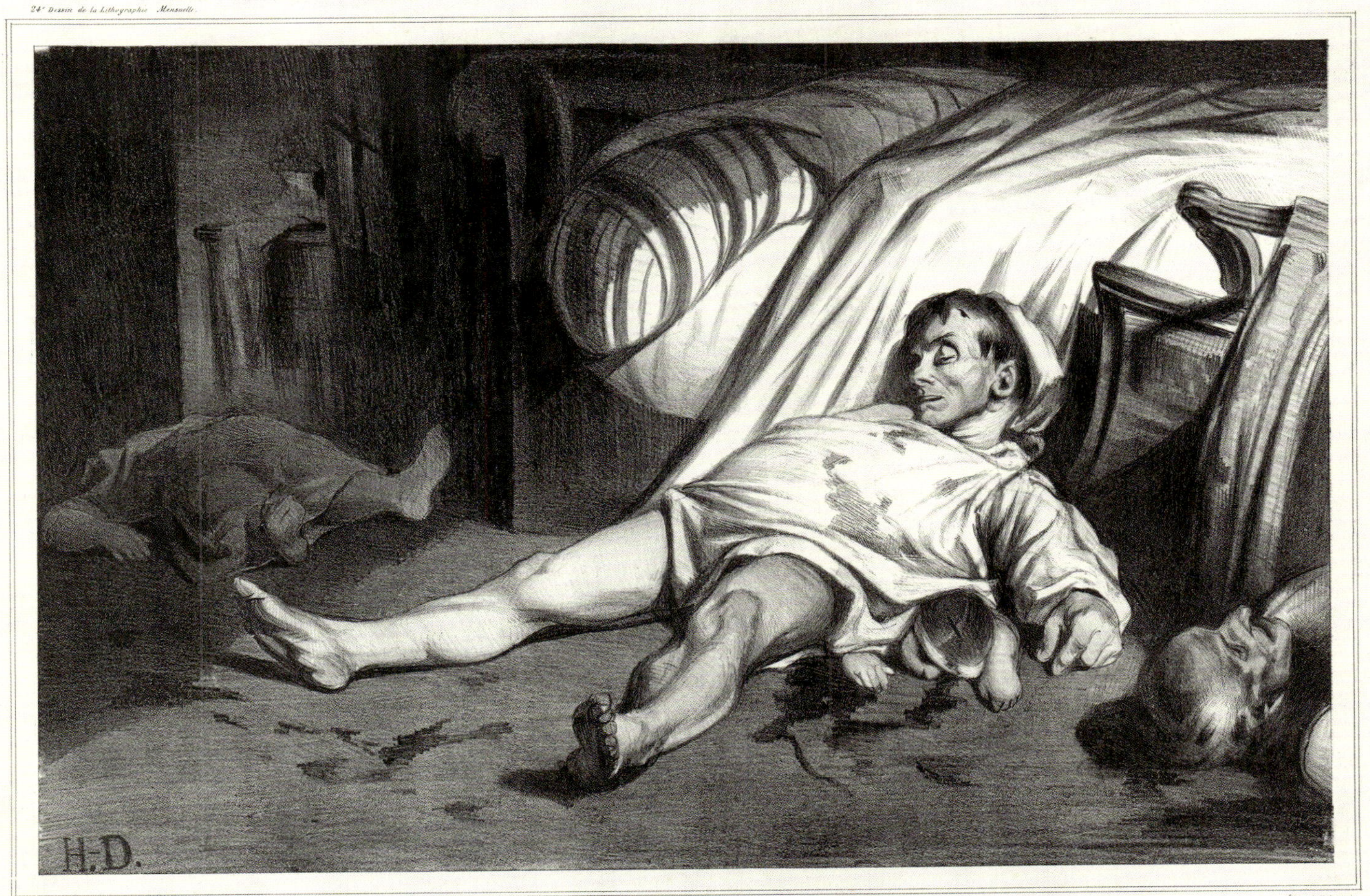

Honoré Daumier, French (1808–1879)

A Gust of Wind Not Predicted by Mathieu (de la Drôme) (Un Coup de Vent non Prédit par Mathieu [de la Drôme]), plate 1 from Winter Sketches (Croquis d'Hiver), 1864

[99]
Lithograph with notations in pen, first state of four (proof before letters), 8½ × 10 in. (21.6 × 25.4 cm)
Harris Brisbane Dick Fund, 1939 (39.45.1)

Provenance: Charles Saunier (1865–1941), Paris and Lozère sur Yvette; [Jean Goriany, New York]; Department of Prints purchase, 1939

[100]
Published in *Petit Journal pour rire*, Dec. 3, 1864
Lithograph, third state of four, approximately 8⅛ × 11¾ in. (20.7 × 29.9 cm)
Harris Brisbane Dick Fund, 1936 (36.12.7)

Provenance: [Frank Bender, New York]; Department of Prints purchase, 1936

Mathieu de la Drôme (1808–1865), a radical Republican politician and meteorologist who believed that weather information would improve the living conditions of the French people, began publishing annual almanacs in about 1862–63. They were immediately in demand. Daumier capitalized on their popularity and played on the use of parentheses in the almanac title—*Triple Almanach Mathieu (de la Drôme)*—to create this image of a fashionable couple nearly toppled by a strong gust of errant wind. This witty scene—shown here in a proof before letters and in the printed edition for a humorous newspaper—is one of more than four thousand ephemeral prints Daumier carefully made. Although some regarded them as mere comics, Mayor thought Daumier's lithographs, which "appeared weekly or oftener, year in and year out, in editions of thirty-five hundred or more," had "an original-ity of vision that helped to show the impres-sionist painters what to paint and how to put it on the canvas" (Mayor, "A Bequest of Prints by Callot and Daumier," 1958: 15–16).

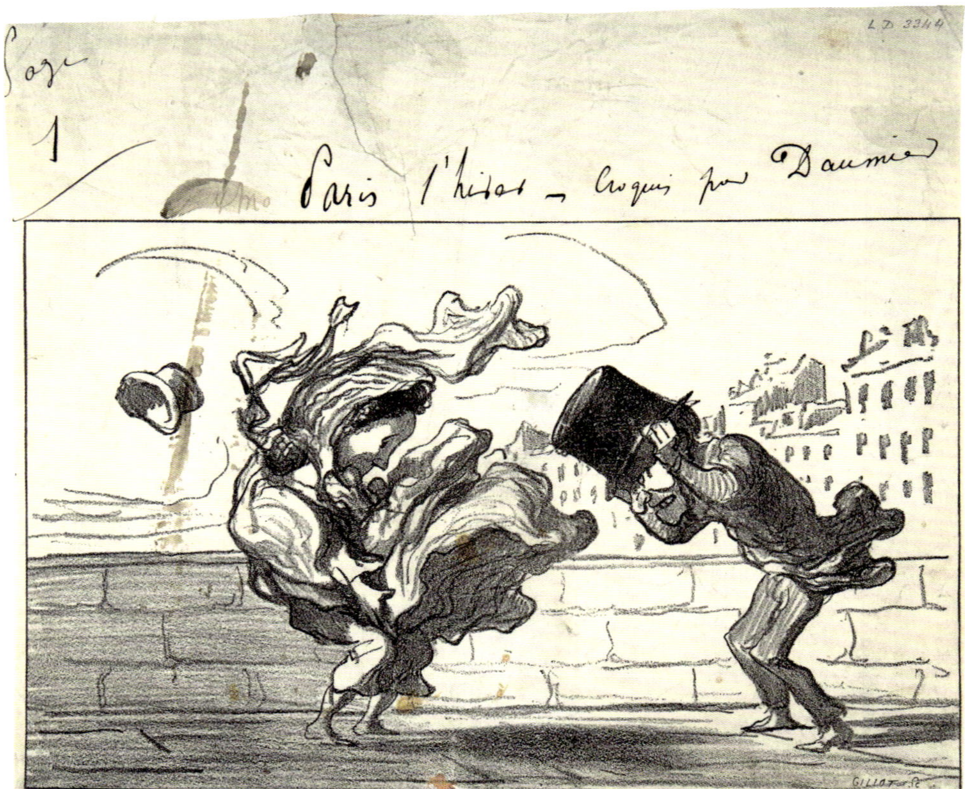

99

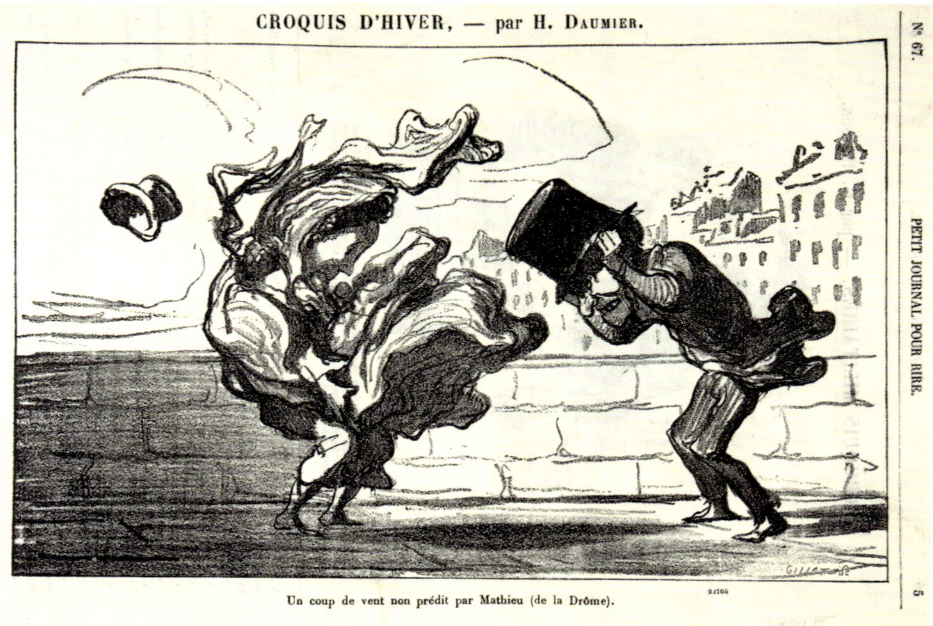

100

101

Honoré Daumier, French (1808–1879)

European Equilibrium (Équilibre Européen), from Actualités (News), published in *Le Charivari,* April 3, 1867

Lithograph, 12 × 11⁵⁄₈ in. (30.5 × 29.6 cm)
The Elisha Whittelsey Collection, The Elisha Whittelsey Fund, 1962 (62.650.405)

Provenance: William M. Ivins Jr. (1878–1964), New York and Woodbury, Conn.; Barbara Ivins (1913–1991), Woodbury, Conn.; Department of Prints purchase, 1962

Executed late in Daumier's career as a workaday lithographer, this print demonstrates how, "by working from the resources of his sculptural memory, he gradually developed an emphatic shorthand of lines that often define shadow and shape in one stroke—lines like an actor's makeup, that follow forms and project expressions surprisingly far. His late work shows no more erasure or redrawing than a Chinese painting on silk. Like a Chinese painter, Daumier must have had to sit still until the clearing of his inner eye discharged an accumulated energy into a few lines flowing deliberate and free" (Mayor, "Lithographs," 1948: 90).

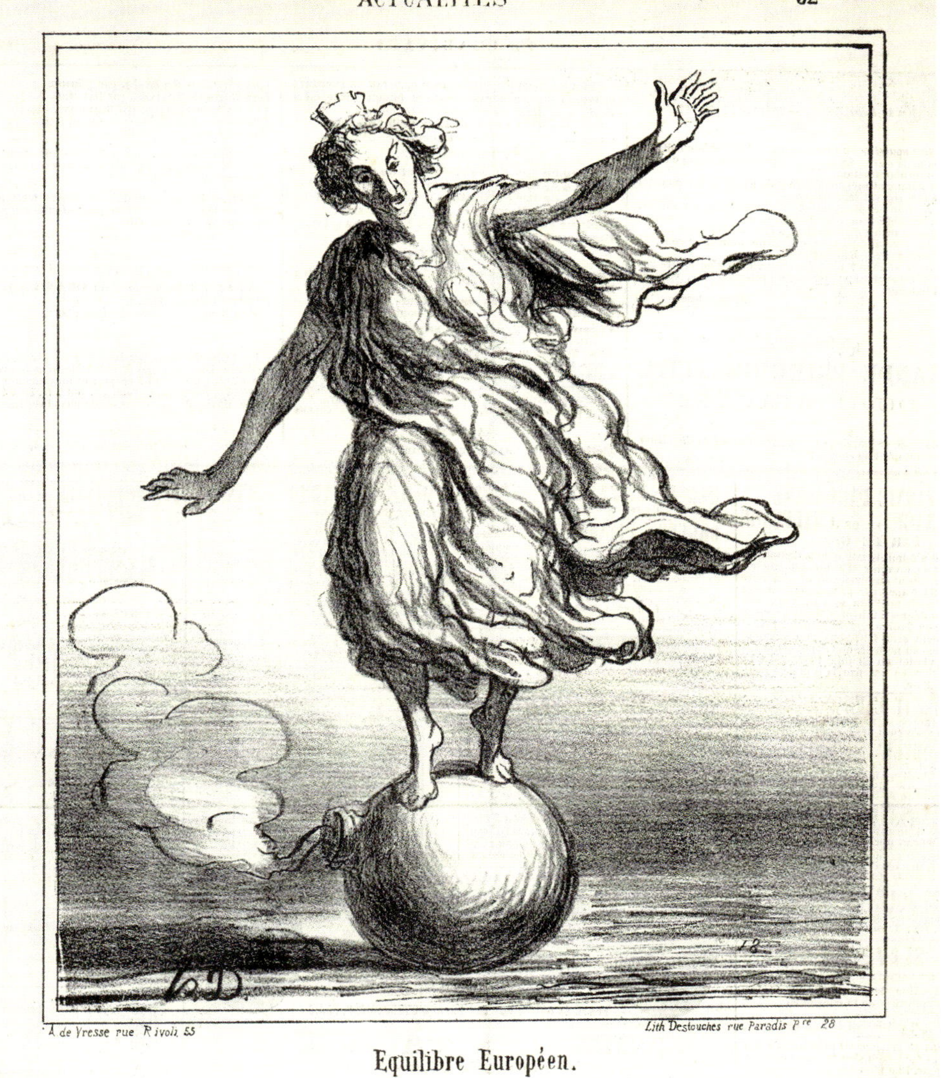

ur, 25 à 30 ans, air aisé, gants de chien, stick — Je désirerais me procurer les photographies rtistes du Palais-Royal.

comme un fumiste et a été à Turin la reine du théâtre français. Aussi regrette t-elle ce beau ciel bleu qu'elle a tant aimé. Prenez également le portrait de Zulma Bouffar,

L'acheteur. — Cette dame mûre, est-ce leur mère ?
La marchande. — Que nenni ! c'est Mᵐᵉ Dellille, duèg de talent, qui soupire de regret chaque fois qu'on lui par

Honoré Daumier, French (1808–1879)

The War Council (*Conseil de Guerre* or *Les Témoins*), 1872

Lithograph, proof of unpublished print, 11⅜ × 9¼ in.
(28.9 × 23.3 cm)
Purchase, Jacob H. Schiff Bequest, 1922 (22.63.7)

Provenance: [Maurice Le Garrec (died 1937), Paris];
Department of Prints purchase, 1922

A unique impression likely intended for a
print run in the thousands as part of the 1872
series Actualités (News), Daumier's powerful
image on the grave issues of war seemingly
did not escape censorship. This lithograph,
also known as *The Witnesses*, shows a group of
dead and decaying figures nearing the door to
a war council that was to try François Achille
Bazaine, a general and marshal of France
accused of treason for surrendering to the
Prussians in Metz. This late print, created with
vehement scrawls that reflect Daumier's night-
marish vision, displays the artist's confidence
in the medium and his ability to create a sense
of foreboding with very few strokes.

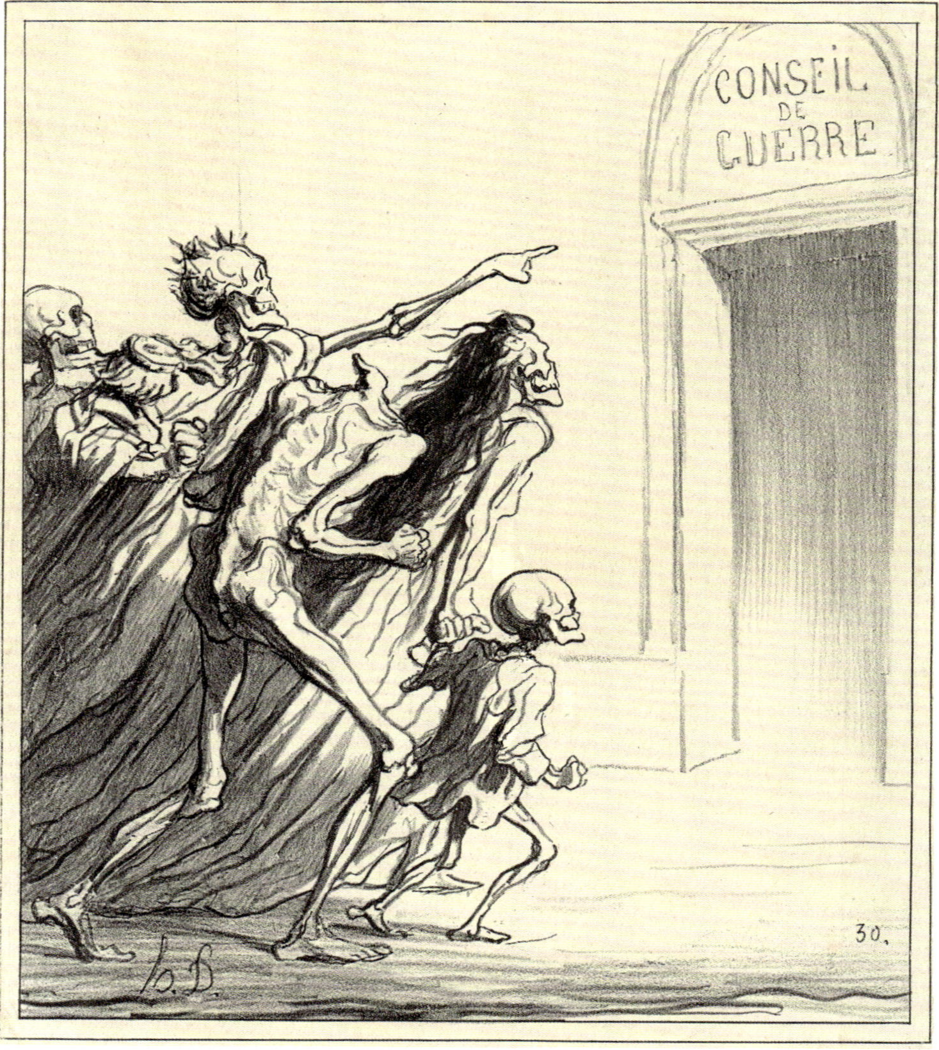

*Nothing Is so Beautiful as a Fairy Tale, or so
Sad as the Truth!* (*Rien N'est si Joli que la Fable,
si Triste que la Vérité!*), plate 30 from Les
Lorettes, published in *Le Charivari*, Oct. 21,
1842 [103]

Printed by Aubert et Cie, Paris
Lithograph, first state of three, before letters, 14¼ ×
10⅛ in. (36 × 25.5 cm)
Inscribed by the artist in brown ink: Rien n'est si joli
que la Fa a a a ble e e, si / tris te que la vérité!; écrivez
plus lisiblement / s'il vous plaît. / appuyez un peu
plus / — marquez ici, comme / il faut les places des /
lettres séparées. (write more legibly please. press a little
more — mark here, as is necessary for the spacing of
the letters.)
Rogers Fund, 1922 (22.61.7)

Collector's mark: Albert Maroni (Lugt 150b)

Provenance: Albert Maroni (1852–1923), Paris; [Galerie
Marcel Guiot, Paris]; Department of Prints purchase,
1922

Look Lodie! Look . . . (*Voyons Lodie! Voyons . . .*),
plate 44 from Les Lorettes, published in *Le
Charivari*, Feb. 13, 1843 [104]

Printed by Aubert et Cie, Paris
Published by Pannier et Cie, Paris
Lithograph, third and final state, 13¼ × 9¾ in.
(33.7 × 24.7 cm)
The Elisha Whittelsey Collection, The Elisha Whittelsey
Fund, 1957 (57.581.15)

Provenance: [Paul Prouté, Paris]; Department of Prints
purchase, 1957

Under the nom de plume he adopted in
his early twenties, the prolific writer and
lithographer Gavarni produced some 2,700
lithographs that reflected and often shifted
perceptions of life in Paris in the 1840s. A sort
of pictorial journalist, "When he was 29 he
began to explore the wiles of women for *Le
Charivari* in [his series of] the lorettes" (Mayor,
Prints & People, 672). *Lorette* was a colloquial-
ism for a new type of prostitute who was kept
in relative luxury in the apartment buildings
that had recently been constructed near the
Notre-Dame-de-Lorette church. Gavarni's
sharp-eyed observations of Parisian society
in works like these demonstrate his value as a
documentarian of his times.

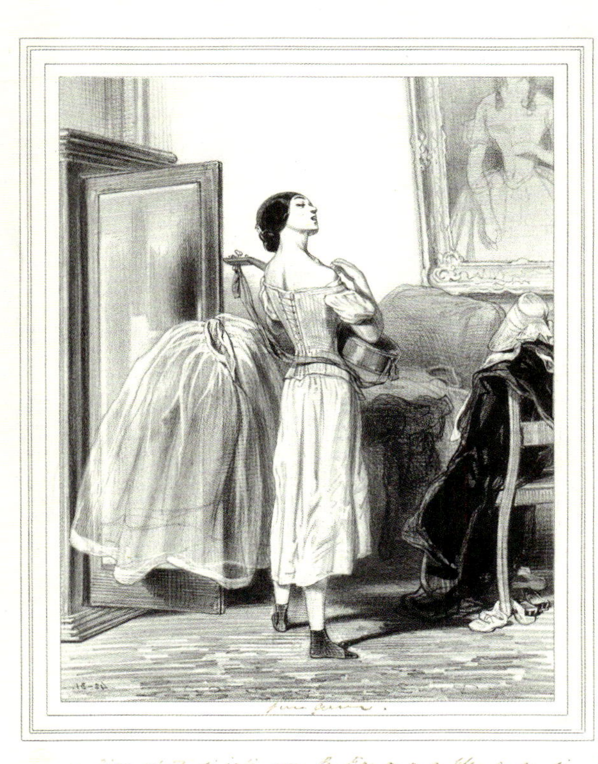

« Rien n'est si joli que la Fa a a ble e e, si
tris te que la vérité! »

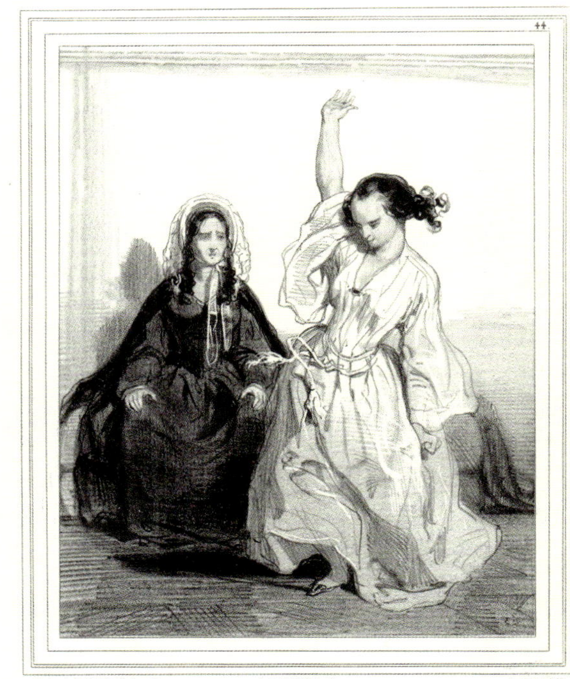

-Voyons Lodie! voyons!.......
- Lariflaflafla! lariflaflafla!
- Faut penser au solide........
- Larifla! fla! fla!
- Habille-toi!........
- Lariflaflafla! lariflaflafla!
- T'as ton terme à payer, ma fille........
- Lariflafla! fla! fla!!!

103

104

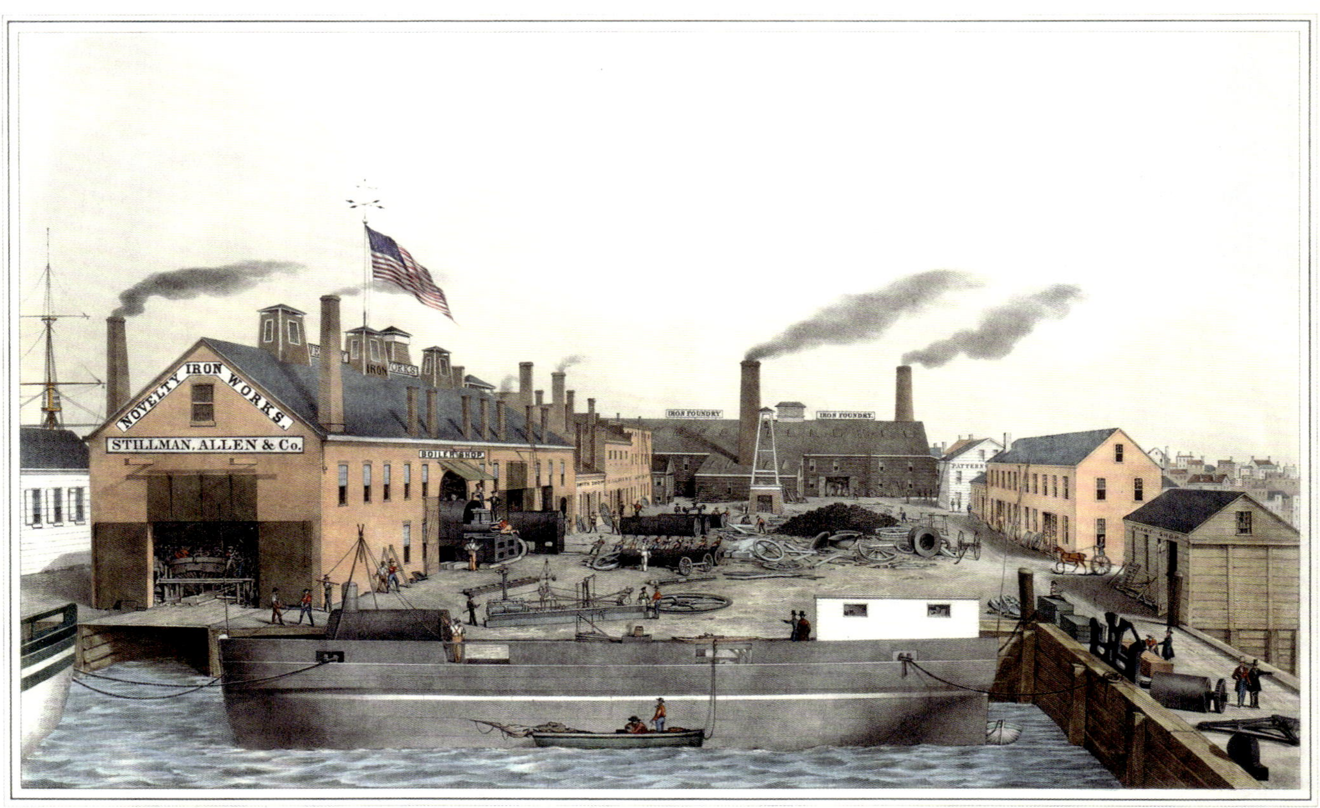

105

John Penniman, American (1817–1850)

Novelty Iron Works, Foot of 12th St. E.R. New York. Stillman, Allen & Co., Iron Founders, Steam Engine and General Machinery Manufacturers, 1841–44

Published by George Endicott, New York
Lithograph printed in colors with additional hand coloring, 25³⁄₈ × 37 in. (64.5 × 93.8 cm)
The Edward W. C. Arnold Collection of New York Prints, Maps, and Pictures, Bequest of Edward W. C. Arnold, 1954 (54.90.588)

Provenance: Edward William Cameron Arnold (died 1954), New York; his bequest to the Department of Prints, 1954

During the nineteenth century prints such as *Iron Works*, produced for the mass market, hung on the walls of homes and public spaces almost everywhere; even Charles Dickens alluded to their pervasiveness in his *American Notes* of 1842. Printed by George Endicott, a well-respected purveyor who competed with the renowned New York firm Currier & Ives, this brilliantly colored and finely wrought lithograph advertises the largest manufacturer of steam engines in New York. More generally, it illustrates how the city's superior port, warehouses, and highly trafficked river facilitated the conduct of business.

Édouard Manet, French (1832–1883)

The Execution of the Emperor Maximilian,
June 19, 1867, 1868

Printed by Lemercier, Paris
Lithograph on chine collé, first printing without letters,
17½ × 23¾ in. (44.5 × 60.3 cm)
Rogers Fund, 1921 (21.48)

Collector's mark: unidentified collector's mark
(Lugt 2631a)

Provenance: [Gutekunst and Klipstein, Bern];
Department of Prints purchase, 1921

Napoléon III of France installed the Habsburg emperor Maximilian to power in Mexico in 1864, an endeavor that failed miserably, ending with the execution of Maximilian and two of his generals by firing squad three years later. News of the execution quickly reached Paris, and Manet, a Republican ideologically opposed to Napoléon, set to work almost immediately on a series of works depicting the event: three paintings, an oil sketch, and this lithograph, which does not exactly correspond to any of the paintings. Inspired by photographs and newspaper reports of the execution, Manet's dispassionate and simplified composition, with its contrasting areas of light and dark, enhances the scene's dramatic impact. He shows the executioners in uniforms very similar to those worn by the French army. As Ivins noted, "[Manet] saw everything broadly and simply as befitted a temperament that habitually found ease in splotches of tone, and as often as possible evaded the discomfort and concentration required to focus attention upon a line" (Ivins, "French Black and White of the Last Half-Century," July 1921: 152). Manet produced this lithograph for wide distribution, but when the printer, Lemercier, tried to register the print, he was ordered to suppress it. Manet then had a public squabble with Lemercier, who wished to destroy the stone but in the end returned it to the artist.

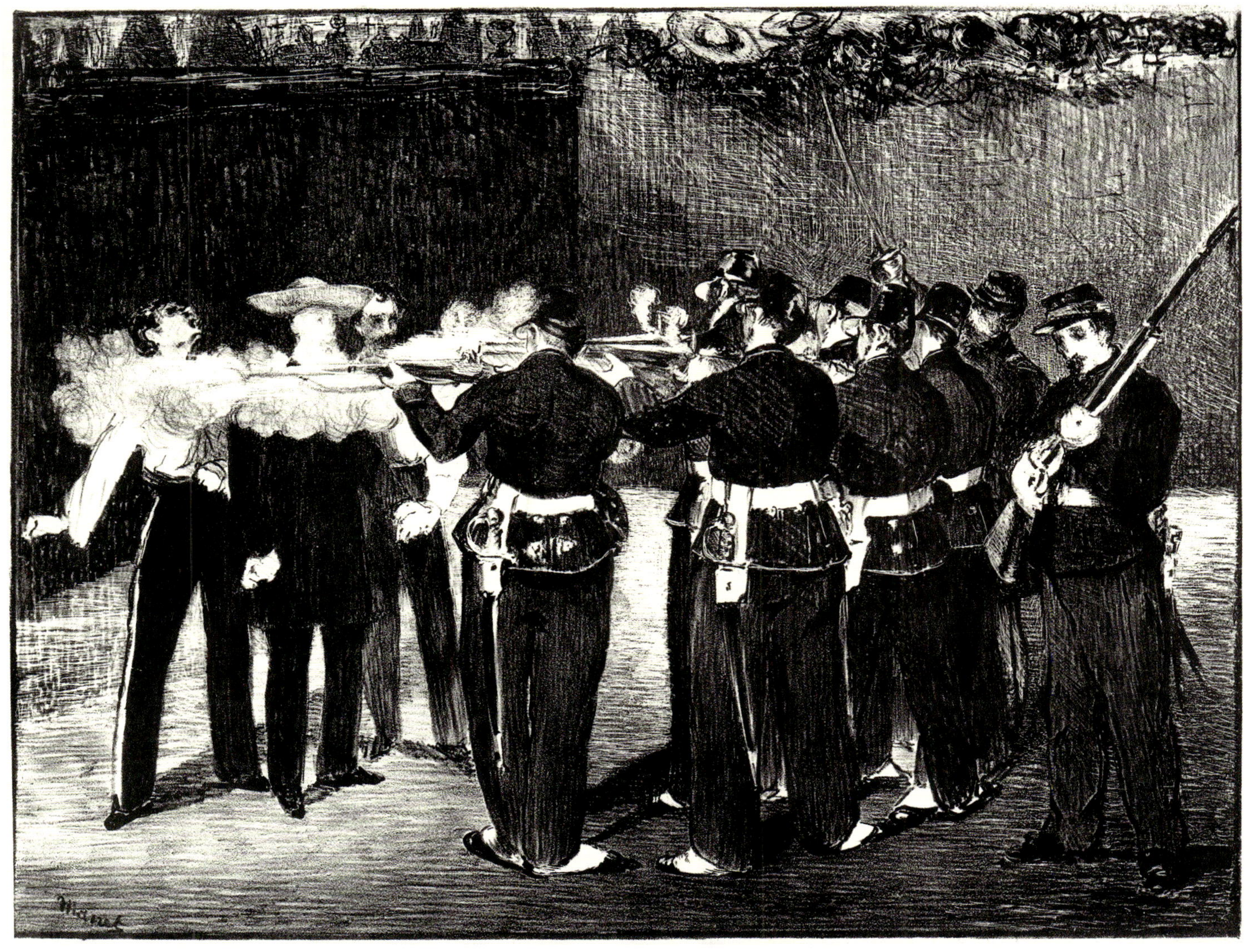

Emmanuel Wyttenbach, American, born Switzerland (1841–1903)

Ship Owners & Merchants Tug Boat Company, ca. 1882

Published by H. S. Crocker and Co., San Francisco
Lithograph, 14¼ × 11¼ in. (36.1 × 28.5 cm)
The Elisha Whittelsey Collection, The Elisha Whittelsey Fund, 1948 (48.120.258)

Provenance: [Richard S. Wormser (died 1975), Bethel, Conn.]; Department of Prints purchase, 1948

"Although chromolithographs for home decoration became common a decade or so after the end of the Civil War, commercial advertising was the big patron of color lithography" (Mayor, *Popular Prints of the Americas*, 15). This small-scale poster printed by one of the earliest and most successful San Francisco printers promotes the Ship Owners & Merchants Tug Boat Company, featuring the firm's capabilities, the names of its acting directors, and its boats with their trademark red funnel with black tops.

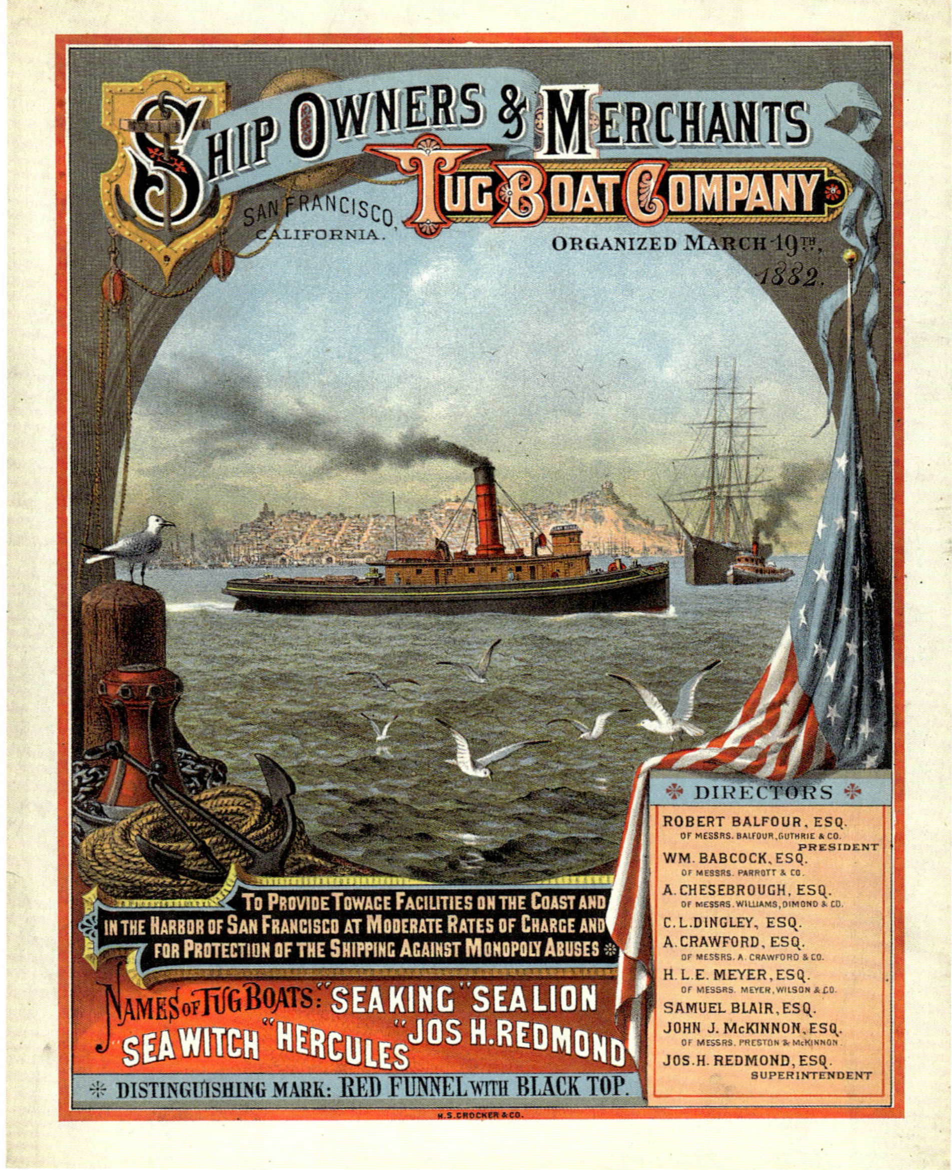

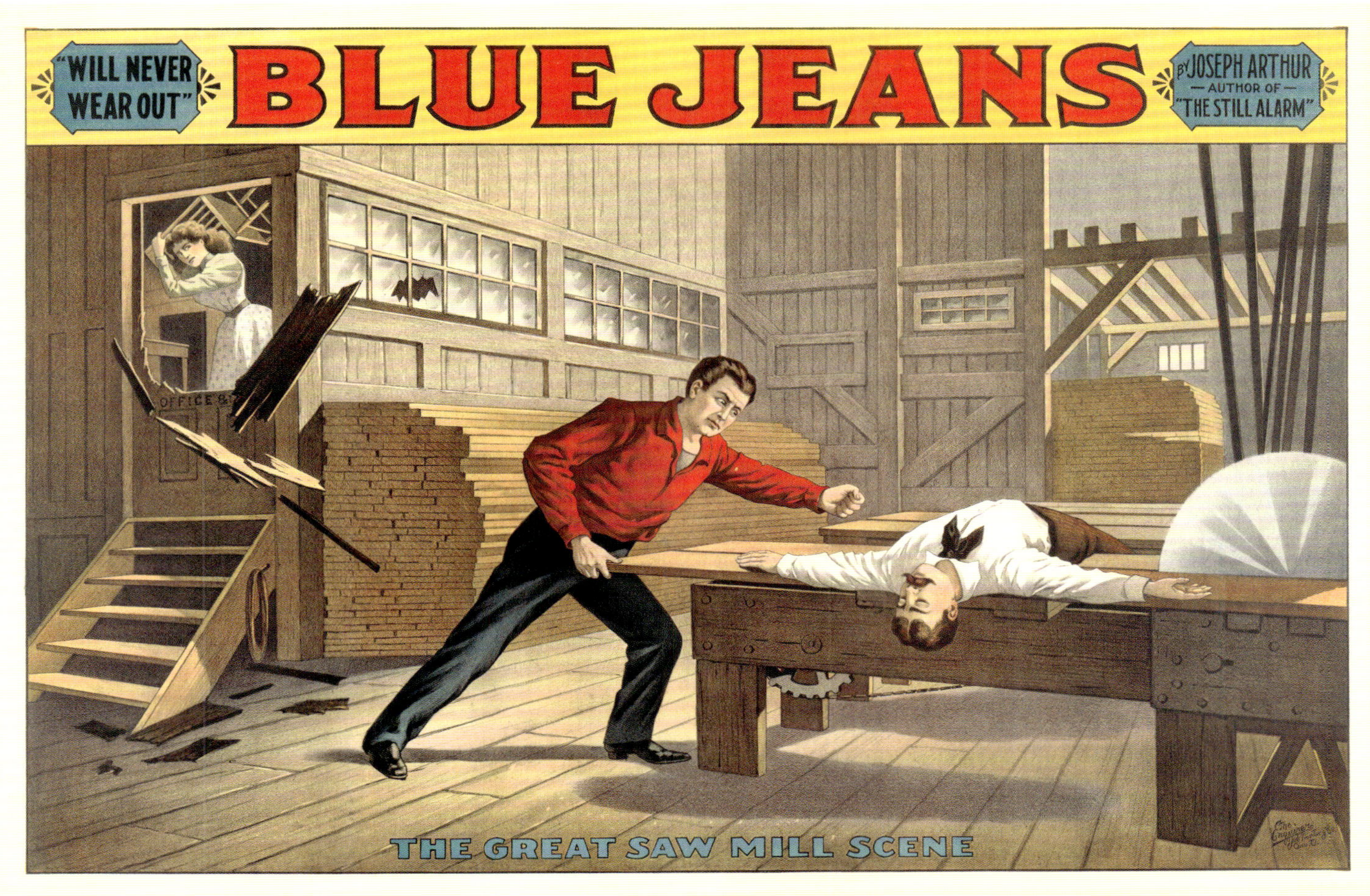

108

Saw Mill Scene from *Blue Jeans*

United States, ca. 1890
Lithograph, 28¼ × 42 in. (71.8 × 106.7 cm)
Gift of Ferdinand H. Davis, 1952 (52.596.3)

Provenance: Ferdinand H. Davis, New York; his gift to the Department of Prints, 1952

Depicting the most memorable and oft-imitated scene in Joseph Arthur's melodrama *Blue Jeans*, this poster celebrated the success of the play's first run at the Fourteenth Street Theatre in New York. The poster illustrates the sensational buzz-saw scene in the last act, when the villain, wearing a fiendishly red shirt, stands over the protagonist, who is about to be cut in two by a large and menacing buzz saw working at full speed. In the theater production, the villain cuts thick boards into lengths just prior to this encounter, proving the sharpness of the blade. This scene reportedly left audiences breathless and excited but agitated by its conspicuous realism, which broke through the artifice of theater and brought it to life—an aspect of theater that always fascinated Mayor. *Blue Jeans* had several revivals and in 1917 was adapted into a silent film.

Henri de Toulouse-Lautrec, French
(1864–1901)

Moulin Rouge: La Goulue, 1891

Printed by Affiches Américaines, Charles Lévy, Paris
Lithograph, second state of four, 74⅞ × 45⅞ in.
(190 × 116.5 cm)
Harris Brisbane Dick Fund, 1932 (32.88.12)

Provenance: [Maurice Le Garrec (died 1937), Paris];
Department of Prints purchase, 1932

Hailing from an aristocratic family but plagued
by physical ailments, Lautrec pursued his artistic ambitions in Paris, where he made a home
in Montmartre, a rundown neighborhood that
catered to the poor, criminals, and prostitutes
as well as artists and bohemians. He found his
greatest inspiration in the nightclubs where he
was a nightly fixture. Creating this poster for
the famed cabaret theater the Moulin Rouge,
Lautrec became an overnight sensation, and
so did the lithographic poster. Mayor found
Lautrec's work compelling because "[he] had
a fellow feeling for the people who have to put
on a good show whatever they suffer, like the
actor, the prostitute, the lawyer, or the circus
performer" (Mayor, "Toulouse-Lautrec," 1951:
90).

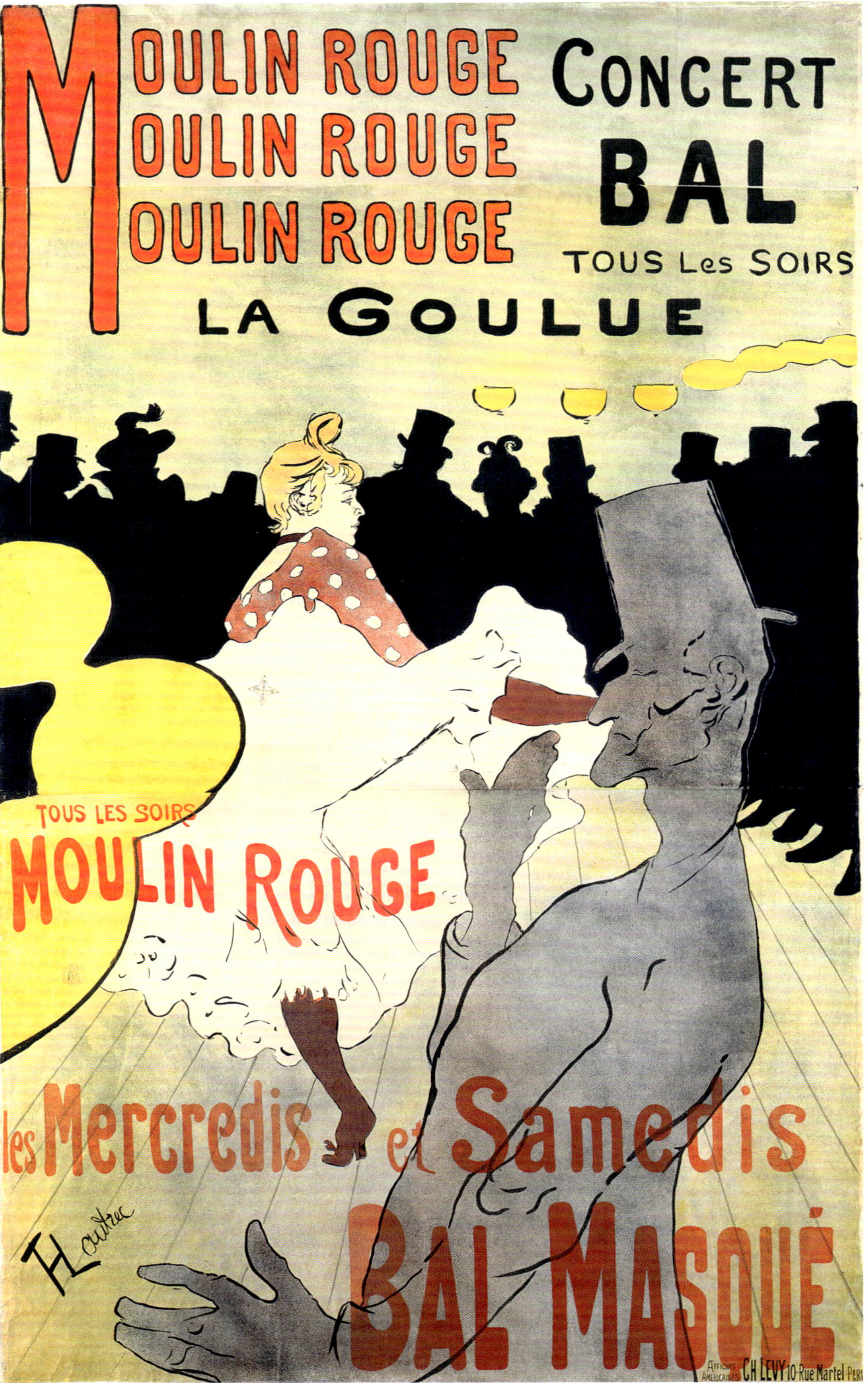

Henri de Toulouse-Lautrec, French
(1864–1901)

The Photographer Sescau (*Le Photographe
Sescau*), 1894

Lithograph, second state of three, 24½ × 31⅛ in.
(62.1 × 79.1 cm)
Harris Brisbane Dick Fund, 1932 (32.88.4)

Provenance: [Maurice Le Garrec (died 1937), Paris];
Department of Prints purchase, 1932

"Lautrec created the modern poster. He jumped to fame when his huge lithographs appeared on every billboard to startle Paris with their simplified colors and calculated design. When his posters first flared their yellows and oranges and blacks in the gaslight, they must have impressed themselves unforgettably, for nothing like them had ever decorated any street before. Even today they are apt to be the first pictures that spring to mind when we think of Paris in the 1890's. Lautrec made them the most memorable of all posters by the exactitude of his attack, not by the brutal smash that has become the commonplace of advertising and propaganda" (Mayor, "Toulouse-Lautrec," 1951: 89). This poster, which Lautrec made for his friend the photographer Paul Sescau, hints at the latter's reputation for using his studio to shoot not only posed portraits but also erotica. The tripod's splayed legs are mirrored by his own, between which dangles the pointed drapery of the camera cover.

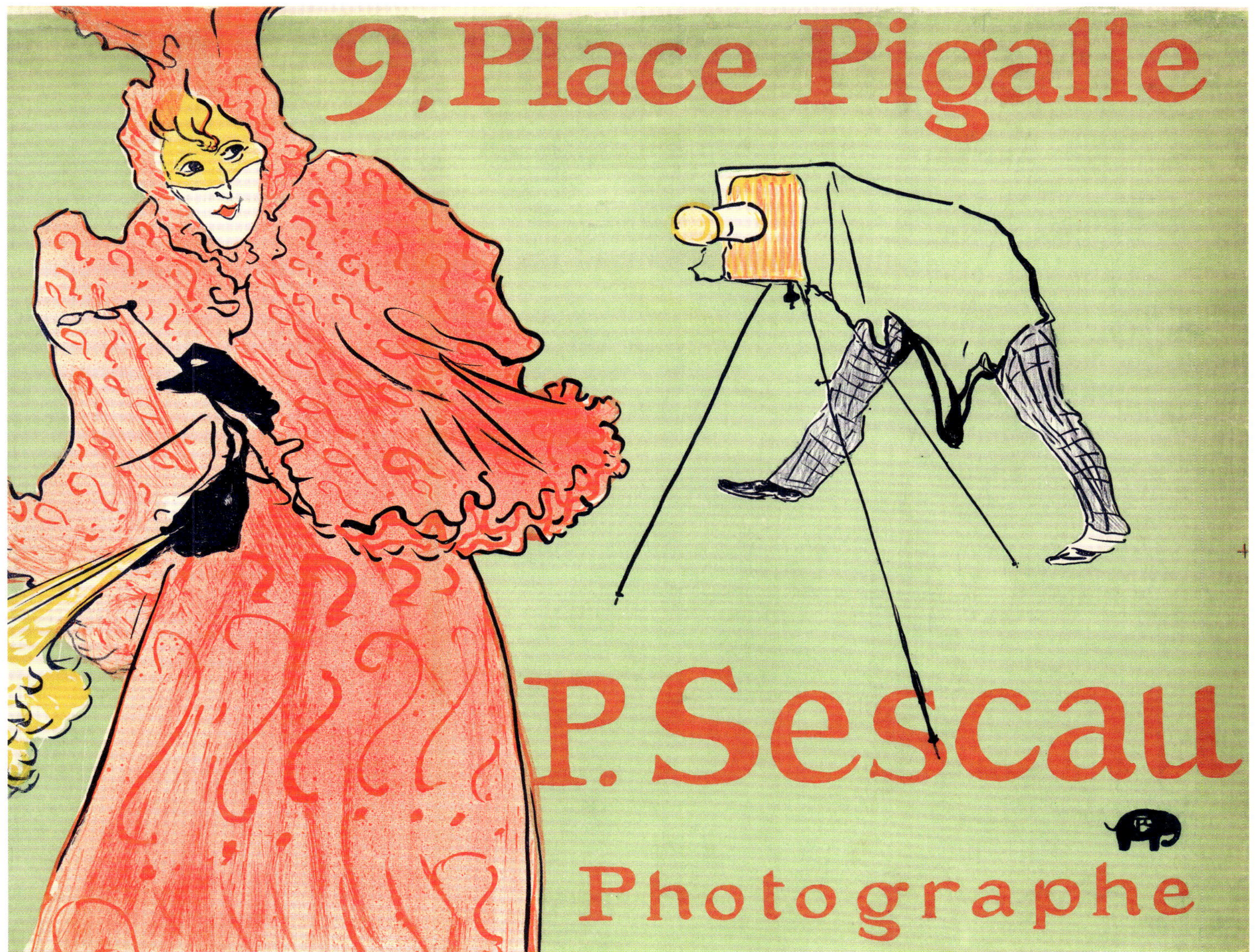

Pantomimes Lumineuses, Théâtre Optique de E. Reynaud, 1892

Printed by Imprimerie Chaix (Ateliers Chéret), Paris
Lithograph, 46½ × 34⅝ in. (118 × 88 cm)
Gift of Bessie Potter Vonnoh, 1941 (41.12.119)

Provenance: Bessie Potter Vonnoh (1872–1955), New York;
her gift to the Department of Prints, 1941

The history of printed advertisements dates
to broadsheets selling indulgences in the mid-
fifteenth century, but with the mid-nineteenth-
century phenomenon of the pictorial poster,
advertising spread "to infest the walls" of Paris
(Mayor, *Prints & People*, 641–42). Jules Chéret,
one of the earliest proponents of the lithographic poster, "advertised theaters, musical
halls, cigarettes, and champagne with about
1000 outdoor posters, at first in three colors
and after 1888 in four, drawn on stones that
became taller than a man by 1890" (ibid.). This
large-scale poster announces the *Pantomimes
Lumineuses*, the first public performance of a
moving-picture show.

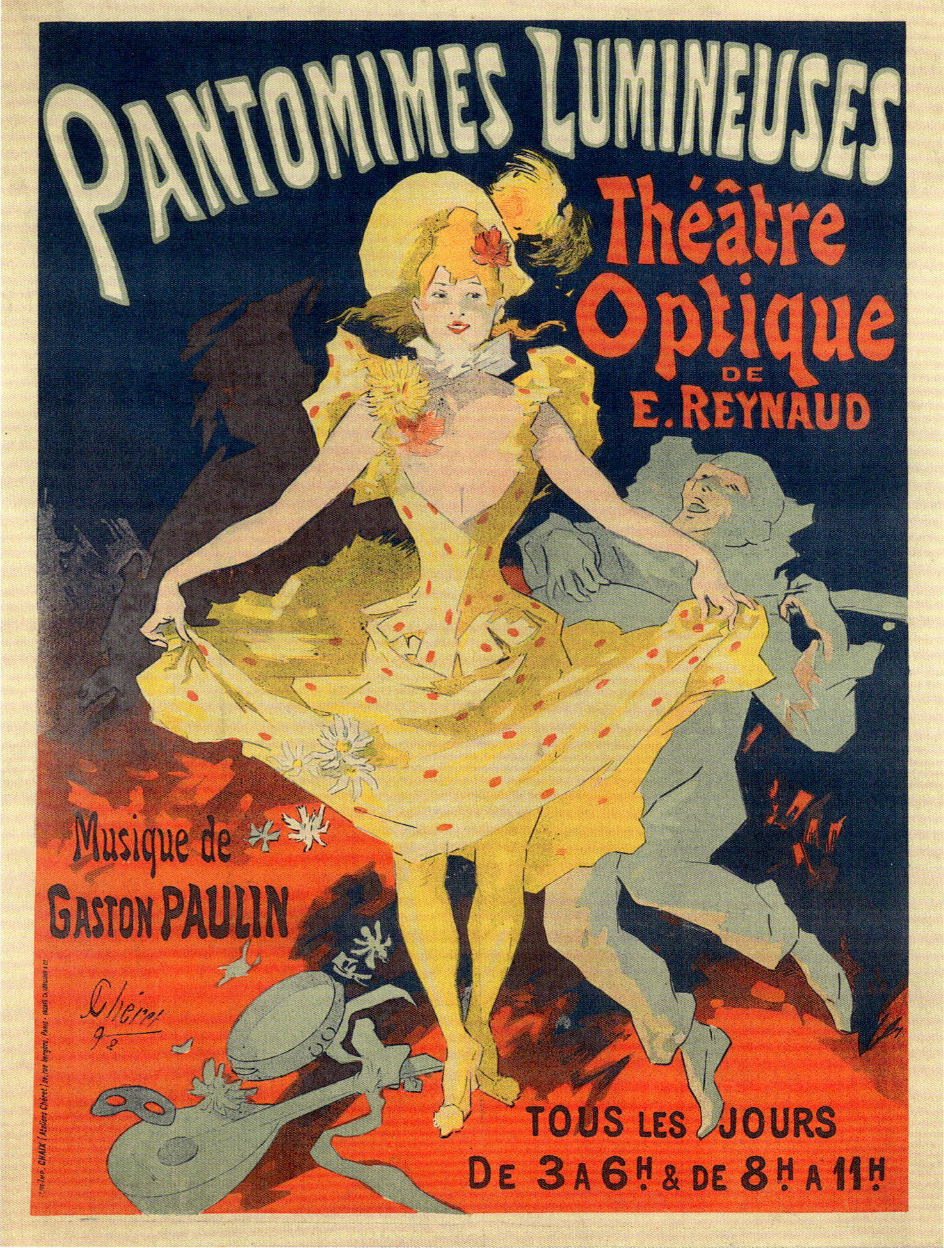

Jules Chéret, French (1836–1932)

Le Rapide, Grand Journal Quotidien, 1892

Printed by Imprimerie Chaix (Ateliers Chéret), Paris
Lithograph, 41 × 34⅝ in. (104 × 87.8 cm)
Gift of Bessie Potter Vonnoh, 1941 (41.12.106)

Provenance: Bessie Potter Vonnoh (1872–1955), New York;
her gift to the Department of Prints, 1941

"Ancestors of the modern advertising art,
colored posters blossomed into spectacular
popularity in the 1890s, when improved
mechanical techniques, chiefly color lithography, made large scale color reproduction
both inexpensive and attractive" (Mayor,
press release for "Posters of the 90's," 1942).
Chéret, often regarded as the originator of the
lithographic poster, employed an innovative
technique known as *crachis*, where he spat-
tered rather than painted a wax resist onto the
lithographic stone, producing a shimmering,
atmospheric effect. Many of Chéret's posters
exploit the images of beautiful women to sell a
daily newspaper or other product.

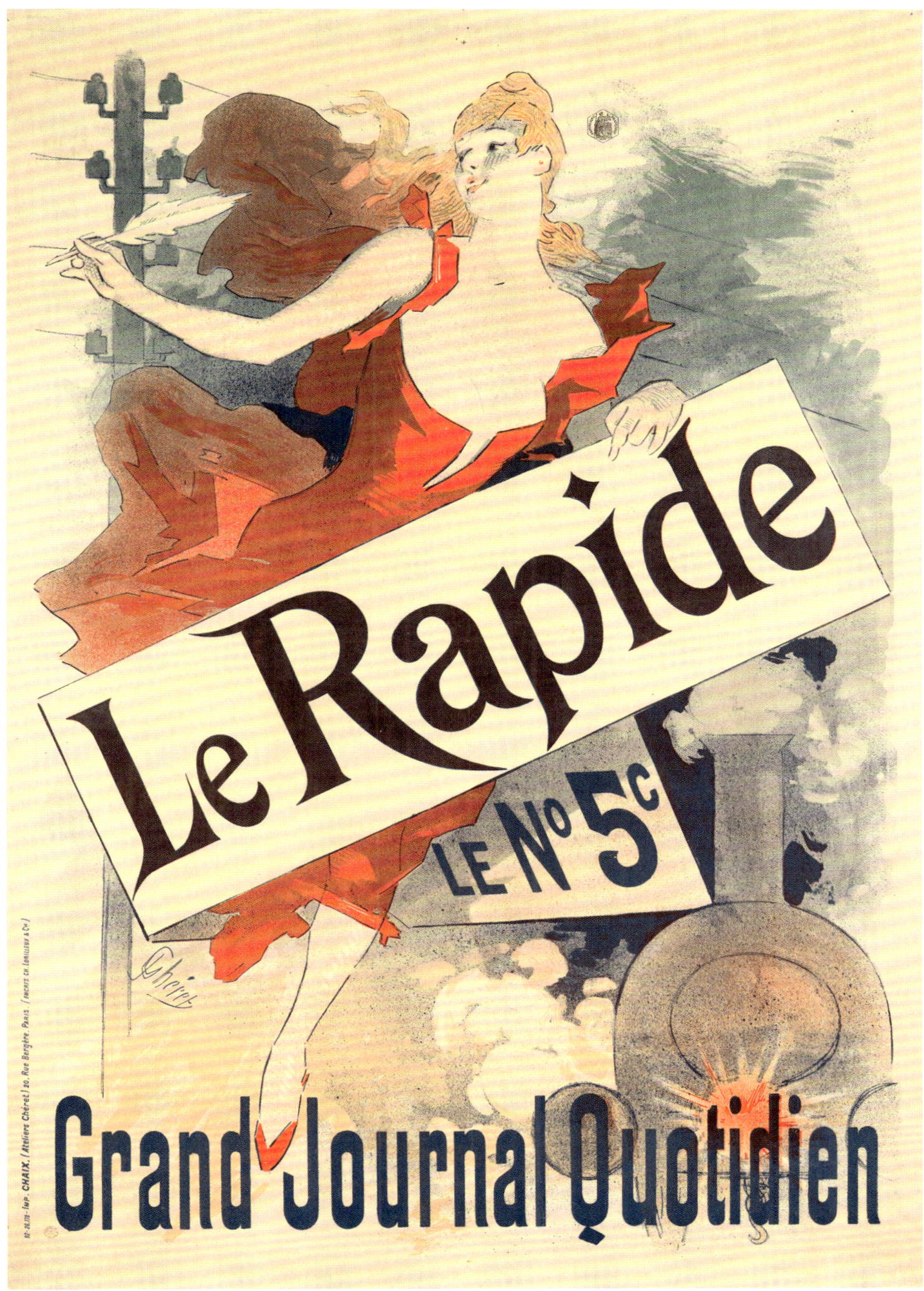

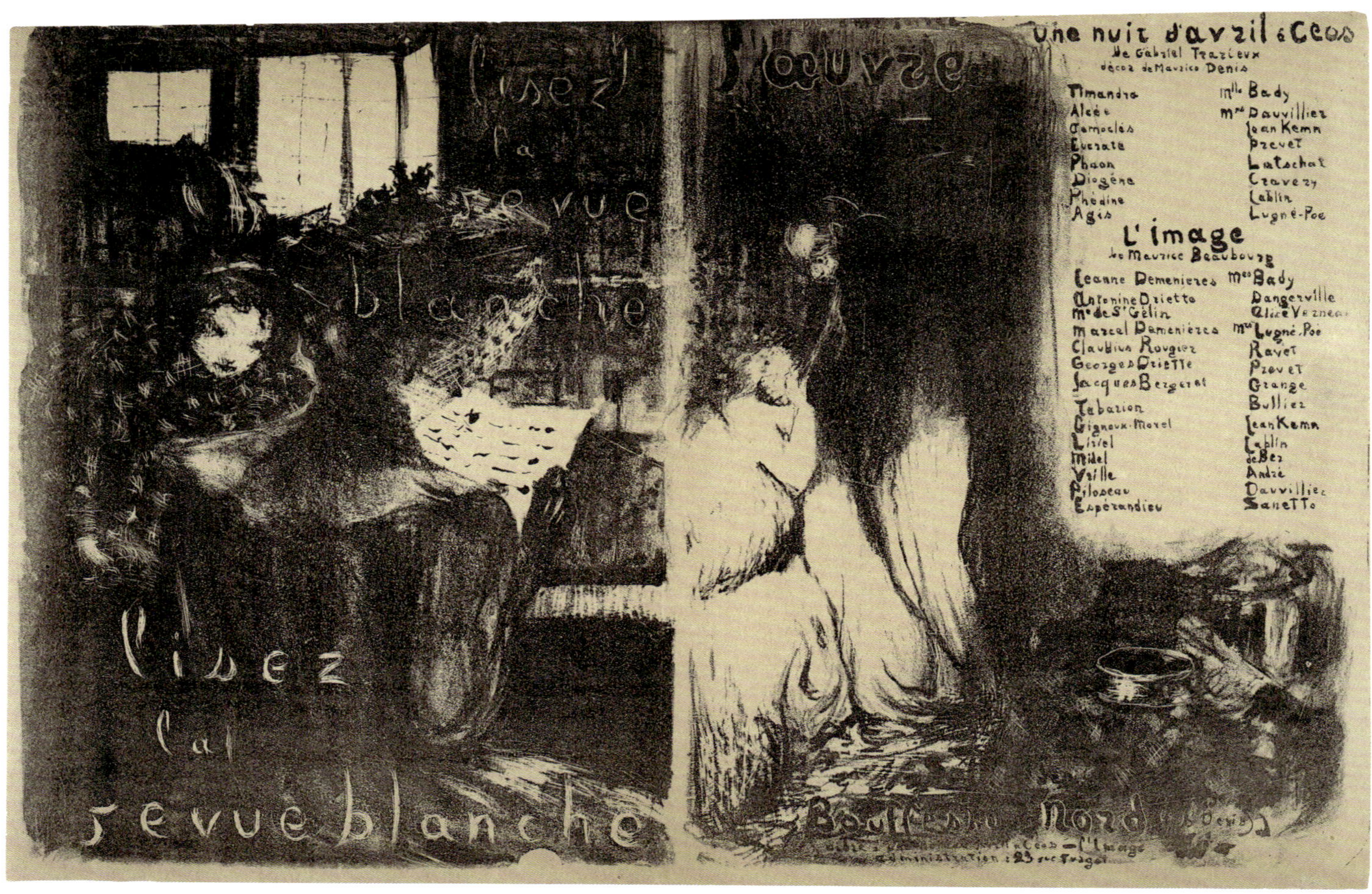

113

113–14

Édouard Vuillard, French (1868–1940)

Programs for Théâtre de L'Oeuvre,
February [113] and May [114] 1894

Lithographs

[113]
12⅛ × 18⅞ in. (30.8 × 48 cm)
The Elisha Whittelsey Collection, The Elisha Whittelsey
Fund, 1951 (50.616.1)

Provenance: [Henry J. Planten (1913–1992), Elmhurst,
N.Y.]; Department of Prints purchase, 1951

[114]
18⅞ × 12¾ in. (48 × 32.3 cm)
The Elisha Whittelsey Collection, The Elisha Whittelsey
Fund, 1966 (66.559.2)

Provenance: [Paul Prouté, Paris]; Department of Prints
purchase, 1966

A founding member of Théâtre de L'Oeuvre, a
showcase for Symbolism, Vuillard not only created the large-scale programs for the productions in the winter and spring of 1894 but also
designed the sets for its second season. With
his codirectors Aurélien Lugné and the writer
Camille Mauclair, Vuillard promoted the
theater with a vigorous campaign of printed
brochures, manifestos, and programs—many
designed and executed by the likes of Edward
Burne-Jones, Félix Vallotton, Toulouse-
Lautrec, Pierre Bonnard, and Théophile-
Alexandre Steinlen. These programs (for *Une
Nuit d'Avril à Ceos* and *L'Image*, at the Théâtre
des Bouffes du Nord, and *Frères*, *La Gardienne*,
and *Créanciers*, staged at the Théâtre de la
Comédie-Parisienne) also tout the avant-garde
journal *La Revue blanche*, one of the most dar-
ing and eclectic periodicals of the 1890s. The
journal often employed artists such as Vuillard
to design its advertising posters.

lisez la Revue Blanche
Frères
pièce en 1 acte de Hermann Bang
traduction de
M.M. de Colleville et Zepelin
Ella   M. Montchazmont
Éric   M. Henri Monteux
Emile   M. Jean Kemn
la Gardienne
poème d'Henri de Regnier
la gardienne   M.lles Lara......Marg.Carlix
le Maitre   M. Lugne-Poe.......Yean Kemn
1er frere d'armes M. Prevet
2e frere d'armes   M.H. Monteux
Conférence de M. Lucien Mühlfeld
Créanciers
tragi-comedie en 1 acte de Strindberg
traduction
de M. Georges Loiseau
Tekla   M.lle Lucienne Dorsy
Gustave   M. Rameau
Adolphe   M. Lugne-Poe
Salle de la Comedie Parisienne   8e soirée de l'Œuvre
administration: 22 r. Turgot

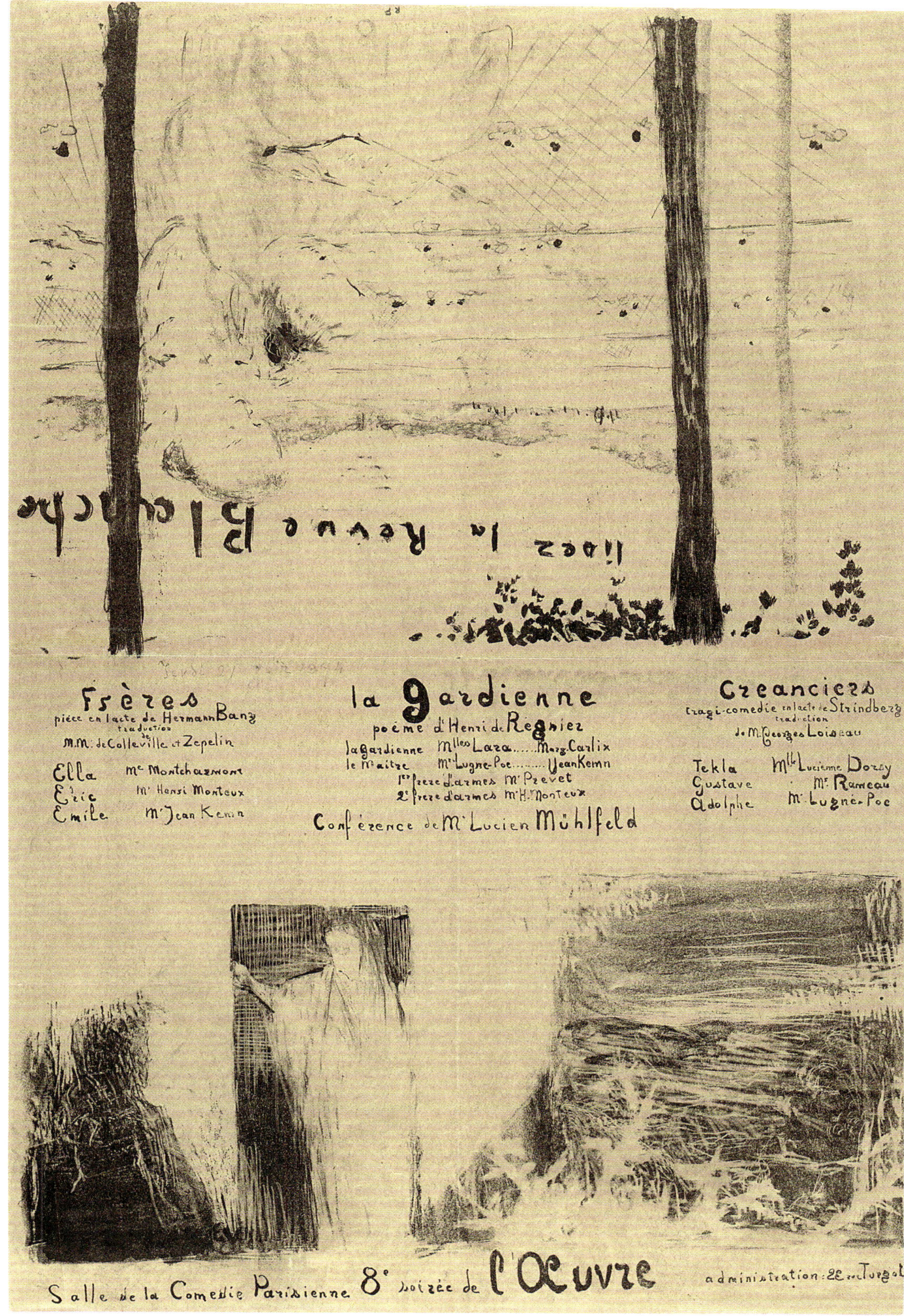

114

William Henry Bradley, American
(1868–1962)

The Echo, Chicago's Humorous and Artistic Fortnightly, 1895

Printed by Ralph Meriman Co. Press, Chicago
Published by *The Echo*, Chicago
Lithograph, 24⅝ × 15⅞ in. (62.3 × 40.3 cm)
Gift of David Silve, 1936 (36.23.22)

Provenance: David Silve, New York; his gift to the
Department of Prints, 1936

Along with Edward Penfield, Bradley, a prolific poster designer, helped fuel the American
poster craze of the mid-1890s. Many "outstanding painters and illustrators of the day
were interested in this new medium and their
posters became not only successful advertisements, but collector's items as well" (Mayor,
press release for "Posters of the 90's," 1942).
Influenced by the designs of the British artists
Aubrey Beardsley and William Morris, Bradley
employed calligraphic lines and decorative
surface patterns that are characteristic of the
Art Nouveau style. The same year that *The Echo*
published this poster, with its sweeping lines
and bold color contrasts, the newspaper noted
that poster art was a democratic art form:
"Appreciation of the poster spreads farther
and farther; business men are beginning to
realize its advantages; artists are more and
more devoting themselves to this specialty. The
result, as it looms on the horizon, is pleasant to
think of: it means art in the street, in the public
eye everywhere" ("Poster Lore," *The Echo* 1,
no. 11 [Oct. 1, 1895]: 258).

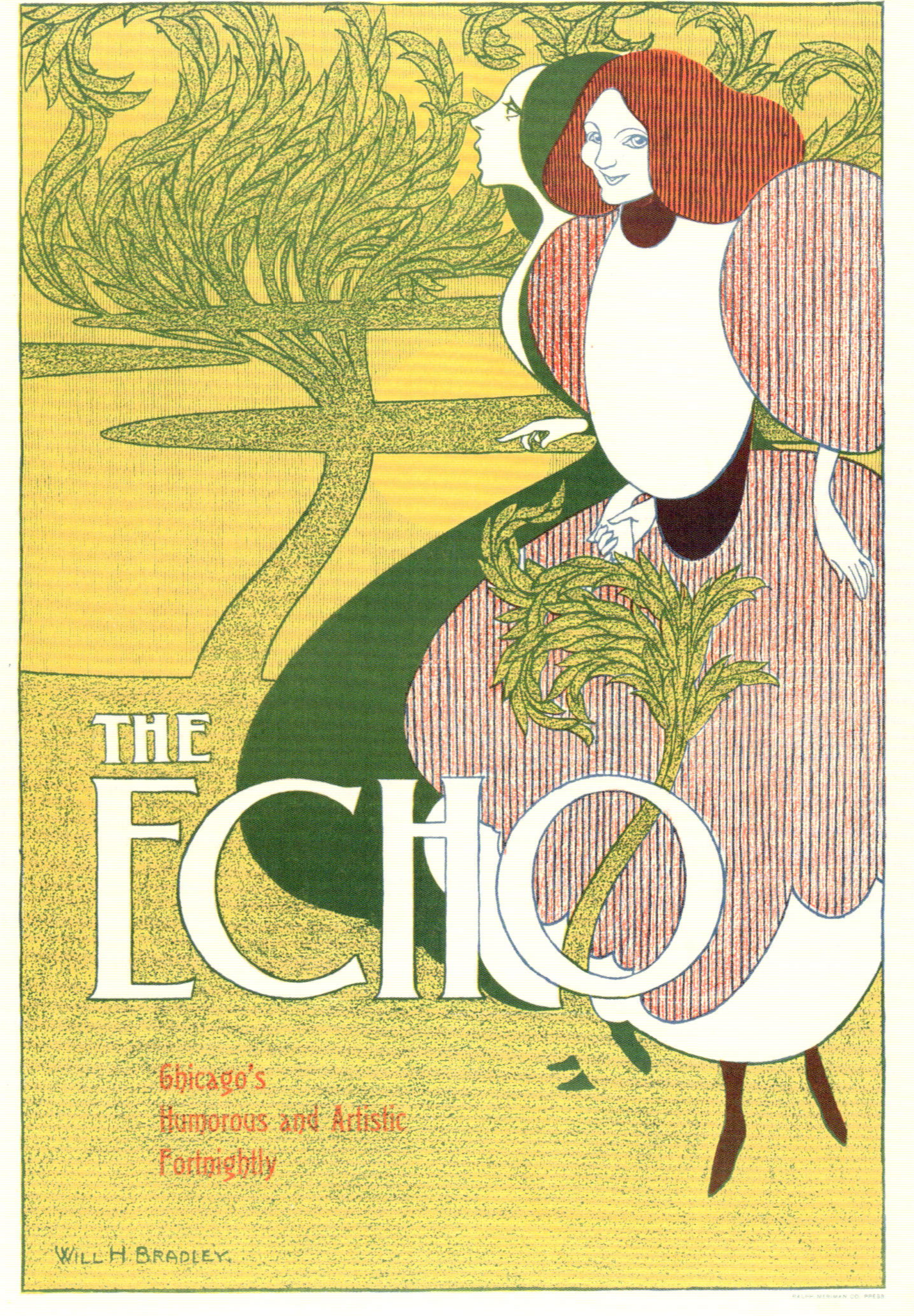

116

Lippincott's, May, 1895

Published by J. B. Lippincott Co., Philadelphia
Lithograph, 18⅝ × 12 in. (47.2 × 30.4 cm)
Gift of Bessie Potter Vonnoh, 1941 (41.12.131)

Provenance: Bessie Potter Vonnoh (1872–1955),
New York; her gift to the Department of Prints, 1941

Between 1894 and 1895 *Lippincott's Monthly
Magazine*, a popular literary journal, commissioned monthly posters from Carqueville that
were meant to compete directly with Edward
Penfield's fashionable posters for *Harper's*. This
small-scale, strikingly colored example is one
of a dozen Carqueville posters that entered
the collection as part of an enormous gift by
the American sculptor Bessie Potter Vonnoh,
a near-contemporary of Carqueville and the
other American and French lithographers
whose work she avidly collected.

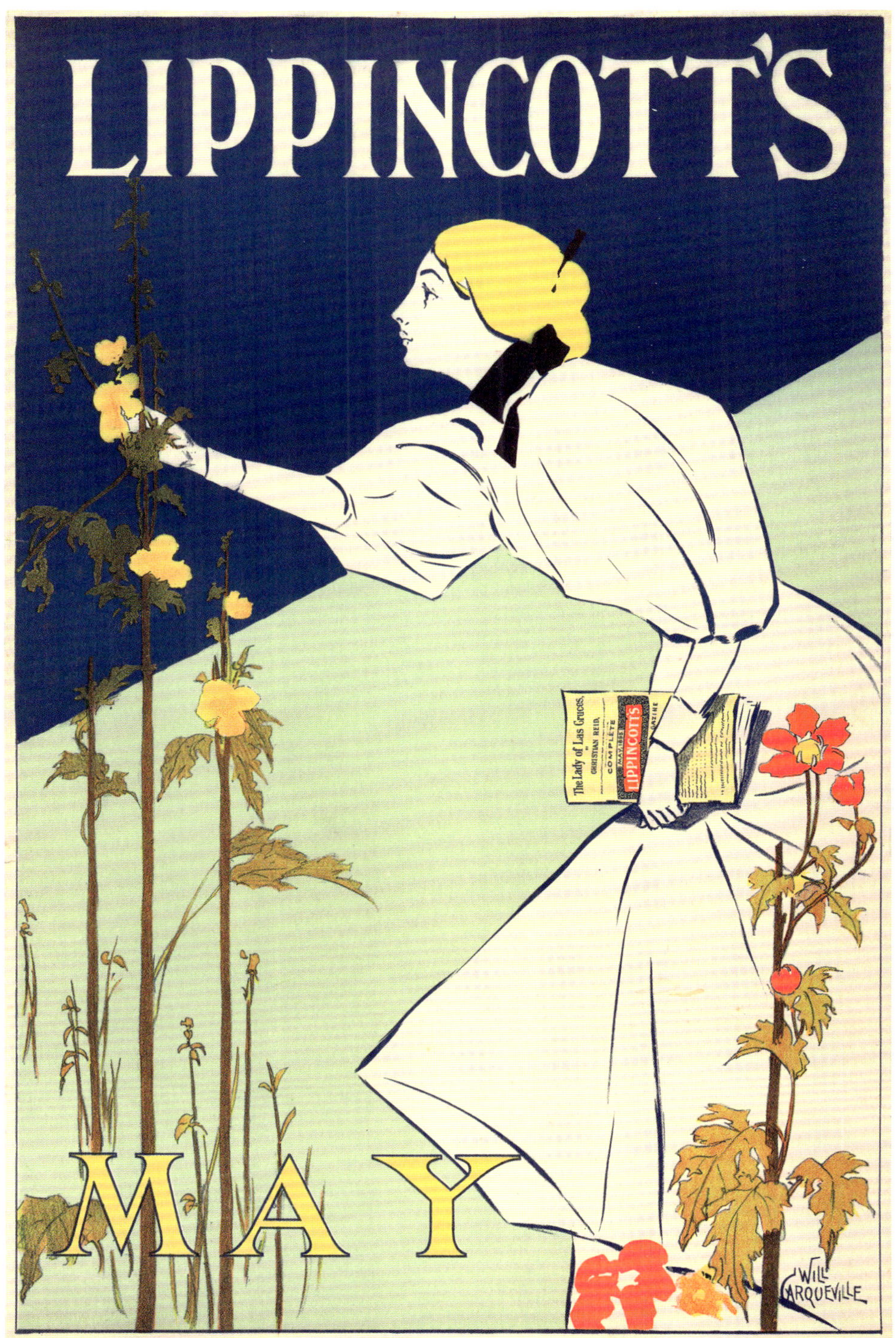

Edward Penfield, American (1866–1925)

Calendar for the Year 1897, printed 1896

Published by R. H. Russell & Son, New York
Lithographs with commercial relief process, each
approximately 14 × 10¼ in. (35.6 × 26 cm)

[117–19]
The Elisha Whittelsey Collection, The Elisha Whittelsey
Fund, 1965 (65.658.40[1–3])

Provenance: [Harvey W. Brewer, Closter, N.J.];
Department of Prints purchase, 1965

[120–21]
Gift of David Silve, 1936 (36.23.1[4–5])

Provenance: David Silve, New York; his gift to the
Department of Prints, 1936

Penfield's 1893 poster for *Harper's* launched the
popularity of American poster art; he would
create monthly posters for the magazine for
nearly a decade. As an acclaimed staff illustrator, Penfield was free to experiment with the
avant-garde styles found in contemporary
French and British poster designs. In this
calendar, one of two made for R. H. Russell &
Son, the influence of Toulouse-Lautrec and
Chéret is evident in the bold and direct style,
but Penfield's figures are uniquely American,
casually but impeccably dressed for a leisurely
afternoon's activities. Penfield's calendar sub-
stantiates Mayor's idea that common prints
such as these are a crucial part of America's
pictorial history.

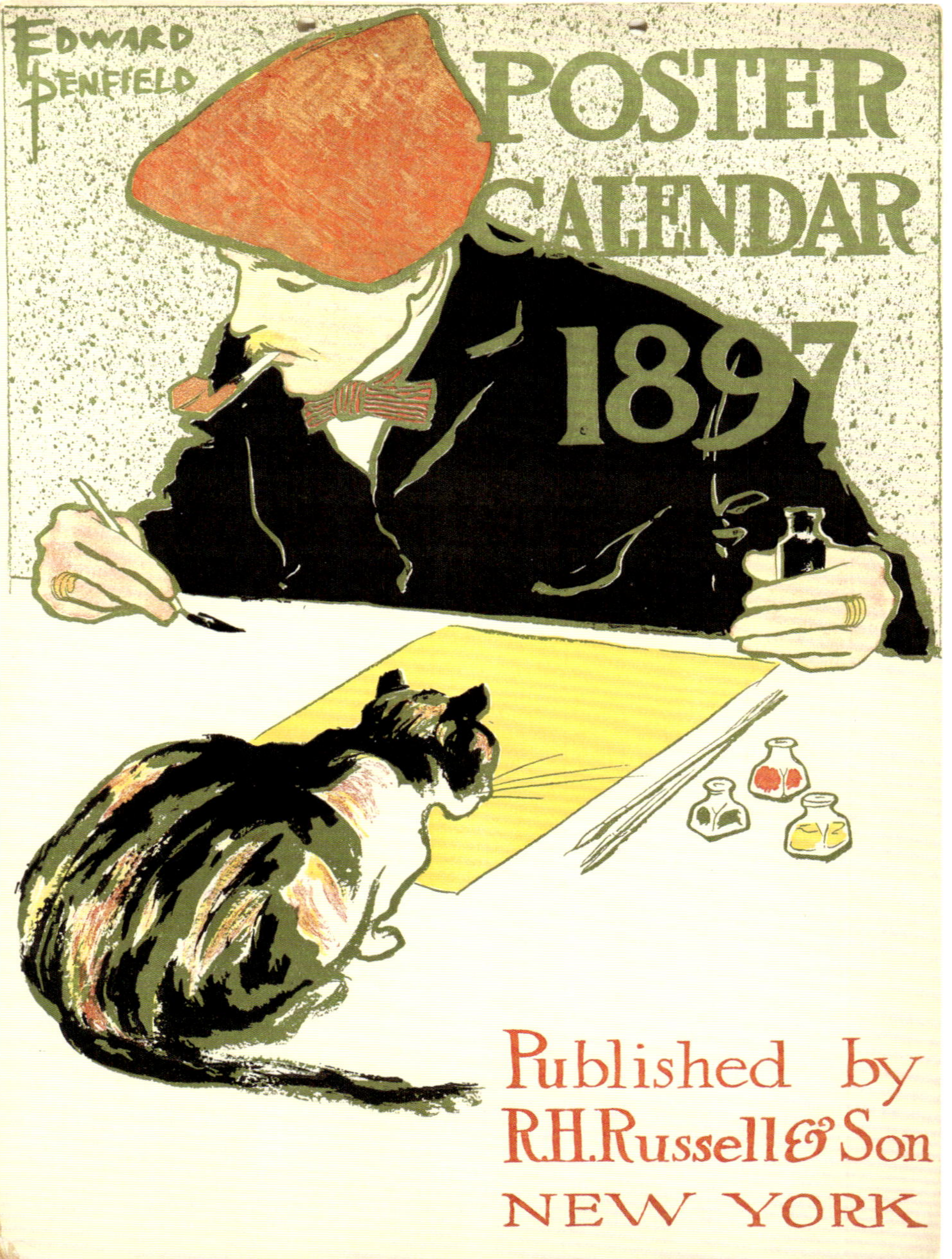

117

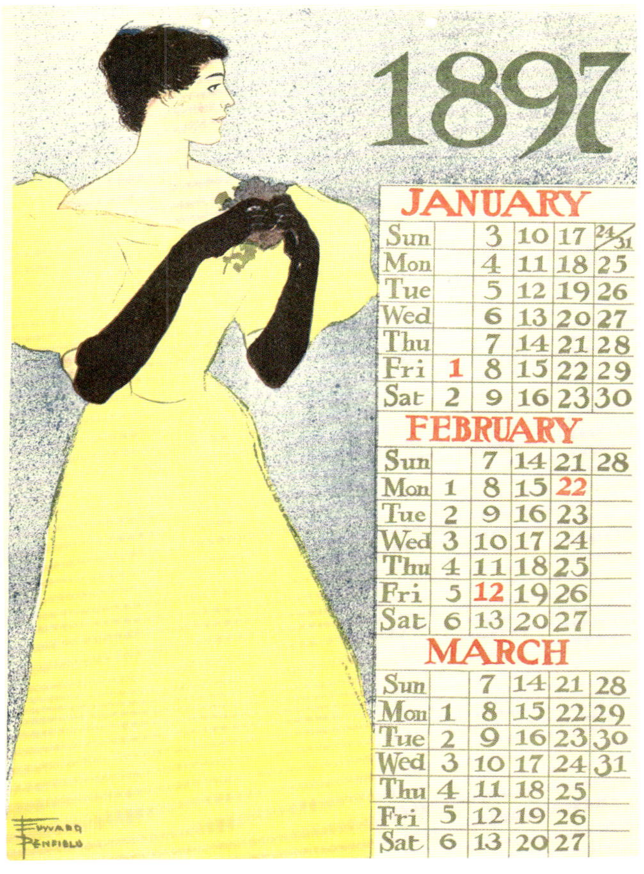

118

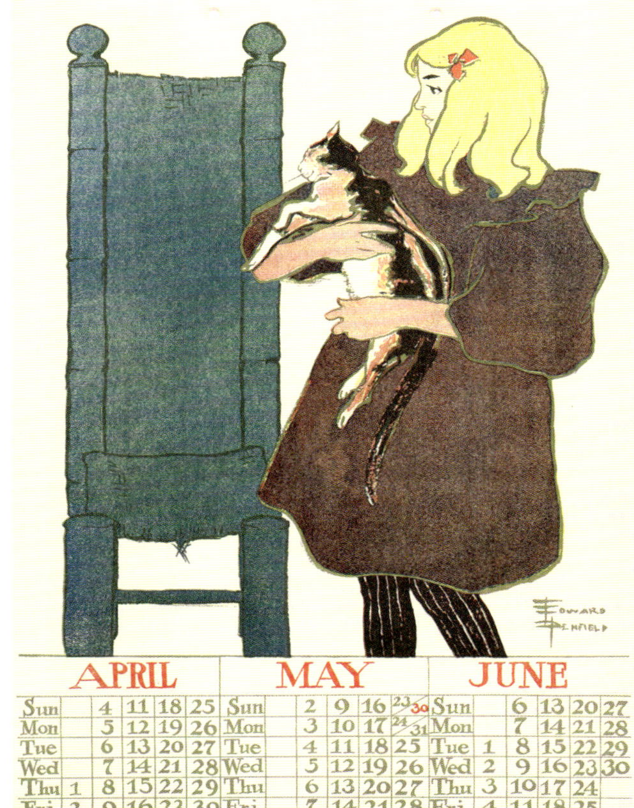

119

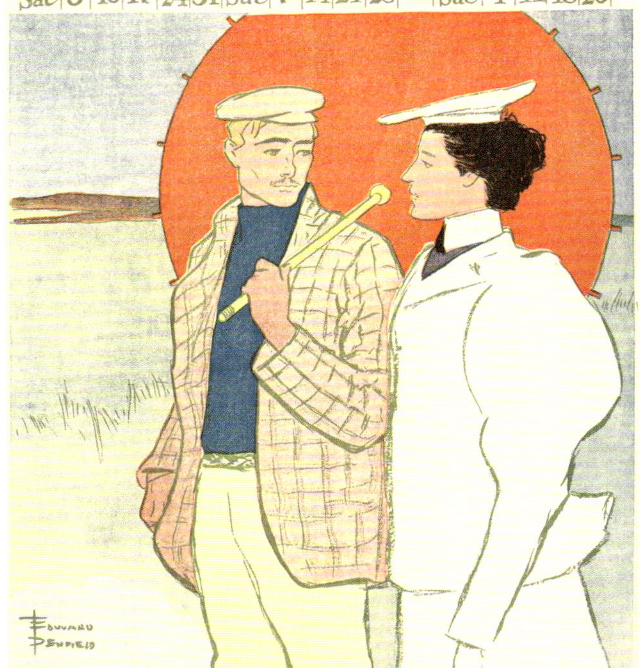

120

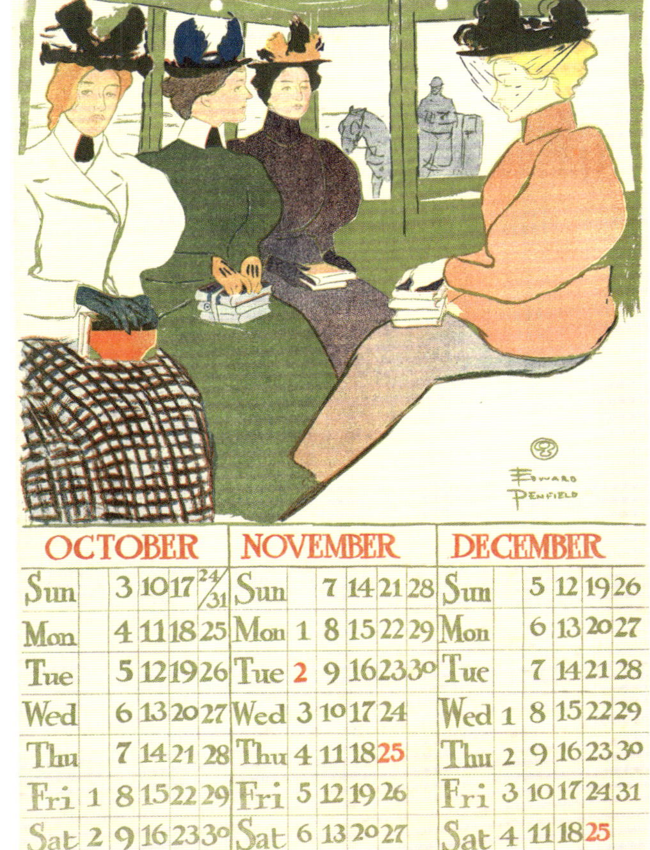

121

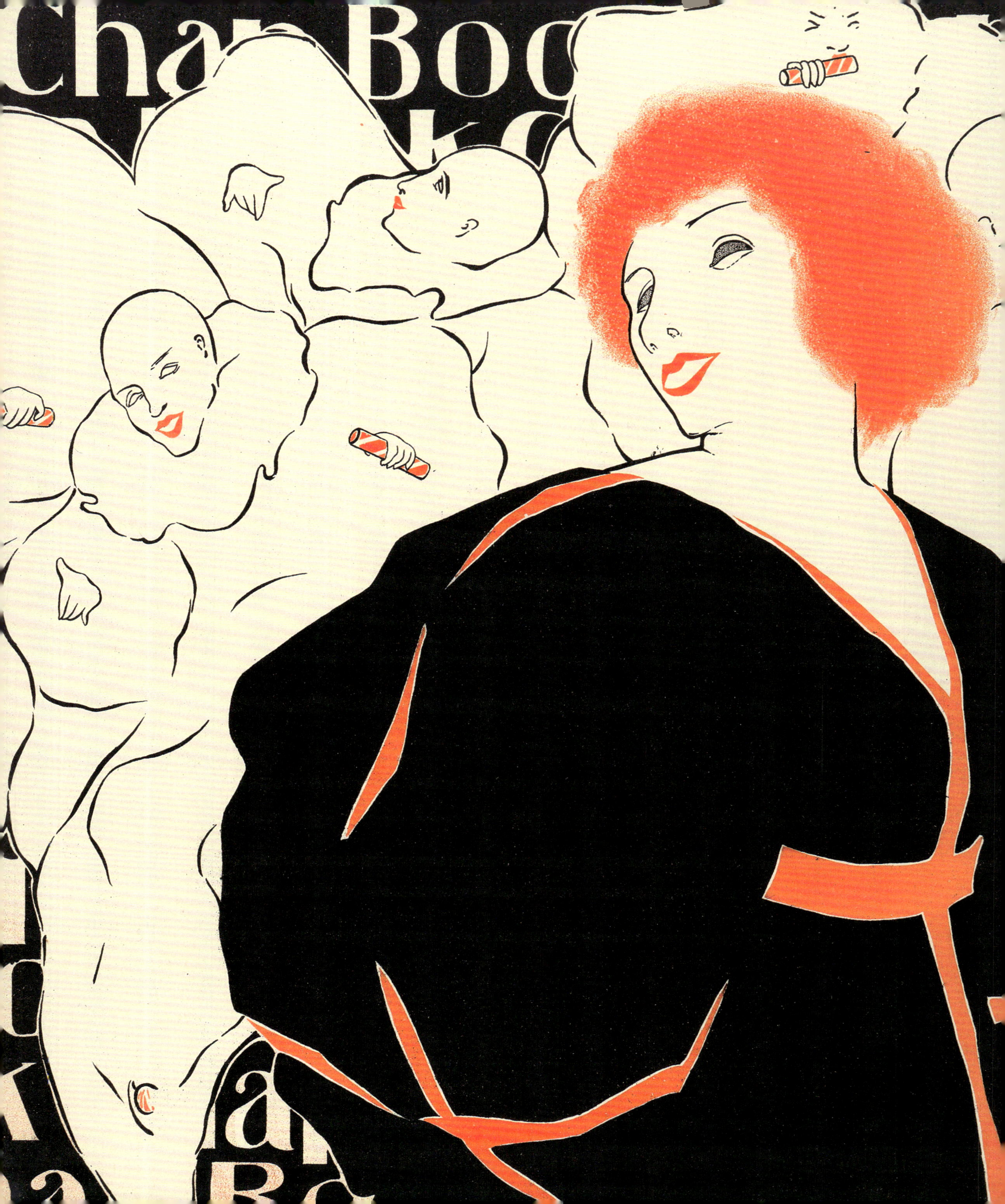
Char Boo

122

Frank Hazenplug, American
(1873/74–1931)

The Chap-Book, 1896

Published by Stone and Kimball, Chicago
Lithograph, 20⅝ × 14¼ in. (52.2 × 36 cm)
Museum Accession, transferred from the Library
(57.627.7[2])

Hazenplug was apprenticed to William Bradley
at the publisher Stone and Kimball but is little
known today. He often preferred to create
forms out of flat areas of color, depending
relatively little on the drawn line. He made this
poster for the influential literary magazine
The Chap-Book, which began to publish posters in 1894 in an effort to compete with larger
journals that deployed artistic posters as their
primary form of advertising. The shock of the
performer's bright orange hair and the cool,
serpentine sweep of her body are reminiscent
of Toulouse-Lautrec's posters of Jane Avril,
while her ease of movement and joie de vivre
recall Georges de Feure's depiction of Loïe
Fuller (see cat. 124).

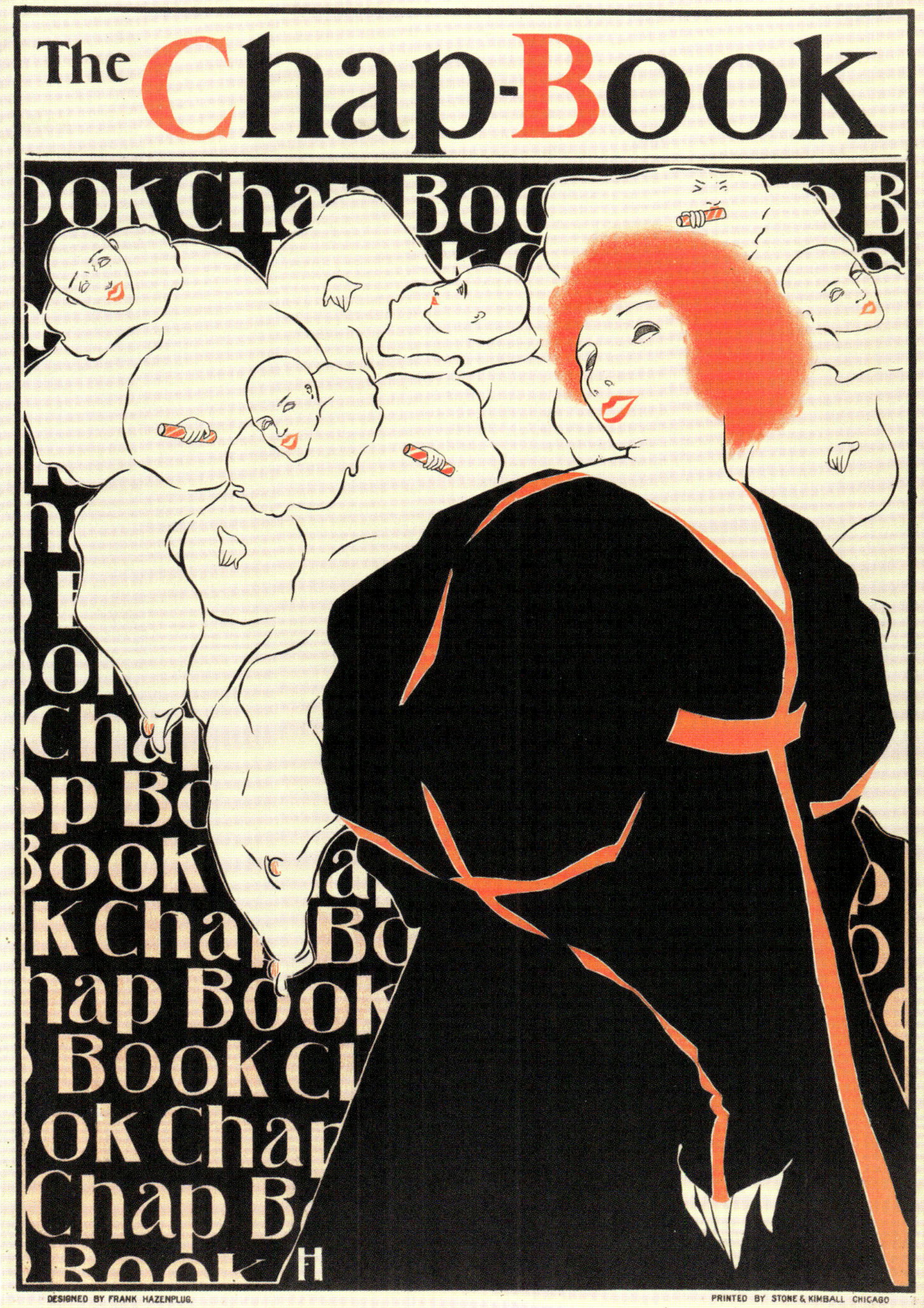

Pierre Bonnard, French (1867–1947)

L'Estampe et l'Affiche (*The Print and the Poster*), 1897

Printed by L'Estampe et l'Affiche, Paris
Lithograph, 32¾ × 24¼ in. (83 × 61.5 cm)
Harris Brisbane Dick Fund, 1939 (39.102.2)

Provenance: [Jean Goriany, New York]; Department of Prints purchase, 1939

Having studied both art and the law, Bonnard decided to focus on his artistic career after selling a design for a poster in 1889. Over the next two years color lithography became central to the output of many artists, including Vuillard and Toulouse-Lautrec, whom Bonnard had initiated into the art of the poster. "For a decade these three painters experimented on the cylindrical billboards of Paris more daringly, promptly, and publicly than in the Salon des Indépendents. The painters' posters of the 1890s so altered all printmaking with their impact of size, design, and color that few printmakers have been content to return altogether to the earlier meditative little monochrome scaled to the collector's portfolio" (Mayor, *Prints & People*, 642).

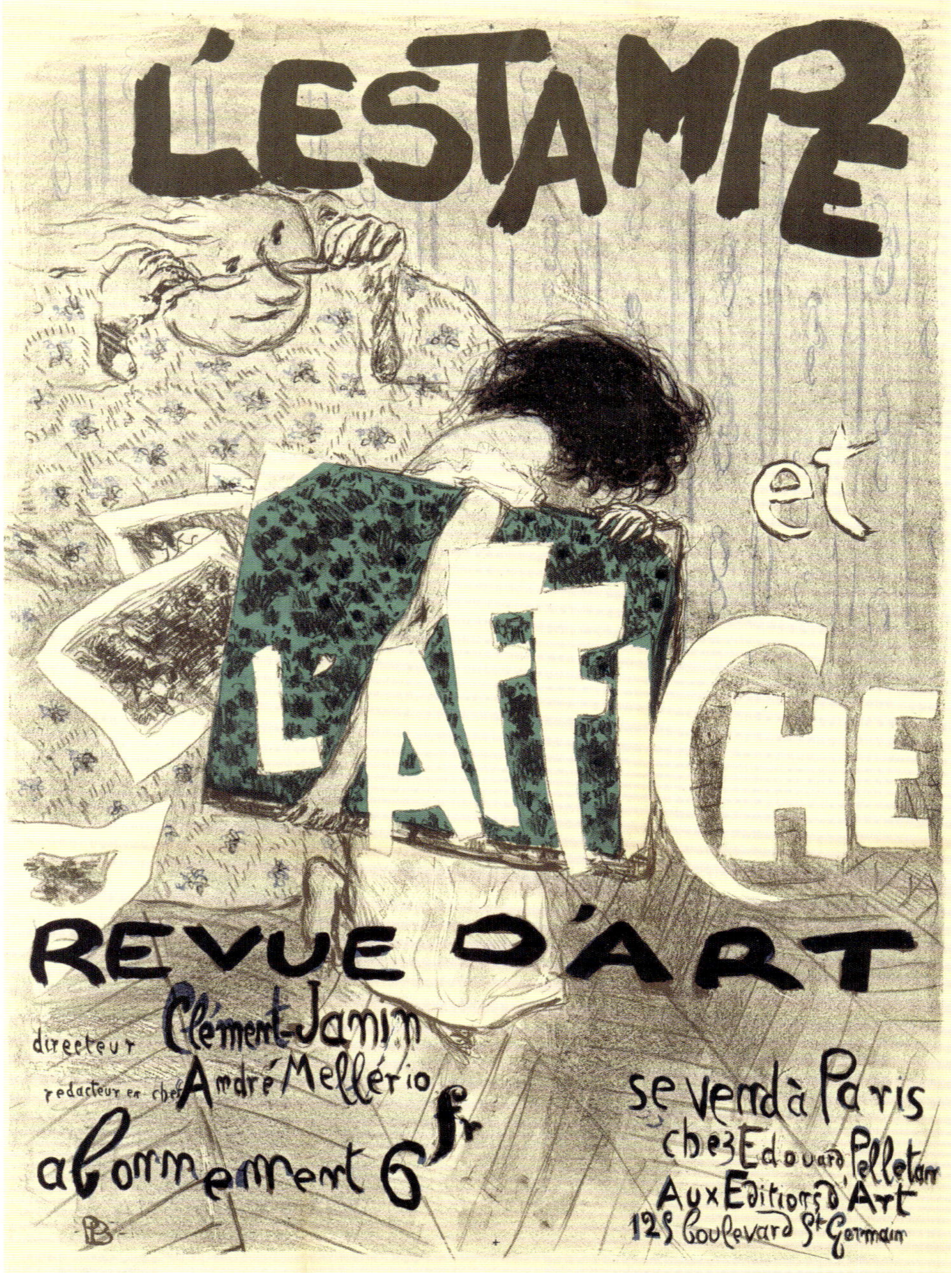

Georges de Feure, French (1868–1943)

*Comédie Parisienne, la Loïe Fuller dans Sa
Création Nouvelle, Salomé,* 1900

Printed by Imprimerie P. Lemenil, Asnières-sur-Seine
Lithograph, 51¼ × 37 in. (130 × 94 cm)
Gift of Bessie Potter Vonnoh, 1941 (41.12.35)

Provenance: Bessie Potter Vonnoh (1872–1955), New York;
her gift to the Department of Prints, 1941

This delightful image of the American dancer
Loïe Fuller captures her exuberant spirit and
the sensuality and excitement of cabaret culture in Paris at the end of the nineteenth century. Fuller's performance at the 1900 world's
fair in Paris attracted considerable attention;
she embodied Art Nouveau style with her
groundbreaking choreography, a seemingly
effortless manipulation of her large, diapha-
nous silk costumes, and her staging, infused
with multicolored electric lights.

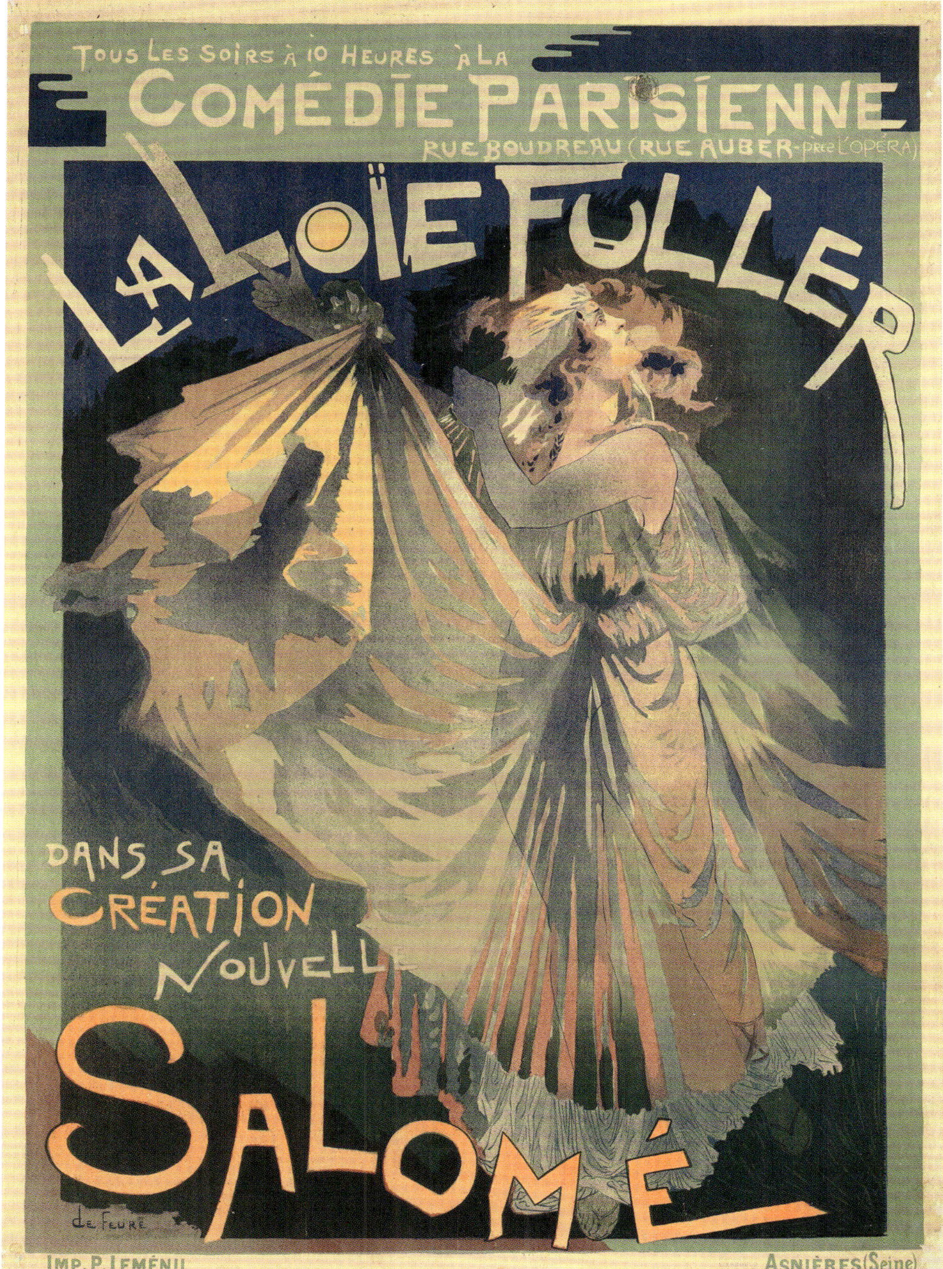

Hassan Cork Tip Cigarettes: The Oriental Smoke

Printed by the American Tobacco Co., Durham, N.C.,
ca. 1910
Lithograph, framed: 29⅛ × 22⅝ in. (74 × 57.5 cm)
The Jefferson R. Burdick Collection, Gift of Jefferson
R. Burdick (63.351.1)

Provenance: Jefferson R. Burdick (1900–1963), Syracuse,
N.Y.; his gift to the Department of Prints, between 1947
and 1963

Still in its original frame, this poster advertising Turkish-blend cigarettes is part of a
collection of more than three hundred thousand works of printed ephemera Jefferson R.
Burdick gave the Museum beginning in 1947.
Burdick spent the last fifteen years of his life in
the Department of Prints cataloguing his gift
of posters, trade cards, and postcards from the
late nineteenth to the mid-twentieth century.
These prints "constitute a continuous record of
design, and a history of the pictorial media that
business has used to present itself to the public" (Mayor, introduction, *Directory of the J. R.
Burdick Collection*, 3). The earliest trade cards
and posters in Burdick's collection, from the
1880s, were created by savvy tobacco compa-
nies, like the conglomerate American Tobacco,
in the wake of the Civil War, when tobacco
products became almost ubiquitous.

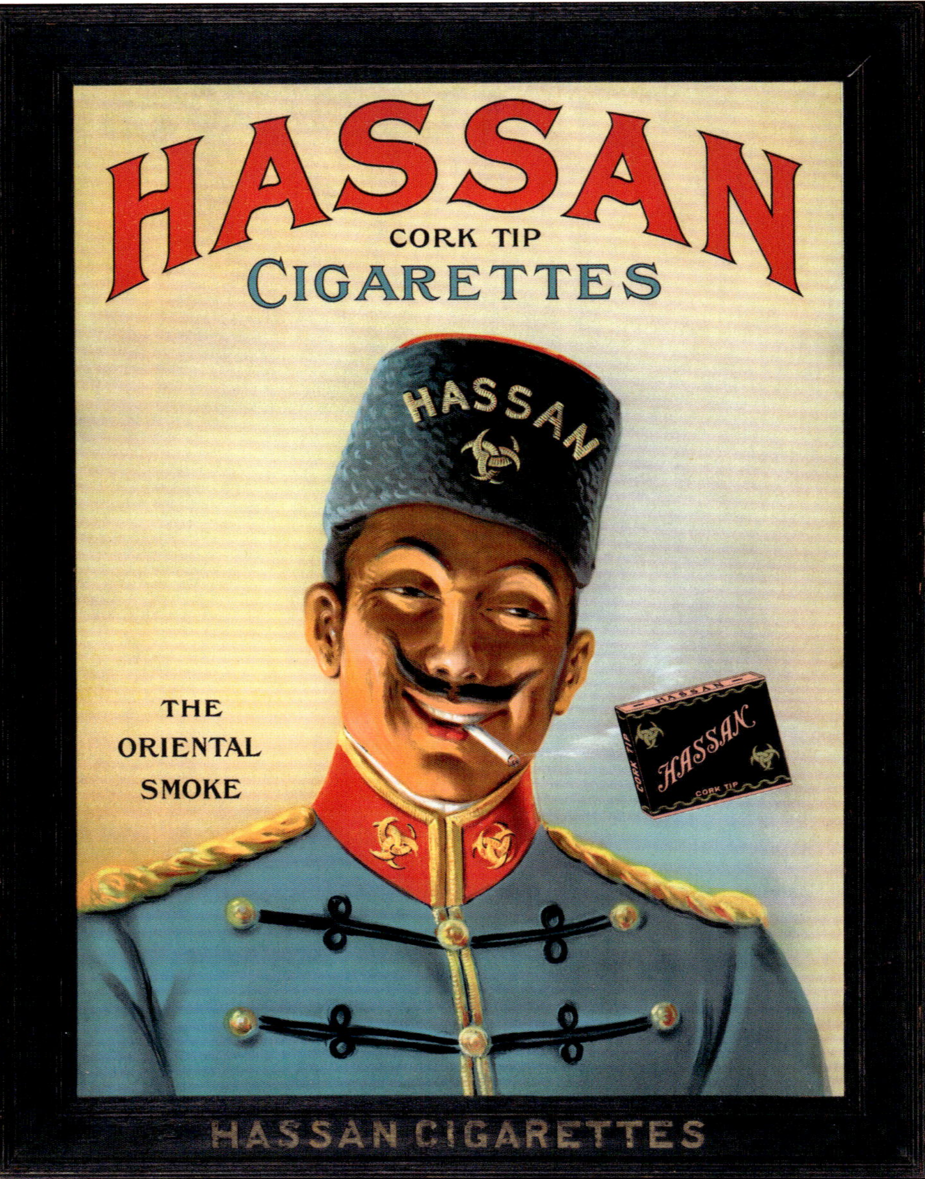

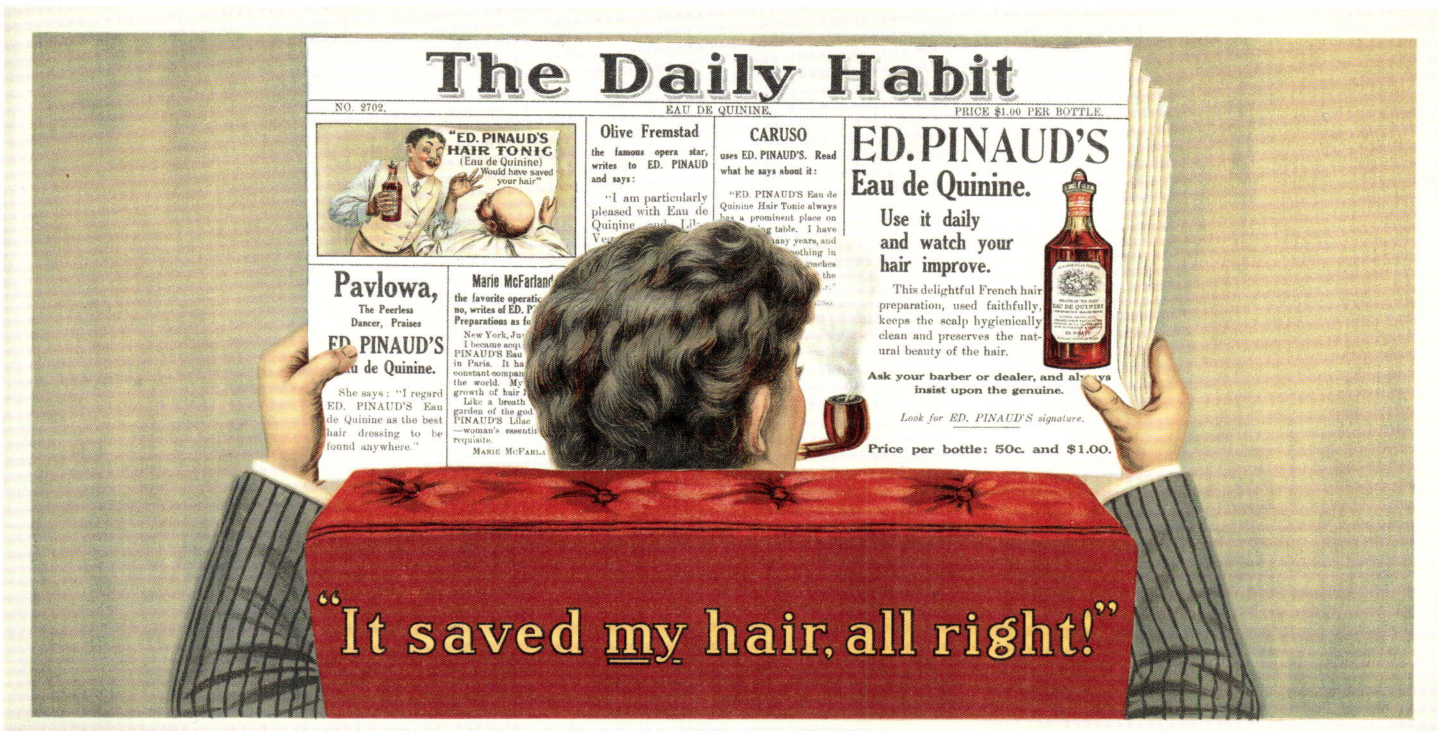

126

Ed. Pinaud's Eau de Quinine

United States, ca. 1920s
Lithograph, 10⅛ × 19⅞ in. (25.5 × 50.5 cm)
Museum Accession, transferred from the Library
(57.627.81)

This poster is part of a collection of more than
seventy popular prints that was transferred
from the Museum's Library to the Department
of Prints in 1957 at Mayor's behest. A New
York subway poster, it advertises the successful
hair tonic Eau de Quinine, which was imported
into the United States from the French per-
fumery. The product remained popular into
the 1960s.

Printed Ephemera

Fʀᴏᴍ ᴛʜᴇ ʟᴀᴛᴇ nineteenth century on, businesses in Europe and the United States exploited the technique of lithography to promote themselves to a broad public through all manner of advertising: billboards and posters, handbills and trade cards, advertisements in newspapers and magazines, and objects such as fans, calendars, and paper dolls that carried their commercial messages.

The small-scale lithographs shown here represent the hundreds of thousands in the Met's collection, which were amassed largely by Mayor. The postcards, trade cards, product inserts, and paper constructions illustrate subjects as varied as screen queens, flowers of the world, opera gloves, and heroes of the Spanish-American War. They often were produced in large sets to encourage collecting and, therefore, repeat buying. Designed in most cases by unknown individuals, these ephemeral printed objects were meant to be collected, carried, traded, and, most important, used.

Harlequin Series 2

Playing cards issued as premiums by Kinney Brothers Tobacco, New York, 1889
Lithographs, each 3½ × 2½ in. (8.9 × 6.3 cm)
Gift of James E. Mason, 1962 (62.581.2)

Benjamin Pollock, British (1857–1937)

Characters and Scenes from *Jack the Giant Killer* for a Toy Theater, 1870–90

Lithographs, each 6¾ × 8½ in. (17 × 21.4 cm)
The Elisha Whittelsey Collection, The Elisha Whittelsey Fund, 1952 (52.541.1[1–24])

Views in Central Park, New York, Part 2

Postcards published by Louis Prang & Co., Boston, 1864
Lithographs, each 4 × 2³⁄₈ in. (10.2 × 6.1 cm)
The Jefferson R. Burdick Collection, Gift of Jefferson R. Burdick, 1947 (47.91.25[26–49])

The Chicago World's Fair Series

Postcards published by Max Rigot Selling Co., Chicago, 1933
Printed by American Colortype, Chicago and New York
Lithographs, each 3⁵⁄₈ × 5½ in. (9 × 14 cm)
The Jefferson R. Burdick Collection, Gift of Jefferson R. Burdick (Burdick 435, PC225-1.2–.48)

Black and White Movie Stars

Bakery inserts issued by E. H. Koester Baking Co., Baltimore, ca. 1920
Lithographs, each 3³⁄₈ × 2 in. (8.6 × 5.1 cm)
The Jefferson R. Burdick Collection, Gift of Jefferson R. Burdick (Burdick 307, D1)

How to Do It Series

Bakery inserts issued by Welle-Boettler Bakery, St. Louis, early 20th century
Lithographs, each 2½ × 1½ in. (6.4 × 3.8 cm)
The Jefferson R. Burdick Collection, Gift of Jefferson R. Burdick (Burdick 307, D45)

Sports Cars

Bakery inserts issued by Mother's Cookies, Oakland, Calif., 1955
Lithographs, each 3½ × 2½ in. (8.9 × 6.4 cm)
The Jefferson R. Burdick Collection, Gift of Jefferson R. Burdick (Burdick 307, D72)

Pullman Kids in Wonderland

Bakery inserts issued by Weber Baking Co., Irvington, N.J., early 20th century
Lithographs, each 3¼ × 2 in. (8.2 × 5.1 cm)
The Jefferson R. Burdick Collection, Gift of Jefferson R. Burdick (Burdick 307, D69)

Ballerina and Bloomer Girls (Prima Donna)

Paper dolls published by Littauer and Boysen, Berlin, 1890–1905
Distributed by Dennison Manufacturing Co., New York
Lithographs, each overall 14³⁄₈ × 6⅛ in. (36.5 × 15.5 cm)
Gift of D. Lorraine Yerkes, 1959 (59.616.403a–g)

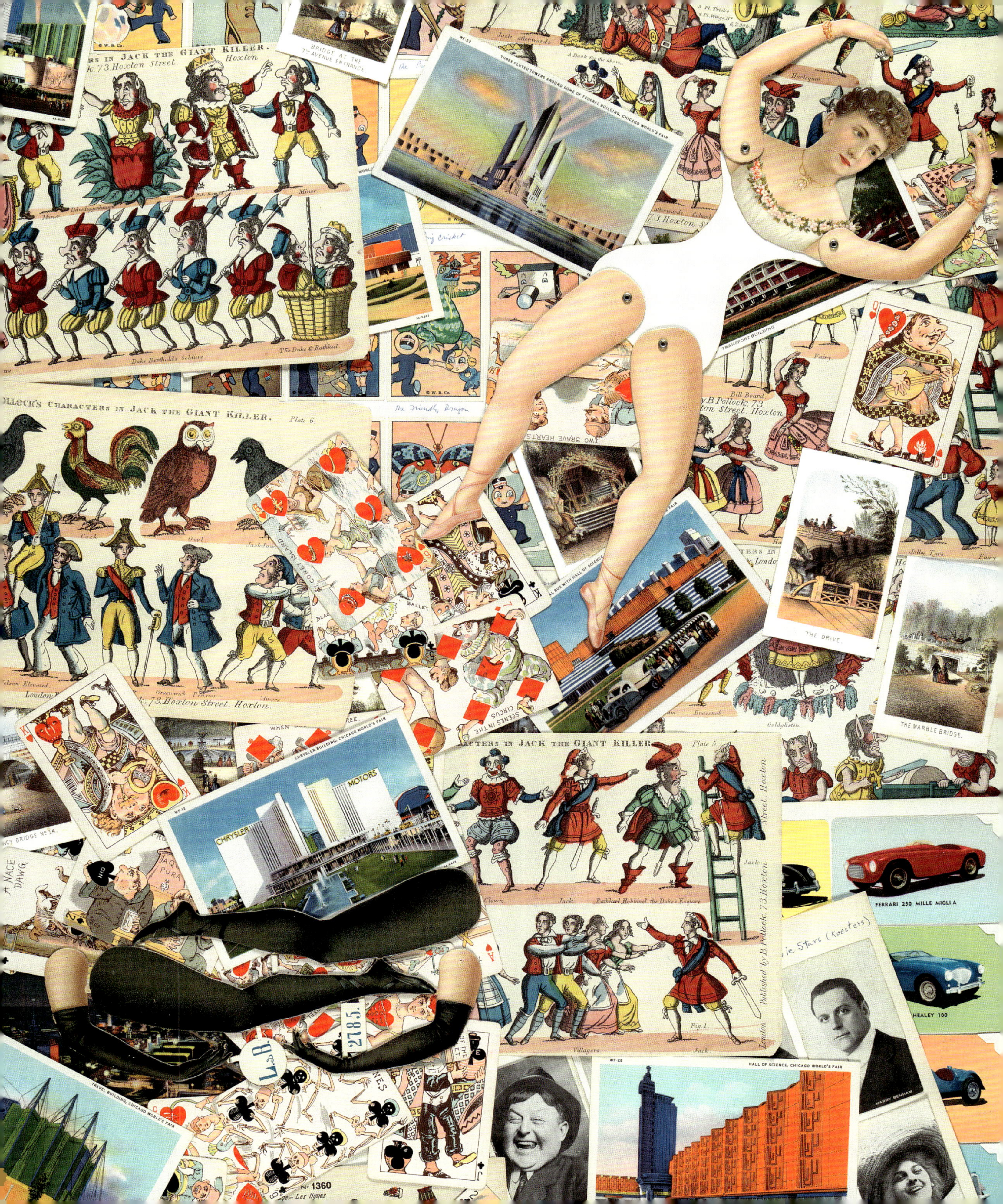

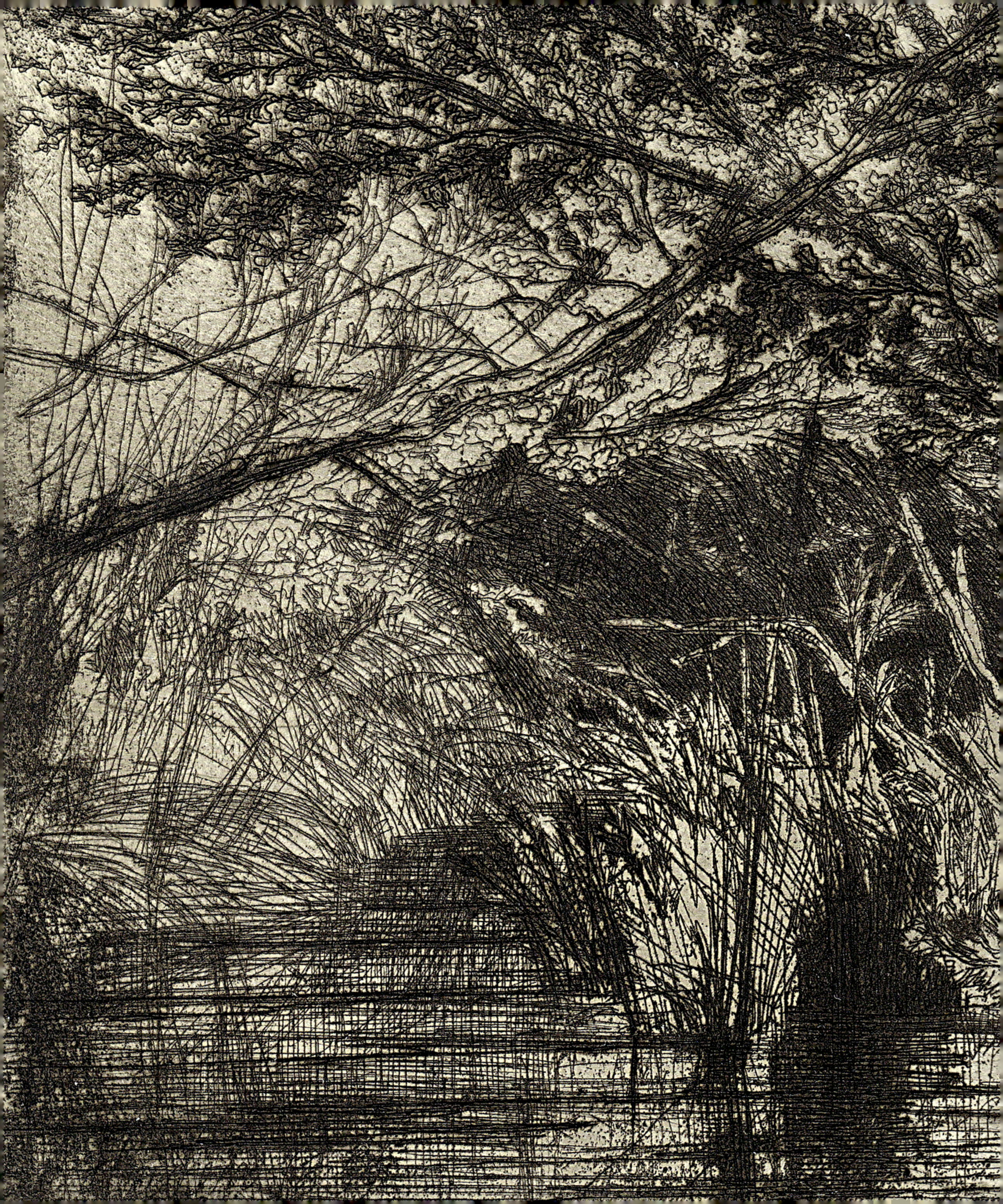

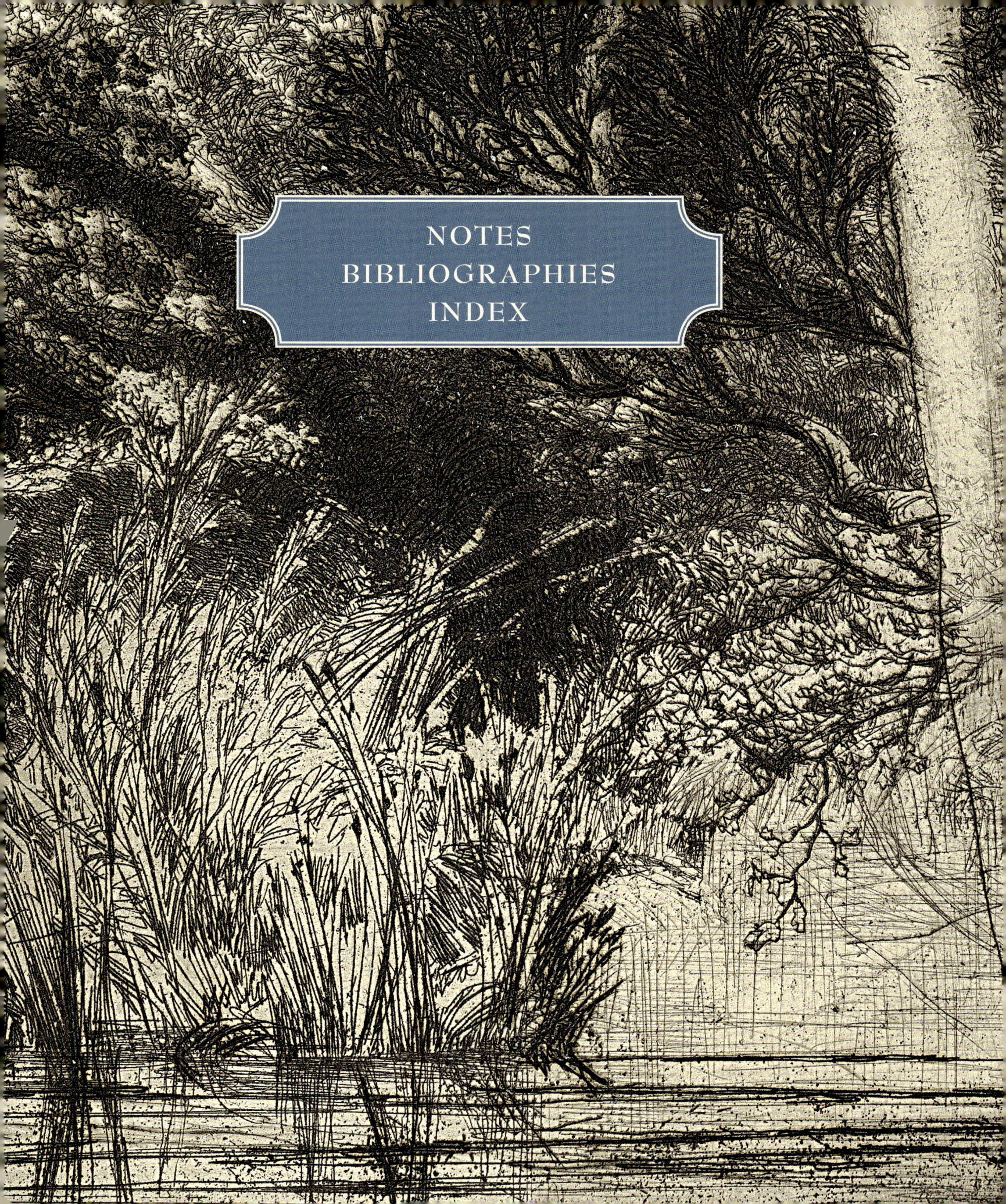

NOTES
BIBLIOGRAPHIES
INDEX

NOTES

Introduction

1. William M. Ivins Jr., "The Museum Department of Prints," *Metropolitan Museum of Art Bulletin* (hereafter, *MMAB*) 12, no. 2 (Feb. 1917): 24.

2. The Museum of Fine Arts, Boston, opened a department of prints, drawings, and photographs in 1889. The Fogg Museum received its founding gift in 1857 but did not open until 1895; its prints department opened in 1897.

3. "The New Department of Prints," *MMAB* 12, no. 1 (Jan. 1917): 2.

4. Ivins, "Museum Department," 1917: 23.

5. Sachs to Edward Robinson, Nov. 25, 1916; Prints Department, 1916–21, 1930–31, 1933, 1943–46, 1949, Office of the Secretary Records, The Metropolitan Museum of Art Archives.

6. Ibid.

7. Ivins, "Museum Department," 1917: 23.

8. Ivins to Paul J. Sachs, Feb. 26, 1916; Harvard Art Museums Archives.

9. Ivins, "A Note on Aesthetic Theory," *Arts* 8, no. 6 (Dec. 1925): 310. William James's radical empiricism influenced Bertrand Russell and Ludwig Wittgenstein, who loomed large in Ivins's scholarship; see "The Education of a Curator" in this volume.

10. Ivins to Paul J. Sachs, March 18, 1921; Harvard Art Museums Archives.

11. Ivins, "New Tastes in Old Prints," *MMAB* 27, no. 9 (Sept. 1932): 204.

12. Ivins, "An Early Aesthetician," *MMAB* 24, no. 9 (Sept. 1929): 229.

13. Ivins, *Prints and Visual Communication* (Cambridge, Mass.: Harvard University Press, 1953).

14. A. Hyatt Mayor, "William Mills Ivins, Jr., 1881–1961," *Print Review* 3 (1974): 48.

15. Ibid.

16. Ivins, *Notes on Prints: Being the Text of Labels Prepared for a Special Exhibition of Prints from the Museum Collection*, exh. cat. (New York: The Metropolitan Museum of Art, 1930), 173.

17. Mayor, *Prints & People: A Social History of Printed Pictures* (New York: The Metropolitan Museum of Art, distributed by New York Graphic Society, 1971), 683.

The Education of a Curator

1. See the obituaries by A. Hyatt Mayor, "William Mills Ivins, Jr., 1881–1961," *MMAB*, n.s., 21, no. 6 (Feb. 1963): 193–201; and Theodore Sizer, "William Mills Ivins, Jr. (1881–1961), 'Fog Dispeller,'" *Yale University Library Gazette* 36, no. 4 (April 1962): 169–75.

2. William Mills Ivins papers, 1878–1964,

Archives of American Art, Smithsonian Institution (hereafter, Ivins papers, AAA, SI), box 11, misc. writings. Ivins to his father on Feb. 8, 1902, making the case for leaving Munich: box 20.

3. William M. Ivins Jr., "Goya's Disasters of War," *MMAB* 19, no. 9 (Sept. 1924): 223.

4. Ivins, "Daumier: The Man of His Time," *Arts* 3 (Feb. 1923): 89–102; "The Art of Rembrandt," *MMAB* 37, no. 1 (Jan. 1942): 3–22; and "A Bruegel Exhibition in the Print Galleries," *MMAB*, n.s., 1, no. 7 (March 1943): 222–30. Ivins found eighteenth-century art to be impoverished by its aloofness from social responsibility.

5. However, Marjorie B. Cohn, "William Ivins's Taste in Prints," *Print Quarterly* 22, no. 1 (March 2005): 31–41, esp. 36–37, dispels the common view that he was unduly conservative in his aesthetic judgments.

6. For Ivins's politics at the time he joined the Museum, see Ivins to Paul J. Sachs, Aug. 22, 1916; Harvard Art Museums Archives. Thanks to Marjorie B. Cohn for a transcription.

7. Ivins to Albert Gallatin, May 29, 1921; Ivins papers, AAA, SI, box 2.

8. Ivins, "'In the Beginning Was the Word,'" *MMAB*, n.s., 4, no. 1 (Summer 1945): 12–17.

9. Ivins, "'Ornament' in the Department of Prints," *MMAB* 15, no. 3 (March 1920): 54, 58.

10. Ivins, "Of Museums," *Arts* 3, no. 1 (Jan. 1923): 31–35, a review of Benjamin Ives Gilman, *Museum Ideals of Purpose and Method* (Cambridge, Mass.: Harvard University Press, 1918; 2nd ed. 1923). See Gilman's brief rejoinder, "Historian versus Artist: Mr. Ivins on Museums," *Arts* 3, no. 2 (Feb. 1923): 157.

11. Ivins, "Art in a University Museum," in *Addresses Delivered at a Convocation Held in Yale University, 18–19 October 1946* (New Haven, Conn.: Yale University, 1947), 13–24; Ivins to Thomas D. Barlow, April 2, 1947 (Ivins papers, AAA, SI, box 1); Ivins to Felix Frankfurter, Sept. 16, 1957 (Ivins papers, AAA, SI, box 2).

12. "Was gezeigt werden kann, kann nicht gesagt werden." Ludwig Wittgenstein, *Tractatus Logico-Philosophicus*, trans. D. F. Pears and B. F. McGuinness (London and New York: Routledge, 2001): 4.1212. Ivins's use of this proposition out of context will raise philosophical objections, but his intent is clear.

13. Ivins, "A Note on Ipseity," *Journal of Aesthetics and Art Criticism* 7, no. 1 (Sept. 1948): 40. Far from just a primer on technique, Ivins's handbook *How Prints Look: Photographs with a Commentary* (New York: The Metropolitan Museum of Art, 1943) is replete with asides on aesthetic and cultural topics.

14. Ivins to Bernard Berenson, Nov. 3, 1933;

Bernard and Mary Berenson Papers [1880–2002], Biblioteca Berenson, Villa I Tatti, Harvard University Center for Italian Renaissance Studies.

15. Ivins, "Of Education in a Museum," *MMAB* 29, no. 9 (Sept. 1934): 150–51. See also Ivins to Francis Henry Taylor, Jan. 12, 1940 (Ivins papers, AAA, SI, box 12), regarding a proposal to write a history of art illustrated by objects in the collection. Ivins was opposed.

16. Ivins, "In the Beginning," 1945; "Free Thought in the Country," *MMAB*, n.s., 6, no. 6 (Feb. 1948): 175–77.

17. Panofsky to Ivins, Jan. 30 and March 14, 1932, and Ivins's response, March 24, 1932; Ivins papers, AAA, SI, box 4. See also *Erwin Panofsky: Korrespondenz 1910–1968: Eine kommentierte Auswahl in fünf Bänden*, ed. Dieter Wüttke, vol. 1 (Wiesbaden: Harrassowitz Verlag, 2001), 481–84; vol. 4 (2008), 1078–79.

18. Erwin Panofsky, "Die Perspektive als 'symbolische Form,'" *Vorträge der Bibliothek Warburg* 1924–25 (Leipzig and Berlin: B. G. Teubner, 1927), 258–330. See Christopher S. Wood, introduction to *Perspective as Symbolic Form*, by Erwin Panofsky, trans. Christopher S. Wood (New York: Zone, 1991), 7–24. Ivins, *Art and Geometry: A Study in Space Intuitions* (Cambridge, Mass.: Harvard University Press, 1946).

19. Erwin Panofsky, *Albrecht Dürer*, 2 vols. (Princeton, N.J.: Princeton University Press, 1945).

20. Alois Riegl, *Stilfragen: Grundlegungen zu einer Geschichte der Ornamentik* (Berlin: G. Siemens, 1893) and *Spätrömische Kunstindustrie* (Vienna: Österreichische Staatsdruckerei, 1927) are cited in Ivins, *Art and Geometry*, 35, 36, and Ivins's essay on museum libraries (Ivins, "In the Beginning," 1945). *Stilfragen* probably encouraged his early interest in ornament.

21. Ivins, "Notes on Three Dürer Woodblocks," *Metropolitan Museum Studies* 2, no. 1 (Nov. 1929): 102–11.

22. Ivins, *On the Rationalization of Sight: With an Examination of Three Renaissance Texts on Perspective*, Papers 8 (New York: The Metropolitan Museum of Art, 1938), 34–43. See also "The Albertian Scheme," *MMAB* 31, no. 12 (Dec. 1936): 278–80.

23. Ivins became acutely interested in Adelbert Ames's psychological and physiological studies of the eye, research that also drew the attention of Alfred H. Barr Jr., who thought it centrally relevant to the origins of abstraction.

24. The argument is nearly identical to that regarding Dürer's woodblocks. Ivins, "The Woodcuts to Vesalius," *MMAB* 31, no. 7 (July 1936): 139–42; "À Propos of the *Fabrica* of Vesalius," *Bulletin of the History of Medicine* 14 (1943):

576–93; "What about the *Fabrica* of Vesalius?" in Samuel W. Lambert, Willy Weigand, and William M. Ivins Jr., *Three Vesalian Essays to Accompany the* Icones anatomicae *of 1543* (New York: Macmillan, 1952), 43–128. Ivins's thesis has been largely ignored. See Francisco Guerra, "The Identity of the Artists Involved in Vesalius's *Fabrica*, 1543," *Medical History* 13, no. 1 (Jan. 1969): 37–50; Martin Kemp, "A Drawing for the *Fabrica*: And Some Thoughts upon the Muscle-Men," *Medical History* 14, no. 3 (July 1970): 277–88; Andrea Carlino, "Representing the Body: The Visual Culture of Renaissance Anatomy," in "Paper Bodies: A Catalogue of Anatomical Fugitive Sheets 1538–1687," supplement, *Medical History* 43, no. S19 (1999): 38–41.

25. Ivins, "A Note on Girard Desargues," *Scripta Mathematica* 9, no. 1 (March 1943): 36. Ivins based his interpretation of Euclid on Federigo Enriques, *Problems of Science*, trans. Katharine Royce (Chicago: Open Court, 1914). Ivins's views on the underestimation of the historical importance of technology drew on Lynn White Jr.'s work: "Technology and Invention in the Middle Ages," *Speculum* 15, no. 2 (April 1940): 141–59, cited in Ivins, *Art and Geometry*, 61n15.

26. Ivins, "A Note on Girard Desargues," 1943: 33–48; "Two First Editions of Desargues," *MMAB*, n.s., 1, no. 1 (Summer 1942): 33–45; *Art and Geometry*, 87–104.

27. Riegl's concept of "will to form" (*Kunstwollen*) probably also contributed to Ivins's concept of "pictorial syntax." But see Ivins to Edgar Wind, June 7, 1947; Ivins papers, AAA, SI, box 6.

28. He delivered his most heated arguments in very public forums: lectures at the Frick Collection and in *Harper's Magazine*. Ivins, "A Few Fallacies about Art," *Harper's Magazine* 195, no. 1167 (Aug. 1945): 114–20; "More Fallacies about Art," *Harper's Magazine* 195, no. 1168 (Sept. 1947): 225–32, where Ivins exposed his long-standing dispute with his respected colleague Gisela M. A. Richter. Berenson is also singled out.

29. Many sought to dissuade Ivins from his more reductive assertions. Vladimir G. Simkhovitch to Ivins, Aug. 27, 1945 (Ivins papers, AAA, SI, box 4); George Sarton to Ivins, Oct.–Nov. 1946 (Ivins papers, AAA, SI, box 4); and George Boas to Ivins, Oct. 26, 1947 (Ivins papers, AAA, SI, box 1). See also the critical review: John L. Caskey and Gaylord M. Merriman, review of *Art and Geometry: A Study in Space Intuitions*, by William M. Ivins Jr., *American Journal of Archaeology* 51, no. 3 (July–Sept. 1947): 330–32. For a brief history of perspective implicitly questioning Ivins's case against Euclid, see Martin Kemp, *The Science of Art: Optical Themes in Western Art from Brunelleschi to Seurat* (London and New Haven, Conn.: Yale University Press, 1990), 53–98. His denunciations of the received wisdom of antiquity drew serious attention and even glee from other quarters.

30. Karl Popper, *The Open Society and Its Enemies*, rev. ed. (1945; repr., Princeton, N.J.: Princeton University Press, 2013). Ivins to George Boas, Oct. 16, 1947; Ivins papers, AAA, SI, box 1.

31. Although a firm supporter of unrestricted trade, Popper appealed to liberal intellectuals in part because he never abandoned certain socialist principles essential to the founding of the European welfare state. Boas, Ivins's closest correspondent during these years, remained sharply on the left and probably did not share his enthusiasm.

32. See the Berenson correspondence from 1922 on; Ivins papers, AAA, SI, box 1, and in the Biblioteca Berenson, Villa I Tatti, Harvard University Center for Italian Renaissance Studies.

33. Ivins participated in a forum on American architecture in 1928, including Lewis Mumford, Walter Pach, and Alfred Stieglitz, in which Ivins and Mumford expressed complementary views on the poverty of contemporary taste. See the transcript of the conversation in Ivins papers, AAA, SI, box 8, 1929 folder.

34. See Meyer Schapiro, review of *Kunstwissenschaftliche Forschungen*, vol. 2, ed. Otto Pächt, *Art Bulletin* 18, no. 2 (June 1936): 258–66. Between 1941 and 1943 Ivins exchanged letters with Schapiro about Pächt's work (Meyer Schapiro Collection; Series II: Correspondence 1920s–2001, Box 135; Rare Book and Manuscript Library, Columbia University Library).

35. Ivins, *Prints and Visual Communication* (Cambridge, Mass.: Harvard University Press, 1953). Ivins's interest in ornament as a linear system and the importance of photography as a measure of objectivity were advanced in writings of the late 1920s. The basic premise of Ivins's argument about the replicated image was already set forth in Ivins, "The Woodcuts to Vesalius," 1936.

36. For critiques of Ivins's thesis, especially regarding photography, see Wolfgang M. Freitag, "Early Uses of Photography in the History of Art," *Art Journal* 39, pt. 2 (1979–80): 117–23; Estelle Jussim, *Visual Communication and the Graphic Arts: Photographic Technologies in the Nineteenth Century* (New York: R. R. Bowker, 1974), especially chap. 1; and Gordon Fyfe, "Art and Its Objects: William Ivins and the Reproduction of Art," in *Picturing Power: Visual Depiction and Social Relations*, ed. Gordon Fyfe and John Law (London and New York: Routledge, 1988), 65–98. Jussim's book is essentially a commentary on Ivins from the perspective of "information theory," which she regards as having been initiated by Ivins. Lewis Mumford's ideas about technology and civilization offer some precedent for Ivins's thinking. Despite his interest in Ivins, Marshall McLuhan's later studies of popular media address sociological and semantic problems not central to Ivins's purpose.

37. See George Boas, review of *The Voices of Silence: Man and His Art*, by André Malraux, *Perspectives USA* 7 (Spring 1954): 137–41. André Malraux, *The Voices of Silence: Man and His Art*, trans. Stuart Gilbert (New York: Doubleday, 1953) was first published in French as *Les Voix du silence* (Paris: Nouvelle Revue Française, 1951).

The first incarnation of Malraux's thesis appeared as *Psychologie de l'art*, 3 vols. (Geneva: A. Skira, 1947–50), revised and translated as *The Psychology of Art*, trans. Gilbert Stuart, 3 vols. (New York: Pantheon, 1949–50).

38. Marshall McLuhan, *The Gutenberg Galaxy: The Making of Typographic Man* (Toronto: University of Toronto Press, 1962). In 1958 McLuhan, apparently much impressed with *Art and Geometry*, made an unsuccessful effort to meet Ivins: McLuhan to Ivins, March 9 and 23, 1958; Ivins papers, AAA, SI, box 4.

39. Thomas S. Kuhn, *The Structure of Scientific Revolutions* (Chicago: University of Chicago Press, 1962). As a point of interest I have found no evidence that Ivins read Walter Benjamin's "The Work of Art in the Age of Mechanical Reproduction." An initial (shorter) version was published in French as "L'Oeuvre d'art à l'époque de sa reproduction mécanisée," *Zeitschrift für Sozialforschung* 5 (1936): 40–63; the extended German version first appeared in Walter Benjamin, *Schriften*, 2 vols. (Frankfurt: Suhrkamp Verlag, 1955). The first English translation appeared in Walter Benjamin, *Illuminations*, trans. Harry Zohn, ed. and intro. Hannah Arendt (New York: Harcourt Brace, 1968), 217–51.

40. Ivins, "Photography and the 'Modern' Point of View: A Speculation on the History of Taste," *Metropolitan Museum Studies* 1, no. 1 (Nov. 1928): 16–24; and especially "Photographs by Alfred Stieglitz," *MMAB* 24, no. 2 (Feb. 1929): 44–45. Both articles, however, stress the importance of photographs as documents first and works of art second.

41. Cohn, "William Ivins's Taste in Prints."

42. Ivins to Theodore Sizer, Easter 1946; Theodore Sizer Papers. Manuscripts and Archives, Yale University Library, file A.

43. Ivins to Theodore Sizer, Jan. 3, 1951; Theodore Sizer Papers. Manuscripts and Archives, Yale University Library, file A.

A. Hyatt Mayor's Life in Art and Letters

1. A. Hyatt Mayor, "A Truth or Two about Art History," *Record of the Art Museum, Princeton University* 36, no. 1 (1977): 24. Mayor's description recalls Ivins, who once referred to himself as a "fog dispeller," according to Theodore Sizer; see "William M. Ivins Jr. (1881–1961), 'Fog Dispeller,'" *Yale University Library Gazette* 36, no. 4 (April 1962), 169–75.

2. Janet S. Byrne, Colta Ives, and Mary L. Myers, foreword to *A. Hyatt Mayor: Selected Writings and a Bibliography*, by A. Hyatt Mayor (New York: The Metropolitan Museum of Art, 1983), 11.

3. Mayor, *Prints & People: A Social History of Printed Pictures* (New York: The Metropolitan Museum of Art, distributed by New York Graphic Society, 1971), foreword.

4. Ibid.

5. Archer founded the Hispanic Society of

America in 1904; Mayor succeeded his uncle as its president in 1955. For more on Archer Huntington, see Shelley M. Bennett, *The Art of Wealth: The Huntingtons in the Gilded Age* (San Marino, Calif.: Huntington Library, Art Collections, and Botanical Gardens, 2013).

6. Anna had exhibited a sculpture of Joan of Arc, which caught the attention of J. Sanford Saltus, an executive at Tiffany & Co. and member of the New York City Joan of Arc Statue Committee. He commissioned her to produce a lifesize version, which was inaugurated in 1915 in a ceremony at Riverside Drive and 93rd Street, where it still stands. See Anne Higonnet, "Anna Hyatt Huntington, Meet New York City," in *Goddess, Heroine, Beast: Anna Hyatt Huntington's New York Sculpture, 1902–1936*, exh. cat. (New York: Miriam & Ira D. Wallach Art Gallery, Columbia University, 2014), 15–17.

7. Mayor to Audella Hyatt, Jan. 2, 1919; A. Hyatt Mayor papers, 1815–1980, Archives of American Art, Smithsonian Institution (hereafter, Mayor papers, AAA, SI). Mayor mistakenly wrote Madame de "Bevigny" rather than Sévigné, a seventeenth-century writer known for her vivid letters.

8. Italian diary entry for Feb. 2, 1925. Mayor, "A. Hyatt Mayor Abroad," *Archives of American Art Journal* 36, no. 4 (1992): 7.

9. Mayor to Berenson, dated April 5 but without a year, most likely written just after his return to New York from Europe, about 1928; Bernard and Mary Berenson Papers (1880–2002), Biblioteca Berenson, Villa I Tatti, Harvard University Center for Italian Renaissance Studies.

10. From the oral history interview with A. Hyatt Mayor, March 21–May 5, 1969, Archives of American Art, Smithsonian Institution (hereafter, Mayor interview, AAA, SI).

11. Richard Boleslavsky, "Creative Theater," trans. Michel Barroy (unpublished lectures, New York Public Library, 1923), 1–2; cited by Ronald Arthur Willis, "The American Laboratory Theatre, 1923–1930" (PhD dissertation, University of Iowa, 1968), 328.

12. Mayor interview, AAA, SI.

13. Mayor, "Gordon Craig's Ideas of Drama," *Hound & Horn* 2, no. 3 (April–June 1929): 236–49.

14. Mayor, "Museums Modern and Metropolitan," *Hound & Horn* 4, no. 1 (Oct.–Dec. 1930): 112.

15. Ibid., 111, 112.

16. Ibid., 112; he is quoting Juvenal's *Satires*, VI: 347–48.

17. Mayor interview, AAA, SI.

18. Mayor, "A Truth or Two," 1977: 23.

19. The exhibition is not listed in the Museum's official calendar, but an exhibition list in the department's files records an exhibition of theater prints taking place between October 1933 and January 1934 in the so-called Basement Hall. This show may have been rehung in the same space in October 1935; see also the Department of

Drawings and Prints Files. There are no exhibition files or checklists for these shows.

20. Mayor, *The Bibiena Family* (New York: H. Bittner, 1945). The ballet premiered in 1941 at the Theatro Municipal in Rio de Janeiro.

21. Originally printed in Mayor, "Carpentry and Candlelight in the Theater," *MMAB*, n.s., 1, no. 6 (Feb. 1943): 198–203. Mayor also honored the Italian invention of stagecraft in the 1951 exhibition "Italian Theatrical Design."

22. Mayor, "The Theater in France," *MMAB*, n.s., 14, no. 2 (Oct. 1955), 48–53.

23. Howard Devree, "America in Perspective, Exhibition at the Metropolitan Presents Wide Range of Interests for Visitors," *New York Times*, July 16, 1939.

24. Mayor interview, AAA, SI.

25. Blythe (last known to be in the National Baseball Hall of Fame and Museum, Cooperstown, N.Y.); Woodville, *Politics in an Oyster House* (The Walters Art Museum); Homer (Saint Louis Art Museum).

26. Hermann Warner Williams Jr., "Life in America for Three Hundred Years," *MMAB* 34, no. 4 (April 1939): 78.

27. Mayor interview, AAA, SI.

28. Erich Auerbach, *Mimesis: The Representation of Reality in Western Literature*, trans. Willard R. Trask (Princeton, N.J.: Princeton University Press, 1953), 551.

29. James Ackerman, "On American Scholarship in the Arts," *College Art Journal* 17, no. 4 (Summer 1958): 357–62.

30. Irving Lavin, "The Crisis of 'Art History,'" *Art Bulletin* 78, no. 1 (March 1996): 13.

31. Taylor to Osborn, Feb. 27, 1943; Box 2, Mayor, A. Hyatt, 1943, William Church Osborn Records, The Metropolitan Museum of Art Archives.

32. Mayor interview, AAA, SI.

33. Mayor, introduction to *Portraits and Masks*, calendar for 1962, prepared by A. Hyatt Mayor and Margaret R. Scherer (New York: The Metropolitan Museum of Art, [1961]).

34. Mayor, "Does Your Art Collection Express Your Community?," *American Federation of Arts Quarterly* 1, no. 3 (1963): 88.

35. Lincoln Kirstein, "A. Hyatt Mayor," *Print Review* 6 (1976): 8.

36. One of the first academic books to look at this kind of material—posters, advertisements, popular prints, scientific illustrations—is Ernst Gombrich's *Art and Illusion: A Study in the Psychology of Pictorial Representation* (London: Phaidon, 1960); it was first in a series of A.W. Mellon Lectures in the Fine Arts at the National Gallery of Art, Washington, in 1956. According to Christopher S. Wood, it prophesied the field of study called visual culture, which elevated images outside the traditional taste for fine art; see Christopher S. Wood, "E. H. Gombrich's 'Art and Illusion: A Study in the Psychology of Pictorial Representation,' 1960," in *The Books that Shaped Art History from Gombrich and Greenberg to*

Alpers and Krauss, eds. Richard Shone and John-Paul Stonard (London and New York: Thames & Hudson, 2013), 116–28.

37. Mayor published some of this material in *Popular Prints of the Americas* (New York: Crown, 1973).

38. Mayor interview, AAA, SI. Mayor was predisposed to accumulate miscellany; unconfirmed stories relate that Mayor would clear off his desk, place the contents in a solander box, and label it with a date, much as Andy Warhol combined art and ephemera in his Time Capsules, which he began making in 1974.

39. Ivins mounted what he called history's first exhibition of reproductive prints in 1931. He also wrote an article on the subject; see William M. Ivins Jr., "An Exhibition of Reproductive Prints," *MMAB* 26, no. 10 (Oct. 1931): 236–39.

40. Recommendation for Purchase, May 26, 1950, Purchases – Authorized – Prints – Colnaghi & Co. (1936–51), 1936–37, 1939, 1949–51, Office of the Secretary Records, The Metropolitan Museum of Art Archives.

41. The Albertina acquisitions are 49.97.1–.696. For correspondence between Mayor and Otto Benesch, director of the Albertina, dating from 1947–49, see Mayor papers, AAA, SI.

42. Mayor, "Prints Acquired in 1949," *MMAB*, n.s., 8, no. 6 (Feb. 1950): 157.

43. Mayor interview, AAA, SI.

44. For the lots of Liechtenstein material, see 49.95.1–.2832; 51.501.1–.7768; 53.600.1–.4833; 53.601.1–.353; 62.602.1–.939. Mayor discusses the distribution of the Liechtenstein collection in his oral history: Mayor interview, AAA, SI. The German-born dealer Richard Zinser (referred to as Hans Zinzer), who was then based in New York, bought the most expensive lots and acted as an intermediary for the transaction. He helped organize the collection into portfolios classifying objects by school, artist, or writer. Mayor mentioned visiting Walter Feilchenfeldt (misspelled Feisenfelt) in Zurich; he had the bulk of the collection, comprising 375 of the red morocco portfolios. These portfolios seem to have held mostly drawings that Prince Franz Joseph II (1906–1989) sold beginning in 1947. P & D. Colnaghi & Co. bought the rest in possibly four large lots between 1949 and 1952. Mayor made the purchases through Colnaghi and referred to his lots as "commercially the trash." For more on the Liechtenstein collection, see [Peter Fuhring], "Fürst von Liechtenstein, L. 4398," in Frits Lugt, *Les Marques de Collections de Dessins & d'Estampes*, online edition by Fondation Custodia, accessed Oct. 14, 2014, http://www.marquesdecollections.fr/detail.cfm/marque/11913.

45. Walter Friedlaender, *Mannerism and Anti-Mannerism in Italian Painting* (New York: Columbia University Press, 1957); Sydney Freedberg, *Parmigianino: His Works in Painting* (Westport, Conn.: Greenwood, 1950); Frederick

Hartt, *Giulio Romano* (New Haven, Conn.: Yale University Press, 1958); John Coolidge, "Vignola, and the Little Domes of St. Peter's," *Marsyas* 2 (1942): 63–123; Craig Hugh Smyth, "Bronzino Studies" (PhD dissertation, Princeton University, 1956) and *Mannerism and Maniera* (Locust Valley, N.Y.: J. J. Augustin, 1963). This shift came from American scholars trained by German émigrés. Interestingly, Arnold Hauser, the great proponent of social history, wrote *Mannerism: The Crisis of the Renaissance and the Origin of Modern Art* (London: Routledge & Kegan Paul, 1964).

46. Gerhard Langemeyer and Reinhart Schleier, *Bilder nach Bildern: Druckgraphik und die Vermittlung von Kunst*, exh. cat. (Münster: West-fälisches Landesmuseum für Kunst und Kulturge-schichte and Aschendorff, 1976).

47. Mayor, "A Truth or Two," 1977: 22.

48. Colin Eisler, "A. Hyatt Mayor: Teacher of Enchantment," *Print Review* 6 (1976): 15–18.

49. Adams to Mayor, Dec. 11, 1962; Mayor papers, AAA, SI.

50. Mayor interview, AAA, SI.

51. Mayor, "Mayor Abroad," 1992: 3; Mayor to Audella Hyatt, Jan. 5, [1925]; Mayor papers, AAA, SI.

52. Mayor interview, AAA, SI.

53. *Portrait of a Zen Master* (63.65) in *Unforget-table People: Names and Addresses*, prepared by A. Hyatt Mayor and Colta Ives (New York: The Metropolitan Museum of Art, 1981).

54. Mayor, commentary on *Portrait of a Zen Master*, in *Unforgettable People: Names and Addresses*.

55. Mayor to Andrew Robison, Sept. 17, 1970. The letter is still in the possession of Andrew Robison, Washington, D.C., who generously shared it with the author.

56. Mayor to Andrew Robison, April 28, 1971; Andrew Robison, Washington, D.C.

Etchings

1. Ivins to Robert W. de Forest, Jan. 17, 1917; Dick, Harris Brisbane - Bequest - Art collection and library, 1916–17, 1972, Office of the Secre-tary Records, The Metropolitan Museum of Art Archives.

2. Ivins to de Forest (op. cit.) records the num-ber of works by each artist: Whistler (153), Haden (227), Cameron (335), Zorn (59), Bone (26), McBey (41), Legros (19), Lepère (21), Frood (14), Pennell (17), Meryon (5), and Dodd (8).

3. Avery gave the collection to the library in 1900; it included 266 etchings. See M. Lee Wiehl, *A Cultivated Taste: Whistler and American Print Collectors*, exh. cat. (Middletown, Conn.: Davison Art Center, Wesleyan University, 1983), 13.

4. J. R. W. Hitchcock, *Etching in America* (New York: White, Stokes, & Allen, 1886), 61. Keppel continued to capitalize on the etching revival with an 1895 exhibition, "Philip Gilbert Hamerton's Favorite Etchings." Hamerton, an English art critic, had written *Etchings and Etchers* (London:

Macmillan, 1868, rev. eds. 1876, 1880), which set the tone for the revival and demonstrated what constituted a cultivated taste for prints.

5. Andrews gave his collection to the Museum's Library, which was then collecting prints (see 83.1.1–.94). The collection was transferred to the Prints Department in 1920.

6. Raymond L. Wilson, *Index of American Print Exhibitions, 1882–1940* (Metuchen, N.J., and London: Scarecrow, 1988), 1–6. The New York Etching Club held annual exhibitions between 1882 and 1893.

7. Koehler wrote extensively on etching; see, among others, S. R. Koehler, *Original Etchings by American Artists* (New York and London: Cas-sell, 1883) and *Etching: An Outline of Its Technical Processes and Its History, with Some Remarks on Col-lections and Collecting* (New York: Cassell, 1885).

8. See Ivins to Sachs, undated but between May 10 and June 7, 1917, Harvard Art Museums Archives, cited and shown by Marjorie B. Cohn, "William Ivins's Taste in Prints," *Print Quarterly* 22, no. 1 (March 2005): 32–33, fig. 16.

9. William M. Ivins Jr., "An Exhibition of Etch-ings," *MMAB* 22, no. 5 (May 1927): 140.

10. Ivins, "The New Department of Prints," *MMAB* 12, no. 1 (Jan. 1917): 2.

11. Ivins's etching shows include "Painter Etchings and Engravings of the Nineteenth Century" (1917); "Etchings in the Print Galleries" (1920); "French Black and White of the Last Half-Century" (1921); "Etched Work of Julian Alden Weir" (1921); "Exhibition of Etchings" (1924); "Memorial Exhibition of the Works of Joseph Pennell" (1926); "Exhibition of Etchings" (1927); "A Whistler Centenary" (1935). Early in the century, even exhibitions at avant-garde spaces such as Alfred Stieglitz's Photo-Secessionist Gallery 291 highlighted works influenced by the British and French etching revival. For more on early shows by Stieglitz and his contemporaries see Reba White Williams, "Prints in the United States, 1900–1918," *Print Quarterly* 14, no. 2 (June 1997): 151–73.

12. Ivins did have a continuing interest in one modern etcher, Mary Cassatt. Adelyn D. Breeskin, the renowned Cassatt scholar, recalled Ivins throwing some of Cassatt's prints on her desk and saying, "Now there's someone you should look into. She's a woman, she's a fine art-ist, and no one's paid any attention to her." Oral history interview with Adelyn Dohme Breeskin, June 27, 1974, Archives of American Art, Smithsonian Institution. Breeskin noted in the acknowledgments to her catalogue raisonné on Cassatt that Ivins himself had, along with Robert Hartshorne, planned to publish on her graphic work: Adelyn D. Breeskin, *The Graphic Work of Mary Cassatt* (New York: H. Bittner, 1948). Cohn also points out that Ivins's estate included three Meryon prints (Cohn, "William Ivins's Taste in Prints," 33).

13. Ivins, "An Exhibition of Etchings," *MMAB* 19, no. 1 (Jan. 1924): 4.

14. Ibid., 5.

15. Ibid., 4–5.

16. Ivins staged two exhibitions, in 1918 and 1936; Mayor staged four, in 1945, 1950, 1955, and 1965. Large groups of prints came into the Museum through gifts and purchases: 18.64(1–80); 21.19.1–.34; and 22.60.25(1–80). The Museum also purchased fifty drawings from members of the Goya family in 1935 (35.103.1–.50). For more on Ivins's pursuit of Goya and his desire to change the taste of the American public, see Susan Alyson Stein, "Goya in the Metropolitan: A History of the Collection," in Colta Ives and Susan Alyson Stein, *Goya in the Metropolitan Museum of Art*, exh. cat. (New York: The Metropolitan Museum of Art, 1995), 34–64.

Engravings

1. William M. Ivins Jr., "Engravings by Four Renaissance Masters," *MMAB*, n.s., 2, no. 10 (June 1944): 293.

2. Ivins to Robinson, Dec. 3, 1916; Ivins, William M. Jr. - Misc. correspondence, 1916–35, 1916, 1919–23, 1925, 1928–29, 1932–33, Office of the Secretary Records, The Metropolitan Museum of Art. See S. R. Koehler, *A Chronological Catalogue of the Engravings, Dry-points and Etchings of Albert Dürer*, exh. cat. (New York: Grolier Club, 1897).

3. Ivins, *Catalogue of an Exhibition of Engravings and Etchings by Albrecht Dürer*, exh. cat. (New York: Frederick Keppel, 1908).

4. Ivins, *On the Rationalization of Sight: With an Examination of Three Renaissance Texts on Perspective*. Papers 8 (New York: The Metropolitan Museum of Art, 1938), 43.

5. Ivins, "Five Years in the Department of Prints," *MMAB* 16, no. 12 (Dec. 1921): 258.

6. The Museum purchased Morgan's col-lection of engravings by Dürer and his con-temporaries (19.73.1–.127); Morgan gave his woodcuts (19.73.128–.254) and two woodblocks (19.73.255, .256).

7. Ivins reiterated his admiration for the British Museum's collecting policies in the purchase papers for a rare group of four prints made in the broad manner of early Florentine engraving and a Mantegna engraving of *The Battle of the Sea Gods*; see Purchase Papers, Oct. 9, 1917, and Jan.15, 1918, in the Met's Department of Drawings and Prints Files. Mayor wrote that Ivins, "like a good lawyer, depended upon the criterion of precedent, consulting past judges of prints whose opinions had stood the test of time. . . . So, if a print had been good enough for Pierre Jean Mariette, Adam Ritter van Bartsch, or the Goncourts, it was good enough for the Metropolitan Museum." A. Hyatt Mayor, "William Mills Ivins, Jr., 1881–1961," *MMAB*, n.s., 21, no. 6 (Feb. 1963): 196. Mariette (1694–1774), a print collector and historian born into a family of engravers and print dealers, amassed and organized the collection of Prince

Eugene of Savoy that is now the Albertina in Vienna. His system of dividing works by periods and then by artists in alphabetical order was later used by Adam Ritter van Bartsch (1757–1821) in his canonical twenty-one-volume *Le Peintre-Graveur* (Vienna: J. V. Degen, 1803–21), revised and reissued as *The Illustrated Bartsch*, ed. Walter Strauss (New York: Abaris, 1978–). The system became the organizing principle for prints in the twentieth century; Ivins certainly followed it at the Museum.

8. Ivins, "Engravings by Four Renaissance Masters," 1944: 296.

9. Ivins, *Prints and Visual Communication* (Cambridge, Mass.: Harvard University, 1953), 64, 66.

10. Mayor, *Prints & People: A Social History of Printed Pictures* (New York: The Metropolitan Museum of Art, distributed by New York Graphic Society, 1971), 336.

11. Ivins, "An Exhibition of Reproductive Prints," *MMAB* 26, no. 10 (Oct. 1931): 236.

12. Mayor, *Prints & People*, 337, 338.

13. For more on the Liechtenstein sale and reproductive prints see "A. Hyatt Mayor's Life in Art and Letters" in this volume.

14. From the oral history interview with A. Hyatt Mayor, March 21–May 5, 1969, Archives of American Art, Smithsonian Institution.

15. The Museum purchased 696 prints directly from the Albertina in 1949 (49.97.1–.696). Ivins wrote about depending on the British Museum and Berlin Kupferstichekabinett as exemplars, but Mayor was more attracted to the collections and organization policies of the Albertina and the Bibliothèque Nationale de France in Paris. See "A. Hyatt Mayor's Life in Art and Letters" in this volume.

Woodcuts

1. William M. Ivins Jr., "Exhibition of the Arts of the Book," *MMAB* 19, no. 5 (May 1924): 116.

2. Ivins, "Reflections upon the Exhibition of the Arts of the Book," *MMAB* 19, no. 7 (July 1924): 169.

3. Ibid., 170.

4. Carl Zigrosser, "Woodcuts of the Italian Renaissance," *Nation* 105, no. 2736 (Dec. 6, 1917): 644. Two years later Zigrosser opened his own shop, the Weyhe Gallery, an outgrowth of the Weyhe Book Store in Manhattan. In 1940 he became curator of prints at the Philadelphia Museum of Art.

5. George Ong and Eric Holzenberg, *For Jean Grolier & His Friends: 125 Years of Grolier Club Exhibitions and Publications, 1884–2009* (New York: Grolier Club, 2009), 60–61. Ivins is not listed as a speaker or curator of the 1912 exhibition "Early Woodcuts," which combined books and single-sheet prints. In 1914 he addressed the club about the revival of the medium, in connection with a show that included illustrated books from 1470 to 1900.

6. Paul Kristeller, *Early Florentine Woodcuts with an Annotated List of Florentine Illustrated Books* (London: K. Paul, Trench, Trübner, 1897); Charles William Dyson Perrins, *Italian Book Illustrations and Early Printing: A Catalogue of Early Italian Books in the Library of C. W. Dyson Perrins* (Oxford: Oxford University Press, 1914); Victor Masséna, *Les livres à figures vénitiens de la fin du xve siècle et du commencement du xvie . . .* (Florence: L. S. Olschki; Paris: H. Leclerc, 1907–15).

7. Many of the works in the show were loans. Ivins went on to acquire many of the earliest printed books in Italy. These works are all now in the collection: see 27.56; 26.71.4; 17.45 respectively.

8. Ivins, *Catalogue of Italian Renaissance Woodcuts*, exh. cat. (New York: The Metropolitan Museum of Art, 1917), 22.

9. Ivins, *Prints and Visual Communication* (Cambridge, Mass.: Harvard University, 1953), 21.

10. Ivins, "Italian Renaissance Prints and Illustrated Books," *MMAB* 32, no. 12 (Dec. 1937): 285.

11. Ivins, "Exhibition of Italian Renaissance Woodcuts," *MMAB* 12, no. 11 (Nov. 1917): 226.

Lithographs

1. For more on Prang and his development of chromolithography, see Katharine Morrison McClinton, *The Chromolithographs of Louis Prang* (New York: C. N. Potter, distributed by Crown, 1973).

2. A. Hyatt Mayor, "Lithographs," *MMAB*, n.s., 7, no. 3 (Nov. 1948): 86.

3. The Dick gift numbers more than 3,600. For the Whistlers, see 17.3.100–.260; for Thornley, 17.3.3385–.3405.

4. William M. Ivins Jr., "An Exhibition of Masterpieces of Lithography," *MMAB* 18, no. 2 (Feb. 1923): 41–45.

5. Mayor, "Lithographs," 1948.

6. Frank Weitenkampf, "Lithography for the Artist," *American Magazine of Art* 9, no. 9 (July 1918): 352.

7. This is the main argument of Ivins's "Masterpieces of Lithography," 1923.

8. Antony Griffiths, "Reflections on the History of Lithography," *Grapheion* 1, no. 1 (1997): 4.

9. Joseph Pennell, "Cantor Lectures: Artistic Lithography, Lecture III," *Journal of the Royal Society of the Arts* 62, no. 3217 (July 17, 1914): 758.

10. This is despite the club's purchase of a printer for its members. For more on Pennell and lithography, see Linda Stiber Morenus, "Joseph Pennell and the Art of Transfer Lithography," *Print Quarterly* 21, no. 3 (Sept. 2004): 248–65.

11. Mayor, "A Bequest of Prints by Callot and Daumier," *MMAB*, n.s., 17, no. 1 (Summer 1958): 15.

12. The exhibition was "Prints by Daumier and Callot from the Bequest of Edwin De T. Bechtel." Bechtel's 1957 bequest included more than five hundred prints by Daumier (57.650.1–.299, .450–.599, .608–.614, and .620–.624). The following year Mrs. Bechtel made a gift of Daumier books (58.580.1–.38).

13. Adele S. Colgate's collection of Currier & Ives (52.632.1–.327 and 63.550.1–.552); the American sculptor Bessie Potter Vonnoh's French and American posters from the 1890s (41.12.1–.224); the Edward W. C. Arnold Collection of New York Prints, Maps, and Pictures (54.90.1–.1311), left to the Museum at Arnold's death after being on loan to the Museum of the City of New York since 1935/40; Bella C. Landauer's gifts of trade cards and ephemera given annually between 1925 and 1954; and Jefferson R. Burdick's collections of trade and postcards (gifts of approximately 303,000 trade and postcards given between 1947 and 1963).

14. Mayor, "A Gift of Currier & Ives Lithographs," *MMAB*, n.s., 10, no. 9 (May 1952): 244.

15. Mayor, *Popular Prints of the Americas* (New York: Crown, 1973).

16. Ibid., 28.

17. In 1942 and 1943 Mayor acquired large groups of material related to World War II and the Great Depression; see 42.117.1–.71 (British posters from Capt. H. P. MacNeal), 43.33.1–.1181 (from the WPA New York Project), 43.46.1–.43 (posters from the Pennsylvania WPA), 43.47.1–.368 (from the WPA Allocation Unit, Chicago), and 43.48.1–.14 (no donor given, South American war posters).

18. Mayor, *Popular Prints of the Americas*, 15.

19. Lincoln Kirstein, "A. Hyatt Mayor," in *A. Hyatt Mayor: Selected Writings and a Bibliography* (New York: The Metropolitan Museum of Art, 1983), 19.

SELECTED BIBLIOGRAPHY OF WILLIAM M. IVINS JR.

Books and Exhibition Catalogues

Catalogue of an Exhibition of Engravings and Etchings by Albrecht Dürer. Exh. cat. New York: Frederick Keppel, 1908.

Catalogue of Italian Renaissance Woodcuts. Exh. cat. New York: The Metropolitan Museum of Art, 1917.

Exhibition of Painter Etchings and Engravings of the XIX Century. Exh. cat. New York: The Metropolitan Museum of Art, 1917.

Guide to an Exhibition of the Arts of the Book. Exh. cat. New York: The Metropolitan Museum of Art, 1924.

Prints and Books: Informal Papers. Cambridge, Mass.: Harvard University Press, 1926.

Notes on Prints: Being the Text of Labels Prepared for a Special Exhibition of Prints from the Museum Collection. Exh. cat. New York: The Metropolitan Museum of Art, 1930.

On the Rationalization of Sight: With an Examination of Three Renaissance Texts on Perspective. Papers 8. New York: The Metropolitan Museum of Art, 1938.

The Unseen Rembrandt. New York: The Metropolitan Museum of Art, 1942.

How Prints Look: Photographs with a Commentary. New York: The Metropolitan Museum of Art, 1943.

Art and Geometry: A Study in Space Intuitions. Cambridge, Mass.: Harvard University Press, 1946.

Prints and Visual Communication. Cambridge, Mass.: Harvard University Press, 1953.

Articles and Essays

"A Note on Goya." *Print-Collector's Quarterly* 1, pt. 2 (April 1911): 204–7.

"The Print Department of the Metropolitan Museum of Art." *Print Collector's Quarterly* 7 (1917): 103–4.

"The New Department of Prints." *Metropolitan Museum of Art Bulletin* 12, no. 1 (Jan. 1917): 2.

"The Museum Department of Prints." *Metropolitan Museum of Art Bulletin* 12, no. 2 (Feb. 1917): 23–25.

"The Harris B. Dick Collection of Prints." *Metropolitan Museum of Art Bulletin* 12, no. 3 (March 1917): 50–56.

"The Department of Prints: Accessions." *Metropolitan Museum of Art Bulletin* 12, no. 5 (May 1917): 107–11.

"Exhibition of Painter Etchings and Engravings of the Nineteenth Century." *Metropolitan Museum of Art Bulletin* 12, no. 5 (May 1917): 104–5.

"The Department of Prints: Gifts." *Metropolitan Museum of Art Bulletin* 12, no. 6 (June 1917): 131–33.

"An Early Book about Etching." *Metropolitan Museum of Art Bulletin* 12, no. 8 (Aug. 1917): 174–76.

"Exhibition of Italian Renaissance Woodcuts." *Metropolitan Museum of Art Bulletin* 12, no. 11 (Nov. 1917): 224–28.

"Department of Prints: Purchases." *Metropolitan Museum of Art Bulletin* 12, no. 12 (Dec. 1917): 249–50.

"Books on Ornament." In "The Application of Arts to Manufacture," special issue, *Metropolitan Museum of Art Bulletin* 13, no. 2 (Feb. 1918): 44–45.

"'Ornament' and the Sources of Design in the Decorative Arts." In "The Application of Arts to Manufacture," special issue, *Metropolitan Museum of Art Bulletin* 13, no. 2 (Feb. 1918): 35–41.

"A Rembrandt Lecture and Exhibition." *Metropolitan Museum of Art Bulletin* 13, no. 3 (March 1918): 66–68.

"Illustrated Books." *Metropolitan Museum of Art Bulletin* 13, no. 6 (June 1918): 130–34.

"Accessions in the Department of Prints." *Metropolitan Museum of Art Bulletin* 13, no. 7 (July 1918): 155–59.

"Goya's Caprices." *Metropolitan Museum of Art Bulletin* 13, no. 7 (July 1918): 162.

"Prints in the Harris B. Dick Collection." *Metropolitan Museum of Art Bulletin* 13, no. 7 (July 1918): 167–68.

"Etchings by Canaletto." *Metropolitan Museum of Art Bulletin* 13, no. 11 (Nov. 1918): 243–44.

"Eighteenth-Century Books of Furniture Design." *Metropolitan Museum of Art Bulletin* 13, no. 12 (Dec. 1918): 268–73.

"Ornament in Old Prints and Drawings." *Scientific American* 120, no. 25 (1919): 673–74.

"Decoration from Louis XV to Our Day." *Metropolitan Museum of Art Bulletin* 14, no. 4 (April 1919): 79–86.

"Notes on the Exhibition of Ornament." *Metropolitan Museum of Art Bulletin* 14, no. 5 (May 1919): 107–11.

"A Further Note on the Exhibition of Ornament." *Metropolitan Museum of Art Bulletin* 14, no. 6 (June 1919): 140–42.

"A First Edition of Breydenbach's Itinerary." *Metropolitan Museum of Art Bulletin* 14, no. 10 (Oct. 1919): 215–21.

"Hans Holbein's Dance of Death." *Metropolitan Museum of Art Bulletin* 14, no. 11 (Nov. 1919): 231–35.

"An Engraved Portrait by Lucas van Leyden." *Metropolitan Museum of Art Bulletin* 14, no. 12 (Dec. 1919): 256, 258–60.

"A Collection of Prints by Albert Dürer." *Metropolitan Museum of Art Bulletin* 15, no. 1 (Jan. 1920): 2–3.

"Engravings and Woodcuts by Albert Dürer." *Metropolitan Museum of Art Bulletin* 15, no. 2 (Feb. 1920): 33–34.

"'Ornament' in the Department of Prints." *Metropolitan Museum of Art Bulletin* 15, no. 3 (March 1920): 53–58.

"Woodcuts by Albert Dürer." *Metropolitan Museum of Art Bulletin* 15, no. 3 (March 1920): 59–62.

"Van Dyck and Rembrandt in the Print Room." *Metropolitan Museum of Art Bulletin* 15, no. 10 (Oct. 1920): 222–27, 238.

"The Baillie Collection of Bookplates." *Metropolitan Museum of Art Bulletin* 15, no. 11 (Nov. 1920): 246–48.

"The Ogden Codman Collection." *Metropolitan Museum of Art Bulletin* 15, no. 11 (Nov. 1920): 250–53.

"A Gift of Renaissance Prints." *Metropolitan Museum of Art Bulletin* 15, no. 12 (Dec. 1920): 271–73.

"The Exhibitions." In *Transactions of the Grolier Club*, pt. 4, 79–96. New York: Grolier Club, 1921.

"Exhibition of Engraved Ornament." *Metropolitan Museum of Art Bulletin* 16, no. 1 (Jan. 1921): 19–20.

"An Exhibition of the Etched Work of Julian Alden Weir." *Metropolitan Museum of Art Bulletin* 16, no. 2 (Feb. 1921): 26–28.

"The Ornament Collection." *Metropolitan Museum of Art Bulletin* 16, no. 3 (March 1921): 64.

and Rudolph Ruzicka. "Contemporary Prints from Dürer's Woodblocks." *Metropolitan Museum of Art Bulletin* 16, no. 3 (March 1921): 53–55.

"Mantegna's Risen Christ: A Fine Impression from a Great Print." *Metropolitan Museum of Art Bulletin* 16, no. 4 (April 1921): 77–80.

"Ornament in the Print Room." *Metropolitan Museum of Art Bulletin* 16, no. 4 (April 1921): 85–86.

"Illustrated Books in the Museum." *Metropolitan Museum of Art Bulletin* 16, no. 5 (May 1921): 107–10.

"French Prints and Drawings of the Last Hundred Years." *Metropolitan Museum of Art Bulletin* 16, no. 6 (June 1921): 126–32.

"French Black and White of the Last Half-Century." *Metropolitan Museum of Art Bulletin* 16, no. 7 (July 1921): 151–58.

"French Black and White of the Last Half-
Century." *Metropolitan Museum of Art
Bulletin* 16, no. 8 (Aug. 1921): 162–68.

"Legros, Lepère, and Zorn." *Metropolitan Museum
of Art Bulletin* 16, no. 11 (Nov. 1921): 229–33.

"Five Years in the Department of Prints."
Metropolitan Museum of Art Bulletin 16, no. 12
(Dec. 1921): 258–62.

"A Scrap-Book of Ornament.'" *Metropolitan
Museum of Art Bulletin* 17, no. 6 (June 1922):
130–32.

"Hans Weiditz: A Study in Personality."
Metropolitan Museum of Art Bulletin 17, no. 7
(July 1922): 156–61.

"French Lithographs." *Metropolitan Museum of Art
Bulletin* 17, no. 10 (Oct. 1922): 216, 218–20.

"Old Woodcuts and Modern Illustrations."
Metropolitan Museum of Art Bulletin 17, no. 11
(Nov. 1922): 240–43.

"Of Museums." *Arts* 3 (Jan. 1923): 31–35.

"Daumier: The Man of His Time." *Arts* 3 (Feb.
1923): 89–102.

"An Exhibition of Masterpieces of Lithography."
Metropolitan Museum of Art Bulletin 18, no. 2
(Feb. 1923): 41–45.

"Daumier as a Lithographer." *Metropolitan
Museum of Art Bulletin* 18, no. 4 (April 1923):
94–98.

"Prints and Illustrated Books." *Metropolitan
Museum of Art Bulletin* 18, no. 5 (May 1923):
114.

"Italian Renaissance Prints." *Metropolitan Museum
of Art Bulletin* 18, no. 6 (June 1923): 146–50.

"'Pleasures of Memory.'" *Metropolitan Museum of
Art Bulletin* 18, no. 7 (July 1923): 174–76.

"The Aldine Hypnerotomachia Poliphili of 1499."
Metropolitan Museum of Art Bulletin 18, no. 11
(Nov. 1923): 249–52.

"The Aldine Hypnerotomachia Poliphili of 1499."
Metropolitan Museum of Art Bulletin 18, no. 12,
pt. 1 (Dec. 1923): 273–77.

"Exhibition of the Arts of the Book." *Metropolitan
Museum of Art Bulletin* 19, no. 5 (May 1924):
114–21.

"Reflections upon the Exhibition of the Arts
of the Book." *Metropolitan Museum of Art
Bulletin* 19, no. 7 (July 1924): 169–72.

"Goya's Disasters of War." *Metropolitan Museum of
Art Bulletin* 19, no. 9 (Sept. 1924): 220–24.

Review of *Etchers and Etching* by J. Pennell. *Arts* 7
(May 1925): 290–92.

"A Gift of Rare Prints." *Metropolitan Museum of Art
Bulletin* 20, no. 9 (Sept. 1925): 211–13.

"A Note on Aesthetic Theory." *Arts* 8, no. 6 (Dec.
1925): 303–10.

"Jean Duvet." In "The Southern Extension of the
Building, Wing K," supplement, *Metropolitan
Museum of Art Bulletin* 21, no. 4, pt. 2 (April
1926): 18–22.

"A Gift of Etchings by John Sloan." *Metropolitan
Museum of Art Bulletin* 21, no. 9 (Sept. 1926):
218–19.

"Joseph Pennell." *Metropolitan Museum of Art
Bulletin* 21, no. 11 (Nov. 1926): 251–54.

"Valturius' De Re Militari." *Metropolitan Museum
of Art Bulletin* 21, no. 11 (Nov. 1926): 267–68.

"Lucas Cranach the Elder." *Metropolitan Museum
of Art Bulletin* 22, no. 3 (March 1927): 84–87.

"An Exhibition of Graphic Techniques."
Metropolitan Museum of Art Bulletin 22, no. 4
(April 1927): 111–13.

"An Exhibition of Etchings." *Metropolitan Museum
of Art Bulletin* 22, no. 5 (May 1927): 139–41.

"A Treasury of Design." *Metropolitan Museum of
Art Bulletin* 22, no. 8 (Aug. 1927): 215–18.

"Titian's Pharaoh in the Red Sea." *Metropolitan
Museum of Art Bulletin* 22, no. 9 (Sept. 1927):
227–31.

"Torquemada's Meditations of 1473." *Metropolitan
Museum of Art Bulletin* 22, no. 12 (Dec. 1927):
316–17.

"Woodcut Books before 1550." *Metropolitan
Museum of Art Bulletin* 22, no. 12 (Dec. 1927):
295–98.

"A Collection of English Trade-Cards."
Metropolitan Museum of Art Bulletin 23, no. 2
(Feb. 1928): 45–47.

"Woodcuts in Chiaroscuro and Color: A Special
Exhibition." *Metropolitan Museum of Art
Bulletin* 23, no. 3 (March 1928): 73–78.

"Albrecht Dürers on Exhibition." *Metropolitan
Museum of Art Bulletin* 23, no. 8 (Aug. 1928):
194–95.

"Beauty in Architecture." *Arts* 14 (Sept. 1928):
130–42.

"A Goya Exhibition." *Metropolitan Museum of Art
Bulletin* 23, no. 10 (Oct. 1928): 230–32.

"Photography and the 'Modern' Point of View:
A Speculation in the History of Taste."
Metropolitan Museum Studies 1, no. 1 (Nov.
1928): 16–24.

"A Gift of Writing Books." *Metropolitan Museum of
Art Bulletin* 23, no. 12 (Dec. 1928): 296–99.

"Photographs by Alfred Stieglitz." *Metropolitan
Museum of Art Bulletin* 24, no. 2 (Feb. 1929):
44–45.

"Early Prints Acquired by the Museum."
Metropolitan Museum of Art Bulletin 24, no. 6
(June 1929): 165–70.

"An Exhibition of Contemporary Prints."
Metropolitan Museum of Art Bulletin 24, no. 7
(July 1929): 183–85.

"An Early Aesthetician." *Metropolitan Museum of
Art Bulletin* 24, no. 9 (Sept. 1929): 227–29.

"Notes on Three Dürer Woodblocks."
Metropolitan Museum Studies 2, no. 1 (Nov.
1929): 102–11.

"Vasari's Lives." *Metropolitan Museum of Art
Bulletin* 25, no. 1 (Jan. 1930): 15–20.

"Notes on Two Woodcuts of the Nuremberg
School." *Metropolitan Museum Studies* 2, no. 2
(May 1930): 171–75.

"Early Italian Prints on Exhibition." *Metropolitan
Museum of Art Bulletin* 25, no. 11 (Nov. 1930):
253–54.

"An Exhibition of Reproductive Prints."
Metropolitan Museum of Art Bulletin 26, no. 10
(Oct. 1931): 236–39.

"Artistic Aspects of Fifteenth-Century Printing."
Papers of the Bibliographical Society of America
26, no. 1/2 (1932): 1–51.

"The McGuire Collection of Early Woodcuts."
Metropolitan Museum of Art Bulletin 27, no. 1
(Jan. 1932): 5–10.

"Early Woodcuts." *Metropolitan Museum of Art
Bulletin* 27, no. 2 (Feb. 1932): 48–51.

"Two Woodcuts of the Virgin." *Metropolitan
Museum of Art Bulletin* 27, no. 4 (April 1932):
109–12.

"The Lübeck Bible, 1494." *Metropolitan Museum of
Art Bulletin* 27, no. 5 (May 1932): 137–41.

"The Lucas-Constable Mezzotints." *Metropolitan
Museum of Art Bulletin* 27, no. 6 (June 1932):
161–64.

"New Tastes in Old Prints." *Metropolitan Museum
of Art Bulletin* 27, no. 9 (Sept. 1932): 202–4.

"Notes on the Exhibition New Tastes in Old
Prints." *Metropolitan Museum of Art Bulletin*
27, no. 10 (Oct. 1932): 227–28.

"The Philosophy of Ornament." *Metropolitan
Museum of Art Bulletin* 28, no. 5 (May 1933):
93–97.

"Plants, Patterns, and Knowledge." *Metropolitan
Museum of Art Bulletin* 28, no. 8 (Aug. 1933):
139–41.

"Some Venetian Renaissance Woodcut Books."
Metropolitan Museum of Art Bulletin 29, no. 3
(March 1934): 46–50.

"An Exhibition of German Prints of the XV and
XVI Centuries." *Metropolitan Museum of Art
Bulletin* 29, no. 5 (May 1934): 77–78.

"Illustrations by Dürer." *Metropolitan Museum of
Art Bulletin* 29, no. 8 (Aug. 1934): 138–41.

"Developments in the Educational Work of
the Museum." *Metropolitan Museum of Art
Bulletin* 29, no. 9 (Sept. 1934): 146.

"Of Education in a Museum." *Metropolitan
Museum of Art Bulletin* 29, no. 9 (Sept. 1934):
148–51.

"A Whistler Centenary Exhibition." *Metropolitan
Museum of Art Bulletin* 30, no. 1 (Jan. 1935): 2–3.

"The Woodcuts to Vesalius." *Metropolitan Museum
of Art Bulletin* 31, no. 7 (July 1936): 139–42.

"Goya's Giant." *Metropolitan Museum Studies* 5,
no. 2 (Sept. 1936): 182.

"The Albertian Scheme." *Metropolitan Museum of
Art Bulletin* 31, no. 12 (Dec. 1936): 278–80.

"Schongauer's Engravings." *Metropolitan Museum
of Art Bulletin* 32, no. 3 (March 1937): 69–71.

"The Master E. S." *Metropolitan Museum of Art
Bulletin* 32, no. 4 (April 1937): 98–101.

"Burgkmair's Prints in the Museum." *Metropolitan
Museum of Art Bulletin* 32, no. 11 (Nov. 1937):
251–55.

"Italian Renaissance Prints and Illustrated
Books." *Metropolitan Museum of Art Bulletin*
32, no. 12 (Dec. 1937): 280–85.

"Italian Baroque Prints." *Metropolitan Museum of
Art Bulletin* 33, no. 7 (July 1938): 158–61.

"The Ketham of 1493." *Metropolitan Museum of Art
Bulletin* 34, no. 2 (Feb. 1939): 44–47.

"The Warburg Collection of Prints." *Metropolitan Museum of Art Bulletin* 34, no. 5 (May 1939): 109–14.

"Of French Prints since 1800." *Metropolitan Museum of Art Bulletin* 36, no. 3 (March 1941): 59–65.

"The Art of Rembrandt." *Metropolitan Museum of Art Bulletin* 37, no. 1 (Jan. 1942): 3–22.

"Two First Editions of Desargues." *Metropolitan Museum of Art Bulletin*, n.s., 1, no. 1 (Summer 1942): 33–45.

"Renaissance Books on Architecture." *Metropolitan Museum of Art Bulletin*, n.s., 1, no. 4 (Dec. 1942): 151–55.

"À Propos of the *Fabrica* of Vesalius." *Bulletin of the History of Medicine* 14 (1943): 576–93.

"A Bruegel Exhibition in the Print Galleries." *Metropolitan Museum of Art Bulletin*, n.s., 1, no. 7 (March 1943): 222–30.

"A Note on Girard Desargues." *Scripta Mathematica* 9, no. 1 (March 1943): 33–48.

"Ignorance, the End." *Metropolitan Museum of Art Bulletin*, n.s., 2, no. 1 (Summer 1943): 2–10.

"The Herbal of 'Pseudo-Apuleius.'" *Metropolitan Museum of Art Bulletin*, n.s., 2, no. 7 (March 1944): 218–21.

"Engravings by Four Renaissance Masters." *Metropolitan Museum of Art Bulletin*, n.s., 2, no. 10 (June 1944): 292–96.

"'But It's Not a Cimabue!'" *Metropolitan Museum of Art Bulletin*, n.s., 3, no. 4 (Dec. 1944): 100–104.

"'In the Beginning Was the Word.'" *Metropolitan Museum of Art Bulletin*, n.s., 4, no. 1 (Summer 1945): 12–17.

"The 'Field' of Prints: Objects vs. Meanings." *Metropolitan Museum of Art Bulletin*, n.s., 4, no. 9 (May 1946): 227–31.

"The Dead Hand." *Metropolitan Museum of Art Bulletin*, n.s., 4, no. 10 (June 1946): 245–48.

"Art in a University Museum." In *Addresses Delivered at a Convocation Held in Yale University, 18–19 October 1946*, 13–24. New Haven, Conn: Yale University, 1947.

"A Few Fallacies about Art." *Harper's Magazine* 195, no. 1167 (Aug. 1947): 114–20.

"More Fallacies about Art." *Harper's Magazine* 195, no. 1168 (Sept. 1947): 225–32.

"Free Thought in the Country." *Metropolitan Museum of Art Bulletin*, n.s., 6, no. 6 (Feb. 1948): 175–77.

"Some Notes on Fakes." *Magazine of Art* 41, no. 5 (May 1948): 168–71.

"A Note on Ipseity." *Journal of Aesthetics and Art Criticism* 7, no. 1 (Sept. 1948): 38–41.

"A Neglected Aspect of Early Print-Making." *Metropolitan Museum of Art Bulletin*, n.s., 7, no. 2 (Oct. 1948): 51–59.

"What about the *Fabrica* of Vesalius?" In Samuel W. Lambert, Willy Weigand, and William M. Ivins Jr., *Three Vesalian Essays to Accompany the* Icones anatomicae *of 1543*, 43–128. New York: Macmillan, 1952.

"What Makes a Masterpiece?" In *Art Treasures of the World: How to Appreciate Art*, 5–22. New York: Harry N. Abrams, 1953.

SELECTED BIBLIOGRAPHY OF A. HYATT MAYOR

Books and Exhibition Catalogues

Sporting Prints and Paintings. Exh. cat. New York: The Metropolitan Museum of Art, 1937.

Catalogue commentary in *Life in America: A Special Loan Exhibition of Paintings Held during the Period of the New York World's Fair*, by Harry Brandeis Wehle. Exh. cat. New York: The Metropolitan Museum of Art, 1939.

The Bibiena Family. New York: H. Bittner, 1945.

Giovanni Battista Piranesi. New York: H. Bittner, 1952.

Goya, 1746–1828. Metropolitan Museum of Art Miniatures. New York: Book of the Month Club, 1953.

Prints & People: A Social History of Printed Pictures. New York: The Metropolitan Museum of Art, distributed by New York Graphic Society, 1971.

Popular Prints of the Americas. New York: Crown, 1973.

Goya: 67 Drawings. New York: The Metropolitan Museum of Art, distributed by New York Graphic Society, 1974.

and Mark Davis. *American Art at the Century*. New York: Century Association, 1977.

Rembrandt and the Bible. New York: The Metropolitan Museum of Art, 1979.

A. Hyatt Mayor: Selected Writings and a Bibliography. Foreword by Janet S. Byrne, Colta Ives, and Mary L. Myers. New York: The Metropolitan Museum of Art, 1983.

Artists and Anatomists. [New York]: Artist's Limited Edition in association with The Metropolitan Museum of Art, 1984.

Articles, Essays, and Miscellany

"Gordon Craig's Ideas of Drama." *Hound & Horn* 2, no. 3 (April–June 1929): 236–49.

"Picasso's Method." *Hound & Horn* 3, no. 2 (Jan.–March 1930): 176–88.

"The 'American Note'?" *Hound & Horn* 3, no. 3 (April–June 1930): 403–9.

"Towards Stronger Reasons for Deploring American Painting." *Hound & Horn* 3, no. 4 (July–Sept. 1930): 568–69.

"Museums Modern and Metropolitan." *Hound & Horn* 4, no. 1 (Oct.–Dec. 1930): 111–12.

"New-York Letter." *Formes* 11 (Jan. 1931): 13–14.

"On the Imitation of Nature." *Hound & Horn* 4, no. 2 (Jan.–March 1931): 265–67.

"American Letter." *Formes* 12 (Feb. 1931): 35–36.

"New York Letter." *Formes* 13 (March 1931): 51–52.

"American Letter." *Formes* 15 (May 1931): 86–87.

"All on the Shoulders of Two." *Hound & Horn* 5, no. 1 (Oct.–Dec. 1931): 91–93.

"Le Monument du Costume." *Metropolitan Museum of Art Bulletin* 28, no. 5 (May 1933): 87–88.

"Three Hundred Years of Landscape." *Metropolitan Museum of Art Bulletin* 28, no. 11 (Nov. 1933): 193–95.

"Goya's Giant." *Metropolitan Museum of Art Bulletin* 30, no. 8 (Aug. 1935): 153–54.

"Goya's 'Disasters of War.'" *American Magazine of Art* 29 (1936): 710–15.

"French Bookbindings." *Metropolitan Museum of Art Bulletin* 31, no. 1 (Jan. 1936): 8–9.

"An Exhibition of Sporting Prints and Paintings." *Metropolitan Museum of Art Bulletin* 32, no. 3 (March 1937): 51–54.

"A Gift of Prints." *Metropolitan Museum of Art Bulletin* 32, no. 6 (June 1937): 140–43.

"Giulio Campagnola." *Metropolitan Museum of Art Bulletin* 32, no. 8 (Aug. 1937): 192–96.

"An Early Whistler Lithograph." *Print Collector's Quarterly* 24, no. 3 (Oct. 1937): 305–7.

"Two Midwinter Print Shows." *Parnassus* 10, no. 2 (Feb. 1938): 13–14.

"A Woodcut in the Style of Veronese." *Metropolitan Museum of Art Bulletin* 33, no. 5 (May 1938): 128–30.

"Piranesi." *Metropolitan Museum of Art Bulletin* 33, no. 12 (Dec. 1938): 279–84.

"Illustrated Books." *Metropolitan Museum of Art Bulletin* 34, no. 7 (July 1939): 174.

"Print Masterpieces of Five Centuries." *Metropolitan Museum of Art Bulletin* 34, no. 7 (July 1939): 184–85.

"Daguerreotypes and Photographs." *Metropolitan Museum of Art Bulletin* 34, no. 11 (Nov. 1939): 240–43.

"Photography's Early Days." *Science Digest* 7, no. 2 (Feb. 1940): 81–84.

"Silhouettes and Profile Portraits: The Mary Martin Collection." *Metropolitan Museum of Art Bulletin* 35, no. 3 (March 1940): 50–54.

"Childe Hassam." *Metropolitan Museum of Art Bulletin* 35, no. 7 (July 1940): 137–39.

"Prints of French Châteaux." *Metropolitan Museum of Art Bulletin* 35, no. 10 (Oct. 1940): 197–200.

"Prints by Living Americans." In "National Art Week and The Museum," supplement, *Metropolitan Museum of Art Bulletin* 35, no. 11, pt. 2 (Nov. 1940): 14–20.

"French Fashions." *Metropolitan Museum of Art Bulletin* 36, no. 2 (Feb. 1941): 40–48.

Foreword to *Artists for Victory: An Exhibition of Contemporary American Art; A Picture Book of the Prize Winners*. New York: The Metropolitan Museum of Art, 1942.

"Renaissance Costume Books." *Metropolitan Museum of Art Bulletin* 37, no. 6 (June 1942): 158–59.

"Rembrandt in Italy." *Metropolitan Museum of Art Bulletin*, n.s., 1, no. 2 (Oct. 1942): 93–96.

"The Artists for Victory Exhibition." *Metropolitan Museum of Art Bulletin*, n.s., 1, no. 4 (Dec. 1942): 141–43.

"Carpentry and Candlelight in the Theater." *Metropolitan Museum of Art Bulletin*, n.s., 1, no. 6 (Feb. 1943): 198–203.

"Old Calling Cards." *Metropolitan Museum of Art Bulletin*, n.s., 2, no. 2 (Oct. 1943): 93–98.

"Jefferson's Enjoyment of the Arts." *Metropolitan Museum of Art Bulletin*, n.s., 2, no. 4 (Dec. 1943): 140–46.

"Photographs by Eakins and Degas." *Metropolitan Museum of Art Bulletin*, n.s., 3, no. 1 (Summer 1944): 1–7.

"Old London." *Metropolitan Museum of Art Bulletin*, n.s., 3, no. 9 (May 1945): 220–23.

"The Bibiena Family." *Metropolitan Museum of Art Bulletin*, n.s., 4, no. 1 (Summer 1945): 29–37.

"The Art of the Counter Reformation." *Metropolitan Museum of Art Bulletin*, n.s., 4, no. 4 (Dec. 1945): 101–5.

"French Renaissance Etchings." *Magazine of Art* 39, no. 4 (April 1946): 135–37.

"The Photographic Eye." *Metropolitan Museum of Art Bulletin*, n.s., 5, no. 1 (Summer 1946): 15–26.

"Goya's Creativeness." *Metropolitan Museum of Art Bulletin*, n.s., 5, no. 4 (Dec. 1946): 105–9.

"Visions and Visionaries." *Metropolitan Museum of Art Bulletin*, n.s., 5, no. 6 (Feb. 1947): 157–63.

"Paris in the 1850s: The Theatre of Daumier." *Theatre Arts* 31 (March 1947): 35–38.

"Renaissance Prints and Drawings." *Magazine of Art* 40, no. 3 (March 1947): 107–9.

"Renaissance Pamphleteers Savonarola and Luther." *Metropolitan Museum of Art Bulletin*, n.s., 6, no. 2 (Oct. 1947): 66–72.

"Northern Gothic Prints." *Metropolitan Museum of Art Bulletin*, n.s., 6, no. 6 (Feb. 1948): 161–65.

"The Greatest Show Down South." *Artnews* 47 (Summer 1948): 46, 61.

"Lithographs." *Metropolitan Museum of Art Bulletin*, n.s., 7, no. 3 (Nov. 1948): 86–94.

"The First Famous Print." *New Colophon* 2, pt. 6 (June 1949): 167–71.

Introduction to *Baroque and Romantic Stage Design*. Edited by Jànos Scholz. New York: H. Bittner, 1950.

"Italian XVIII Century Book Illustration." *Metropolitan Museum of Art Bulletin*, n.s., 8, no. 5 (Jan. 1950): 136–44.

"Prints Acquired in 1949." *Metropolitan Museum of Art Bulletin*, n.s., 8, no. 6 (Feb. 1950): 157–67.

"Change and Permanence in Men's Clothes." *Metropolitan Museum of Art Bulletin*, n.s., 8, no. 9 (May 1950): 262–69.

"Toulouse-Lautrec." *Metropolitan Museum of Art Bulletin*, n.s., 10, no. 3 (Nov. 1951): 89–95.

"The World of Atget." *Metropolitan Museum of Art Bulletin*, n.s., 10, no. 6 (Feb. 1952): 169–71.

"A Gift of Currier & Ives Lithographs." *Metropolitan Museum of Art Bulletin*, n.s., 10, no. 9 (May 1952): 241–44.

"Alive, Alive, O." *Metropolitan Museum of Art Bulletin*, n.s., 11, no. 6 (Feb. 1953): 164–67.

"A Modern Artist of the Eighteenth Century." *Metropolitan Museum of Art Bulletin*, n.s., 12, no. 4 (Dec. 1953): 100–104.

"A Metal Cut Attributed to Francesco Francia." In *Studies in Art and Literature for Belle da Costa Greene.* Edited by Dorothy E. Miner, 197–99. Princeton, N.J.: Princeton University Press, 1954.

"La Scenografia Primo del 1700." In *Tempi e Aspetti della Scenografia.* Edited by Marziano Bernardi, 10–63. Turin: Edizioni Radio Italiana, 1954.

"German Mannerist Drawings." *Art Quarterly* 17 (Summer 1954): 176–78.

"Being Able to Draw the Figure and Know What's Going On." *Artnews* 53 (Oct. 1954): 48.

"Goya's 'Hannibal Crossing the Alps.'" *Burlington Magazine* 97, no. 630 (Sept. 1955): 295–96.

"German Drawing: The Electric Line." *Artnews* 54 (Oct. 1955): 18–21.

"The Theater in France." *Metropolitan Museum of Art Bulletin*, n.s., 14, no. 2 (Oct. 1955): 48–53.

Preface to *Reginald Marsh: Etchings, Engravings, Lithographs*, by Norman Sasowsky. Introduction by Isabel Bishop. New York: Praeger, 1956.

"Two Piranesi Drawings in the Gilmor Collection." *Baltimore Museum of Art News* 20, no. 1 (Oct. 1956): 1–2.

"Great Prints Are Rare." *Artnews* 55 (Nov. 1956): 22–25.

"The Gifts That Made the Museum." *Metropolitan Museum of Art Bulletin*, n.s., 16, no. 3 (Nov. 1957): 85–107.

"A Bequest of Prints by Callot and Daumier." *Metropolitan Museum of Art Bulletin*, n.s., 17, no. 1 (Summer 1958): 8–18.

"First Victorian Photographer." *Metropolitan Museum of Art Bulletin*, n.s., 17, no. 4 (Dec. 1958): 113–19.

"Frank Lloyd Wright's Drawings." In *Frank Lloyd Wright: Drawings for a Living Architecture*, 20–21. New York: Horizon, 1959.

Foreword to *John James Audubon, peintre naturaliste américain, 1785–1851.* Paris: Centre culturel américain, Les Presses artistiques, 1960.

"The Greeks Had No Word for It." *Saturday Review* 43 (May 28, 1960): 38–40.

"Prints Recently Acquired." *Metropolitan Museum of Art Bulletin*, n.s., 18, no. 10 (June 1960): 325–33.

"The Fountain of Delight." *Artnews* 59 (Sept. 1960): 38–39.

"The Flexibility of Drawings." In *Centennial Loan Exhibition: Drawings and Watercolors from Alumnae and Their Families*, xiii–xvi. Poughkeepsie, N.Y.: Vassar College, 1961.

Portraits and Masks. Calendar for 1962, prepared by A. Hyatt Mayor and Margaret R. Scherer. New York: The Metropolitan Museum of Art, [1961].

"Stamps Designed by Fine Artists." *Art in America* 49, no. 4 (1961): 32–39.

"Italian Prints." *Metropolitan Museum of Art Bulletin*, n.s., 19, 7 (March 1961): 206–8.

"Brush and Camera." *Saturday Review* 44 (June 17, 1961): 48–49.

"The Etchings of Jacques Callot." *Massachusetts Review* 3, no. 1 (Autumn 1961): 121–32.

"History of Photography at George Eastman House." *Aperture* 10, no. 2 (1962): 55.

Rembrandt: A Hidden World. Calendar for 1963. New York: The Metropolitan Museum of Art, 1962.

"Rowlandson's England." *Metropolitan Museum of Art Bulletin*, n.s., 20, no. 6 (Feb. 1962): 185–201.

"Pen, Brush, Paper, and Genius." *Saturday Review* 45 (Nov. 3, 1962): 44–45.

Introduction and "Jefferson R. Burdick." In *Directory of the J. R. Burdick Collection: Trade and Souvenir Cards and Other Paper Americana in The Metropolitan Museum of Art*, 3–4. New York: The Metropolitan Museum of Art, 1963.

"Does Your Art Collection Express Your Community?" *American Federation of Arts Quarterly* 1, no. 3 (1963): 85–92.

Preface to *English Publishers in the Graphic Arts, 1599–1700: A Study of the Printsellers & Publishers of Engravings, Art & Architectural Manuals, Maps & Copy-books*, by Leona Rostenberg. New York: Burt Franklin, 1963.

"Painters' Playing Cards." *Art in America* 51, no. 2 (1963): 39–42.

"Stamps Designed by Fine Artists," and "Painters' Playing Cards." In *Art in America: What Is American in American Art?* Edited by Jean Lipman, 156–63, 171–74. New York: McGraw-Hill, 1963.

"William Mills Ivins, Jr., 1881–1961." *Metropolitan Museum of Art Bulletin*, n.s., 21, no. 6 (Feb. 1963): 193–201.

"The Italian Sources of European Stage Design." *Bulletin of the Minneapolis Institute of Arts* 52, no. 1 (March 1963): 2–13.

"A Matter of Opinion." *Saturday Review* 46 (May 18, 1963): 41–54.

"Velázquez Monument." *Artnews* 62 (Oct. 1963): 43.

"Accidents are Inartistic." *Nation* 197, no. 18 (Nov. 30, 1963): 370–71.

Introduction to *Architecture and Perspective Designs: Dedicated to His Majesty Charles VI, Holy Roman Emperor*, by Giuseppe Galli Bibiena. New York: Dover, 1964.

Foreword to *Hispanic Furniture from the Fifteenth through the Eighteenth Centuries*, by Grace Hardendorff Burr. 2nd ed. New York: Archive Press, 1964.

"The Italian Sources of European Stage Design." In *Four Centuries of Theater Design: Drawings from the Donald Oenslager Collection*, by Richard P. Wunder, unpaged. Exh. cat. New Haven, Conn.: Yale University Art Gallery, 1964.

"Notes." *Metropolitan Museum of Art Bulletin*, n.s., 22, no. 5 (Jan. 1964): 184.

"Artists as Anatomists." *Metropolitan Museum of Art Bulletin*, n.s., 22, no. 6 (Feb. 1964): 201–10.

"How to Bake an Exhibition." *Photography in the Fine Arts Bulletin* (Fall 1964): 3–10.

"Prints in Elizabethan Poetry." *Metropolitan Museum of Art Bulletin*, n.s., 23, no. 3 (Nov. 1964): 135–38.

"The Swiss behind the Colors." *Nation* 199, no. 17 (Nov. 1964): 414–15.

"'The Met' from the Inside." *Metropolitan Museum of Art Bulletin*, n.s., 24, no. 1 (Summer 1965): 29–36.

"Aquatint Views of Our Infant Cities." *Antiques* 88 (Sept. 1965): 314–18.

"Practical Fantasies." *Apollo* 82 (Sept. 1965): 241–46.

"Catalogue of Paintings, Drawings, Sculptures, Objects, Medals, Coins, Seals, Engravings, and Etchings." In *Builders and Humanists: The Renaissance Popes as Patrons of the Arts*, 51–129. Exh. cat. Houston: University of St. Thomas, 1966.

Hokusai. Calendar for 1967. New York: The Metropolitan Museum of Art, [1966].

"James J. Rorimer (1905–1966)." *Art Journal* 26, no. 1 (Autumn 1966): 44.

"Drawings for Unidentified Book Illustrations by Tiepolo." In *Homage to a Bookman: Essays on Manuscripts, Books and Printing Written for Hans P. Kraus on His 60th Birthday, October 12, 1967*, edited by Hellmut Lehmann-Haupt, 235–42. Berlin: Mann Verlag, 1967.

Essay in *Sculpture of Gaston Lachaise*, by Hilton Kramer et al., 33–34. New York: Eakins, 1967.

"An Unidentified Ingres Lithograph." *Burlington Magazine* 109, no. 775 (Oct. 1967): 583.

Introduction to *Complete Course of Lithography*, by Alois Senefelder (1771–1834), with a supplement of thirty-one plates from the first German and French editions. New York: Da Capo, 1968.

Preface to *Language of the Print: A Selection from the Donald H. Karshan Collection.* Foreword and essay by Richard V. West. Catalogue commentary by Donald H. Karshan. Exh. cat. Brunswick, Maine: Bowdoin Museum of Fine Art, 1968.

Preface to *American Printmaking: The First 150 Years*, by Wendy J. Shadwell. Foreword by

Donald H. Karshan and introduction by
J. William Middendorf II. Washington,
D.C.: Smithsonian Institution Press for
the Museum of Graphic Art, New York,
1969.

"Early Engraving in Germany and the
Netherlands." In *Late Gothic Engravings of
Germany and the Netherlands*, by Max Lehrs,
1–3. New York: Dover, 1969.

Flowers for All Seasons. Calendar for 1971. New
York: The Metropolitan Museum of Art,
[1970].

"In the Beginning." *Album* 4 (1970): 14–15.

"Prints and People." *Metropolitan Museum Journal*
3 (1970): 357–69.

"The Photographic Eye." *Album* 3 (April 1970): 14.

"Manuel Gómez-Moreno." *Art Journal* 30, no. 1
(Autumn 1970): 82.

Parlors and Palaces. Calendar for 1972. New York:
The Metropolitan Museum of Art, [1971].

"Prints and People: A Social History in Printed
Pictures." *Metropolitan Museum of Art
Bulletin*, n.s., 30, no. 2 (Oct.–Nov. 1971):
92–93.

"Correspondence." *Print Collector's Newsletter* 2,
no. 5 (Nov.–Dec. 1971): 99–100.

Beasts of Earth and Air. Calendar for 1973. New
York: The Metropolitan Museum of Art,
[1972].

"Four Centuries of Spanish Painting." *Apollo* 95
(April 1972): 252–63.

"Rembrandt from 'Prints & People.'" *Metropolitan
Museum of Art Bulletin*, n.s., 30, no. 5 (April–
May 1972): 210–19.

Foreword to *Art of the Playing Card: The Cary
Collection*. Exh. cat. New Haven, Conn.: Yale
University Library, 1973.

Gardens East and West. Calendar for 1974. New
York: The Metropolitan Museum of Art,
[1973].

"Mrs. Gardner Comes to Call." In *Fenway Court:
Isabella Stewart Gardner Museum*. Annual
Report 1972, 40. Boston: Trustees of the
Isabella Stewart Gardner Museum, 1973.

"The Print That Worked a Miracle." *Print
Collector's Newsletter* 4, no. 5 (Nov.–Dec.
1973): 97.

Life in America. Calendar for 1975. New York: The
Metropolitan Museum of Art, [1974].

"William Mills Ivins, Jr., 1881–1961," *Print Review*
3 (1974): 47–55.

"Remembrance of Dealers Past." *Artnews* 73 (Oct.
1974): 35–36.

Secret Gardens. Calendar for 1976, New York: The
Metropolitan Museum of Art, [1975].

"Goya at Boston and Ottawa." *Print Collector's
Newsletter* 5 (Jan.–Feb. 1975): 147–48.

"Prints." In "1776: How America Really Looked,"
special issue, *American Art Journal* 7, no. 1
(May 1975): 43–51.

"Mail Orders in the Eighteenth Century."
Antiques 108 (Oct. 1975): 756–63.

Introduction to *Auguste Edouart's Silhouettes of
Eminent Americans, 1839–1844*, by Andrew
Oliver. Charlottesville, Va.: University Press
of Virginia for the National Portrait Gallery,
Smithsonian Institution, 1977.

"A Truth or Two about Art History." *Record of the
Art Museum, Princeton University* 36, 1 (1977):
22–24.

"Hunt for the Fishing Lady." *Antiques* 112 (July
1977): 113.

"Rembrandt and the Bible." *Metropolitan Museum
of Art Bulletin*, n.s., 36, no. 3 (Winter 1978–
79): 2–48.

Foreword to *Diaries, 1871–1882, of Samuel P.
Avery, Art Dealer*. Edited by Madeleine
Fidell Beaufort, Herbert L. Kleinfield, and
Jeanne K. Welcher. New York: Arno, 1979.

"Introduction: Bookgreen Gardens." In
*A Century of American Sculpture: Treasures from
Brookgreen Gardens*, by Joseph Veach Noble et
al., 15–29. New York: Abbeville, 1980.

Unforgettable People. Calendar for 1981. New York:
The Metropolitan Museum of Art, [1980].
Reprinted as an address book: *Unforgettable
People: Names and Addresses*. Prepared by
A. Hyatt Mayor and Colta Ives. New York:
The Metropolitan Museum of Art, 1981.

"A. Hyatt Mayor Abroad." *Archives of American Art
Journal* 36, no. 4 (1992): 2–18.

INDEX